Post-industrial Labour Markets

Following the increasing interest in the field of comparative labour market studies, this book considers both the characteristics of labour markets and the institutional frameworks which condition how they function. It starts with discussions about the intensified competition in the world economy as a result of globalisation processes and the shift towards a post-industrial service or informational society. The overriding aim is to identify the consequences of these changes, for example, in terms of employment conditions and the gender mix of the labour force, and to analyse how they are modelled by different institutional set-ups.

Four cases are examined: on the one hand, Canada and the United States, generally characterised as liberal and market-directed, and on the other hand, Denmark and Sweden, generally described as social democratic and welfare state-oriented. *Post-industrial Labour Markets* addresses what such institutional differences mean for the development of labour markets. It tries to illuminate the role of national traditions and institutions in four countries deeply involved in the recent social and economic transformations of the world economy.

In the first part of the book, the institutional frameworks of the four countries are in focus. Three different chapters deal with topics such as industrial relations, labour law and employment regulation, and the welfare state and labour market policy. The next part of the book contains six chapters that analyse labour market outcomes, in particular trends in labour force and employment, the shift towards post-industrialism, occupational changes, unemployment, labour market flexibility and wage formation. The final part compares the four case studies with other labour markets in the OECD area.

Featuring contributions from leading scholars within the fields of sociology and economics, this book is a valuable addition to the growing area of comparative labour market research and will prove to be essential reading for those studying the sociology of work and labour markets, organisations and industrial relations at both the under- and post-graduate levels. It will also be of general interest to academics and researchers in sociology and economics.

Thomas P. Boje is Professor of Sociology at Umeå University, Sweden and Professor of Social Sciences (welfare and labour market) at Roskilde University, Denmark. He has been American Studies Fellow at Harvard University, Jean Monnet Fellow at the European University Institute, Florence and Guest Professor at several universities. His research is mainly focused on the welfare state and labour market, labour market flexibility, citizenship and gender and social exclusion.

Bengt Furåker is currently Professor of Sociology at Göteborg University, Sweden. He has previously held positions at the universities of Umeå and Lund. His research is mainly focused on labour market issues, employment and unemployment, labour market policy, the public sector, relationships between the labour market and the welfare state and social stratification.

Routledge Studies in the Modern World Economy

Post-industrial Labour Markets

Profiles of North America and Scandinavia

Edited by Thomas P. Boje and
Bengt Furåker

LONDON AND NEW YORK

First published 2003
by Routledge
11 New Fetter Lane, London EC4P 4EE

Simultaneously published in the USA and Canada
by Routledge
29 West 35th Street, New York, NY 10001

Routledge is an imprint of the Taylor & Francis Group

ML

© 2003 Selection and editorial material, Thomas P. Boje and Bengt
Furåker; individual chapters, the authors

Typeset in Baskerville by M Rules
Printed and bound in Great Britain by
MPG Books Ltd, Bodmin

British Library Cataloguing in Publication Data
A catalogue record for this book is available from the British Library

Library of Congress Cataloging in Publication Data
Post-industrial labour markets: profiles of North America and
Scandinavia / edited by Thomas P. Boje and Bengt Furåker.
   p.   cm.
Includes bibliographical references and index.
1. Labor market – United States. 2. Labor market – Canada. 3. Labor
market – North America. 4. Labor market – Denmark. 5. Labor
market – Sweden. 6. Labor market – Scandinavia. I. Boje, Thomas P.,
1944–   II. Furåker, Bengt, 1943–
HD5724.P577 2002
331.1′0948–dc21   2002068248

ISBN 0–415–21809–8

Contents

Figures

Tables

Contributors

Thomas P. Boje is Professor of Sociology at Umeå University, Sweden and Professor of Social Sciences (welfare and labour market) at Roskilde University, Denmark. He has been Jean Monnet Fellow at the European University Institute, Florence, Italy and American Society Fellow at Harvard University, Cambridge, MA, USA. His research is mainly focused on labour market development, social inequalities, citizenship and gender, welfare state and civil society and gender and family. He is the Swedish team leader for two EU-TSER research projects on precarity and social exclusion and on household, work and family.

Bengt Furåker is currently Professor of Sociology at Göteborg University, Sweden. He has previously held positions at the universities of Umeå and Lund. His research is mainly focused on labour market issues, employment and unemployment, labour market policy, the public sector, the relationship between the labour market and the welfare state and social stratification.

Anne Grönlund is Researcher in Sociology at Umeå University, Sweden. Her research is focused on labour market flexibility, family and gender.

Lars H. Hansen is Assistant Professor of Sociology at Göteborg University, Sweden. His main research interests are in the fields of occupational and labour market sociology and the organisation of work in contemporary Western societies.

Rafael Lindqvist is Professor of Social Work at the Department of Social Welfare, Umeå University, Sweden. He has previously held positions in sociology at Umeå University. His research is focused on the formation of the Swedish welfare state, industrial relations in the public sector, labour market policy and vocational rehabilitation.

Per Kongshøj Madsen is Associate Professor of Economic Policy in the Department of Political Sciences at the University of Copenhagen, Denmark. His main research interests are comparative labour market policy and European employment policy. Since 1997 he has been the Danish correspondent to the Employment Observatory of the European Union.

Preface and Acknowledgements

The origin of this book dates back to the first half of the 1990s and arises out of an interest in North American labour markets and in how they differ from the ones in our own native countries, Denmark and Sweden. At this time many social scientists debated intensely issues such as the American 'employment miracle' in contrast to European unemployment, American labour market flexibility in contrast to the 'sclerotic' European labour markets, the international trend towards increasing female labour force participation, and the rise of post-industrial or information society with its consequences for the industrial and occupational structures.

With so many interesting issues – and with all the differences and similarities that we could identify in relation to the North American and Scandinavian labour markets – it seemed to be a highly relevant and important task to carry out systematic comparisons between them. We expected to find two different labour market models, a 'liberal' North American one and a 'social democratic' Scandinavian one, but we were at the same time aware that important differences exist between Canada and the United States on the one hand and between Denmark and Sweden on the other.

Draft versions of the chapters in the book have been discussed at internal seminars in which Rafael Lindqvist and Lars H. Hansen have often participated alongside us. However, the work has also benefited both directly and indirectly from members of the labour market research communities at the Department of Sociology, Umeå University, and the Department of Sociology, Göteborg University, i.e., our workplaces during the crucial years of planning the book. Thus many people – who cannot be mentioned individually but whom we want to thank collectively – have contributed in one way or another to making up the final versions of the different chapters.

A book cannot be produced without resources. For part of the work, grants from the Swedish Council for Work Life Research and the Swedish Council for Research in the Humanities and Social Sciences have been available. In addition, our home universities in Göteborg and Umeå have supplied us with funding. We want to express our gratitude for all this support.

Since none of the authors has English as his/her native tongue, most of the chapters have needed language correction. We want to thank Accent Language Service, Umeå, Sweden for an excellent job in improving our texts.

Thomas P. Boje and Bengt Furåker
Copenhagen and Göteborg, August 2002

1 Introduction

Thomas P. Boje and Bengt Furåker

This is a book about the labour markets and the institutional frameworks that con-dition how they function in four countries: Canada, the United States, Denmark and Sweden. In the last decades, the world economy has undergone significant social and economic transformations, and the four countries in our study have been profoundly affected by these. Since our examples represent rather different societal models, we may ask whether they have been affected in the same way. Their dif-fering socio-economic institutions can be expected to have some impact on these changes. North America is generally characterised as liberal and market-directed and Scandinavia as social democratic and welfare state oriented. A crucial question is what this means for the development of their labour markets. However, there are also important differences between Canada and the United States on the one hand and between Denmark and Sweden on the other. We may therefore more carefully examine what nation-specific patterns exist or remain in a world that seems to become more and more subjected to a common social and economic development. What do different national traditions and institutions mean in such a world?

The purpose of this introduction is to spell out some ideas and questions about the changes taking place in the contemporary advanced economies and their labour markets. We will call attention to two general trends that are now often the focus of the economic and political debate: the intensification of competition related to the internationalisation of economies and the shift towards post-industrialism.

Labour markets under intensified competition

The process of globalisation (internationalisation is perhaps a better term) of modern economies is certainly not new, but it appears to have accelerated in the last decades (see Bélanger, Edwards and Haiven 1994; Castells 1996; Drache and Gertler 1991; Hall and Jacques 1989; Piore and Sabel 1984; Thurow 1996). It would be extreme to argue that there is only one global economy, but international trade has grown, markets have expanded, and firms have increasingly become transnational, that is to say they have also established themselves outside their nation of origin, often in a large number of countries. These changes have been promoted by the remarkable economic performance of the newly industrialised countries (NICs), the fall of state socialism in the Soviet Union and Eastern Europe, the shift towards market solutions in China, the development and enlargement of the European Union, and the birth of NAFTA (the North American Free Trade Agreement). Today, many national borders that used to be closed are open, trade tariffs are lower, customs restrictions have been weakened or eliminated, and capital, money, people, goods and services move more freely between countries than ever before.

Internationalisation has been facilitated by the development of new technologies, above all computer-based technologies (cf. Castells 1996; Thurow 1996). Compared to 25 years ago, it is now much easier for people and companies in different parts of the world to communicate with each other. In almost no time at all, they can exchange all kinds of information with each other. This does not mean that communication is of equal benefit for everyone. The new technologies create new inequalities by reshaping the division of labour. They make it possible for companies to locate the manufacturing of goods in areas with inexpensive labour, while at the same time keeping administrative headquarters in a few business centres.

With the internationalisation of economies, competition between firms has intensified (Castells 1996: ch. 2; Drache and Gertler 1991; Porter 1990; Thurow 1996). There are simply more competitors trying hard to increase their share of the markets. This means stronger pressure upon workplaces to reduce costs which in turn make managers demand more flexibility in terms of work organisation, number of employees, work hours, wages, etc. Flexibility can generally be defined as 'the capacity to adapt to change' (Meulders and Wilkin 1987: 5, italics removed), i.e., it refers to the ability and readiness of the firm or the individual worker to adjust to new conditions.

There is now a vast amount of literature contrasting 'Fordist' with 'post-Fordist' work organisation (see Boyer 1988; Hall and Jacques 1989; Piore and Sabel 1984; Sabel and Zeitlin 1997). The old Fordist type of industrial production is usually characterised as based on Tayloristic principles of management with a fragmentation of tasks and a hierarchical, vertically integrated division of labour. It is said to have been organised around standardised products for mass consumption. Cost reduction was accomplished by large-scale solutions. Post-Fordism implies that the traditional mass production regime has been abandoned and succeeded by 'flexible specialisation', vertical disintegration of the organisation, small batch production, more diversified products, and 'just-in-time' production. This reasoning has, however, been questioned by many researchers arguing that the transition from Fordism to post-Fordism has not really taken place or is too much of a simplification of the ongoing processes (see Kumar 1995: ch. 3; Sayer and Walker 1992: chs 4–5; Vallas 1999; Williams *et al.* 1987). A more reasonable hypothesis might be that different production regimes coexist.

Different forms of flexibility often have very different consequences for employers and employees. The introduction of a given type of flexibility may thus become a matter of conflict between the two parties. Generally speaking, it seems that the intensified competition in world markets has given employers an advantage over employees. In an internationalised economy, companies can move production or at least let new investments go to countries where wages are low and employment contracts insecure. Workers in the West, who are used to relatively high wages and stable employment conditions, may therefore have to lower their demands or risk losing their jobs. In the last few decades, it appears that the working class and its organisations, above all the trade unions, have been weakened in the economically advanced world. This process is far from uniform. Most dramatically, it can be observed in countries like the United States and New Zealand, while it is less noticeable in Denmark and Sweden – countries with a high degree of unionisation among workers and an institutionalised negotiation system in the labour market.

It has often been argued, but sometimes also contested, that North America, or at least the United States, has much more flexible labour markets than Western Europe (see Auer 1995; Freeman 1992; Graafland 1989; Lindbeck and Snower 1988; Korpi 1996; Schmid 1994b). The background to this discussion is that, after the recessions in the mid-1970s and the early 1980s, the United States quickly returned to its previous growth pattern with regard to both economic performance and jobs, while Europe was haunted by low economic growth and stagnating employment. Thus, the 'American employment miracle' has been contrasted with 'Eurosclerosis', a 'disease' referring to the alleged lack of labour market flexibility due to regulations imposed by governments or collective agreements and to sup- posedly rigid wage structures created by strong labour unions and welfare state arrangements. A trade-off has been assumed to exist between employment pro- tection and small wage differentials on the one hand and insufficient job growth and high levels of unemployment on the other. From this point of view, Eurosclerosis can be cured only if employment relations become deregulated and higher wage differentials are allowed. These arguments have now become less persuasive with the current economic growth and the decreasing unemployment figures in Europe over the last few years. Moreover, Europe is far from a homoge- neous continent. Since there is a great deal of variation across its countries, it would be very misleading to treat single cases as exponents of the same institutional pattern.

Employment protection has been subjected to several studies (see Buechtemann 1989, 1993; Emerson 1988; Mosley 1994; OECD 1993: ch. 3; OECD 1999b: ch. 2). The idea that restrictive legislation may lead to lower employment is that if it is difficult or costly for companies to make workers redundant, they become afraid of taking on more than a minimum of personnel. There are, of course, counter- arguments. One is that if there is no or little employment protection and employers take advantage of this, then probably more people will also be fired. If more people are recruited to jobs but at the same time more people are dismissed, the effects on employment and unemployment rates may be rather insignificant. Furthermore, at least large companies need to have some management plans and these plans must include calculating the consequences of legislative measures or agreed-upon rules. The really small firms often have a very different situation, but in most countries there are also various exceptions for them.

The arguments concerning wage differentials are rather similar. If people lower the price of their labour enough, the chance presumably increases that someone becomes willing to employ them (see OECD 1994c: part II, ch. 5). The problem is often defined as 'too high real wages and downward wage rigidity, too narrow wage differentials, and too high nonwage labour costs' (Schmid and Schömann 1994: 26). Most often unions and governments are blamed for this state of affairs. Unions prevent wage flexibility by enforcing collective agreements making it impossible that anybody be employed without being paid a certain minimum. Governments keep up wages not only by legislated minimum wages but also, and perhaps more importantly, by generous welfare arrangements providing people with alternatives to carrying out paid work.

There is, however, another aspect to consider in relation to government programmes. So-called active labour market policies are aimed at preparing the unemployed for employment and providing them with jobs. Their underlying idea is the opposite of many other welfare state measures that instead offer people a chance to leave the labour market, such as early retirement programmes. Active labour market policies include public employment services, labour market training, job creation programmes, etc. The question is whether they help lower unemployment or not, and, if the answer is yes, whether they do this at reasonable costs (for overviews on these issues, see Calmfors 1994; Calmfors and Skedinger 1995; Martin 2000; OECD 1993: ch 2; Robinson 2000; Scarpetta 1996). There may, for example, be 'dead-weight', substitution or displacement effects, taking away much of the gross employment effect.

The discussion has also dealt with the consequences of the American model. It is often maintained that even if people are poorly paid, it is still better for them to have a job than to be on the dole. But if wages do not even reach the minimum standard level, is this still a good solution? Does this not imply that the government has to intervene anyway, providing the poor with supplementary resources? Moreover, some have suggested that not only are a lot of Americans unable to support themselves on the basis of full-time jobs, but the level of unemployment is not as related to the high wage differentials as is commonly believed (Mishel and Schmitt 1995). Instead, other factors must be emphasised, for example the size of the home market and the technological advantage.

Furthermore, there may be a specific 'Euro-efficiency'. It has been argued that 'short-term institutional inflexibilities – such as advanced notice of mass redundancies, generous unemployment compensation, further training obligations, the persistent linkage between wages and skill status – can in many cases serve as both a requirement and a stimulus for long-term adaptability'; i.e., 'supposed cases of eurosclerosis prove to be a specific "euro-efficiency"' (Schmid 1994a: 8). The functioning of the labour market is always a matter of the interplay between various actors within the framework of certain institutions. The welfare institutions at hand may promote co-operative relations and perceptions of 'fairness', thus creating better long-term conditions for flexibility and change than if the market mechanisms are allowed to operate in a more uncontrolled way.

The shift towards post-industrialism

It is often assumed today that we – the people in the economically advanced societies in the West – live in a post-industrial era, or at least at its dawning (Bell 1968, 1976; Block 1990; Toffler 1980; Touraine 1971). A common assumption is also that the people of the former state socialist societies in the East are following in our footsteps. And, of course, there are many other countries in the world allegedly moving in the same direction.

The hypotheses of the post-industrial trajectory may seem plausible at least in their more sophisticated versions. However, the economic and social development in Western economies as well as in other parts of the world are more diversified and contradictory than assumed in interpretations arguing that all countries are taking the same post-industrial route. If there were only one route to follow, it might be argued that history is more or less over. Although, in this book, we restrict ourselves to a small number of Western countries – Canada, the United States, Denmark and Sweden – we believe that there is more variety between these four countries than is recognised by many post-industrial theorists. One purpose of our book is thus to spell out various aspects of this diversity.

The author perhaps most often associated with post-industrialism is Daniel Bell. In particular, his book *The Coming of Post-Industrial Society* (1976) developed the main themes of this theory. Bell's point of departure is that the concept of post-industrial society is an analytical construction aimed at catching ongoing changes in modern Western nations (Bell 1976: 483 ff.). It thus does not deal with any specific nation but with tendencies against which existing countries could be measured. In other words, post-industrialism can be understood as an 'ideal type'. Bell is guided by a Weberian principle making him generalise certain features from reality to grasp the basic characteristics of a phenomenon.

Bell's analysis (1976: 9–10) strives to identify 'axial principles' within various societal spheres. It is not a matter of finding causal relationships but of determining 'centrality'. The idea is to figure out how a given society is held together and through conceptual devices to identify the essential elements in its development. Bell makes a distinction between three social spheres: the social structure, the polity and the culture. The development of the post-industrial society is above all a matter of changes within the social structure, i.e., the economy, the occupational structure and the relationship between science and technology (Bell 1976: 12–13). Parenthetically, it could be asked why the latter relationship is not a part of the cultural sphere.

What, then, does Bell focus upon in his analysis? Allowing ourselves some simplification, we could summarise his ideas in the following way (Bell 1976: 14 ff.). First of all, the development towards post-industrial society is characterised by a transition from production of goods to production of services. Second, there is a restructuring of the class composition implying that occupations based upon professional and technical knowledge will expand and gain importance. Finally, Bell argues that theoretical knowledge becomes increasingly significant. Thus, the strategic aspect in society is the production and control of codified knowledge. An 'intellectual technology' will develop and universities will become key institutions.

The analysis is partly conducted by contrasting post-industrial society with its industrial and pre-industrial predecessors (Bell 1976: xii, 116 ff.). Characteristic of the pre-industrial world is that the economy is extractive, i.e., based upon agriculture, fishing, forestry, mining, etc. In contrast, industrial society means production of goods with the help of energy and machines. The key feature of post-industrialism is the 'processing' of knowledge and information. Bell describes the ideal-type 'design' of pre-industrial society as a 'game against nature', and the corresponding industrial and post-industrial designs are characterised as a 'game against fabricated nature' and a 'game between persons'.

According to Bell (1976: 15), services are central to post-industrial development, but they also exist in pre-industrial and industrial societies. The context, however, is very different in the three systems. In pre-industrial society, services are above all a matter of work in private households. Industrialism brought with it an expansion of a service sector related to the production of goods, i.e., transportation, communication, financing, etc. Finally, in post-industrial society, services are a matter of education, health care, and other professional activities.

As has been said, the concept of post-industrial society is an analytical construction aimed at grasping tendencies of development. Thus, Bell (1976: xvi) emphasises that post-industrial society will not replace industrial society totally any more than the latter replaced pre-industrial society. Instead, the three types of systems coexist. Therefore, strictly speaking, we should talk about a pre-industrial, industrial and post-industrial *sector* rather than society.

For Bell, the post-industrial development is characterised by the decisive role given to knowledge and technology. Of course, knowledge has been important in all societies, but in post-industrial society there is a primacy of theoretical knowledge (Bell 1976: 20). Theory triumphs over empirical information and is codified in abstract systems of thought. Universities become crucial institutions. With the increasing role of knowledge, the possibilities for societal planning in various spheres expands, implying a greater role for the state.

The growing proportion of services and the strengthening of theoretical knowledge are accompanied by changes in the composition of occupations and in the class structure. Professional and technical occupations, based upon education and knowledge, have a key position. Therefore, power relations in society change. Those who were powerful previously due to their ownership of material resources have to make concessions to other groups. In post-industrial society, a new class of professionals and technical intelligentsia becomes dominant, which does not exclude internal ideological conflicts (Bell 1976: 358–9).

Although the concept of service is crucial in his book, Bell never explicitly tells the reader what he means by it. The word 'service' is not included in his index (but we find the words 'service occupation'). This is no doubt a remarkable omission in the analysis. However, Bell implicitly departs from the distinction between 'services' and 'goods'. The assumption is perhaps that our daily language provides a general conception of what is meant and that no more is needed.

Several authors have criticised Bell's (lack of) treatment of the service concept (e.g., Gershuny 1978: 55–9; Offe 1985: ch. 4; Sayer and Walker 1992: 56 ff.). It is common to advocate a rather narrow definition of the crucial concept. In Gershuny's words (1978: 56), 'services . . . are immaterial, non-permanent, made by people for people ("post-industrial society" is essentially a game between persons) and can only be consumed in the moment of production. When a good is acquired by the consumer, it is a *thing* while a service is a *state* or an *activity* or a *sensation*.' From a definition of this kind, a number of activities that are usually considered to be services, such as sending out pay cheques for a company or revising its financial situation, have to be excluded. This also means that the idea of the expanding service sector appears as much exaggerated.

However, many social scientists agree on the importance of growth in service activities, although they may quarrel over the definitions of services and service work. There is of course a need to find a label for the activities for which we gave two examples above and that do not fit in with Gershuny's definition. The proper way of proceeding appears to be to define a general service concept and then distinguish different kinds of services. This is also a very common solution in the literature (see Elfring 1988; Esping-Andersen 1990: 195–7; Forsman 1984: 31–3; Singelmann 1978a). We could talk about a wider and a narrower concept of service (Furåker 1987: 124–9). The narrow definition would then be close to the concept used by Gershuny and others, and the wide one could include, more or less, everything else that is commonly referred to as services.

Along with the debate over his concepts of service and service work, Bell's general propositions have also been widely discussed and criticised. It would take us too far to scrutinise all the questions that have been brought up, but a few more points need to be noted. One of the most important criticisms is that intellectual technology is also closely related to industrialism (Kumar 1988: 29–30, 81; see also Giddens 1989: 649–50). Of course, the gigantic technical development that has taken place during the industrial era and that has made industry so highly productive is based upon knowledge and the exchange of knowledge. The results of research and technology have been continuously applied within industry. It cannot reasonably be argued that the transition to intellectual technology appeared only with the decline of the industrial sector.

Some service work involves great responsibilities and/or a high degree of autonomy for the incumbents of the jobs. It thus creates a demand for highly qualified labour. However, the service sector is very heterogeneous. A significant number of service jobs do not require much theoretical knowledge but are above all a matter of manual labour (Giddens 1989: 649; Harrison and Bluestone 1988). The whole idea of a new class of professionals and technical intelligentsia has been highly debated and contested over the years (for some discussion on this topic, see Esping-Andersen 1993).

In spite of the criticisms that can be directed against his analysis, Bell provides a picture of certain changes occurring in most advanced capitalist societies and these changes must be taken seriously. The relative size of the service sector has grown and will probably continue to do so, while the industrial sector is headed downwards. Science and technology have become increasingly more important and this appears to be an irreversible process. Even though they may not form a dominant class, occupational groups based upon theoretical knowledge have gained relatively strong positions in society. Nevertheless, we certainly find significant differences between countries in terms of the speed and scope of these processes. Moreover, there are many other aspects that need to be taken into account in an analysis of modern labour market developments. In the following section, we will bring up some such ideas.

The focus of this book

Several years before the concept of post-industrialism was introduced, Clark Kerr and his co-authors argued that the 'logic of industrialism' made modern nations increasingly similar (Kerr *et al.* 1960). Industrialism would lead to certain changes in terms of the division of labour, urbanisation, the development of the educational system and the expansion of certain cultural values related to science and technology (see also Feldman and Moore 1962; Levy Jr. 1966). For some analysts, the Soviet Union and other state socialist societies were considered to be part of the same development (e.g., Mills 1958; Sorokin 1964). The ideas of Kerr and others have been criticised by many (e.g., Badham 1986; Ellman 1980; Goldthorpe 1971; Meyer 1970; see also Giddens 1989: 647). For example, it has been pointed out that there are still great differences between industrialised nations and that similarities and differences between them may not derive directly from the level of industrialisation.

In addition, there is not even agreement among social scientists concerning the concept of post-industrialism and how to determine when a given society has reached this stage of development. Although Bell (1976: xii) is solicitous to argue that there are no 'unilineal sequences of societal change', no 'laws of social development', there may be some temptation to interpret his analysis as implying a process of convergence between nations. In a self-critical note in his book *Postindustrial Possibilities*, Fred Block (1990: 7, n.16) takes an earlier text by himself and his co-author Larry Hirschhorn as an example of this tendency to regard post-industrialism as 'an inevitable process of social development'. In order to avoid deterministic evolutionary assumptions, which Bell never entertained, Block argues for a reformulation of the theory.

Post-industrialism is thus regarded as 'the historical period that begins when the concept of industrial society ceases to provide an adequate account of actual social developments' (Block 1990: 11). It seems, however, that this statement can be interpreted in exactly those terms that the author wants to criticise. Block argues that this definition has two virtues. First, it does not take a stand concerning what the most fundamental elements are for the constitution of the society. Second, it is a way of emphasising that post-industrialism is an ongoing process. Although it is difficult to see that they follow from the above-mentioned definition, these arguments are reasonable. Therefore, we will be looking for alternative post-industrial routes and their possible determinants.

This book will deal with the structure and functioning of labour markets. A guiding question is how they are shaped by the intensified competition due to the globalisation or internationalisation of economic activities and by the changes in the direction of a service, information or knowledge society. We are at the same time interested in whether the ongoing changes take different forms depending on the institutional frameworks furnished by the individual countries. The relationship between market forces and social institutions is thus a crucial dimension. Above all, attention will be paid to the role of organised interests (unions) and of government (welfare state) legislation and policies. These institutions can be expected to have some, presumably rather material, impact on the functioning of labour markets.

First, we will briefly discuss unions and collective bargaining. The influence of the trade unions is very different in the four countries to be dealt with here. Sweden and Denmark have high degrees of unionisation, whereas Canada and in particular the United States score much lower (for details, see Chapter 2). Not only do the Danish and Swedish trade unions have a much larger proportion of employees as members and a much wider coverage of collective agreements, they also have substantially more political influence than their North American counterparts. The key to this is their relationship with the strong national social democratic parties. In both Denmark and Sweden, social democracy has long been the most powerful political force. Through the union–political party nexus, the interests of the Scandinavian wage earners have been better looked after than probably any other wage earners in the capitalist world. The North American situation is radically different. To be sure, the Democratic Party in the United States has certain ties with the trade unions, but these ties are comparatively weak and complicated. In Canada, the New Democratic Party has been successful for some time in some of the provinces, but its role has been considerably more modest than that of social democracy in Scandinavia.

Second, we will deal with some aspects of government intervention in the labour market. To some extent, the role of the state reflects the power of the unions and the working class or, rather, the balance of power between contending social forces in society. Thus, a strong labour movement can be expected to push public policies towards improving the work conditions of ordinary workers, protecting their jobs, creating a generous social security system, and decreasing income differentials among them (see Esping-Andersen 1985, 1990; Korpi 1983; Korpi and Palme 1998; O'Connor and Olsen 1998; Stephens 1979).

On a general level we can distinguish three different functions fulfilled by the state in modern capitalist societies (Furåker 1987: 39–47). The word 'function' does not here imply a functionalist interpretation of the world but is used in a descriptive way only. First, the state maintains law and order. This is done through legislation and other kinds of rule making, ultimately sanctioned by a police and a judicial system. External defence and the maintenance of international relations can be included under this function. In terms of the labour market, employment protection legislation is also an example. Second, the state redistributes resources, mainly through taxation and transfers. Finally, it has an important role as the organiser of service and, to a much lesser extent, goods production. All three of these forms of state intervention are indeed important for the functioning of the labour market, and since there are significant differences in these respects among the countries to be analysed, we will have to come back to them repeatedly.

Applying these general distinctions to the labour markets in Western countries, we find that the first type of state intervention mentioned above corresponds to labour legislation. The state intervenes in different ways by establishing and maintaining rules for the interaction between employers and employees. Labour law is oriented towards employment protection, job safety, work-time regulation, etc. It provides legal standards for the hiring and firing of personnel and for the physical and psychosocial work environment, including decision-making processes in the workplace.

The second type of state intervention is redistribution through taxation and transfer payments. It involves social protection for individuals when they become ill, unemployed, old, etc. A crucial issue is the impact of transfer payments on people's needs or intentions to be gainfully employed. By providing subsistence in case of illness, unemployment, old age and so on, the welfare state also furnishes those who cannot work with basic security. This may imply that some individuals who in fact could work do not because they are supported anyway. The debate over possible work disincentives created by the welfare state is probably endless. However, the general goal is not to make people leave the labour market, but to support them when they cannot earn a living themselves or, as regarding old-age pensions, are considered to have done their part. Social policies may have different consequences for the labour market in affecting people's capacity for, and willingness to, work. Among other things, we are interested in the unemployment insurance (sometimes referred to as passive labour market policy) and in measures aimed at putting people (back) into work (i.e., active labour market policies).

Third, the state is not only a legislator and a redistributor of resources but also a provider and producer of goods and services. Government goods production should not be completely ignored, but it usually has a rather limited scope in the Western world, in particular after the privatisation campaigns of the last decades. It is above all in the service sector that the government acts as producer. Welfare state research has been criticised for mainly focusing on transfer payments and thus neglecting social service production (see Olsen 1994: 5; Sainsbury 1996: 37). For those of us interested in the relationship between the welfare state and the labour market, it is important to pay attention to the government's producer role.

In producing services like health care, education and care for children and the elderly, the state acts in the labour market as employer. In most economically advanced countries in the West, public sector employees make up a fairly large, although varying, proportion of total employment (see Alestalo, Bislev and Furåker 1991; Cusack, Noterman and Rein 1989; Furåker 1989; Rose 1985; Saunders and Klau 1985; and the account in Chapter 6). Sweden and Denmark have a leading position as regards the proportion of public employees (close to one-third of total employment), whereas Canada is clearly lower in this respect and the United States much lower. The welfare state expansion especially in Scandinavia has involved recruitment of large numbers of people, primarily women, to jobs in the government social service sector.

Labour markets cannot just be treated as simple economic structures. In analysing them, we have to take into consideration the different institutional frameworks. The trade unions, the system of collective bargaining and the welfare state are examples of important institutions. Of course, there are also others that need to be considered. For example, we should not forget the role of the family. There will be relatively little focus on the family in this book, but we do not want to play down its significance. No doubt, it has a decisive role in relation to, among other things, female labour force participation. This will be more extensively discussed in some of the analyses to come.

Why this four-country comparison?

There are different reasons why we have selected our four cases: Canada, the United States, Denmark and Sweden. A decisive factor is that Denmark and Sweden are the home countries of all the authors in the book. Thus, these two countries are best known to us. Most of the authors have also long been interested in events in North America. This interest has been developed during longer or shorter visits to Canada and the United States and through direct collaboration with North American colleagues in research projects (see van den Berg, Furåker and Johansson 1997).

Another aspect must also be mentioned. Denmark and Sweden are members of the European Union (EU). Denmark has been a member since 1973 and Sweden since 1995. The EU has gradually expanded and will continue to do so. Its internal processes of reorganisation and integration have garnered much attention in both Denmark and Sweden. The public debate has become oriented towards European issues, perhaps more than would be justified if we think in terms of more general societal developments. Danes and Swedes may have just as much or even more to learn from what is going on in North America than from the European scene. (Of course, we should not forget other parts of the world.) At least some of the EU member states appear to be further away from the Scandinavian setting than the two North American countries. Developments occurring 'over there' often become a part of our debates more rapidly than changes taking place in southern Europe.

Our selection of countries is also based upon theoretical considerations. Canada, the United States, Denmark and Sweden are at about the same stage of post-industrialism and their economies are all deeply involved in the internationalisation process. Nevertheless, the four countries are very different in many respects. As noted above, one crucial difference is that North America and Scandinavia represent rather opposite poles in the way their labour markets are regulated. The two Scandinavian neighbours have much stronger trade unions and a much more interventionist welfare state.

Researchers of the welfare state tend to classify Canada and the United States as belonging to a 'liberal' model and Denmark and Sweden as belonging to a 'social democratic' model. This is exemplified by Gøsta Esping-Andersen's (1990: 26–9) well-known typology of three worlds of welfare capitalism. Canada and the

United States are regarded as liberal models characterised by strong reliance on the market and low levels of welfare spending, means-tested assistance and small numbers of citizens eligible for benefits. Denmark and Sweden are examples of the social democratic model with universal income-related benefits combined with a strong ambition to diminish inequality and poverty. There is also a third, a corporatist or conservative model, typified by Germany. It differs from the social democratic regime in being more oriented towards preserving social and economic differentials as well as the family institution and from the liberal welfare state regime in not having the same reliance on the market.

Others who have used different typologies by, for example, arguing for a fourth category – be it Antipodean, Mediterranean, or East Asian (cf. Esping-Andersen 1999: 88–92) – have nevertheless most often classified Canada, the United States, Denmark and Sweden in the same way as Esping-Andersen. However, there are exceptions to this. In Walter Korpi and Joakim Palme's work on the welfare state and social insurance systems, Denmark is associated with the liberal or market countries (Korpi and Palme 1998; Korpi 2000). Without going into details, we observe that the authors classify not only Canada and the United States but also Denmark as belonging to the basic security model in which eligibility is based on contributions or citizenship and flat-rate benefits are applied. Only Sweden among our four cases is included in the encompassing model, where citizenship and labour force participation form the basis for eligibility and benefits are flat-rate or income related.

In his book *American Exceptionalism*, Seymour Martin Lipset (1996) develops the idea that the United States is in fact economically, politically and culturally unique compared to the rest of the world. He has previously analysed the differences between Canada and the United States, arguing that Canada has many European features making it very unlike its southern neighbour (Lipset 1990). We will not go into a debate about whether Lipset's conclusions are right or wrong, but we think it is important for researchers to keep an open mind and, if warranted, modify or go beyond existing typologies of societal models. Social and economic transformations are usually shaped by a combination of factors that may be difficult to capture in simple analytical categories.

There has been a lot of discussion of, and criticism against, the ambition to create welfare state typologies (Castles and Mitchell 1990; Olsen 1994; Sainsbury 1996: 9–14; Stephens 1994). Here we can note one such criticism. By placing countries in predefined categories, we may underestimate their differences. Ideal types rather than specific countries are being compared. If Canada and the United States are both classified as liberal, the differences between them may remain hidden. Moreover, welfare state models tend to neglect the differences between various programmes in a single country. For a given country, we may find a rather heterogeneous picture. One programme is perhaps best classified as 'social democratic', whereas another is typically 'liberal'. Even within a given programme, there may be different elements that are akin to different models.

We do not think welfare state typologies should be avoided. On the contrary, we believe that these typologies have greatly contributed to the development of welfare state research and that they will continue to play a crucial role. Of course, when we chose between one or the other typology the decisive issue will always be what purpose a given study is supposed to attain. Whenever classification schemes are applied there is a risk that important nuances will be neglected, but we must live with this if we are to do comparative research involving several nations.

In our four-country comparison, we can allow ourselves to be rather open to differences. Still, as a starting point, two main models can clearly be distinguished, a North American and a Scandinavian model, because, in significant respects, Canada and the United States cluster as do Denmark and Sweden. At the same time, in the course of this book it will become evident that North America is far from being a homogeneous continent. This can also be said about Scandinavia. There are significant differences between Canada and the United States as well as between Denmark and Sweden. Since this is just the introduction to the book, though, we should not say too much about the relative distances between the four countries.

These issues will not be discussed further now, but we will return to them later in the book. To summarise, large differences can be found among countries that have reached approximately the same level of economic development. The post-industrial world is far from uniform. There are several good reasons for comparing the two North American and the two Scandinavian neighbours. North America is considerably closer to the ideal of the 'free' market and Scandinavia is much more regulated by unions and governments. However, we must be careful not to forget the differences within each of the two camps. In some respects, Canada is more similar to Europe than to the United States, and Denmark is sometimes closer to Canada (and even the United States) than to Sweden, such as in terms of legislated employment protection. Thus, we need to analyse the differences between nations carefully. The remainder of the introduction will briefly outline the rest of the book.

The structure of the book

Part I, consisting of Chapters 2, 3 and 4, deals with institutions that are important for how the labour markets in the four countries function. Though North America and Scandinavia have gone through economic and technological developments with many common traits, we find significant differences in the way national labour markets work. We will therefore take a closer look at some of their institutional frameworks. Three crucial topics are to be examined: industrial relations, labour law, and the welfare state and labour market policy.

Part II, consisting of Chapters 5 to 10, explores a number of labour market indicators in Canada, the United States, Denmark and Sweden. These include labour force participation, employment rates, part-time work, industrial structures, the occupational composition of the work force, unemployment, various types of flexibility and income differentials. We will examine these indicators in relation to the topics discussed in the preceding chapters. A crucial issue is whether differences between the four labour markets can be understood in terms of the institutional set-up in each country. In Part III, Chapter 11 compares the two North American and the two Scandinavian cases with other labour markets within the OECD.

Thomas P. Boje and Rafael Lindqvist are the authors of the first chapter on institutional frameworks. In Chapter 2, they outline the general patterns of industrial relations in the four countries. They start out from the late nineteenth century and trace how different traditions have developed up to the present. A main argument is that the early formation of blue-collar workers' trade unions and their counterparts' associations – and the early interplay between these organised interests – must be considered crucial also for organisational developments in the service sector and among white-collar workers. Furthermore, it is emphasised that organisations representing the working class have played a much more significant role in Denmark and Sweden than in Canada and the United States. In addition to describing these divergent patterns, the authors also spell out some of the most important differences within North America and Scandinavia.

One part of the institutional framework of labour markets is labour law, which is dealt with in Chapter 3. Written by Rafael Lindqvist, this chapter focuses on rules related to hiring and firing procedures and to co-determination. It turns out that the two Scandinavian countries differ from North America, and in particular the United States, but also from each other. Sweden has the most severe restrictions concerning hiring and firing, and it has the most developed co-determination legislation. Denmark is much more 'liberal' in both of these respects and does not differ greatly from Canada. However, the differences between Denmark and Sweden become less obvious when we take collectively negotiated solutions into consideration. Collective agreements also have some significance in North America.

Chapter 4, jointly written by Bengt Furåker and Rafael Lindqvist, is an attempt to adopt a wider perspective on the role of the state, especially the welfare state. This chapter has three main objects of study: transfers, service production and labour market policy. The welfare state is to a large extent a re-distributor of resources, i.e., it gathers resources primarily through taxation and distributes them according to politically determined criteria as pensions, illness benefits, unemployment benefits, etc. Furthermore, it is an important producer of services, e.g., childcare, health care, education and care for the elderly. In doing this, the state enters the labour market as employer. This chapter's final section touches on labour market policy as a special kind of state intervention in the labour market. This includes both transfers (such as unemployment benefits) and services (such as placement services). Sometimes the state also takes a direct employer role for the unemployed as is the case in certain job creation programmes.

From Chapter 5, the book concentrates on labour market outcomes. Chapter 5, authored by Thomas P. Boje, presents detailed information on labour force participation and employment. Boje shows us the differences and similarities between the four countries in these respects. The main characteristic they all share is that male labour force participation and employment rates tend to decline slowly, whereas the corresponding female rates are increasing at a relatively high pace. Even if Scandinavian women seem to be ahead of their North American sisters, the similarities are more striking than the differences. There is no doubt that the feminisation of employment is a common feature of the post-industrial labour market.

In Chapter 6, Thomas P. Boje explores the distribution of the workforce across sectors and industries. Agriculture has long since been reduced to a tiny fraction of total employment in all four countries, whereas about one fourth of all employees work in industrial production (including construction), and the rest, about 70 per cent or more, are engaged in service production. This general pattern applies to all four countries, but there are also differences. One of the most important of these is the relative size of public employment. The two Scandinavian neighbours have about 30 per cent of the workforce employed in the public sector compared to less than 20 per cent in Canada and less than 15 per cent in the United States.

In Chapter 7, Lars H. Hansen examines the occupational distributions in the four countries. There are several striking similarities but also some disparities. One main conclusion is that high-skill occupations are growing more rapidly than other occupational groups in all four countries, which strengthens the notion of a more or less universal process of post-industrialisation. One specific trait that sets the countries apart is that the occupational structures of Canada and the United States are characterised by larger shares of managers than are those of Denmark and Sweden. Gender segregation is also considered in this chapter. To achieve an equal distribution of both men and women across occupations, more people would have to switch jobs in Scandinavia than in North America.

Chapter 8, authored by Bengt Furåker, is an analysis of the unemployment patterns in our four countries. Unemployment is of course related to business cycles; it usually decreases in boom periods and rises during recessions. So far, the four countries resemble each other, but they nevertheless show some very significant differences. During the 1980s, Sweden had by far the lowest unemployment rates, but the situation changed dramatically in the 1990s. Sweden then even passed the level of Canada, the country with the highest rates most of the time since 1980. Accordingly, Denmark and the United States had the lowest unemployment levels most of the 1990s. Towards the turn of the millennium unemployment began to decline in all four countries. Furåker discusses these changing patterns in relation to various theories on what makes unemployment occur.

The book then addresses the issue of labour market flexibility. In Chapter 9, Thomas P. Boje and Anne Grönlund present some of the literature dealing with this topic. In particular, they concentrate on the predictions that theorists have brought forward about labour market flexibilisation. The authors above all use the distinction between numerical, working time and functional flexibility. It turns out to be very difficult to find relevant and reliable empirical indicators on the different flexibility types. Although labour market statistics are generally well developed, they provide surprisingly little help for this purpose. The few relevant indicators that exist, however, do not lend much support to the various predictions about a thorough-going flexibilisation of labour markets, although obviously certain changes have occurred.

Chapter 10 – by Thomas P. Boje and Per Kongshøj Madsen – focuses on earnings inequality, earnings mobility and low pay as well as on the relationship between wage growth and changes in unemployment. During the past three decades, the two Scandinavian countries and Canada have had strong changes in wage growth, while the United States shows a more stable pattern. Earnings inequalities are, however, far more pronounced in Canada and the United States than in Denmark and Sweden. There is no clear evidence of a correlation between employment among precarious groups of employees and level of payment. Furthermore, nearly the same degree of earnings mobility is found in the four countries, but the move out of low-paid work was significantly higher in Scandinavia than in the United States; as a consequence far more US workers were living in poverty even if they had a full-time job.

Finally, in Chapter 11, Bengt Furåker extends the country comparisons more systematically to other OECD countries. This gives us a broader perspective on the question whether our four cases are similar to or different from each other. It appears that Canada, the United States, Denmark and Sweden are very often closer to each other than to many other countries, for example southern European countries. However, the four countries are sometimes divided into different clusters and this is often related to the role of the welfare state. The chapter is also an attempt to characterise post-industrial societies – North American, Scandinavian and others – in terms of employment, female employment, service production, self-employment and a number of other aspects.

Part I

The institutional framework of national labour markets

2 Labour movement and industrial relations

Thomas P. Boje and Rafael Lindqvist

Introduction

Union membership and the number of labour strikes decreased across most of the economically advanced world throughout the 1980s and into the early 1990s. Trade unions and the organised working class seemed to be in trouble because their organisations were by-passed by a high-tech age of globalisation, knowledge work, fragmentation and flexibility in work organisation. A strong wind of neo-liberal market economics has influenced all capitalist countries. For the most optimistic supporters of trade unions, the possible solution for increasing political influence seems to be increased involvement of unions in the 'negotiated economy' of tripartite institutions or 'social partnership' agreements between the institutional actors in the labour market (Moody 1997/2001).

Obviously, as shown throughout this book, the labour market has changed. For a long time, male industrial workers dominated the working class and its institutions and were the impetus for union organisation, but they no longer comprise the majority of the working class. Women now play an important role in the labour force and in the labour movement. Increasingly, immigrant workers have entered the workforce, the organisation of work has changed with a growing number of contingent jobs, and the organisation of the production process itself has been transformed through strategies that encourage flexibility, subcontracting and outsourcing. In the spirit of human resource management, the old forms of labour protection have been replaced by quality circles, participation and empowerment of the individual workers often in an attempt to decrease the influence of trade unions (Crouch and Streeck 1997; Tilly and Tilly 1998; Moody 1997/2001: 11). In all industrial countries, the shift from national economies to global industries, the shift from 'Fordist' production chains to flexible knowledge-based network production, and the shift towards a more diversified labour force have changed industrial relations. However, these changes have not altered the basic relationship between workers and employers. This relationship remains uneven and dominated by the capital owners. In *Economy and Society*, Max Weber describes this one-sided relationship as 'the more powerful party in the market, i.e., normally the employer, has the possibility to set the terms, to offer the job "take it or leave it", and, given the normally more pressing economic need of the worker, to impose his terms on him' (1978: 729 f.).

In industrial relations literature, several hypotheses have been developed concerning the possible influence of trade unions and the institutional framework based on negotiations between capital and labour with respect to labour market performance. In this chapter, some of these hypotheses will be reviewed based on the differences in labour market outcomes in Scandinavia and North America. However, trade unions have in all countries at least three functions: (1) they are the institutions which provide collective bargaining with the employers on wage and work conditions; (2) they are part of a social movement aimed at improving the living conditions of workers; (3) they are pressure groups that influence parliaments, governments and public administrations. Throughout the twentieth century, the position of trade unions has been accepted and typically they have become stronger and a more integrated part of the institutional framework for negotiating wages, work time and living conditions of the workers.

Despite the growing institutionalisation of unions, their role is still highly debated and in several countries strongly contested. In discussing the role of trade unions, two completely different approaches are often confronted (Freeman and Medoff 1984). On the one hand, the unions are viewed as a monopoly that negatively influences the market because it undermines the country's competitive position. This view claims that unions protect the insiders in the workforce from the outsiders – those who are unemployed are excluded from getting gainful employment. On the other hand, the unions are praised because they provide employees a voice and ensure their concerns are heard when employment terms and working conditions are negotiated. By participating in determining the employment conditions, workers do not need to exit from negotiations in case of disagreement between workers and employers, but they might still – through their voice – be able to influence the negotiations through their trade unions. This alternative of voice through negotiation is, according to those arguing for the integration of the unions into the economy, more efficient than the alternative of exit because that alternative typically means labour conflicts, strikes, etc. (Visser 2001: 189–90).

The four countries included in this study are markedly different in their approach to industrial relations. Unions and employer organisations are different and so is the type of collective bargaining system used in each country. In this chapter we analyse how these differences have emerged during the development of the industrial relation systems. In this respect, the industrial structure of the economy and the composition of the labour force greatly influence the system of industrial relations. Even more important for the development of industrial relations and for the role of unions in policy-making on wages, work conditions and employment terms are the political orientation and ideological values of the working class and its organisations. How the political and social institutions incorporate individual freedom, egalitarianism, collectivism and state interventionism are crucial in defining the position of the working class and the influence of the labour movement. A conventional distinction is evident between countries characterised by adversarial industrial relations (Canada and the United States) and countries with more consensual industrial relations (Scandinavian countries). For countries with adversarial industrial relations, the adaptation of the labour market and its institutions that change economic conditions occurs more slowly than in countries with consensual industrial relations (Bamber 1998).

In studies about labour movements and the process of unionisation, a variety of factors have been identified in understanding the differences in structure and political position of national union movements. Poole (1981) and Visser (1991, 1994) identify in their studies of unionisation the most important dimensions that influence the system of industrial relations: structural economic characteristics such as the industrial development; the role of small firms; foreign ownership and international competition; institutional factors such as government support for or antagonism against unionisation and how the unions are regulated by government; ideological opinions about trade unions such as the workers' attitude about collective organisations and action; the influence of religious organisations on trade union; and managerial strategies for labour relations.

This chapter does not allow for an analysis of all the dimensions mentioned above. We start with a brief account of the formation, structure and development of industrial relations in the two Scandinavian and North American countries. Following the historical description of the present industrial relations in the four countries, we localise them in relation to other OCED countries with respect to unionisation and collective bargaining. The chapter concludes with a discussion on the future of industrial relations that influence globalisation, diversification and flexibility of the position of the trade unions in the society.

Organisation of the labour movement – the socio-political background

Historically, trade unions can be seen as broad counter-movements that attempt to modify the economic and social inequalities created by the prevailing market distribution in emerging capitalist societies. However, such labour market conditions have not always resulted in unionisation and employer representation. Variations among national labour movements concerning the relation between unions and working-class parties can take various forms. Valenzuela (1994: 54–5) claims that the Scandinavian countries fit into the *social democratic* type in which 'the unions link up to basically one national organisation that in turn connects itself with a single relatively strong party'. The US labour movement, and the Canadian to some extent, can be characterised as the *pressure group* type in which unions link themselves to individual politicians or fractions of pre-existing parties.

The historical differences of the North American and European working classes and the absence of social democratic parties especially in the United States have been a curiosity for many labour market researchers. During most of the industrialisation process, the European working class has been 'included' in the political establishment through a variety of institutional organisations. Despite profound differences in the level of class conflicts and in the tradition for, and level of organisation of, the working class, all European societies have well-organised labour movements. Moreover, the European unions have typically been integrated in the welfare system through corporatist institutions. In Europe, the relationship between capital and labour has been mediated and regulated through a large number of collective self-formed institutions at the economic, social, political and cultural level. Even during the postwar period of increasing globalisation, individualisation and flexibility of production and work processes, institutional class co-operation in industrial relations has been maintained in most countries and remained a dominant feature of the European industrial relation systems (Davis 1987: 7–8).

The American working class, on the other hand, has developed in a fundamentally different direction. The working class has never been integrated in the political and social institutions. Instead, it 'has been increasingly integrated into American capitalism through the *negativities* of its internal stratifications, its privatisation in consumption, and its disorganisation *vis-à-vis* political and trade-union bureaucracies' (Davis 1987: 8). During a crucial period in the formation of the labour movement – the world crisis of the 1930s and the postwar economic restructuring period of the 1940s – the American working class was characterised by fragmentation and increasing depolitisation. The Western European working class, however, succeeded in encouraging economic and political co-operative institutions and in remaining a reformist social force influencing the political decision-making process. This occurred especially in the Scandinavian countries characterised by strong labour movements closely integrated into the welfare state apparatus.

The history of the US and Canadian working class is by no means identical. Canada has had a somewhat stronger socialist and trade union movement than the United States. Despite obvious similarities in economic and social development in the United States and Canada, the strength of the two labour movements and the institutional framework for regulating the capital–labour system are different although they have come closer during the recent decades of internationalisation. Lipset (1990) describes this as a 'continental divide'; the US is part of British North America that successfully broke from the British Commonwealth, while Canada remained highly influenced by British politics. Lipset (1996) traces this difference back to the period when the two North American nations and their economic and political institutions were formed. These different outcomes of the de-colonisation process resulted in markedly different socialist and labour movements and in different views on state intervention and labour legislation.

The United States had a liberal revolution that created a general value system based on rationalism and individualism without 'the traditional values of rigid social classes derived from feudalism' (Lipset 1996: 87). In this political culture, it was not the fight against an old-fashioned political system nor a struggle for political voting rights that was crucial, but instead the virtues of hard work and the need to exploit nature were emphasised. In the United States, the population attained the right of suffrage prior to being organised into class-based parties; one of the consequences of this was that a European type of labour movement and party structure never developed. This political culture also reflects the attitudes of the dominant US unions. They have generally accepted the capitalist market ideology and rejected socialist ideas. Unlike the Scandinavian unions, the American unions have not been active in forming a major socialist political party nor were they affiliated with any political movement. Instead, political action of unions took the form of exchanging electoral and financial aid for the promise that individual candidates would support their agenda. That is, the unions expect candidates to support sympathetic legislative and governmental initiatives. The major aim of American unions has thus been to improve the material living conditions of their members on a day-to-day basis and for specific groups of workers.

Canada, on the other hand, is the country of a counter-revolution. It remains British and its political institutions grew out of the British Tory tradition. In Canada, Lipset (1996: 92) reminds us that 'the Tory tradition has meant support for a strong state, communitarianism, group solidarity, and elitism'. In reality, this is manifested in public enterprises, in more and earlier introduced social programmes, and in more restricted support for *laissez-faire* capitalism. During the 1930s, many Canadian labour activists took part in the formation of the first viable social democratic party, which was a relationship that became stronger over the years. This relationship resulted in the formation of a renewed party, the New Democratic Party, which was established in the early 1960s (Lipset 1996: 96). *Laissez-faire* market capitalism, which rejects any form of capital–labour regulation, dominates in the United States, whereas state intervention and regulation through co-operative institutions are important parts of the Canadian political culture. Consequently, the Canadians adapt social democratic ideas and use them as a comprehensive industrial relation system to produce a 'civilised' capitalist economy (Lipset 1990).

Compared with North America and the rest of Europe, the similarities rather than the differences characterise the formation of the Scandinavian industrial relations system. In both the Scandinavian countries trade unions initiated the formation of social democratic parties. The labour movement predated universal suffrage and the socialist parties had to appeal to the workers for support before the universal suffrage was instituted. Indeed, class consciousness followed from the political organisational efforts and social democracy grew through the struggle for electoral democracy. The formation of a labour movement was secured through early collective bargaining and politically moderate reforming leadership. Capitalists, as the possible organisers of governments, also soon accepted labour parties (Valenzuela 1994: 69). The welfare state became a function of a strong, centralised and unified working-class movement (Esping-Andersen 1990; Korpi 1983; Stephens 1979). With their broad and well-organised unions and central collective bargaining systems, social democratic regimes formed a breeding ground for neo-corporatism in the 1970s when governments faced the challenge of rising inflation coupled with growing recession and unemployment. Trade union strength in both the state and the industrial arena helped deal with grievances and demands (Korpi 1983).

Three common traits characterise the formation and growth of the Scandinavian labour movements. First, the formation of the Scandinavian labour movement was based on a largely homogeneous class of workers. Second, the labour movement was accepted early by the employers and the state authorities considered the movement as the legitimate representatives for the workers. Third, in both Denmark and Sweden the labour movement was closely connected to the social democratic movement. They can be considered as two pillars of the same structure. Trade unions were in fact the organisational basis upon which the social democratic parties in both countries were built (Elvander 1980: 35–49).

However, there are also differences between Denmark and Sweden in the organisation of the system of industrial relations and these differences can be traced to the fact that industrialisation and societal changes developed differently in the two countries. Denmark was urbanised and industrialised earlier than Sweden, and Denmark's industry was built around small enterprises and typically oriented towards home-market and consumer goods. Even today, more than 80 per cent of all Danish firms have less than 10 employees. This industrial structure has favoured a craft-based union organisation rather than an organisation along industrial lines (Scheuer 1998: 152–6) and resulted in the Danish labour movement growing more slowly and becoming more moderate than the Swedish labour movement. From its beginning, the Danish labour movement was decentralised and fragmented, which from time to time created tension within the labour movement between craft unions organising skilled workers in small firms and general unions organising unskilled workers employed primarily in larger firms.

Swedish industry was export-oriented, based on natural resources, and characterised by large firms with a production based on a number of strategically important technical inventions and with a more centralised structure of ownership than in Denmark (Elvander 1980: 23–8). The late but rapid industrialisation in Sweden meant that Swedish trade unions were organised around industries rather than along narrow craft interests. Consequently, from the early beginnings of Swedish unionisation, craft unions formed a minority in comparison with the vast groups of workers organised along industry lines. This resulted in wide-spread unionisation and led to centralisation for both employee and employer organisations, which came much earlier than in Denmark.

The historical development of industrial relations – formation of unions and their recognition

The formation of the unions and the conditions under which they are recognised in the four countries is the focus of this section. This needs to be addressed in order to understand how the position of the working class in the individual countries differs and to evaluate the influence of unions on industrial relations. The collective bargaining process and the system of employment regulation will be described later in this and the next chapter.

Formation of unions

In Denmark, the union structure was established by the end of the 1800s and the Trade Union Federation (LO) was established in 1898. The unions were organised around traditional crafts. Vocational education has been the dominant principle for union organisation in Denmark until recently. However, the craft unions soon faced fierce competition from general unions established by primarily unskilled workers who were excluded from craft unions and their jobs.

Unskilled Danish workers still have their own unions and they have organised male and female workers separately since the beginning of the twentieth century. The general union for unskilled male workers (*Specialarbejderforbundet* (SiD)) is the most powerful and it was established as a national union in 1897. Among the general unions for unskilled and skilled salaried employees at lower occupational levels, the Union of Commercial and Clerical Employees (HK) is the largest and most powerful. Both these general unions are members of the Danish LO and together with the Metal Workers Union, they constitute the dominant group in the federation (Table 2.1 and Scheuer 1998: 152–6).

During the 1960s, a growing number of salaried employees created independent unions that were primarily organised along educational lines. These unions have established their own confederations partly outside the Danish LO. Salaried employees at middle or higher levels are organised in professional unions and affiliated with the Central Confederation of Salaried Employees (FTF). Supervisors or salaried employees in managerial positions form their own occupational unions and the unions for university graduate professionals are organised in the Central Confederation of Professional Associations (AC). Unions outside these national confederations include only 4 per cent of the total unionised labour force. The structure of the trade union movement in Denmark is highly diversified and decentralised. Negotiating power is placed in the individual unions while the

Table 2.1 Composition of Danish and Swedish trade unions in the late 1990s

Denmark		**Sweden**	
Organisation	*% of total union members*	*Organisation*	*% of total union members*
Federation of Trade Unions (LO)	70	Federation of Trade Unions (LO)	56
of which		of which	
HK (salary employees)	17	Municipal workers	19
SiD (unskilled workers)	14	Metal (skilled workers)	9
KAD (female workers)	4	Handels (Commercial workers)	5
Metal (skilled workers)	7	SEKO (Service employees)	4
Conf. of Salaried Employees (FTF)	16	Byggnads (construction)	3
Conf. of Professional Ass. (AC)	6	Conf of Prof. Employees (TCO)	31
Supervisors' unions	4	of which	
Other unions	4	SIF (Clerical and technical)	9
		Lärerf. (teachers' union)	5
		SKTF(Local Governm. Empl.)	5
		Conf. Of Professional Ass. (SACO)	10
		Others	3
Total (%)	100	Total (%)	100
Total (million)	2.2	Total (million)	3.3

Sources: Ebbinghaus and Visser 2000 and Kjellberg 2000.

confederations have only co-ordinating tasks. This organisational structure of the Danish unions results in very little political radicalism and a weaker bargaining position compared to trade unions in the other Nordic countries.

Since the early 1970s, the Danish union movement has tried to solve the problem of diversity. In 1971, a proposal to form nine industrial unions was approved by the LO but never implemented. Neither the Metal Workers Union nor the SiD was prepared to compromise. In the late 1980s, a proposal to form five industrial cartels was approved by all unions just after the employers had changed their organisation (Scheuer 1998). This proposal met with heavy opposition from the SiD and a compromise that included six cartels was implemented in the mid-1990s mainly as a counterpart to changes on the employers' side. The LO has constantly been weakened and today the negotiation power is placed completely in the six industrial cartels. In addition, the division in the Danish union organisation between the LO and the two confederations for technicians and professionals – the FTF and the AC – has weakened the labour movement. On the other hand, the Danish LO has been defending its share of the total labour force better than in the other Scandinavian countries (Visser 2001: 201).

In Sweden, the formation of unions started just after the introduction of freedom of trade in the latter half of the nineteenth century. Unions for craft and skilled workers were established in the mid-1880s and some years later unions for unskilled and factory workers were established. By 1900, the first unions for publicly employed workers were established (Åmark 1986: 84). At the turn of the century, three principles of organisation were represented in the Swedish trade union movement: pure craft unions, industrial unions and general unions for unskilled workers. This situation was similar to the Danish labour market. However, already by the early twentieth century industrial unions became the dominant mode of organisation. In 1898, a number of federations formed the Swedish Trade Union Federation (the LO) in order to increase co-ordination in collective bargaining and to influence the political arena.

The Swedish union movement has developed into three main union confederations. The largest union confederation is the LO, organised on an industrial basis, which covers more than 90 per cent of blue-collar employees and 56 per cent of the total unionised labour force (Hammarström and Nilsson 1998: 229; Table 2.1 and Kjellberg 1997: 78). The second largest confederation, the Central Organisation of Salaried Employees (TCO), was formed in 1944. This organisation dominates the white-collar sector and covers 31 per cent of the total unionised employees. The third largest confederation is the SACO, a confederation of professional unions that represents employees having academic training. The largest unions within the LO are the Swedish Municipal Workers' Union and the Swedish Metal Workers' Union. Today, neither the LO nor the TCO take part in the bargaining process, which is the responsibility of the individual federations. However, both peak organisations represent the individual trade unions in negotiations with the government on general economic and social interests. Although the Swedish union movement is centralised in structure, federations rely on active local organisations (union clubs) to perform the day-to-day bargaining work with employers.

The Swedish model of industrial relations has therefore been characterised as centralised 'self-regulation' (Kjellberg 1998: 79 and 104–5).

As an immediate response to the formation of the peak organisation for workers, both the Danish Employers' Confederation (DA) and the Swedish Employers' Confederation (SAF) were established in 1896 and 1902, respectively. From the very beginning, the employers' peak organisations developed a strategy of centralisation. It was the federations alone and not its industrial divisions or the individual employers that had the power to decide on lockouts. By the beginning of the twentieth century in both Denmark and Sweden, the collective labour contracts agreed upon between employers and trade unions had to be approved by the executive committees of the Employers' Confederations. The parallel organisation of employers and workers in both countries was a pre-condition for a broadening of collective agreements and led to a concentration of bargaining power in the hands of the peak organisation on both sides. Moreover, this influenced the centralisation of the Danish and Swedish industrial relation system as a whole. During the late 1980s and early 1990s, the Danish system of industrial relations has been transformed and has clearly become more decentralised than the Swedish system. This was mainly a response to changes in the employers' organisation. In a development referred to as 'centralised decentralisation', a merger of local trade unions and employers' associations has taken place simultaneously with a decentralisation of decision-making with respect to pay and working conditions (Due, Madsen and Jensen 1997: 127).

In the United States as in many other countries, skilled and craft workers were the first who formed trade unions in order to protect themselves from both employers' arbitrary decisions and from the competition from unskilled labour. A constant immigration of cheap labour into the United States fuelled fierce tensions between various groups of workers and created a more heterogeneous labour movement than in Scandinavia. The formation of the Knights of Labor in 1869, was the first attempt to create a national federation. The Knights included all categories of workers and was very successful in the mid-1880s. However, its broad social movement soon led to inter-union rivalries and to its decline when craft unions formed the American Federation of Labor (AFL) in 1886 in an attempt to co-ordinate the unions' efforts (Bernstein 1960: 78).

In 1905, a new and more radical organisation, the syndicalist oriented Industrial Workers of the World (IWW), was established in reaction to the reformist AFL. The IWW preferred direct strike action rather than collective bargaining and labour contracts (Galenson 1986: 46). It soon became the major union among unskilled migration workers in the western part of the United States. However, its militancy and reluctance to co-operate in the war preparations during World War I led to its collapse after 1917. The IWW had difficulty attracting workers and was fiercely attacked by employers and the political system. By 1920, the AFL had become the dominant organisation in the United States.

Because the AFL was mainly a federation of craft unions, problems arose when large factories were organised. The AFL strategy implied that skilled workers should be divided by occupations instead of organising them according to industrial lines. This strategy was opposed by workers in the large industrial firms and in an attempt to develop industrial unions the Congress of Industrial Organization (CIO) was established through a split in the AFL in the mid-1930s (Galenson 1986: 54). The strategy of this new and more radical union federation was to organise semi-skilled and unskilled workers in basic industries such as steel and automobile manufacturing. Reacting to this split, the AFL also began an organisational drive among the unskilled workers and succeeded especially among the Teamsters and Machinists. During nearly two decades, these two federations of unions competed for members among the United States workers and when they re-merged in 1955 the AFL was twice as large as the CIO.

Since the merger of the AFL and the CIO there has been a steady decline in union influence on industrial relations in the United States and a decrease in bar-gaining power and in total membership (Western 2000; Clawson and Clawson 1999). Compared with the union structure in the Scandinavian countries, the American union movement is loosely organised and decentralised in its bargaining procedure, which take place at the enterprise level and with no co-ordination between the individual agreements.

US employers did not create nation-wide employers' organisations that have authority to speak for the business community in matters of industrial relations similar to employers' organisations in Scandinavia. In general, most major com-panies have rejected bargaining on the industrial level. There are a few exceptions; for example, the steel industry has organised into a multi-employer bargaining committee that involves the major firms and who negotiate through a loose, infor-mal committee rather than an association (Derber 1984: 105–10). In the political arena there are, on the other hand, numerous employer associations opposing labour organisation. The US National Association of Manufacturers (NAM) cre-ated at the turn of the century is perhaps the major organisation focusing on industrial relations. It raises political campaign funds and lobbies in order to combat unions and to prevent companies entering collective bargaining with unions.

During the 1980s, hostility towards unions increased worldwide; this has been especially the case in the United States. Already by the mid-1970s, the US labour market saw an emergence of anti-union activities by employers ranging from maintaining workplaces free from unions and relocation of enterprises in 'union free zones' to open violation of labour laws and the creation of pay systems favour-ing non-union employees (Wheeler and McClendon 1998: 72). One indicator of the increasing employer resistance to unionisation was a constant decline in elec-tions accepted by the employers from the late 1970s to the early 1990s (Clawson and Clawson 1999: 102).

A characteristic feature in the history of labour movement in Canada is the dominant influence from the US-based (international) unions. Most of the original labour organisations in Canada were part of the US-based unions primarily affil-iated with the AFL (see Table 2.2 and Thompson 1998: 93). By the end of the nineteenth century, however, the Canadian unions had a much more politically ori-ented perspective than their US counterparts. They were actively fighting to

Table 2.2 Composition of Canadian trade unions in the late 1990s

Organisation	% of total union members
Canadian Labor Congress (CLC)	72
of which	
International (AFL-CIO/CLC)	28
National unions	44
Confederation of National Trade Unions (CNTU)	21
of which	
CSN	6
Centrale des syndicats du Quebec	3
Unaffiliated unions	12
Others	7
Total (%)	100
Total (million)	4.1

Source: Statistics Canada 2001.

improve the living conditions of their members by means of political involvement and did not advocate 'pure and simple unionism' as American unions did (Smucker 1980: 183–4). Canadian unions were first established in construction and transportation mainly on a craft basis. During the 1930s and 1940s, industrial unionisation spread to primary industries and manufacturing, but here the Canadian unions did not have a major breakthrough similar to that which happened for the CIO in the United States. Controversies regarding Canadian workers' membership in US-controlled unions have remained an important issue throughout the history of the Canadian labour movement. The spread of public sector unionism in the 1960s and 1970s changed this situation of dependence; the relative share of membership in the US-influenced international unions declined and simultaneously a mobilisation and larger national consciousness appeared among union members in the private sector.

The most important central confederation in Canada is the Canadian Labour Congress (CLC), which represents more than half of all union members in most industries except construction (Table 2.2). It has no role in bargaining and it has practically no decision-making power over the affiliated unions. In Quebec, the Confederation of National Trade Unions (CNTU) – including the CSN and the CSQ – is the dominant peak organisation that represents virtually all unionised French speaking employees. In its early days, the Catholic Church sponsored the union, but it has now become more leftist in its approach. Consequently, it has become more centralised in its organisation. Today this confederation is the most radical and politicised labour organisation in North America (Thompson 1998: 94–5).

In Canada, no nation-wide employer's organisations developed for the purpose of collective bargaining. Instead organisations developed to articulate management's view in the political sphere and to the public (Adams 1985). The Canadian Manufacturer's Association (CMA) provides services for individual company members. However, the CMA has little bargaining power compared to the Scandinavian employers' associations. It has no capacity to decide on collective agreements. Other business organisations have been established but none of them has the same firm stance against unions as seen in US business organisations for employers (Atkinson and Coleman 1989: 41–8). Although most Canadian employers prefer a non-union status, a majority of unionised firms accept unions, albeit reluctantly, and open attacks on established unions seldom occur (Thompson 1998: 95).

In summary, unionisation in the United States is extremely low compared both with Canada and most European countries. Unions in the United States, and to a lesser extent in Canada, mainly focus on economic issues. The scope of Scandinavian unionism is broader and provides a wide range of work conditions. Their unions are normally active at the local, industrial and national level. Unions in the US and Denmark until recently, and to a lesser extent Canadian unions, are basically built around (narrow) occupational groups, while Swedish unions are associated with each industry. Scandinavian organisations exert a significant influence within the corporatist framework of decision-making while American unions rely on strength at the shop floor level. In labour market segments, where unions have gained a steady foothold, their influence may be quite substantial. Since employers' organisations play no role in collective bargaining in both the North American countries, negotiations take place primarily at the single-employer level. In the Scandinavian countries, bargaining takes place according to industrial lines between central organisations formed by employees and employers.

Recognition of union rights

The criteria and procedures for recognition of trade unions by the state and the employers differ strongly between Scandinavia and North America. In Denmark and Sweden, recognition of unions happened early in the history of the union movement and took place with relatively little conflict. In the United States, unions were continuously and fiercely fighting with employers and governments. A strong opposition against unions still exists in the United States and they have to fight for acceptance at all levels of industrial relations.

In 1899, just a couple of years after the first workers' organisations had been founded, the main principles for union recognition and collective bargaining in the Danish labour market were agreed upon between the Employer's Confederation (DA) and the Federation of Trade Unions (LO) in a main agreement (*Septemberforliget*). This agreement has been negotiated and revised several times (1960, 1973 and 1993) but not radically changed (Due, Madsen and Jensen 1997). As part of the 'main agreement' the parties created an arbitration court that made decisions concerning violations of the agreement. This court was a forerunner to the Danish Labour Court (*Den faste Voldsgiftret*) that was agreed upon in 1910. Together these two agreements have formed the basis of industrial relations in the Danish labour market. When the collective action organisations entered into an agreement, industrial conflicts were not tolerated during the contracting period (Boje and Kongshøj Madsen 1994).

In 1906, a similar agreement, the *December Compromise*, was reached in Sweden between the peak organisations. The content of the two agreements was roughly the same. The employers agreed to respect the workers' right to organise and negotiate. In addition, the two national LOs agreed to give the employers discretion rights. They accepted the employers' rights to hire and fire manual workers, to manage and distribute work, and to hire workers from any trade union whatsoever, i.e., no closed shop clauses were allowed. In both Sweden and Denmark any group of employees is free to form its own unions. Unions need not be registered or accepted by government authorities or courts and once established they will automatically be covered by industrial relations legislation. This applies as well to minority unions and to supervisors and public employees. Employers formally have to negotiate with minority unions, although labour contracts in such cases are frequently duplicated from the majority unions (Hammarström and Nilsson 1998: 229).

In both countries, the main agreements regulating union recognition and bargaining procedures were born in an era where the labour market was tormented by frequent labour conflicts between the newly established central organisations. While the Danish main agreement between employers and employees from 1899 specified the procedures for collective bargaining and how to restrict coercive measures, no such issues were dealt with in the Swedish agreement, the *December Compromise*. Instead, the legal principles for collective bargaining in Sweden were codified in a *Law on Collective Agreements* in 1928. Simultaneously, a special Labour Court was set up composed of lawyers and representatives of the parties to handle disputes on correct interpretations or applications of agreements (Edlund and Nyström 1988: 8). Legislation as well as case law strongly emphasised the peace-keeping function of collective agreements. During the term of an agreement, the parties were not allowed to use coercive measures, not even threats, on issues that they had agreed upon (Göransson 1988).

In both Scandinavian countries, the salaried employees faced greater difficulties than blue-collar workers did in achieving union rights. They were too few and unionisation was weak. During the 1930s, private salaried employees started unionisation in both Denmark and Sweden while public salaried employees first obtained legal rights to negotiate and exercise coercive measures in the 1960s (Jägerskiöld 1971; Furåker and Lindqvist 1992: ch. 2; Petersen 1987: 67). In both countries, these rights were restricted concerning the scope of agreements and the right to strike. However, in broad terms, in both Sweden and Denmark, a homogenisation of union rights has taken place; i.e., private and public employees have roughly similar rights to form unions, to take part in collective bargaining, and with some exceptions to engage in coercive measures. Such developments reflect that Scandinavian governments have had positive attitudes towards unions during most of the post-World War II era.

In North America, trade union rights were instituted a good deal later than in Scandinavia. In the second half of the nineteenth century, unions in the United States were looked upon as 'criminal conspiracies' to raise prices of goods and work. At the end of the century, however, this doctrine of conspiracy lost most of its practical importance. Instead, employers used another weapon, injunctions, to combat organised labour. Injunctions meant that claims could be made to the courts that a specific strike should be declared illegal under the pretext of protecting common interests of trade and business. Such judicial involvement in labour–capital conflict occurred against the backdrop of increasing strike calls and boycotts. Initiatives taken by judges, facilitated by the fact that common law principles gave leeway for different interpretations, made courts a hostile place for unions during this era (Forbath 1991: 63, 171–2). Injunctions in combination with 'yellow dog' clauses hit especially hard since workers who did not abstain from trade union membership could be fired. The Norris-LaGuardia Act of 1932 made such interventions by injunction illegal.

From the mid-1930s in the United States, union rights and collective bargaining were regulated by legislation. The overall aim of The National Labor Relations Act (NLRA) of 1935, the Wagner Act, was to reduce the number of labour market conflicts and to improve wages and purchasing power of the workers. This was to be achieved by eliminating barriers for organisation and by providing labour with bargaining rights once the employees had chosen their representatives. In order to realise these intentions, the employees were given rights of association, collective bargaining, and the right to engage in coercive measures. The employers were forbidden to assault the employees' right of association; such measures were considered unfair labour practices and they were requested to negotiate with the trade unions for which the majority of employees had voted. A special administrative authority, the National Labor Relations Board (NLRB), including a panel of experts appointed by politicians, was given the task of enforcing the Wagner Act. This Board was given the power to determine when elections were to be held, the basic unit in which to vote, the eligible voters, confirmation of election results, and how to determine a suspected unfair labour practice (Getman and Pogrebin 1988: 2).

If workers want to form a union, they must obtain signatures of at least 30 per cent of the employees. Then the union files the Board for an election. After the Board has set the election date, the campaign period (15 to 30 days) begins and ends in a secret ballot. Employers need not recognise and deal with the union unless an election is held. If the majority of the workers vote for the union, the Board certifies the union as the bargaining agent and a bargaining order is issued (Goldfield 1987: 86–7). The next problem that faces the union is to win a first contract in negotiations with the employer. However, NLRB has no power to penalise an employer who refuses to bargain with a union that won the election. In such cases, the Board has to petition a court, which in turn has to decide whether the Board's order should be enforced or modified. Enforcement proceedings in a court of appeal may take years. Consequently, the union often was weakened and its membership discouraged when the process of certification or de-certification lasted for some years.

The doctrine of exclusivity, allowing only the union chosen by a majority to represent everyone in a bargaining unit, is another specific trait of the US system of labour relations. This makes it almost impossible for non-majority groups of employees to establish unions with bargaining powers even on behalf of its members. Another specific trait is that the line between management and workers must not be blurred. The exclusion of supervisors from union rights and bargaining have deterred salaried employees such as middle managers, technicians and the vast group of semi-professionals from unionising. The line between management and labour was not sharply drawn in the Wagner Act. However, in 1974 the US Supreme Court ruled that the NLRA should not protect unionisation for anyone who had authority to 'formulate and effectuate management policies by expressing and making operative the decisions of the employer' (Heckscher 1988: 78). This meant that union representation only included employees having little or no responsibility, i.e., those working in routine jobs.

The Taft-Hartley Act of 1947 reflected a shift towards more anti-union sentiments in American industrial relations. The law limited the use of coercive measures and strikes. In contrast, the employer has gradually become permitted to continue operating during a strike by hiring strikebreakers permanently to replace the regular workforce. Goldfield (1987: 184–5) contends that Taft-Hartley made life harder for unions in four ways: (1) new legal rights for employers to sue unions for damages in connection with banned coercive measures; (2) certification of unions by card checks and other informal methods (permitted by the Wagner Act) were eliminated and elections after a campaign period became the only legal way by which unions could be certified; (3) employers were granted 'free speech' rights during campaign periods; and (4) it became legal for states to pass laws banning the union shop, i.e., a system where all workers must become union members for a short definite period of time after they start working for the employer.[1]

However, also in North America a process of homogenisation of private–public union rights has taken place. Bargaining rights for public sector employees were instituted in the early 1960s. A presidential order in 1962 authorised such rights to federal employees, a principle that later became incorporated in federal law. In the 1970s, most states adopted similar legislation (Lewin 1986: 248–9). Despite the right of employees to form unions and elect their own representatives, the scope of bargaining is more restricted than in the private sector and clauses restricting the union's role are often inserted in the collective agreements as a matter of law.

In Canada, worker's associations were given status as voluntary associations in 1872. Consequently, workers had a legal right to become members, but the union itself was not recognised as a legal representative with bargaining rights for the individual workers (Smucker 1980: 242). A nation-wide labour code was first proposed in the early 1940s. This code, modelled after the US Wagner Act from 1935, included recognition of a worker's right to join a union, encouragement of collective bargaining, and compulsory conciliation in case of disputes. However, the unions were not legally recognised as negotiating representatives for workers; without such certification, employers were not forced to negotiate. By 1943, the federal government passed an act that guaranteed workers the right to organise and the right to select the units for collective bargaining, to define the groups to be covered by agreements, and certification of bargaining agents. Shortly after this Act was approved, most Canadian provinces enacted their labour legislation in accordance with its guidelines (Smucker 1980: 244–5).

Canadian procedures allow unions to establish more rapidly, and, more importantly, provide employers little or no opportunity to conduct lengthy anti-union campaigns before the representation election. In Canada, unions are normally certified after demonstrating that they have recruited 50 per cent of the workers as dues-paying members. In the United States, however, the employer has the right, and typically uses it, to request a secret ballot election before a union can be certified. The Canadian unions can be certified automatically by the labour board once unions are able to prove that its membership has reached a majority. Furthermore, due to Canadian labour laws, labour management consultants who specialise in defeating unions in certification elections are not a dominant feature in the industrial relations scene as is the case in the United States.

The industrial relations procedure for Canadian public employees significantly changed in the mid-1960s. Because of the Public Service Staff Relations Act (1963), collective bargaining rights were granted to federal civil service employees. Similar legislative provisions were made in provincial jurisdictions one by one, and by the mid-1970s nearly all public employees were granted collective bargaining rights (Ponak 1982: 350). However, the right to strike for public employees became circumscribed and in the 1980s the federal government increasingly narrowed the scope of industrial action by defining certain jobs as 'essential for the safety and security of the public' (Panitch and Swartz 1988: 36).

The North American institutional setting and regulatory procedures for unions differ significantly from the Scandinavian institutional setting and procedures. However, there are also important differences between the two North American countries. The labour laws in the Canadian provinces and at the federal level are markedly more pro-union than corresponding laws in the United States. In Canada, bargaining rights in several provinces can be obtained based on authorisation cards whereas in the United States contested elections must take place. Both countries use national labour relation boards for adjudicating disputes concerning the interpretation of labour laws. While the NLRB in the United States is a quasi-judicial body composed of political appointees (lawyers and public officials), Canadian provinces have tripartite boards consisting of representatives of labour, management and the public (Block 1990: 255). The two countries also differ with regard to government involvement in contract negotiations and labour conflicts. In Canada, most jurisdictions make it difficult for an employer to opt out of the collective bargaining relationship and it requires conciliation before a legal strike or lockout; this is not the case in the United States. The United States and Canada also differ in their view on hiring permanent strike replacements. In the United States, it is legal to hire replacements. Legally striking workers in much of Canada (Ontario) have the right to return to their work until six months after the beginning of the strike (Gould 1994: 230–1). Moreover, Canadian employers are less inclined to engage in unfair labour practices than American employers (Weiler 1990: 254–5).

In Scandinavian countries, unions are permitted to establish quite freely. There are no procedures that require certification elections or authorisation cards in order to form a union. In contrast to the American principle of exclusivity,

Scandinavian unions organise broad occupational groups according to industrial lines. In most workplaces, in addition to a number of unions, supervisors and employees in managerial positions are free to join unions. In Scandinavia, union rights for public employees have gradually become similar to the standards for private employees. In the post-World War II era, both governments and employers in Scandinavia have regarded the unions as an integral part of the 'associative corporatism' whereas this is not the case in the United States. The Scandinavian peak organisations are closely linked to the state apparatus since tripartite negotiations have become common in most societal sectors. This Scandinavian version of associative corporatism is characterised by large representation from capital and labour, a dispersion of decisional authority and autonomy to the local organisational level, a dense network of representation as the basis for decision-making, and a strong reliance on dialogue for conflict resolution and policy consensus (Amin and Thomas 1996; Jessop, Nielsen and Pedersen 1993).

A comparison of industrial relations and collective bargaining

A major purpose in many comparative studies that scrutinise the structure of collective bargaining and trends in unionisation has been to analyse the influence of the institutional setting of the labour market on the performance of the national economy (OECD 1991b, 1994a, 1997d and 1999b). However, a large majority of these analyses do not find statistically significant relationships between measures of economic performance (productivity, wage formation and rates of unemployment and employment) and the structure of collective bargaining. In two respects, a relationship is found. First, a negative relationship between earnings inequality and centralised/co-ordinated bargaining structures. Second, a weak tendency that centralised/co-ordinated bargaining systems tend to have lower rates of unemployment and higher employment rates. Both relationships are not surprising considering the Scandinavian labour market experiences, but these relationships strongly disagree with the prevailing neo-liberal hypotheses that non-market institutions and regulations might harm an efficient performance of the economy and especially the labour market.

Our aim with this section is primarily to position the bargaining structure of the four countries in comparison with other industrial OECD countries. Four different measures are chosen to illustrate the bargaining system of the individual countries: trade union density; rate of coverage in collective bargaining; centralisation in bargaining; and co-ordination of bargaining. *Trade union density* is the number of employed persons who are union members as a percentage of the total wage and salary employment. *Coverage of collective bargaining* is the number of employees covered by collective agreements as a percentage of the total wage and salary employment. *Centralisation* is the formal structure of bargaining. Collective bargaining can take place on three different levels: the national level between the peak organisation covering all unionised members; the regional level between unions and employers' organisations for individual industries or crafts; and the firm level between the unions and management. By *co-ordination*, we focus on the degree of consensus between the collective bargaining actors. The co-ordination can be more or less tight, with bargaining taking place at both a centralised and decentralised organisational level. In Table 2.3, the countries are ranked by these four measures.

The power of the unions depends largely on their capability to organise the employees and to improve their earnings and working conditions. In this respect, the level of unionisation and coverage of collective bargaining are important empirical indicators. The pattern of industrial bargaining is characterised by centralisation; that is, the organisational level at which the bargaining takes place and by co-ordination measuring to what extent collective agreements for one group of workers are imposed on other groups. The level of strike activity is another indicator, which might illustrate the type of industrial relations and the power of unions. In the following section, we will look briefly at these indicators for the four countries in comparison with other industrial countries.

Table 2.3 Comparing the industrial relations systems in selected OECD countries

Country	Union density %	Country	Coverage of collective bargaining %	Countries ranked by degree of centralisation (highest first)	Countries ranked by degree of co-ordination (highest first)
Sweden	80	Austria	97	Austria	Austria
Finland	78	Ireland	90	Belgium	Germany
Denmark	76	Belgium	82	Finland	Japan
Belgium	60	Italy	82	Norway	
Norway	54	Greece	80		Italy
Ireland	49	Germany	80	Denmark	Norway
Italy	44	Netherlands	79	France	
Austria	39	France	75	Germany	Denmark
UK	33	Sweden	72	Italy	Finland
Canada	32	Portugal	71	Netherlands	
Germany	29	Finland	67	Portugal	Belgium
Portugal	26	Spain	67	Spain	France
Netherlands	26	Norway	62	Sweden	Portugal
Japan	24	Denmark	52		Spain
Greece	24	UK	40	UK	Sweden
Spain	19	Canada	37	Canada	
United States	14	Japan	25	Japan	Canada
France	9	United States	11	United States	United Kingdom
					United States

Sources: OECD 1997d: 71; Visser 1998, 2001: 191; and the Scandinavian countries adjusted according to Kjellberg 2000: 27.

Notes
Union density: unionised wage and salary workers in proportion to the total number of employees.
Coverage of bargaining: the proportion of the total number of employees covered by collective agreements.

Union density

Unionisation is generally higher in Europe than in the rest of the world. The exception is France and to some extent Spain, which have some of the lowest levels of unionisation among all OECD countries. Three other conclusions can be drawn from this comparison of unionisation. First, the level of unionisation tends to be higher in small countries than in the larger ones. The four Scandinavian countries have a high level of unionisation. These are homogeneous countries with a high level of corporatism; that is, they have a social partnership between labour and capital intended to solve labour conflicts (Lehmbruch 1984). Second, unionisation is high in the labour markets where the trade unions control the administration of the unemployment insurance system. This is the case in Sweden, Finland, Denmark and Belgium (all countries with a high level of unionisation). Third, union density tends to be higher in countries with 'consensual' industrial relations than in countries with the 'adversarial' system (OECD 1991b: 100). Countries with consensual industrial relations are typically characterised by numerous corporative institutions and a widespread network of institutions for conflict resolution that demand high levels of representation on both sides of industrial relations. The Scandinavian countries represent this consensual type of industrial relations while France, the United States, Spain and Japan are characterised by a system that relies more on industrial conflicts and an adversarial system. In this respect, Canada, the UK and Italy are exceptions; they have medium levels of unionisation but also a relatively adversarial industrial relations system.

Whereas the 1970s appeared to be the decade of union membership expansion, especially in western Europe, the 1980s were the years when employers regained the initiative in a period of recession and rising unemployment, which in many countries weakened the position of the employees' organisations. This shift in favour of employers occurred not only in the field of industrial relations but also politically in terms of a move towards neo-liberal political values, supply-side economic policies and unregulated marketplace ideologies (Kochan 1985; Visser 1994). Table 2.4 illustrates the development in unionisation rates during the last three decades.

Table 2.4 Rates of unionisation in Canada, Denmark, Sweden and the United States, 1970–98 (%)

	1970	1975	1980	1985	1988	1990	1994	1998/99
Canada	31	34	35	36	35	35	35	32
Denmark	60	67	75	77	75	76	76	76
Sweden	68	75	78	81	84	82	85	80
United States	–	23	23	18	17	16	16	14

Sources: OECD 1997d: 71; Traxler 1994; Visser 1991: 101. For 1990–98/99 see Kjellberg 2000.

Note
Canada: union membership as a percentage of the non-agricultural paid workers.

The trends in unionisation and consequently the impact of the economic recessions in the 1980s and 1990s differ markedly in the four countries. Denmark and Sweden have had high rates of unionisation during this period. In both countries, the level of unionisation has been constantly growing until the mid-1980s when a minor decrease took place in the rate of unionisation but not in the total number of organised employees. For both countries, this fall in union density can be explained by difficulties in unionising private salaried employees especially in consumer and business services, industries that rapidly grew in the late 1980s. In the early 1990s, the level of unionisation increased again in all four countries and particularly in the two Scandinavian countries.[2]

The United States represents another extreme with a low level of unionisation. In 1945, unionisation in the United States reached its peak with one-third of the labour force unionised. Since then the US rate has been constantly falling and only about 14 per cent were unionised by the late 1990s. As noted above, the industrial relations climate in the United States has not favoured unions. The Taft-Hartley Act of 1947 in combination with a strong ideological anti-unionism created hostility among US employers towards any kind of collective organisation and this made unionisation extremely difficult for US workers (Davis 1987: 146–7).

The Canadian unionisation is markedly higher than the US level. This reflects the different development in the industrial relations climate in the two countries described earlier in this chapter. In the early 1950s, the industrial relations system in the two countries was generally the same and so was the level of unionisation among workers. Then it started differing and the trends in unionisation did the same (Davis 1987: 146). The rate of unionisation in Canada has been constant at about one-third of the employees during most of the postwar period. It started growing in the late 1980s, but then it decreased in the late 1990s. An important factor in explaining the different development in unionisation in Canada and the United States is the attitude of government towards unionisation in the two countries. The Canadian government has not taken any strong actions against unions and has not pursued an industrial policy of deregulation, as has been the case in the United States.

Here we have looked only at the total rates of unionisation. A closer look at the sector and demographic composition of the unionised employees shows marked changes during the post-World War II period. The traditional male industrial workers in manufacturing, construction and transport dominated the unions throughout the first half of the twentieth century. Today, these groups of workers are a minority while the wage and salaried employees in the services industries have become the dominant group and in countries with the highest union density such as Sweden and Finland women are the majority among the unionised. In most OECD countries, union density in manufacturing is still higher than the average level of unionisation in the labour force and this is especially the case in the high density countries like Denmark and Sweden. However, the level of unionisation is higher among public sector employees than manufacturing workers in countries with low or medium union density such as in Canada and the United States (Western 2000).

Collective bargaining – organisation and coverage

Typically, the proportion of employees covered by collective agreements is higher than the proportion belonging to unions. The OECD rate of unionisation is on average 38 per cent and the rate of agreement coverage is as high as 68 per cent. Two reasons can explain the higher rates of collective bargaining coverage: (1) employers tend to extend collective agreements to non-union employees in the firm; and (2) collective agreements are often extended by legal regulation to third parties (OECD 1997d: 70).

The coverage of collective bargaining is an important indicator that demonstrates the extent the unions are able to negotiate wages and other working conditions for their members. The bargaining process can take place at different levels: between trade unions and individual companies (single-employer bargaining); and between union federations and employers' associations (multi-employer bargaining) at the industrial or the national level. When the bargaining process is centralised and co-ordinated, we can expect a high rate of coverage. This is the case especially in France, Spain and Italy where significantly more workers are covered by the collective agreement than organised in trade unions because the negotiations take place at the national level and are highly centralised often involving the peak organisations as well as the state. The reversed relationship – higher unionisation than rate of bargaining coverage – we find in the Scandinavian countries. These countries are characterised by high unionisation; however, this is combined with relatively low levels of co-ordination and often decentralised bargaining procedures that means modest rates of bargaining coverage (Table 2.3 and OECD 1994a; OECD 1997d).

Among the four countries, the United States, Sweden and, especially, Denmark are characterised by the reverse relationship – higher rates of union density than collective bargaining coverage. In Denmark, a significant number of employers are not organised and no legal extension arrangements exist. Consequently, a large number of the unionised employees are not covered by the collective agreements negotiated between organised employers and the unions. Another reason for a low level of bargaining coverage in Denmark may be the large number of small and medium size enterprises (SME) that are not organised and where the workers even if they are members of a union are not covered by a collective agreement (Scheuer 1997).

In both the Canadian and the US labour market, collective bargaining takes place between trade unions and individual employers and only in the companies that are unionised. The low level of unionisation is combined with a decentralised and uncoordinated bargaining system, which means that only a minority of North American employees are covered by collective agreements and they are not extended to other groups except the unionised workers.

As already mentioned, centralisation reflects the level at which collective bargaining takes place: enterprise, industrial sector, or nation-wide. The countries with a highly centralised bargaining system are typically small European countries such as Austria, Belgium, Finland and Norway. In these countries, more employees are covered by collective agreements than are unionised (Table 2.3). In the rest of Europe, including Denmark and Sweden, the dominant bargaining system is the industrial sector level. Canada, the UK, Japan and the United States are characterised by an enterprise level bargaining system.

Co-ordination implies the synchronisation of collective bargaining across individual unions and is often correlated with the level of centralisation, but this is not always the case. In Japan, there is a highly decentralised enterprise level bargaining system, but the employers' associations usually closely co-ordinate their bargaining strategies among the individual enterprises. The general pattern, however, is a high level of co-ordination in countries that are characterised by a relatively centralised system of collective bargaining such as in Austria, Norway and, to some extent, in Germany. The other Scandinavian countries are placed in an intermediate position on both centralisation and co-ordination of bargaining. At the bottom, and far below the other countries we find Canada, the United Kingdom and the United States with a low level of centralisation and nearly no co-ordination between unions and employers in collective bargaining.

Strikes – the level of labour conflict

The level of strike activity is a rough indicator of both the types of industrial relations dominating the labour market and the capability of the unions to enforce their demands. A low level of strike activity may indicate that the unions are able to enforce their demands through a well-functioning collective bargaining system, which normally is the case in the Swedish system. However, it can also mean that the unions are extremely weak and do not have the necessary support among employees to enforce their demands for better wages or work conditions through a strike, which is the case for most unions in the United States. The United States and Sweden are the two countries with the lowest level of strike activity (Table 2.5).

Until recently, Canada was characterised by a high level of strike activity but this has changed during the 1990s. The unions have been weakened during the long period of economic recession and high levels of unemployment and this has

Table 2.5 Number of employees involved in strikes or lock-outs as a percentage of the total employees in Canada, Denmark, Sweden and the United States, 1975–98

Country	1975	1980	1985	1990	1995	1998
Canada			4.1	2.1	1.1	1.7
Denmark	2.7	3.6	22.8	1.4	4.8	18.6
Sweden	0.6	17.7	2.9	1.6	3.1	0.3
United States	1.1	0.8	0.3	0.2	0.2	0.3

Source: ILO: Laborsta (2000).

Note
The figures include only strikes and lock-outs lasting at least one day with more than 100 days lost.

reduced their ability to influence employers by striking. In Denmark, the general level of strike activity is surprisingly high considering that the unions are closely connected to a strong social democratic party, which often participates in the government and through this connection they are well integrated in a system of associative corporatism. On the other hand, the Danish bargaining system is relatively decentralised; that is, the individual unions negotiate independently from the peak organisation and this often leads to major strikes associated with the bargaining negotiations. This happened in 1985 and 1998. The Swedish situation is similar to the Danish situation, but the Swedish unions clearly are in a more powerful position with respect to the social democratic party. This means that they are in a better position to enforce their demands through negotiation and through the system of consensus policy-making. In the United States, the level of strikes is lower than in the other three countries, but this reflects the extremely low level of unionisation more than a low level of industrial conflict among the organised workers (Moody 1997/2001).

Industrial relations – different institutional models

The national industrial relations systems have been under heavy pressure during the recent decades. The trends towards globalisation, flexibility and the market deregulation have weakened the trade unions during the 1980s. The increase of cross-border activities of firms and the fragmentation of the labour markets moved the emphasis in collective bargaining from the national or industrial level to the company level. This has restricted the power of national unions. These structural trends together with the prevailing neo-liberal market discourse arguing for deregulation, privatisation and flexibility present enormous problems for the trade unions 'whose very existence necessitates the restriction and regulation of labour markets' (Clawson and Clawson 1999: 101).

Despite the pressures on industrial relations mentioned above and among the European countries, the influence from the EU integration on social and economic affairs, the historical differences in the system of industrial relations as well as the organisation of the social and economic institutions persist (see Crouch 1993; Esping-Andersen 1990 and 1999; Gallie and Paugam 2000). Relying on the comparative research of industrial relations, Ebbinghaus and Visser (1997) have developed a typology describing four 'ideal types'. Our four countries represent two of these models – the Nordic welfare corporatist model for Denmark and Sweden and the Anglo-Saxon pluralist market model for the United States and Canada (Table 2.6).

The Anglo-Saxon model, represented by Canada and the United States, is characterised by a low level of unionisation. Union membership is concentrated on the workers employed in the traditional manufacturing industries. The low level of unionisation is combined with low coverage of collective bargaining, a decentralised negotiation system with bargaining at the firm level, which takes place in an adversarial climate, and with no co-ordination between the individual bargaining units. This is a highly fragmented and individualised industrial relations system.

Table 2.6 Models of industrial relations

	Nordic welfare corporatist model	*Central European social partnership model*	*Latin Europe conflict dual model*	*Anglo-Saxon pluralist market model*
Organised interests (unions and employers)	Cohesive Disciplined Comprehensive	Segmented Segmented Partial	Rivalry Volatile Variable	Fragmented Volatile Variable
Relationship	Labour-led/ balanced	Employer-led/ balanced	Weakness on both sides	Alternating/ unstable

Bargaining
  Dominant level
  Coverage
  Depth
  Style
	Sector
	High
	Significant
	Integrative
		Sector
		Medium/high
		Moderate
		Integrative
			Alternating
			Medium/high
			Limited
			Contestational
				Company
				Small
				Significant
				Adversarial

Co-ordination	High	High	Variable	Absent
Centralisation	Moderate	High	Moderate	Absent
Level of conflict	Medium to low Highly organised	Low Highly organised	High Spasmodic	Medium to high Dispersed
Role of the state	Facilitating Collective labour rights	Facilitating/ regulating Individual/ collective labour rights	Intervening Individual/ collective labour rights	Abstaining Voluntarism
Countries	Denmark Sweden Finland Norway	Austria Germany Belgium Netherlands	France Italy Spain Portugal	United States Canada United Kingdom

Sources: Ebbinghaus and Visser (1997; and Visser (2001).

Canada differs in some respects from this pattern. Canadian workers have been more successful in unionisation than their US counterparts, but on several of the other dimensions Canada is similar to the United States (Western 2000: 40–1).

The Nordic model, represented by Denmark and Sweden, is characterised by a high level of unionisation. All groups of employees have high rates of unionisation and even private service employees have relatively high rates of unionisation. In the Scandinavian countries, there has been a tendency towards decentralisation – most obviously in Denmark and Sweden where the negotiations are still rather co-ordinated. This co-ordination takes place at the industrial level, but it is carefully monitored by the national industrial unions. This is contrary to the corporatist model that dominates the Continental European countries where co-ordination takes place at the national level involving the peak organisations and the state. The

Scandinavian unions are integrated strongly into the state apparatus through their close contacts with the political representatives in the social democratic parties and therefore have a large influence on many aspects of national policy.

There are two other models of industrial relations in Continental Europe. The 'social partnership' model is found in Germany and Austria. Here the level of unionisation is medium or low, but it is combined with relatively high coverage rates for collective bargaining because of centralised procedures for negotiation and strong co-ordination both among unions and the employers' organisations. This type of industrial relations is a traditional corporatist model with strong relationships between unions and employers' organisations and with comprehensive intervention in the collective bargaining from the government authorities. Often concessions at the bargaining table are co-ordinated with state legislation. The other Continental European industrial relations model is the conflict dual model found in Southern Europe – France, Italy, Spain and Portugal. This model is characterised by low or moderate levels of unionisation, several competing unions, and typically adversarial industrial relations. Because of highly centralised collective bargaining, far more workers are covered by the agreements than are unionised. The industrial relations system is a dual system because it strongly protects the insiders (those already employed) with respect to earnings, employment conditions and social protection, but excludes the outsiders (young people, women and the unemployed) from all the negotiated benefits.

National characteristics and general trends – comparing Scandinavian and North American industrial relations

In analyses dealing with national characteristics for comparative purposes, generalisations about trade union behaviour and industrial relations systems cannot be avoided. Such generalisations may come into a different light depending on which countries are compared. Therefore, it is important, as has been concluded by many analysts, to understand the union movement and industrial relations systems in terms of their historical origin. Furthermore, its institutional framework needs examination as we have tried to do above (Baglioni and Crouch 1990; Bamber and Lansbury 1998; Ferner and Hyman 1998; Golden, Wallerstein and Lange 1999; Regini 1994).

Differences between the national labour markets in level of union density as well as in the type of union organisational structure have not converged but rather widened during the last two decades (see also OECD 1997d). A number of theories have been offered in order to explain these variations in level, structure and trends in unionisation. These theories and their hypotheses do not provide a comprehensive and fully plausible explanation of the development in industrial relations; they should be seen as complementary. Here we shall discuss some of these theories and present evidence for or against their explanatory power.

The logic of industrialism or the convergence thesis

The idea of the convergence of unionisation and industrial relations systems has a long tradition (Kerr *et al.* 1960). At the core of this functionalist hypothesis lies the assumption that the logic of the industrialisation processes will create a convergence of social institutions. Kerr *et al.* argue that

> the industrial system tends to develop a common set of rules under common technological and economic conditions. Cultural and national differences are less significant to the web of rules, the further the country is along the road towards industrialism.
>
> (Kerr *et al.* 1960: 42)

In line with this argument Kerr *et al.* find that industrialization everywhere creates organizations of workers although with differing structure, leadership and ideology depending on the type of industrializing elite (1960: 215). Although there is variation, such functionalist explanations may be questioned based on empirical evidence. Differences in industrial relations system and in the level of unionisation are much larger than warranted by differences in economic development, industrialisation, social structure or public spending (Visser 1994: 18). Although employers and workers are forced to co-operate in one way or another, there is considerable variation across nations in the structure and functions of industrial relations systems. Countries such as France and Belgium that have very similar industrial structures and welfare regimes differ radically in union organisational structure and in union density because of different historical backgrounds with respect to their labour movements and have a different set-up for collective bargaining (Table 2. 3).

The convergence thesis, however, has recently gained renewed interest because of a supposed inevitable trend towards disorganisation in industrial relations imposed by the globalisation of economies and intensified market competition followed by a need for more flexible employment relations. This development is characterised by decentralisation of collective bargaining, deregulation of industrial relations, and adjustment to market forces that result in a weakening of the organisational power of labour unions and to some extent also of the employers' organisations (Lash and Urry 1987; Traxler 1994: 3). The logic behind this type of explanation is that structural changes in the world economy and the growing international competition will result in a shift in industrial relations and employment regulation towards decentralisation and deregulation. Traxler (1994: 4–8) criticises this argument and states that it is divergence rather than convergence in industrial relations that has been the prevailing trend during the recent decades. Variation across countries may therefore be larger than is predicted by the disorganisation thesis. In this context, it is important to take into account the intervening institutional variables such as the organisation of the unemployment benefit system, the relationship between unions and political parties, the degree of corporatism, and the power position of the labour movement in the individual countries.

The structural-change hypothesis

Another type of theory, closely related to the convergence thesis, tries to explain the decline in unionisation and indirectly the changes in the industrial relations systems by focusing on broad economic changes affecting the labour force. Such changes may have reduced the size of the workforce in industrial sectors that are traditionally highly unionised and increased the number in sectors with traditions for low or no unionisation. Thus the decline is tied primarily to structural change in the economy and not linked to union or management behaviour. According to Freeman and Medoff (1984: 226–7), this explanation has three serious problems.

First, the structural changes in the labour market, including the growth of white-collar jobs, decline of manufacturing, and the feminisation of the labour force have occurred in nearly every major Western economy without causing a general decline in unionisation. Perhaps most telling are the diverging trends in union membership between the United States and Scandinavia. Countries have reached nearly the same level of post-industrial labour market structure with the large majority of the labour force employed in the services industries and in knowledge-related occupations (Chapter 6 and 7 in this volume). In the Scandinavian labour markets, white-collar groups, women and public employees have been more organised than in the two North American countries. However, even in the United States and Canada, where many of the same unions and firms operate, there are marked differences in the organisation of the labour movement and in level of unionisation. Since the 1950s, the level of unionisation in Canada has increased from well below to markedly above the US level despite a similar development in the structure of the labour force in the two countries.

Second, the structural-change hypothesis assumes that the proportion of unionised workers in specific sectors does not change over time. This is not correct in light of Scandinavian experience because for white-collar and public employees unionisation has increased during the recent decades and this is a main reason for the growing union density in Scandinavia (Western 1995: 182). On the other hand, part of the explanation for the low union density in the United States is that the large majority of white-collar employees in private services are not unionised (Clawson and Clawson 1999). In the future, there might be a decrease in unionisation because of a growing number of employees working on a contract basis, outsourcing, self-employment, telephone work, etc. In addition, there are differences in the unions' capacity to organise these groups of workers, depending on the institutional settings and the political attitudes towards unionisation.

Third, the structural argument is not compatible with the fact that many workers want to become union members; the crucial point here is whether employees are free to form and join unions. Consequently, the focus should instead be on the legal procedures and the role unions and managers play in the certification of unions in the countries where such legal arrangements exist. Freeman and Medoff (1984: 228) conclude that a more realistic assessment is that 'structural factors increase or decrease the difficulty of organization but do not determine unionization'. Goldfield (1987: 189 and 210) comes to a similar conclusion, but Goldfield specifically stresses the growing capitalist anti-union offensive and the 'lack of aggressiveness and allocation of resources by US trade unions themselves'.

Different institutional (legal) settings

Many analysts argue that variations in union membership can be explained by differences in labour legislation and the role of governments in industrial relations systems. A larger level of membership in Canadian unions compared to the US has been explained by the fact that labour laws in Canada *encourage* union formation and collective bargaining, while in the United States the labour laws *allow* unions to act (Huxley, Kettler and Struthers 1986: 131). Goldfield (1987: 217) goes further, stating that the policy towards unions in the United States, particularly in the private sector 'poses more difficulties for union organization than in any other economically developed capitalist country'. Such policies are made possible by the anti-union legislative framework that permits resistance of employers to unionisation. Under legal provisions guaranteeing free speech, employers are allowed to regularly contest elections favouring union representation. Organised managerial opposition to unionism, including illegal campaign tactics, discourages US workers from joining and becoming politically active in unions (Bronfenbrenner 1994: 75–89; Freeman and Medoff 1984: 233). Weiler advances this argument by pointing to the crucial role that the different legal systems in the United States and Canada play in connection with union density:

> Canada has a far lower incidence of employer unfair labour practices, in particular discriminatory discharges, a much higher rate of union success in obtaining certification under its legislation, and a union density ratio that has moved, for the last quarter-century, in the opposite direction from the trend we have observed in the United States.
>
> (Weiler 1990: 254–5)

Unions and unemployment benefits

The role of unions in organising and running the administration of the unemployment benefit system has been seen as an important factor leading to a high level of unionisation. Most labour markets with high union density have a system of union-organised unemployment benefit funds. By combining the members' unemployment funds and unions, it is much easier to recruit employees for unions and those employees who become unemployed or are employed in contingent jobs do not leave the unions as often happens when unions and unemployment funds are separated. This is the case for both Sweden and Denmark, but is not the case for the two North American countries. Historically, unemployment benefits together with financial aid in case of strikes and lockouts have played an important role for the consolidation of unions in periods of high unemployment and increased industrial conflicts. Both unemployment benefits and financial aid with strikes make it more difficult for employers to find workers willing to take jobs during strikes and lockouts (Kjellberg 1997: 22).

Over the past two decades, the level of union density has been affected by the level of unemployment. A growing level of unemployment tends to increase the level of unionisation (Figure 2.1). Finland, Sweden and Spain (all countries with rapidly growing unemployment) have experienced a growth in unionisation while Portugal, the Netherlands and the United Kingdom (countries with decreasing unemployment) have experienced a decline in unionisation. Union density started to recover in Sweden at the beginning of the 1990s when the unemployment rate went up. In Denmark, union density increased during the 1970s, which was a period of mass unemployment (Scheuer 1998: 157–8). Such findings are in line with other comparative studies contending that countries with stable or increasing union density normally have trade unions in control of, or linked to, unemployment funds (Golden, Wallerstein and Lange 1999).

How can we interpret the development of the labour movement and the industrial relations systems in the four countries in the light of the previously discussed theoretical perspectives? The convergence thesis obviously provides us with a framework that points to broad long-term trends concerning the continuing development of industrial societies. However, these four countries have moved towards post-industrialism in quite different ways. Although the countries have similar structural changes (globalisation, flexibility, etc.), unionisation and industrial relations have diverged more than might be expected with respect to the convergence thesis. Similarly, structural change (the decline of industrial sectors and the growth of the service sectors) affects unionisation in different ways. Unionisation among service workers is extremely difficult in the United States because there are legal barriers and political resistance to unionisation. In the Scandinavian countries with longstanding traditions of union rights, collective bargaining and corporate decision-making as structural change avenues have not significantly affected union

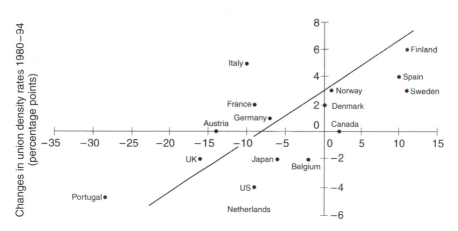

Changes in unemployment from 1980–85 and 1990–95 (percentage points)

Figure 2.1 Changes in unemployment and union density among OECD countries, 1980–95
Sources: OECD 1985; 2000a.

density among groups of employees in the new service sector. In connection with structural change in labour markets, the organisation of unemployment funds plays an important role for unionisation. The two Scandinavian countries have unemployment insurance funds administered by, or closely linked to, unions implying that claims for such benefits are facilitated by union membership. This brings us to the conclusion that institutions do matter in explaining unionisation. However, labour law alone does not result in unionisation. Different political cultures and social values concerning individualism–collectivism create different preconditions for unions. Here we can point to the historical relationship between the Scandinavian unions and working-class parties that have paved the way for unions as integrated societal and political actors. Such relationships have produced early pro-union legislation and make it easy to form and run unions, engage in collective bargaining and, if necessary, take coercive action. Unionisation will therefore prevail at a high level in the associative democracies where the industrial relation system obviously is less sensitive to neo-liberal offensives and globalisation than in societies characterised by adversarial systems of industrial relations.

Conclusion

Pronounced differences exist in the history of the North American and the European working classes. During most of the industrialisation process, the European working class has been included in the political establishment through a variety of institutional agencies. The relationship between capital and labour has been mediated and regulated through a large number of collective self-formed institutions at the economic, social, political and cultural level. This co-operative system of mediation has probably reached its highest level in Scandinavia.

The American working class developed in another direction. As a class, it has never been integrated into the political and social institutions. Instead, it has been increasingly integrated into American capitalism on an individual basis. During the postwar economic restructuring period, the American working class was characterised by fragmentation and increasing de-politicisation. In North America, however, there are significant differences in the history of the US and Canadian working classes. Canada has had a stronger socialist tradition and trade union movement than the United States. The institutional framework for regulating the capital and labour system fundamentally differ in the United States and Canada and this is probably the main reason for the differences in unionisation. In the United States, the right to form unions was guaranteed for a restricted group without supervisory functions. This hampered collective organising among the growing groups of professionals and salaried employees and the US rate of union density has become one of the lowest in the OECD from the early 1980s.

In Canada, there is greater confidence in unions. Usually, they are automatically certified by the state authorities when the union membership exceeds a certain level. The Canadian unions are also more autonomous *vis-à-vis* the state in dealing with their own internal affairs compared with the US unions. Canada is similar to the Scandinavian model; its unions are expected to maintain peace in the labour market and to refrain from coercive measures during the life of collective agreements. Today the Canadian level of unionisation is nearly double the US level and comes close to most European countries.

Denmark and Sweden, on the other hand, have experienced nearly the same historical conditions for formation of the union movement and the industrial relation system. In both countries, the labour movements were the most important social forces behind the democratisation process. Trade unions were the driving forces upon which the social democratic parties were established. During the early 1900s, the industrial relations system was constituted in both countries through main agreements between employers' and employees' peak organisations outlining the procedures for collective bargaining and industrial conflict. This development is also reflected in the level of unionisation, which in both Denmark and Sweden has increased almost uninterruptedly since the first decades of the twentieth century. During the 1980s, unionisation and the strength of the unions diminished in most Western countries, but in the Nordic countries the unions held their position relatively well.

Several explanations can be given for the high Scandinavian level of unionisation. First, and probably most important, both the Danish and Swedish labour movements are united organisations characterised by common political goals and without rival organisations. Second, the political and industrial part of the Scandinavian labour movement has been co-operating closely in organising the welfare society and establishing the system for negotiating industrial conflicts. Third, there exists in both countries a close connection between the trade unions and the unemployment security system and this has been a great impetus in the unions' efforts to recruit new members. The OECD countries with the highest rates of unionisation – Denmark, Sweden and Finland – are all characterised by a system of unemployment insurance which is voluntary and organised in close connection with the unions. This seems to result in the willingness to join a union during periods of growing unemployment and this trend is higher than in countries where the unemployment insurance system is part of the public benefit system.

In both the North American and the Scandinavian countries, the aim of the unions was to protect workers from pure arbitrariness by the employers. The vehicle for this was granting of trade union rights and measures facilitating collective agreements. While unions in North America, notably the United States, have typically been committed to pure trade unionism, i.e., a gradual improvement of wages and material living conditions, the Scandinavian unions have developed in tandem with social democratic parties. This has enabled unions to exert influence on a number of issues. The attitude of Scandinavian governments *vis-à-vis* unions has been permissive in comparison with the North American unions. Unions and employers' organisations in Sweden and Denmark were given responsibility to establish a centralised collective bargaining system, although under supervision of the state authorities. The premise was that conflicts of interest should be solved peacefully with a minimum of strikes and lockouts. Consequently, the state has also provided the parties with mediation and arbitration bodies and labour tribunals in order to solve conflicts. Unlike the United States, the state hardly intervenes in a union's internal affairs. This arrangement constituted fertile ground for unionisation; in both countries, union density for workers and salaried employees reached extremely high levels.

3 Labour law and employment regulation

Rafael Lindqvist

Introduction

Labour law is an important instrument for structuring the relations between employers and employees. It supports and restrains the power of management and organised labour by defining the conditions for payments, employment security and negotiations in the workplace. In this regard, labour law has historically developed along different avenues in various countries. Legislation and collective agreements have had various influences due to the strengths of organisational interests, constitutional factors and political preferences. The interwoven social relations of capital–labour, property rights–employee rights, and state regulation versus the free play of market forces create country-specific patterns. This chapter describes the main differences and similarities in the developments of jurisdictions and practices in employment regulation and workers' participation in North America and Scandinavia. The aim is also to relate the respective patterns of labour legislation to the debate on labour market flexibility and unemployment. The point of departure is that labour laws must be seen as limitations in the traditional prerogatives of capitalists to freely recruit and dismiss employees and to exercise management without encumbrance from unions. This chapter examines the different routes taken by the respective countries.

Market society, labour law and civil rights

The development of labour law in industrial societies must be seen in the light of the self-regulating market society emerging in the latter half of the nineteenth century. Industrial society certainly brought labour power into the orbit of the market system implying that labour was dealt with as a commodity, subject to supply and demand and sold at prices called wages (Polanyi 1957). Under such circumstances, the central issue for workers was to mitigate the dependence and arbitrariness of the employers by regulating payments, hours of work and other working conditions. From this point of view, according to Otto Kahn-Freund (1972: 8), labour law can be seen as 'an attempt to infuse law into a relation of command and subordination'. Labour became in a certain aspect a commodity, but it is unique in that its sale is carried out only within the employment contract (Wheeler 1992: 18).

However, this transaction takes place within a relationship in which the players have different power resources. Therefore, the superior position of the employer in terms of social and economic status needs to be taken into account because it renders the employment relationship open for exploitation.

Seen from the viewpoint of employers, institutions of labour legislation were usually related to the overall goals of efficiency and assessed in terms rendering the firm more profitable and viable. From a business perspective, an unregulated market society harboured many risks in terms of strikes and extortion of productive resources including labour power. However, if labour laws granting union rights and collective bargaining were perceived to restrict the performance of functions in which employers have a strong interest, then such laws would likely be modified or abolished, particularly if employers are sufficiently powerful to force such change against the will of weak labour movements.

Scandinavia: collective agreements and labour law

The Scandinavian countries have typically chosen a collectivist route by allowing unions to interfere in the free play of market forces by granting extensive rights to organise and negotiate on a wide range of issues. However, the achievement of such rights was the result of intense pressure from the unions. Important elements in this respect were central agreements negotiated by employers and unions in the two countries (the *September Agreement* in Denmark, 1899 and the *December Compromise* in Sweden, 1906). Such agreements granted the workers the right of association and certain rudimentary guarantees against dismissal for trade union activists. In the 1930s, the *Saltsjöbaden Agreement* established by LO and SAF expanded union rights for Swedish workers in 1938. This agreement gave the trade unions some influence over lay-offs and dismissals because notice had to be based on a just cause and a brief period of notice must be observed. These rights only applied to workers. When Swedish salaried employees began to unionise, they wanted union rights similar to those granted to manual workers at the turn of the century (see Chapter 2). In response to the number of dismissals in the 1930s enacted by employers in order to resist white-collar unionisation, controversies and increased pressure from the growing white-collar unions resulted in the passing of the *Act on Rights of Association and the Right of Collective Bargaining* in 1936. It granted all salaried employees, except public officials in administrative and managerial positions, the legal right to organise in trade unions and to negotiate wages and other working conditions. Indirectly, such steps strengthened the protection against arbitrary dismissal. In 1966, negotiation rights were granted to public civil servants in general except for a small number of top-level employees (Furåker and Lindqvist 1992; Jägerskiöld 1971; Tobisson 1973).

In Denmark, union rights for workers were expanded within the framework of the *September Agreement*. This agreement remained in force until 1960, when it was replaced by the *Basic Agreement* (Hovedaftalen) containing more elaborated rules on coercive measures, peacekeeping obligations and restrictions in managerial prerogatives concerning allocation of work and dismissals. Because both public and private sector salaried employees pressured for union rights in the 1930s, the state anticipated tendencies towards homogenisation of trade union rights between workers and white-collar workers. The state chose to include the latter group within a separate legal framework, *The White Collar Act* (Funktionærloven) of 1938 (Petersen 1987: 48). Thus, a considerable part of the Danish white-collar employees were granted union rights although not in the same comprehensive ways as the basic agreement granted such rights to workers. However, the idea behind this law was also to demarcate *vis-à-vis* other categories of employees by laying down minimum (but comparatively favourable) standards of terms and conditions in the employment relationship (including employment protection).

The guiding principle that evolved during the first half of the twentieth century, accepted by the state, employers and trade unions in Denmark and Sweden, declared that labour market organisations should reach agreements on employment conditions for blue-collar workers instead of the state intervening. Towards the end of the 1960s, however, the general attitude in Sweden was steadily developing in favour of state intervention and regulation by law in employment protection. In the beginning of the 1970s, the union movement succeeded in pressuring the Social Democratic government to pass two laws in order to improve employment protection for older employees. Employers were required to implement prolonged notice periods for older employees, and also to keep and recruit disabled persons. These two laws were followed by the *Employment Protection Act* that was enacted in 1974. This act required the employer to objectively demonstrate reasons for employee termination – e.g., shortage of work (or shortage of money to have the work done) or personal reasons like misconduct, lack of competence, etc. In case of redundancy, the employer is obliged to observe certain priority rights according to the principle of 'first in – last out', unless otherwise agreed to by the relevant union. In case of discharge due to personal reasons, the character and circumstances have to be carefully documented and proven. The law also covers public sector employees. However, a special law, *The Public Employment Act* (1976), provides for some additional regulation concerning the discharge of public employees.

In Denmark there is no general legislation specifying conditions for dismissals. Statutory regulation on these matters covers only white-collar workers, while blue-collar workers have to rely on employment protection and seniority principles in collective agreements (Nielsen 1992: 99). Hence, a vast majority of all employers must have an objective ground for firing an employee. Without protective legislation, the strength of unions constitutes a crucial precondition for employment security.

Since the 1970s, legislation similar to the North American civil rights acts has been introduced in Scandinavia. Denmark introduced sex equality legislation in the late 1970s, partly as a result of the membership in the EC, and Sweden introduced an equal opportunity act in 1980. Since 1999, Sweden has also enacted legislation prohibiting discrimination of disabled people in the world of work and an act prohibiting discrimination of people on grounds of race, ethnicity and sexual preference. An ombudsman advocates for the rights of the people the law intends to support and monitors the implementation of each law.

North America: common law and civil rights

Given a comparatively weak labour movement, North America has embarked on an individualist route relying on common law practices and civil rights regulation to cope with employment protection and other work place issues. The origins of employment regulation are to be found in the British common law tradition requiring a reasonable amount of notice. However, the two countries responded in different ways to such traditions. The United States gradually adopted the employment at will for all workers, including white-collar workers. Canada, on the other hand, kept much of the British notions of reasonable notice, implying that in practice the definition of what was reasonable became more generous for high wage white-collar workers than for blue-collar workers. Canada's longer attachment to the British system has been cited as a possible cause for this difference (Kuhn 1993: 284; see also Jacoby 1982).

In contrast to Scandinavia, where employment protection developed on a broad basis within the framework of collective bargaining actively promoted by the state, neither the *Wagner Act* nor the *Canadian Labour Code* became vehicles for employment protection for North American workers (except for union members). Instead, both Canada and the United States experienced a substantial growth in legislation, from the 1930s onwards, setting minimum standards for employment in terms of minimum wages, vacations, public holidays, weekly rest, etc. In the postwar period, developments in minimum standards legislation seemed to slow in the United States while continuing to grow in Canada. Part of this trend was the gradual development during the 1970s and 1980s of statutory minimum notice requirement for individual termination and later special requirements for mass termination by Canadian provinces (Kuhn 1993: 287). Unlike the Scandinavian development of employment protection, where efforts by trade unions and labour parties have played a crucial role in the introduction of mandatory and collective agreements regulation, the only significant pattern in Canada seems to be 'a process of diffusion from the large, central provinces [Ontario and Quebec] to smaller more remote provinces' (Kuhn 1993: 287).

This gradual adoption of individual and group notice laws in Canada over the past 30 years, which can be seen as an outgrowth of other minimum standards legislation, was largely unparalleled in the United States. What occurred instead was a growing pressure for plant closing laws regulating mass termination, which peaked in the federal *Worker Adjustment and Retraining Notification Act* (WARN) of 1988. While notice provisions for mass lay-offs are rather similar in the two countries, the United States does not have statutory minimum levels of notice for individual dismissals and no severance pay requirements.

The major focus of federal legislation in the United States has been employment discrimination by means of civil rights legislation supplemented by affirmative action, i.e., programmes to include minorities and women in the work force by making private employers and government entities take positive action. Canada has adopted similar legal measures. However, instead of affirmative action Canada uses the term 'employment equity'.

The North American employment regulation thus has two central features. The first is a continual increase in formal legal requirements (improved human rights legislation, employment standards, and occupational health and safety), which has narrowed the gap between the rights of different groups (Adell 1993: 583; Finkin 1994: 5). The second is a sharp divide between organised and unorganised employment. Organised employment has protection clauses and the grievance arbitration processes laid down in the union–management collective bargaining agreements often give union members substantial protection. Unorganised employment relies on the doctrine of employment at will, especially in the United States, giving the employers a substantial amount of freedom to terminate contracts for any reason. However, during the last two decades, this principle has been eroded by various court decisions dealing with wrongful dismissals.

Employment regulation regimes

Employment regulation in Western countries usually has a number of formal requirements in order to prohibit discriminatory employment policies, unjust dismissals, and to ease the economic burden of those dismissed due to a shortage of work. In this section, we compare regulations concerning recruitment and employment procedures, then we will look at legislation and practices concerning individual dismissals by examining just cause, notice periods and consultation (negotiation) with unions and labour market authorities. Next, we will look at the same issues as far as collective redundancy is concerned. First, however, we intend to put the four countries in a broader framework by comparing them to the other OECD countries.

Employment protection in Western countries

Legislation and practices in the field of employment protection differ substantially across Western nations. In general, employment protection laws are most strict in southern Europe, France and Germany and less strict in English-speaking countries, notably North America. The Scandinavian countries place themselves somewhere in between (see Chapters 2, 8 and 9). This picture has not changed very much since the late 1980s although some countries have liberalised or tightened specific components of their legislation (OECD 1999b: 49–51). Whereas Sweden and Germany liberalised their regulation on fixed-term employment and temporary agency contracts during the 1990s, Spain tightened its restrictions. Only in France has overall strictness of employment regulation increased during this period. Canada and the United States have the least restrictive regulations although waiting periods and notification periods in case of mass lay-offs have been tightened by legislation. In Table 3.1, the strictness of employment legislation in selected OECD countries is shown. The employment protection legislation (EPL) in overall terms is less strict in both Denmark and Sweden in the late 1990s compared to ten years earlier. This is mainly due to the abolition of legal restrictions for temporary work agencies, and in the case of Sweden less legal restrictions for employers to take on employees on fixed-term contracts.

Table 3.1 Summary indicators of the strictness of employment protection legislation, EPL (selected OECD countries)

	Overall EPL strictness	
	Late 1980s[a]	Late 1990s[a]
Central and Western Europe:		
France	2.7 (10)	2.8 (21)
Germany	3.2 (14)	2.6 (20)
Southern Europe:		
Italy	4.1 (18)	3.4 (23)
Spain	3.7 (17)	3.1 (22)
Nordic countries:		
Denmark	2.1 (7)	1.5 (8)
Sweden	3.5 (15)	2.6 (18)
North America:		
Canada	0.6 (3)	1.1 (4)
United States	0.2 (1)	0.7 (1)

Source: OECD 1999b: 66.

Note

a Average of indicators for regular contracts, temporary contracts and collective dismissals (only late 1990s). The summary scores can range from 0 to 6. Figures in brackets show country rankings of OECD members. All rankings increase with the strictness of employment protection. The number of countries ranked in the late 1980s was 19 and in the late 1990s it was 26. Indicators on which summary scores are calculated are as follows: (a) regular contracts – procedural inconveniences, notice and severance pay for no-fault dismissals and difficulty of dismissal; (b) temporary contracts – requirements for fixed-term contracts and temporary work agency employment; (c) collective dismissals – type of definition, additional notification requirements, delays involved and other costs for the employer (see OECD 1999b: 118 for further details on the construction of indicators).

Although the above EPL ranking is based on a number of indicators of strictness for regular and temporary contracts, it is important to note that the institutional environment has grown increasingly complex. For example, concurrent with the existence of standard employment contracts there has in many countries been an increase in less protected (part-time and temporary) jobs that lack a well-defined juridical status. Beside the need to update such rankings, Bertola, Boeri and Caxes (2000: 57–72) argue in favour of developing new measures in order to capture the interactions between legal provisions and the enforcement procedures applied in various countries. The degree and nature of enforcement may turn out to be as important as nominal strictness in determining labour market flows into and out of unemployment. However, lacking such sophisticated measures we have to rely on indicators of strictness produced by OECD. Consistent with earlier studies the OECD (1999b) holds that there seems to be little or no association between strictness in employment regulation and overall unemployment (see Chapters 1 and 8, this volume). Such regulation, however, may be strongly associated with the demographic composition of employment and unemployment; i.e., strict laws might raise employment for prime-age male employees and lower employment for youths and women, and lower turnover rates in the labour market. Once unemployed, the risk of remaining in a stagnant pool of unemploymentincreases. However, evidence is insufficient and there is a need for more robust analysis.

Hiring and the employment contract: laws and policies

Several strategies can be adopted in order to influence recruitment procedures and the way employment contracts are designed. In countries where unions generally are weak and few, unions may find it proper to try to gain control over recruitment policies within firms or branches in order to survive or expand by getting the right people. Closed shops or union shops can be seen as adequate measures in this strategy. If unions are weak (and the proportion of employees covered by employment protection clauses in collective agreements is low), a larger arena will be opened up for potential civil rights legislation compared to cases where union coverage is high. If unions are strong and union density high, then unions do not need to control recruitment at the plant level. From a union perspective, it might be more rational to try to achieve general principles favouring a wider collective of workers. Preferably, such rules would focus on conditions for short-term workers or part-time workers in aiding them to obtain permanent full-time work and procedures for communication with unions in case of redundancy or lay-offs.

Denmark

Danish employers are not legally obliged to give preference to any particular person or category of persons when hiring. Legislation does not exist that prohibits an employer from hiring a temporary worker, or that forbids the hiring for a specific job or as replacement for another worker. However, contracts for specific jobs are common in some sectors of the labour market (for instance construction) and collective agreements generally hold such contracts to be legal (Jacobsen 1993: 78). According to the *White Collar Act*, salaried employees may be engaged for temporary work such as seasonal assistance or substituting for another employee if the period does not exceed three months. It is legally permitted to prolong contracts for an additional three-month period in case of probation periods (Borch 1996: 25).

Danish statutes prohibit employers from discriminating against an applicant on the grounds of sex, married status, race, religion or obligation with respect to military service (Borch 1996: 19). Such regulation limits the scope of managerial freedom because it pressures employers to base management decisions on objective and justifiable reasons. Since the mid-1970s, Denmark has had equal pay legislation. The present statute, the *Equal Treatment Act* (1990), bans discrimination and promotes equality planning and positive action (Nielsen 1995: 15–17). Under circumstances where sex discrimination may be suspected, the employer must show valid reasons for decisions.

Sweden

In principle, Swedish employers are free to choose the persons they want to employ, provided they do not violate bans on discrimination against designated groups. However, employment on fixed-term contracts is strictly regulated. The *Employment Protection Act* (1974, amended 1982) states that a job is to be considered as permanent unless other terms have been agreed upon. Probation periods are permitted for a maximum of six months. In addition, detailed regulations were created specifying in which situations temporary employment contracts are valid. This legislation regulates work such as seasonal work, temporary jobs, substitutes, or in the case of peak periods. Despite such formal restrictions, typically many employees work as substitutes over many years. In the 1990s, regulation on such matters was relaxed: temporary work agencies have been permitted since 1993 and from 1997 fixed-term contracts are possible without specifying an objective reason, where no more than five employees are covered by such contracts simultaneously (OECD 1999b: 53). The free choice to recruit is also regulated by the requirement stipulating that when an employment contract is terminated due to shortage of work, the discharged worker has the right to be re-employed in the job that he had earlier if the employer needs to take on new employees within a period of 12 months. The labour market authorities may also set up selective hiring criteria for companies that apply for certain government subsidies.

Discrimination in work life on grounds of sex was not banned in Sweden until 1980 when the first *Equal Opportunity Act* was passed. Such a late emergence of equal opportunity legislation between men and women has been explained by the fact that the state has always been careful not to interfere in the collective bargaining process because equality issues in the labour market generally have been handled by agreements between employers and unions. This kind of Swedish politics of solidarity, according to Bacchi, has 'produced a narrow space within which claims can be made for "women"' (1996: xiii) because corporate politics operates to protect the prerogatives of industry and unions and thereby to determine the scope of positive action. When the Swedish law was introduced in 1980, it took the form of a compromise between the government and the social partners where the latter became responsible for promoting equal opportunity within the frame of collective agreements (Xu 1997: 30–2). In 1992, the law was sharpened by reducing the impact of collective agreements. The new Act requires that every employer, having ten or more employees, make detailed annual equality plans including a review of pay differentials. The task of the *Equality Ombudsman (JämO)* is in the first instance to seek to persuade employers to follow the provisions of the Act voluntarily (SFS 1991:433). Individuals who feel that they have been discriminated against on grounds of sex, as a job seeker or as an employee, can turn to *JämO* for help. However, the unions have an obligation to help their members in such disputes, which means that *JämO* must always ask a union whether it wishes to represent its member in a dispute. Positive action, formulated in gender-neutral language, is reflected in the Act's provision requiring employers to 'make special efforts, when taking on new employees, to obtain applicants of the underrepresented sex' (SFS 1991: 433).

The United States and Canada

In the United States and Canada there is no specific regulation governing fixed-term employment. Such jobs are in principle subject to free hiring and firing conditions. In both countries the major focus of federal legislation has been employment discrimination. The *Civil Rights Act* of 1964, title VII, bans such discrimination on the grounds of race, colour, national origin, religious preference or sex. This statute specifies a series of unlawful employment practices but does not explicitly define the term 'discriminate'. Instead, an *ad hoc* approach has developed as to the content of the concept. The *Age Discrimination in Employment Act* (1967) prohibits employment discrimination on the basis of age. The *Rehabilitation Act* (1973) and the *Americans with Disabilities Act* (1990) prohibit employment discrimination against the disabled. The *Equal Employment Opportunity Act* (1972) broadened the coverage of title VII (to state and local governments) and made it possible to seek enforcement of the law in the courts. Affirmative action, i.e., programmes that require private employers and government entities to take positive actions to include minorities and women, dates back to the late 1960s (Jones 1985: 219; Marable 1996: 3–14). Essentially, such plans require self-analysis and determination of areas where women and minorities are under-utilised and goals and timetables to achieve appropriate representation of the excluded classes in the job categories in which they are found lacking.

In both the North American countries, *Federal Contractors' Programmes* exist which require contractors to sign a certificate of commitment to design and carry out an employment equity programme. The purpose is to identify and remove artificial barriers to the selection, hiring, promotion and training of women, aboriginal people, people with disabilities and visible minorities. Failure to comply with the requirements does not result in the loss of a contract; it only means that the firm in question is not allowed to take part in the bidding process in the future. In the United States such programmes include contractors with 50 employees or more which bid on federal government contracts for goods and services of a certain economic value. Regulation in Canada covers companies with 100 or more workers as well as subcontractors (Jain 1992: 402–7).

The *Canadian Human Rights Act* (1978) adopts a similar legal definition of discrimination as legislation in the United States does. It bans individual acts of discrimination in employment and the pursuit of discriminatory employment policies and practices based on the following grounds: race, religion, colour, national or ethnic origin, sex, marital status and age. Provincial jurisdictions may have further proscriptions such as physical and mental disability and sexual orientation (Jain 1985: 71–3). Almost all jurisdictions have Human Rights Commissions in order to enforce the laws. The Act also allows organisations to adopt and carry out special programmes (affirmative action) designed to prevent or eliminate disadvantage related to any of the grounds of discrimination (Raskin 1994: 76).

As in most other anti-discrimination legislation, affirmative action constitutes an explicit exemption that allows legislative intervention on behalf of what is thought of as disadvantaged groups. At the federal level, the *Employment Equity Act* (1986) and the Federal Contractors' Programme together encompass Canada's approach to affirmative action. The Act requires the covered employers to report and prepare annual employment equity plans with goals and a timetable in order to improve the representation of the designated groups. Employers are legally obliged to consult with designated employee representatives, or with bargaining agents in the relevant unions (Jain 1992: 401). However, there are no enforcement provisions, and employers are only required to send an annual report to the responsible Minister; there is no penalty for non-compliance with such plans and nothing in the statutes obliges companies to improve their efforts.

Canadian affirmative action is, like its counterparts in the United States, understood as assistance to disadvantaged groups to catch up. But the Canadian discussion has not condemned affirmative action as 'reverse discrimination' to the same extent as in the United States. There seems to be more willingness to discuss sex equality in the language of 'equal results' and in terms of result-oriented policies admitting that 'disadvantaged' groups require a range of special measures and reasonable accommodation to achieve equality in work (Bacchi 1996: 61).

To conclude, Scandinavian countries have approximated the North American system of giving credit to anti-discrimination laws. Such legislation has become such an important element that employers have to pay attention to it when hiring. However, in contrast to North America, the Scandinavian equal opportunity legislation is inserted in the collective bargaining system because the social partners have been given a substantial role in the implementation of the regulation. The idea of taking proactive steps, by means of affirmative action, in order to dismantle prejudice is another difference between the countries. In Scandinavia the softer variant 'positive action' is held to be sufficient.

Protection against individual dismissals

Preventing arbitrary dismissals has been a vital interest for blue-collar as well as white-collar employees. Strong unions may try to negotiate better terms for collective agreements or attempt to channel demands into the political machinery to achieve favourable labour legislation. This would typically be the case if unions have close links to a strong political party. In the case where unions are weak, the option of legislation is still open; however, one might expect legislation to be designed in broad terms not necessarily focusing on what unions perceive to be the most urgent issues.

Denmark

In line with Denmark's dual structure of employment protection, statutory regulation concerning dismissals in Denmark covers only white-collar workers, whereas blue-collar workers have to rely on rules laid down in the *Basic Agreement* between peak organisations and sector collective agreements that regulate procedures for discharge, notice periods and severance pay. Such agreements cover a vast majority of employers and provide a partial functional alternative to white-collar statutory rules. For white-collar employees, the notice period will generally be longer than for blue-collar workers. According to the *White Collar Act*, the minimum notice required is one month for six months of employment. For employment periods that last for longer, notice periods are as follows: additional months for each three years of service up to a maximum of six months when the employee has obtained a seniority of nine years (Jacobsen 1993: 79). Employers are not required by law to consult with trade unions before deciding to dismiss an employee. However, this may be regulated in various collective agreements. Maximum compensation for unfair dismissal in Denmark, according to the collective agreements, is 39 weeks of pay (Borch 1996: 40).

Sweden

Basic statutory regulation on employment protection in Sweden embraces all wage earners, stipulating that an employer must have an objective ground for giving an employee notice. Hence, termination of employment contracts in case of redundancy is strictly regulated. Written notice must be given to the worker in person, including instructions concerning the procedure to be followed by the employee if he wishes to refer the matter to the Labour Court. Shortage of work is always considered an objective ground, and in such cases the employer is obliged to observe certain priority rights according to seniority principles, unless otherwise agreed to by the relevant union. In 1993, employers were given the legal option to retain two workers of their own choice in redundancy situations. However, a couple of years later the 'first in – last out' principle was reinstated in its strict form. Instead, possibilities to modify the order of dismissals through collective bargaining were strengthened (OECD 1999b: 52). The *Employment Protection Act* requires notice of one to six months depending on the age of the employee and employment record in the firm. The longest period of notice is six months for people aged 45 or more (provided that they have been working for the employer for at least six months). Compensation for unfair dismissal renders the employee 16 to 48 months of pay depending on age of employee and length of service.

Consultation with the trade union is requested before dismissals are decided in Sweden. Every trade union employing at least one union member has the right to negotiate with an employer. Consultation should begin at the earliest opportunity and the unions should be given a fair chance to influence the employer's decision. Hence, trade unions have a legal role in determining whether a dismissal is reasonable. The central labour market organisations can conclude agreements on alternative priority rights. The Labour Court (Arbetsdomstolen) is the first and supreme court in dismissal disputes in which employers or employees are bound by collective agreements. In other cases involving non-union members or when the union is unwilling to represent the employee the settlement first goes to the district court whose decision can be lodged to the Labour Court.

United States

Although there is no statutory law of general application that alters the employment at will doctrine, there are within the United States common law concepts of wrongful termination, good faith and fair dealing that require an employee to be given advance notice. What constitutes objective grounds and reasonable notice may depend on factors such as the employee's position, his length of service, written agreements, oral assurances and past practices in similar situations.

In at least three areas courts have abandoned the ultra-free firing model and set restrictions for discharge grounded on theories of contract. First, several courts have held that statements in a personnel manual or employee handbook, providing that discharge will be for cause only, may constitute an implicit promise of continued employment. Such promises by the employer, may become part of the employment contract because of an employee's legitimate expectations. Second, courts may take into consideration factors like length of service, employee performance as demonstrated by regular wage increase, positive performance evaluations, past practices concerning bonuses, promotions and so on, as employer assurance that employment would continue (Carr Jr., Cathcart and Kruse 1991: 81–2; Grenig 1991: 573). Third, public policy exceptions of the employment at will doctrine mean that the employer is prohibited from dismissing an employee at will in case the employee reports an employer's violation of state or federal laws or in case the employer undermines a firmly established principle of public policy.

Many grievances in the non-union sector end up in courts because laid-off employees initiate efforts to uncover a firm's illegal practices. The number of wrongful termination lawsuits has increased steadily because many legal experts consider such cases easy to prosecute and economically rewarding for the employee and the lawyer. Depending on the type of law suit, this kind of conflict solution may be very expensive for the employer in terms of reinstatements, additional compensation, tort damages for emotional distress, etc. The costs for this 'freedom' to dismiss staff can therefore be very high for individual companies compared to the statutory provisions in Europe (Emerson 1988: 788). In recent years, a number of employers have developed various systems for providing hearings before impartial arbitrators, neutral hearing officers, sometimes chosen by the fired employee, in order to develop swift procedures for employees who do not have union representation (Grenig 1991: 578).

Another body of regulation is employee rights legislation in the different states, which puts various restrictions on employee dismissal. While a few states have statutes codifying the employment at will rule most states have laws restricting the right to discharge or discriminate against their employees because of race, age, sex, handicap or religion. Some states protect employees who report employer violations of state or federal laws to enforcement agencies and most states protect employees from dismissal because of exercising citizenship rights like voting or jury duty. Some states also limit the right to dismissal because of an employee's refusal to take a lie detector test. A few states have adopted statutes requiring 'good cause' for the dismissal of an employee (Grenig 1991: 570).

A third type of regulation is to be found in the unionised sector. Nearly all collective bargaining contracts provide that covered employees may be discharged only for just cause. However, the meaning of just cause is rarely defined in the contracts and it is seldom specified what kind of conduct is considered suitable for dismissal. It is therefore important that almost all such contracts provide for arbitration of grievances, i.e., a method for the union and the employer to resolve conflicts of dismissal. Usually such an arbitrator is selected on an *ad hoc* basis to decide a single case although in settings where grievances often occur the parties use the same arbitrator or a panel of arbitrators. The employer must prove that the dismissal was correct and many collective agreements require that both the employee and the union be given notice of the dismissal. However, a key principle in just cause determination under collective agreements is that discipline should be progressive and corrective before the ultimate sanction of dismissal is taken. The degree of penalty should be related to the seriousness of the offence (Grenig 1991: 577).

Canada

In many respects Canada has similar regulatory systems governing employer's obligations when labour contracts are terminated. Like the United States, Canada uses common law, which governs the interpretation and enforcement of private employment contracts. Accordingly, contracts without explicit fixed duration could be terminated by the employer in one of the two following ways: by giving notice or by termination for cause (for instance wilful misconduct, dishonesty, etc.). In the common law context the courts have set the standard that an employer must meet in order to dismiss an employee. In contrast to the United States, there has been a history implied in the contract of hiring that an employer is obliged to give reasonable notice of an intention to terminate employment (Christie, England and Cotter 1993: 609). The typical remedy in the non-unionised sector of the labour market is a civil suit. In such cases courts frequently hesitate to decide on reinstatement orders fearing that this would be too hard to enforce against reluctant employers. However, courts will usually grant damages equivalent to the wages the employee would have earned during a period of reasonable notice.

The second main body of employment protection law consists of federal and provincial legislatures with statutes guaranteeing all workers a minimum amount of notice for individual termination. Canadian federal law and most provincial jurisdictions therefore require that a minimum period of notice be given to an employee who is to be dismissed. Canada differs significantly from the United States. Depending on the length of the worker's service, the periodicity of payment and customs in the branch the notice period is generally one to eight weeks in advance (Arthurs *et al.* 1988: 133–9; Kuhn 1993: 280). Immediate termination of an employment contract, without giving either adequate notice or pay in lieu of notice, may be carried out in cases of serious misconduct (Craven Hoglund 1996: 59–60). Federal unjust dismissal legislation generally supplies unorganised employees with public mediation, which is considered to be of substantial help for those who cannot afford lawyers in helping to pursue complaints. No labour legislation (and rarely collective agreements) claims that dismissed or suspended employees be kept on the job while their complaints are being investigated (Adell 1993: 598–9). In most Canadian jurisdictions, employee remedies for non-compliance with minimum notice statutes are swift and relatively cheap. Within the administrative machinery of the province's *Labour Standards Acts*, which set minimum standards for a wide variety of working conditions, it is fairly easy for workers to have claims investigated. If liable, the employer may be ordered by a judge to pay back wages for the required notice period.

The third body of regulation is the system of collective agreements and grievance arbitration in the organised sector, which provides a framework of substantive and procedural rights. In Canada unionised workers usually have contract provisions regulating dismissals; collective agreements usually include a clause that employees may not be discharged except for 'just cause' (Arthurs *et al.* 1988: 62). Every collective agreement must provide an arbitration procedure for the resolution of rights and disputes arising during the term of an agreement. In the organised sector, arbitrators (usually chosen and paid jointly by the employer and the union) have statutory authority to reinstate unjustly dismissed employees and often do so. This is backed up by the refusal of courts to deal with wrongful dismissal actions by unionised employees (Adell 1993: 587). Some jurisdictions have taken steps towards statutory provision for speeding up arbitration procedures with more government involvement in the choice of arbitrators, and more use of pre-adjudicative mediation.

Collective redundancies

Regulation of collective redundancies in the four countries follows very much the same principles as the respective regulation in case of individual discharge, with the exception of more and stricter requirements on employers in terms of notice periods, information to labour market authorities and negotiation with unions. The reason for such requirements is found in the severe social consequences of mass termination.

Denmark

In Denmark no statutory selection criteria exist when carrying out large-scale dismissals, but it is not unusual that in the course of negotiations trade unions press for certain principles or priority rules. Practices depend on the strength of the relevant union. However, prior consultation in the company's work council is required for the purpose of avoiding the announced redundancy or alleviating its consequences. The employer is not only obliged to consult with employee representatives, but also to provide them with all the necessary information (in written form) about the number of dismissals, the reasons for them and the timetable. The same information has to be communicated to the appropriate national labour market authorities. Salaried employees can claim statutory severance payments from one to three months, while blue-collar workers can receive payments according to collective agreements – the amounts vary considerably from one trade to another (Borch 1996: 34–5).

Sweden

In Sweden there are detailed rules in case of collective redundancy. As a first step, *The Employment Protection Act* states that all employees of the relevant category of workers should be considered, and as a second there are rules that guide how to choose which workers among those affected by shortage of work will be dismissed. In the latter aspect, the law relies on the principle of seniority in terms of length of service, provided the workers in question have 'sufficient qualification' for the job. Special protection is afforded employees above 45 years of age and disabled workers on special employment contracts (Numhauser-Henning 1988). It is important to note that the above mentioned principles apply also for employees who are not members of a trade union or at workplaces where no union is involved. Employers are required to give information to labour market authorities according to strict procedures and timetables.

Canada

The Canadian federal government and a number of the provinces have introduced special legislative measures relating to plant closures and cutbacks. Most jurisdictions stipulate that where 50 or more employees in an industrial establishment are terminated within a period not exceeding four weeks, the employer must give notice by writing to the labour market authorities and the trade unions representing the employees affected. The employees should be given at least eight weeks notice in the smallest lay-offs covered by these regulations and up to a maximum of 18 weeks for large closures. With growing numbers of intended dismissals, the periods of notice increase accordingly (Arthurs *et al.* 1988: 137).

Most Canadian jurisdictions with mass termination laws also require the employer to set up and fund a 'manpower adjustment committee' with worker representation in order to create adjustment programmes for assisting workers to find new employment (Kuhn 1993: 282). One drawback to this legislation on mass termination is that the notice need be given only after the employer has actually finalised the decision to implement lay-offs. There are no requirements to negotiate or even contemplate major changes in production that are likely to entail terminations. Nor have any of the provinces enacted a right for redundant employees to be re-hired if the former employer again hires workers with comparable qualifications (Christie, England and Cotter 1993: 584, 593).

United States

Companies in the United States traditionally have been free to close a plant without notification and bargaining with the trade union, unless the collective bargaining contract contains a preservation of work clause. Under the pressure of increased competition during the 1980s many US companies granted job security provisions in exchange for concessions on work practices or wages. In return for employers' demand for increased flexibility to organise and assign work, unions often bargained for improved job security or for income protection or improved early retirement benefits for those terminated. Although such changes are confined to a modest number of companies mostly in the automobile, steel and electrical machinery sectors, some unions have gained new forms of job security (Kassalow 1992: 152–3). However, such achievements must not overshadow the fact that the majority of American employees lacked employment protection in case of plant closings or cut downs in the 1980s. In 1988, the *Worker Adjustment Retraining and Notification Act* was passed, which states that employees affected by plant closures involving mass lay-offs must be given 60 days notice. It applies to plant closures involving 50 or more workers, or to any lay-off of six or more months involving either at least one-third of the work force at a given site or 500 or more workers. In a number of states, laws regulating plant closures exist stipulating various periods of advance notice and severance pay (Carr Jr., Cathcart and Kruse 1991: 89, 92–7). Affected workers or relevant unions must be notified as well as state and local authorities. However, no law requires that that the employer negotiates with unions (OECD 1999b: 114).

Table 3.2 shows the main features of employment protection regimes in the four countries.

Co-determination and industrial democracy

Demands for industrial democracy or worker's participation have long been one of the union's most urgent issues. Because of its intrinsic values, employment protection and workers' participation go together and the latter may be seen as a vehicle to improve protection against arbitrary dismissals. The idea of co-determination is generally accepted in Scandinavia. In both Sweden and Denmark, regulation gives unions various rights to exert influence on the employer's decisions. Union representatives play a crucial role in the co-determination system that is constructed as a two-level system – the shop floor level and the top level of the company. In North America, concepts of co-determination or workers' participation in management are by tradition alien to labour law, which emphasises the bargaining process as the favoured method for resolving conflicts.

Denmark

In Denmark the principles of co-determination and reduction of managerial prerogatives were expressed early in the *September Agreement*. Today regulation is laid down in the *Basic Agreement* which states that systematic co-determination between management and employees at all levels is a vehicle for increased competitive strength as well as increased work satisfaction and well-being of the employees. According to the Agreement, information should be given at such an

Table 3.2 Main features of employment protection regimes in North America and Scandinavia

	Canada	United States	Denmark	Sweden
Recruitment				
• Anti-discrimination	Civil rights	Civil rights	Anti discrimination laws – designated groups	Anti discrimination laws – designated groups
• Assistance to disadvantaged groups	Affirmative action by Employment Equity Law Federal Contractor's Programme	Affirmative action by Equal Employment Opportunity Act Federal Contractor's programme	'Positive action' by collective agreements	'Positive action' required by law
• Fixed-term employment	No restriction	No restriction	No restriction – blue collar Minor restrictions – white collar	Regulated by legislation
Individual dismissal	Common law (reasonable notice) Federal and provincial law on notice Collective agreements in union sector	Common law Employment at will (circumscribed by courts) Employee Rights legislation Collective agreements in union sector	Collective Agreement Seniority principles Statute – white-collars	EPL 'first in – last out' Collective agreements may provide alternative priorities
Collective dismissal	Provincial jurisdiction regulates mass termination Employers must engage in 'manpower adjustment committees' Negotiation with unions not required	Federal law (WARN) regulates notice in case of mass lay-offs Negotiation with unions not required	Collective agreements Prior consultation in work council Communication to labour market authorities	EPL 'first in-last out' Collective agreements may provide alternative priorities Negotiation required by statute Communication to labour market authorities

early stage that the views of, and suggestions from, the employees could form the basis of the decisions. In enterprises with more than 35 employees, a special works council (*samarbejdsutvalg*) consisting of representatives of the employer and the employees should be set up on request of one or both of the parties. In addition, each side should have equal representation (Flodgren 1992: 69–72). Such work councils typically supplement and reinforce the regular bargaining activities performed by shop stewards. Shop stewards are normally entitled to short-time paid leave for union work. Both parties in the work councils are required to strive towards consensus and then to act according to what has been agreed. Management has a duty to continuously give information about the economic situation of the firm and prospective major changes. According to similar agreements in the public sector, work councils are also set up in the government and in the municipal sector.

Sweden

Co-determination has a long tradition in Sweden. In collective agreements a general model of co-determination within advisory joint councils in the enterprises (*företagsnämnder*) was developed from the late 1940s. Backed up by left-wing currents in public debate, it was not difficult for Swedish trade unions to demand extended rights of negotiation from the late 1960s. Increased market competition, lay-offs, unemployment problems and regional labour turnover were problems that employees felt they should have an impact on by democratisation in working life. A militant wild-cat strike in the mine-fields in northern Sweden in the winter of 1969–70, which later spread to manufacturing industry, played an important role in pushing trade union leaders and labour politicians into taking initiatives in the parliament to prepare a new law on extended co-determination (SOU 1975:1).

In 1977, the *Co-Determination Act*, applicable for both the private and the public sector, was enacted. It substantially modified the old principle (codified in the *December Compromise* from 1906) that the employers had the right to manage and allocate work. Thereafter, the employer was obliged to inform and to negotiate with the local union before important changes in the workplace that affected workers were introduced. If the employer and the local trade union are unable to agree, the employer must on request also negotiate with the employees' central organisation. The employer, however, has the final say. The Act marks out the company as an arena where conflicts of interest between capital and labour are to be solved. However, it does not explicitly change the power resources of the parties. Because the Act only provides a framework of rules, the intention was also that the parties should work out models of co-determination adjusted to the various sectors of the labour market. Such Development Agreements have been elaborated for both the public and private sector. In the latter the parties agree to further the company's efficiency, economic viability and competitive strength and to promote secure and enriching employment conditions for the employees (Flodgren 1992: 79–82). In order to strengthen the position of the unions at the workplace level, the *Act Concerning the Status of Shop Stewards* was passed in 1974 in connection with the strengthening of employment protection legislation. The shop stewards are thereby entitled to paid leave from their work for reasonable periods of time to undertake their union functions. They also enjoy special job security in case of redundancy if it is important for the trade union that the shop steward retains his job (Edlund and Nyström 1988: 22–4).

During the 1970s, other laws were also passed in order to strengthen the position of wage earners. In 1973, a temporary law (made permanent in 1976) was introduced that gave wage earners in joint-stock companies and economic associations representation on the boards. Employees in public authorities obtained similar rights in 1974. However, restrictions in co-determination were set concerning the employees' influence on the goals, direction, scope and management of the activities of the official authorities (Lindqvist 1992: 53). In the light of the increased union concern about structural unemployment and difficulties influencing decision-making in increasingly transitional companies, unions pressured in the 1970s for 'economic democracy' by claiming 'wage-earner funds'. Such union-controlled funds were established by a profit tax and would build up stock holdings in the companies that would give wage earners substantial influence over management and investment policies. The 'wage earner fund' issue was highly contested, and against the backdrop of the recession in the early 1980s, pressure from the New Right, and a declining interest in economic equality the Social Democratic government in 1983 took a more 'realistic' position and implemented a drastically watered-down version of the wage earner fund (Pontusson 1987). Hence, workers were never given any substantial influence over capital's decision-making. In the early 1990s, the funds were phased-out and the accumulated economic assets were distributed to various research funds and to national knowledge and competence development programmes aimed to strengthen conditions for economic growth and the competitiveness of Swedish firms.

United States

In the United States the only channel of employee participation is the union. Non-union employees have no right to be informed or consulted about decisions that affect them. This tradition dates back to the *National Labour Relations Act* (1935) that instituted the employee's right to associate in unions and to engage in industrial action for the purpose of furthering collective bargaining (Bellace 1992: 242–3). The underlying assumption is that co-determination may be an outcome of the bargaining process, but it must not modify the basic division of interest between employers and employees. The *Wagner Act*, according to Heckscher (1988: 77), became a barrier to progress because it does not meet the need for effective representation of diverse white-collar employees or the need for increased strategic flexibility and the needs of multiple interests of management. The parties have been keen on upholding this division of interest between management and unions. Trade unions have frequently also been opposed to representation in the managerial boards, fearing that the trade union representatives might become managerial employees. Where trade unions have been represented on boards, this has been part of the settlements where unions have agreed to concessions in order to salvage the company. No statutory or common law duty exists granting employees the right to participate in management. However, collective bargaining may provide for worker's participation in specific areas such as safety and technological changes.

Given the restrictions posed by labour law, workers' participation has developed along an alternative avenue outside the collective bargaining system. Since more than two decades ago a number of non-union firms have developed what by now have become a variety of employee involvement programmes (EI). Job rotation, quality circles, quality-of-working-life (QWL) committees and a team system of production have been elements in these programmes. Non-union EI programs have gradually inspired unions to join in negotiated EI programmes in order to influence decision-making in managerial issues. Notwithstanding there is a marked ambivalence about EI among trade unions and serious activity in this domain has occurred in only a limited number of union settings like the auto industry and the telecommunication industry. In these sectors there has been a need on the part of management for EI and a union leadership interest in trying to develop new models of labour management relations (Weiler 1990: 29–36).

Canada

In Canada, there is neither a statutory nor a common law that grants employees the right to participate in management. However, collective agreements may provide for worker's participation in specific areas such as safety and technological changes (Craven Hoglund 1996: 113). As in the United States, QWL has been promoted as an attempt to create harmony between workers and management. In the mid-1970s, the federal government actively stimulated such experiments in Ottawa and Toronto in order to help workers redefine their jobs, increase independence on the shop floor, and to enhance group decision-making. However, the ultimate aim was to increase productivity. As in the United States, labour leaders have been suspicious of participating in such programmes because some companies have used them as a means to resist unionisation. QWL programmes never involved more than a tiny fraction of the labour force and the success of such programmes has been quite limited (Heron 1989: 133). Another attempt to establish participation at the workplace was the joint labour–management committees developing in the aftermath of occupational health and safety legislation first enacted in the province of Saskatchewan in 1972. As other provinces followed, such committees spread quickly and the federal labour department encouraged the creation of similar committees. The object was primarily to cope with consequences of new technology because such issues had rarely been dealt with in collective agreements (Heron 1989: 133). The predicament from a union perspective is that such committees, as is the case for QWL programmes, are outside the bargaining structure.

Although Canadian labour was slow to respond to work reorganisation issues in the 1970s, auto, steel and communication workers' unions in the first half of the 1990s articulated goals for active intervention in workplace change. In order to

Table 3.3 Main features of co-determination regimes in North America and Scandinavia

	Canada	United States	Denmark	Sweden
Scope	Limited Not integrated in collective bargaining	Limited Not integrated in collective bargaining	Wide All major changes No explicit duty to negotiate Partly integrated in collective bargaining	Wide All major changes Explicit duty to negotiate Integrated in collective bargaining
Type	EI and QWL programmes Health and safety, technological change (Encouraged by federal government)	EI and QWL programmes Health and safety, technological change	Work councils	No special co-determination body Union-based at local and central level
Regulation	No regulation	No regulation	Basic collective agreement	Co-determination Act
Status of shop steward	Weak	Weak	Medium Collective agreement Short time paid leave accepted	Strong Regulated by law Right to paid leave for union functions

affect positive outcomes for workers all the three unions adhered to the adversarial framework of labour–management relationships and insist that workplace changes have to be negotiated. Major improvement in work environment, training and a union voice in strategic and shop floor decision-making were other important goals. Interestingly, these unions also believe that collective bargaining activities need to be supplemented by legislative and political initiatives to reinforce labour's influence beyond the workplace sphere. Notwithstanding employers' reluctance to extend union voice in these areas, there is at least some evidence of increasing frequency of negotiations over work reorganisation issues with greater union influence over workplace issues (Kumar 1993).

The main features of co-determination regimes in our sample are set out in Table 3.3 (page 71).

Employment protection laws and labour market flexibility

The interest in labour market efficiency and regulations concerning recruitment and dismissals has recently increased among social scientists and policy-makers. The issues brought up for debate are very much discussed within a binary conceptual framework: rigidities in terms of strict employment regulation is thought to be correlated with high unemployment, while flexibility and de-regulation are thought to be a precondition for low unemployment (Nickell 1997; Schömann, Rogowski and Kruppe 1998). Hence, the broad spectrum of conflicting arguments brought to the fore in the debate rests on competing notions of the advantages of market and policy. While the proponents of market solutions emphasise the supremacy of unconstrained voluntary contractual arrangements in terms of economic output, the proponents of employment protection laws demonstrate greater trust in policy-makers, labour legislation and corporate arrangements (Buechtemann 1993: 14).

According to Buechtemann (1993: 9–12), proponents arguing in favour of market solutions take their point of departure in the assumed correlation between stagnating employment and heavy regulation in western Europe and relatively low unemployment and few regulations in the United States. The fact that job protection laws in some European countries became stricter in the early 1970s, about the time when unemployment and productivity problems began to arise, has been contrasted to the 'American job miracle' and the traditional North American doctrine of employment at will. The argument is that labour market rigidity in many western European countries has made the European economy unable to adapt to changing economic conditions. Such rigidities are supposed to have occurred as a result of difficulties restraining lay-offs in periods of reduced demand. Hence, firms that must reduce the work force due to decline in demand must adjust more slowly to their new optimal level and thus have to bear costs in terms of labour hoarding, severance pay and early retirement plans. Strict employment security legislation is also thought to have negative effects on technological innovation and structural change because high dismissal costs curb a firm's effort to adjust its work force to upgraded skills linked to the use of new technologies. Moreover, such legislation discourages entrepreneurs from setting up new firms in unexplored markets.

Another argument put forward by pro-market proponents holds that strict employment security is supposed to make firms more inclined to offer atypical forms of employment such as part-time, fixed term contract, outsourcing, etc. This leads to the relative growth of a two-tier labour market, one with decent job security for the core employees and one with poor employment security for the peripheral work force. Employment security legislation might therefore bring about a segmentation of labour markets between permanently employed insiders and the long-term unemployed outsiders facing increasing difficulties becoming an insider (Lindbeck and Snower 1988: 252). Difficulties of substitution further worsen the prospects for the long-term unemployed. Dismissal protection is also thought to largely fail for those groups who need statutory protection most – the unskilled, the severely handicapped, older workers, etc.

On the other hand, there are also arguments in favour of employment security policies (Buechtemann 1993: 12–13). One argument points to the economic advantages of long-term employment relationships, the encouragement of co-operative labour relations, the higher degree of internal flexibility, and the willingness of employees to accept technological change. Seen in this perspective statutory employment protection might stimulate various arrangements to human capital investment; i.e., it might help upgrade and train the staff and thereby create a potential for more rational decisions because firms may abstain from or reduce trial and error methods in employment policies. Employment security regulation is also assumed to be an important element of a strategy to create long-term human resources development, which is necessary in order to direct the economy into future-oriented areas. Pfeffer makes this point clear:

> Security of employment signals a long-standing commitment by the organization to its workforce. Norms of reciprocity tend to guarantee that this commitment is repaid, but conversely, an employer that signals through words and deed that its employees are dispensable is not likely to generate much loyalty, commitment or willingness to expend extra effort for the organisation's benefit.
>
> (Pfeffer 1994: 31)

Others among the labour legislation proponents argue that employment protection standards introduce principles of fairness and help workers to overcome difficulties of subsistence when there are no jobs. In addition, labour markets are characterised by a fundamental power asymmetry between employers and employees because the latter normally have fewer resources, less information and fewer alternatives than the former. Hence, labour markets are not fully competitive and employment security legislation is needed to constitute a balance between workers and firms, i.e., preconditions for efficient market transactions (cf. Wheeler 1992: 20).

In overall terms, the United States and Canada fit more into the market model, while Scandinavia, particularly Sweden fits the policy model. According to theoretical market models, strict employment protection would have a constraining effect on lay-offs and employment, job creation and destruction in individual firms. However, other parameters may be important to grasp the overall effects on inflows and outflows in the labour market. Legal provisions in other policy areas need to be taken into account as well as interactions between different legal provisions when focusing on factors circumscribing or enhancing labour market flexibility. According to Derckson (1992: 95–8), it is reasonable to see an active labour market policy as a functional alternative to job protection because the creation of new jobs contributes to employment security. In fact, a combination of active labour market policy and weak employment protection laws may be more effective than strict employment regulation and passive labour market policies.

Employment protection and labour market flexibility are not necessarily conflicting aims. In this connection it is useful to make a distinction between numerical and functional flexibility (cf. Atkinson 1987: 90–2). Numerical flexibility includes measures to adjust the number of workers (or the working time of the workers) to the firm's demand for labour. Functional flexibility addresses the company's capacity to re-allocate the labour power by changing a worker's job assignment to meet the needs of the firm (see Chapter 9 for more details). North American labour law seems to accept the necessity of numerical flexibility, but with certain types of restrictions. In the unionised sector, seniority principles have strong support and human rights legislation in general is intended to put some limits on the free hiring and firing of employees. Hiring procedures in the United States and Canada are relatively free and unregulated, provided that the employer does not discriminate against people on any of the grounds enumerated in the human rights legislation. This 'freedom' is also to some extent restricted by pressure to engage in affirmative action programmes and federal contractors' programmes in order to include under-represented groups in the labour market up to a regional average. Notwithstanding, American employers are comparatively free to adjust the size of their work force. North American functional flexibility is (except in the unionised sector) provided for in a manner that does not involve labour law. In other words, the potential that lies in tying the work force closely to the firm by means of employment protection laws is not exploited. Neither is the commitment of the employees made use of by means of formalised worker's participation arrangements.

Swedish regulation, on the other hand, firmly limits the scope of numerical flexibility. It is true that decisions concerning the size of the company's work force, what type of goods and services to produce, and many other things rest with management. However, employers no longer have the discretionary and exclusive right to dismiss their employees. The law puts pressure on the employer first to relocate workers, and if that is impossible, bring up the question of dismissal for negotiation with the union. This is an explicit impetus to go for functional flexibility, i.e., to look for the broadest possible use of the work force. Restrictions concerning fixed-term contracts works the same way. The Danish plethora of regulations in collective agreements operates in the same way. Strict employment protection laws can be said to promote a long-term relationship between employer and employees, and can thus be regarded as a vehicle to advance vocational education and human resources policies in the firm. Functional flexibility depends on measures to ensure that the employees have sufficient qualifications for the job. Scandinavian labour market policies, especially Swedish policies, aim towards 'life-long learning' as a relevant interacting legal provision (Stephens 1996). Regulation on co-determination may also work as a vehicle to increase functional flexibility and thereby involve workers in accomplishing the necessary economic goals of the firm.

During most of the period, from 1974 onwards, strict statutory employment protection legislation has been in force and unemployment in Sweden has been comparatively low, a fact indicating that the law is not to be blamed for causing high unemployment. This is consistent with Nickell's (1997: 72) finding that labour market rigidities in terms of strict employment protection legislation and general legislation on labour market standards 'do not appear to have serious implications for average levels of unemployment'. The kind of economic, educational and labour market policy pursued is probably far more important. It is true that high unemployment in the 1990s occurred at the same time as trade unions were forced to take on more defensive strategies, i.e., to accept hiring and firing strategies proposed by employers in order to avoid firms closing down. Job security has also been weakened (though the core labour force still enjoys adequate protection) due to recent employer-oriented changes in the law. Now, in the dawn of the new millennium, Scandinavian unemployment has decreased steadily and the primary concern has become how to expand the post-industrial service sectors with labour power. Strict employment protection laws or general demands on employers to negotiate with unions evidently have not hampered the success of many IT-based Swedish firms in the late 1990s.

Discussion

Employment protection systems differ significantly between North America and Scandinavia. In fact we can talk about an individualistic route implying a continuous juridification of employment protection regimes in North America. This avenue contrasts sharply with the collective and corporatist route taken by the two Scandinavian countries. In North America the dominant ideology, although now substantially circumscribed by federal, state and provincial law, is based on employment and firing at will. Employment protection is not an integral part of industrial relations because collective agreements cover only a minor part of the labour market. Co-determination has not been accepted as a legitimate element in North American labour law. The failure to guarantee a reasonable amount of job security through collective bargaining has opened up an array of legislative measures, notably civil rights legislation, that aims to improve employment protection. Many employment issues are dealt with by courts and not by labour market organisations in bargaining arrangements. Hence, new barriers have been created while the employment at will doctrine has been limited. However, there are important differences between the two North American countries. Employment at will leaves management with relatively free hands in the United States, whereas Canadian federal and provincial legislatures require notice periods unseen in the United States and also provide relatively swift and cheap procedures for non-compliance with notice statutes. The interwoven relations between capital–labour and property rights–employee rights are not dealt with in corporate decision-making models, but are articulated and handled within the judicial system as individualised problems. Within an increasingly de-unionised industrial relations system employees have to act in their role as citizens in order to have their employee rights sustained.

Labour legislation in Sweden and Denmark is structurally embedded in the tripartite system of labour relations. Although it sets up a number of material rights for employees, labour law is closely connected to the preconditions of the trade unions, thus underpinning corporatist culture. The right in Sweden to negotiate over employment protection for instance when determining priority lists in case of dismissals is an example illustrating how labour law promotes and facilitates corporatist solutions. In both countries, employment protection and co-determination rights are linked to each other insofar as issues concerning dismissals must always be negotiated: in Sweden according to statute and in Denmark according to collective agreements. In Sweden, it has been an explicit aim that employment protection legislation should be of help for older workers who are especially vulnerable when industry is being restructured. Notice and severance pay periods, as well as priority rules in cases of dismissals, are all constructed according to seniority principles. Trade unions are also given a central role in the implementation of this regulation.

The Scandinavian route, notably the Swedish route, is indeed a route that, as Kahn-Freund states, can be seen as 'an attempt to infuse law in a relation of command and subordination' (1972: 8). However, this attempt has been very much oriented towards the collective interests of workers implying that the social partners are the players expected to solve employment problems. Law has therefore become elastic in the sense that trade unions and employers can (and are permitted to) deviate from what are the basic goals stated in key paragraphs. Unions and not the individual are given certain rights. It is also important to note that the infusion of law in the institution of the employment relationship is restricted by the fact that this relationship is indeed a relationship of power and different social status. The existing power imbalance makes transactions in the labour market like hiring and firing, collective redundancy, and workers' participation in management quite unlike what takes place in other markets. The challenge for labour law is therefore to recognise the full humanity that follows from the fact that the commodity of labour cannot be separated from the provider of this commodity, namely the employee.

4 The welfare state and labour market policies

Bengt Furåker and Rafael Lindqvist

In the introductory chapter of this book, the state in contemporary advanced societies is described as fulfilling at least three different functions or roles (see also Furåker 1987: 39–47). To be very concise, the argument can be summarised in the following way: The state maintains internal order and external relations, redistributes resources, and organises production. We can add that the state concept here refers to the political-administrative apparatuses not only on the central level but also on regional and local levels.

With respect to the labour market, the first one of the three functions mentioned above refers to labour legislation and maintenance of labour law. The state intervenes in the labour market by making and upholding rules for the interaction between buyers and sellers of labour power. It provides legal standards and sanctions for such phenomena and activities as the hiring and firing of personnel, working time and work schedules, minimum wages, and the physical and psychosocial work environment, including decision-making processes in the workplace.

Second, via tax collection and transfers the state redistributes resources between various categories of the population or – perhaps to put it more adequately – between different periods in individuals' lives. It provides resources for people in case of sickness, old age, unemployment and other situations when they cannot support themselves. The transfer state performs a social insurance function, but its activities are sometimes also aimed at making the income distribution more even. In addition, there are transfer payments to companies such as subsidies within the framework of regional policies.

The state has a third role as a producer of goods and services. This means that it appears in the labour market as employer. In all advanced capitalist societies government goods production is of a rather or very limited proportion. Public enterprises are mainly found in infrastructural activities like the supply of water, electricity, gas, transportation, communication, etc. Because the international statistics on public enterprises (as well as on public employment in general) are underdeveloped, cross-country comparison is restricted. There is some effort within the OECD to remedy this (for national statistical sources on public sector employment, see OECD 1994d), but much remains to be done. The principal producer role of the state is, however, a matter of social services such as health care, education, and care for children and for the elderly. In the West, not to mention the former socialist world, there has been a pronounced trend towards privatisation of both goods and service production in the last few decades. Nevertheless, public organisations continue to be important producers and thus are important employers.

This chapter will deal with the relationship between the (welfare) state[1] and the labour market in the four countries that we have selected for comparison: Canada, the United States, Denmark and Sweden. Labour law has already been treated by Rafael Lindqvist in Chapter 3 and will not be discussed here. We shall concentrate on the role of the state as a redistributor and employer and pay extra attention to labour market policy that is of particular interest in a study dealing with employment and unemployment.

Labour market policy is a specific type of state intervention in the labour market. A distinction is often made between 'passive' and 'active' measures. Passive measures refer to unemployment benefits and other kinds of financial support for the unemployed. Active programmes involve efforts to find people jobs through, for example, placement services, labour market training and job creation. There is no simple way of placing labour market policy in one of the three state functions outlined above. Labour law – with its impact on hiring practices, firings and unemployment – might be considered an aspect of labour market policy, although it is seldom treated in this way. Both active and passive measures imply legislation, but their distinctive features refer to other dimensions. Cash benefits to the unemployed are part of the social insurance system and thus of the state's redistributive role. Moreover, many active programmes consist of subsidies – transfers – to firms. The activities of the public employment service and labour market training organisers can be regarded as service production for both employers and job searchers. Other active measures, such as certain job creation programmes, imply that the state acts as an employer by, for example, organising sheltered workshops.

In the discussion about the welfare state, two concepts often appear: commodification and decommodification. According to Gøsta Esping-Andersen (1990: 37), decommodification is not a matter of 'the complete eradication of labour as a commodity; it is not an issue of all or nothing', but it 'refers to the degree to which individuals, or families, can uphold a socially acceptable standard of living independently of market participation'. This in turn means that commodification is a matter of making individuals dependent on the market. In order for a welfare state to be decommodifying, it should allow its citizens 'freely, and without potential loss of job, income, or general welfare' to 'opt out of work when they themselves consider it necessary', which 'would, for example, require of a sickness insurance that individuals be guaranteed benefits equal to normal earnings, and the right to absence with minimal proof of medical impairment and for the duration that the individual deems necessary' (Esping-Andersen 1990: 23). Thus, in Esping-Andersen's perspective, the emancipatory role of the welfare state is embodied in its capacity to diminish or abolish the dependence of individuals and families on the market.

There has been much discussion about these concepts and about the role of the welfare state in relation to them. Some have pointed out that the advanced welfare state is not only oriented towards decommodification but also towards commodification or recommodification (Furåker 1989; Offe 1984). With full employment as a central goal of the welfare state, the ambition is rather to help people support themselves via the market (Furåker 1989; Furåker, Johansson and Lind 1990; Sainsbury 1996: 88). For example, Sweden – one of the model decommodifying countries according to Esping-Andersen's analysis – for a long time has had an active labour market policy strongly oriented towards putting people to work. This has been a key element in the so-called Swedish model, and it has been considered – at least by its architects – an emancipatory strategy.

Another criticism against Esping-Andersen's treatment of decommodification and the welfare state argues that it does not take women's unpaid work into account (Sainsbury 1994, 1996: 36).[2] Ruth Lister (1994: 37, 1997: 173) has suggested that we use the concept of 'defamilialisation' to supplement the decommodification concept in the evaluation of social rights (see also McLaughlin and Glendinning 1994). Defamilialisation is regarded as a parallel concept to decommodification. It is a matter of 'the degree to which individual adults can uphold a socially acceptable standard of living, independently of family relationships, either through paid work or through the social security system' (Lister 1994: 37). Ann Orloff (1993: 318–19) has similarly argued that in order better to assess the quality of social rights we need to take into account 'access to paid work' and 'the capacity to form and maintain an autonomous household' (italics removed). These are of course relevant criticisms if we are looking for criteria to assess the emancipatory role of the welfare state; this obviously requires something more than the concept of decommodification.

The welfare state is often associated with disincentives for the labour force. Its benefits and other measures are assumed to be detrimental to work motivation and thus to the volume of work and to the standard of living in society. From an alternative perspective, the welfare state is seen as a correcting mechanism needed to produce a better outcome than the market produces alone. Using statistics from the OECD countries (in the mid-1980s), Stefan Olafsson (1992) has tested whether there is a negative relationship between each of three welfare state aspects – social security expenditures, proportions of public employment, and tax levels – and volumes of work. The empirical evidence supports the hypothesis that social security reduces work volumes, but the other two hypotheses are rejected.

The purpose of this chapter is not to answer questions like the ones raised by Olafsson but to provide some basis for the analyses to be done later in the book. Here we shall describe a few crucial dimensions of the state's relationship to the labour market in Canada, the United States, Denmark and Sweden. The chapter is divided into three main sections. The first one is devoted to the redistributive role of the welfare state, i.e., to what could be called the transfer state. In the second section, we shall briefly touch on the government's role as employer, in particular in the service sector. Finally, we will pay attention to labour market policies.

The transfer state

Let us begin this section by looking at some statistics on social security transfers. According to the OECD definition, these transfers include, among other things, benefits for sickness, old age, family allowances and social assistance. One problem with this type of information is that countries differ from each other because of the technical solutions they use to improve people's standard of living. Sometimes, instead of receiving benefits, people get a tax deduction, which means that the redistribution is more or less kept invisible. However, the data on social security transfers are still helpful and we find it worthwhile to supply such information. This is done in Table 4.1 where figures represent percentages of GDP for a number of countries.

It goes for all the countries that social security transfers make up a higher proportion of GDP in the end than in the beginning of the period covered by the table. In 1996 or 1997, seven of the countries spent between one-fourth and one-fifth of their GDP on such transfer payments and both Sweden and Denmark are found in this group, although not at the top. Sweden comes fifth in the ranking after the Netherlands, France, Belgium and Finland, while Denmark is seventh.

Table 4.1 Percentage of government expenditures for social security transfers as a percentage of GDP, selected years, 1974–97

	1974	*1987*	*1992*	*1996 or 1997*
Netherlands	20.7	25.7	26.4	23.9
France	15.5	21.6	22.4	23.5
Belgium	18.0	24.2	23.7	23.4
Finland	7.6	15.4	23.7	22.7
Sweden	14.3	18.7	23.4	22.5
Austria	15.5	20.9	20.2	21.8
Denmark	12.0	16.2	19.6	21.5[a]
Italy	13.7	17.3	19.3	19.3
Germany	14.6[b]	16.2[b]	17.0	18.4
Spain	9.5	15.3	17.5	17.2
Greece	7.1	14.9	15.3	16.9[a]
UK	9.2	12.8	14.4	15.4[c]
Norway	13.3	13.2	17.1	14.8
Portugal	5.3	11.0	12.5	14.2[a]
Japan	6.2	11.6	11.3	13.8
Ireland	11.4	16.7	14.9	13.2
US	9.5	10.7	12.9	12.6
Canada	7.5	10.2	13.6	11.9
Australia	7.0	9.3	11.3	11.3

Source: OECD 1999c: 71.

Notes
a 1995.
b West Germany.
c 1994.

Canada and the United States, on the other hand, both appear in the bottom of the table with roughly 12–13 per cent. There is no doubt that – in terms of government spending on social security transfers – North America differs quite substantially from our two Scandinavian cases.

In terms of Esping-Andersen's (1990: 26–9) well-known typology of welfare capitalism, Canada and the United States belong to the 'liberal' model and Denmark and Sweden to the 'social democratic' model. The North American neighbours are characterised by a strong reliance on the market and low levels of welfare spending, means-tested assistance and small proportions of the population being eligible for benefits. In Scandinavia, there are universal income-related benefits combined with an endeavour to diminish inequality and poverty. The emancipatory ambitions are directed both against the market and the family. These two models – the liberal and the social democratic – are both contrasted with the 'corporatist' or 'conservative' model. The latter category (exemplified by Germany) is characterised by rather generous welfare arrangements – based on occupational status divisions – and by support for the family. It differs from the liberal model by placing much less reliance on the market and from the social democratic regime by being more oriented towards preserving social and economic differentials as well as the family institution.

Based on pension, sickness benefit and unemployment insurance schemes, Esping-Andersen (1990: 47–54) calculates a decommodification score for various countries. For each of the schemes, replacement rates, eligibility requirements and similar criteria are used. Generally, the liberal countries receive the lowest scores and the social democratic countries obtain the highest, with the conservative ones somewhere in between. In other words, labour is less dependent on the market in countries like Denmark and Sweden than it is in Canada and the United States. However, we also find a large difference between the latter two, with Canada showing a clearly higher decommodification score.

In their analysis of welfare state and social insurance systems, Walter Korpi and Joakim Palme (1998; see also Korpi 2000) make a slightly different classification, in which Denmark is connected with the liberal or market-governed countries. The authors' typology is supposed to reflect the organisation of welfare state institutions as 'intervening variables' in the process of income distribution and is based on two fundamental social insurance systems: the pension system and sickness insurance. Three dimensions are included: eligibility for benefits, levels of benefits and forms for governing social insurance programmes. Five categories are identified. Without going into details, we can observe that Denmark is brought together with Canada, the United States and other Anglo-Saxon countries in what is called the basic security model, while Sweden and two other Nordic countries, Finland and Norway, are classified as belonging to the encompassing model.

Nevertheless, in the final empirical analysis (based on income measures from 1990; see Korpi 2000) Denmark is rather close to the encompassing (Nordic) model that has the lowest inequality and poverty of all, whereas the basic security systems of Canada and the United States entail among the largest income gaps. Fifteen countries are ranked in terms of their average position on various income inequality and poverty measures. The United States is the most unequal country and Canada comes third. Denmark is tenth and Norway, Sweden and Finland rank number 13 to 15 (least unequal) (Korpi 2000: 165).

Beside the pension system and sickness insurance, there are also certain differences in terms of labour market policies between Denmark and Sweden. In this respect, it seems that for a long time Denmark put much less emphasis on full employment and active labour market programmes (see Furåker, Johansson and Lind 1990). However, in the 1990s there was a shift in Danish labour market policy towards a much more 'active' profile (for further discussion, see Boje and Åberg 1999; and below in this chapter). Thus, Denmark has come much closer to the Swedish model and it is, in fact, rather difficult to judge which of the two countries is putting the strongest emphasis on active policies.

Compared to Scandinavia, both the United States and Canada 'rely on more intensive use of means-tested (residual) forms of welfare on the one hand, and private, market-based insurance on the other' (Myles 1996: 121). Still there are important differences between the two North American countries. In an interesting piece of research, it has been estimated what would have happened with poverty levels in the United States had it had the transfer system of an average Canadian province (Blank and Hanratty 1993). It turned out that the United States would have had much lower poverty rates both among single-parent families and among all families – even lower than in Canada.

In an article on family policy and health care, Gregg Olsen (1994) has emphasised that Canada cannot simply be treated as a welfare laggard like the United States but is in some respects very far from it. In terms of health care, for example, Canada is positioned somewhere in between Sweden and the United States, when three crucial criteria are applied. Looking first at the organisation (public/private sector), it shows a pattern that is rather close to that of the United States, i.e., private sector solutions play a dominant role. However, with respect to the second criterion – universalism or selectiveness in coverage – Canada is instead similar to Sweden with its universal coverage system. The degree of orientation towards intervention or prevention was applied as a third criterion. On this dimension, Canada appears as halfway between the United States and Sweden, more strongly oriented towards prevention in health care than the United States but less so than Sweden. Moreover, also in terms of expenditures and outcomes Canada takes a position in the middle.

In the last decades, 'workfare' has often been debated in relation to social policy. This concept generally refers to 'attempts to introduce work requirements for claimants of public income support; that is claimants will have their cash benefits reduced or withdrawn if they are not willing to participate in some sort of work or training programme' (Hvinden 1999: 29). There may be different motives behind such attempts, for example to cut back costs for social welfare or at least prevent them from rising, to promote people's integration in the labour market, to avoid welfare traps and, perhaps, to enforce moral standards upon welfare recipients.

Workfare programmes were launched in the United States during the Reagan presidency, with the purpose of deterring employable people from receiving welfare (Mead 1992: 167). The Clinton administration advanced these policies further by making social assistance for the able-bodied conditional on work or training and by strictly limiting the duration of welfare (King 1999: 274–86; Mishra 1999: 47). In Canada, workfare programmes have been implemented since the late 1980s and – under pressure to reduce costs for family allowances and employment benefits – they have continued in the mid-1990s (Shragge 1996).

During the 1990s, both Denmark and Sweden have shown a shift in emphasis regarding social policies towards 'activation' which is a concept similar to that of workfare. For example, in Denmark we find a strengthening of the work requirements in labour market policy (Boje and Åberg 1999; see also below) and one of the acts on social assistance is now directly called 'The activation act' (Abrahamsson 1999: 412). In Sweden, for the purpose of activating people, work rehabilitation measures have been developed and the possibilities of becoming compensated – through, for example, early retirement, sickness, unemployment and work injury schemes – have been tightened (Lindqvist and Marklund 1995; Stephens 1996: 48–9).

Summing up our observations on the role of the state as redistributor, we can conclude that there are great differences between the Scandinavian and the North American systems. The transfer state is generally much more generous in Denmark and Sweden than in Canada and the United States – and we can therefore distinguish two clusters. However, the patterns are more complicated. Canada is, at least in some respects, rather unlike the United States, i.e., more 'European', whereas Denmark, at least in some accounts, has been treated as rather liberal. Still we may distinguish a Scandinavian model with Sweden as the most 'social democratic' or 'transfer-oriented' model and a North American cluster with the United States as the most 'liberal' or 'market-oriented' case.

There is a continuous debate about how labour markets and people's willingness to work are affected by a generous transfer state. Do munificent benefits have a decommodifying role; i.e., do they make people withdraw – temporarily or permanently – from the labour market? It should be emphasised that welfare states often maintain rules requiring people to work (long) before they receive benefits and/or in order to obtain the maximum benefits. When the systems are designed in such a way, it becomes advantageous for people to work a great deal because that will entitle them to be supported if or when the need emerges. There may be what is called an 'entitlement' effect (Hamermesh 1979, 1980). In other words, we must take their full complexity into account when considering the effects of generous welfare arrangements on the labour market.

The producer state

Being an organiser of production – be it goods or services – the state appears in the labour market as an employer. As pointed out above, in most Western countries state ownership of goods-producing companies is not very common. Public sector enterprises may be responsible for infrastructural activities like the supply of water, electricity, gas, transportation and communications, but they usually make up only a small proportion of total employment (Rose 1985; Saunders and Klau 1985: 75–8). As a producer, the state is mainly engaged in the social service sector. It often has a decisive role in social services such as health care, education, and care for children and the elderly.

Although many countries in the West have experienced large-scale privatisation over the last decades (see, e.g., Kamerman and Kahn 1989; Martin 1993; Saunders and Harris 1994; Whitfield 1992), their governments continue to have a significant role as employers. Public employees constitute a large – albeit varying – proportion of total employment in most advanced nations. Sweden and Denmark belong to those nations that have the largest proportions of public employees, whereas Canada is much lower in this respect and the United States even more so (for more detailed information, see, e.g., Alestalo, Bislev and Furåker 1991; Cusack, Noterman and Rein 1989; Furåker 1987; and Chapter 6 in this book).

Public service production is an important feature of the welfare state expansion in Scandinavia and in many other countries. This has meant that large numbers of people – above all women – have been recruited to jobs in the public sector. They are employed in services like education, health care, care for the elderly, childcare, etc. Beside the recent trend of privatisation, there have also been public-sector cuts in many Western nations, leading to a stagnation or decrease in the number of jobs. Nevertheless, in countries like Denmark and Sweden, government employment – excluding state-owned enterprises – make up about one-third of total employment.

The state is thus an important employer in the labour market. It can, then, be said to have a commodifying role in relation to labour because it recruits people to jobs. The transfer of certain functions (above all caring tasks) from the family to the public sector has been accompanied by a commodification of female labour. Public services are provided if not entirely free, at least at low, subsidised fees. Thus, when certain services are decommodified – provided for independently of the market – somewhat paradoxically female labour is at the same time commodified (Sainsbury 1996: 102–3). Many women working in the public service sector carry out the same type of work as before, but they are trained in this work, they get paid for it (although their wages or salaries are often rather low), and they have often joined unions.

With respect to childcare and certain other forms of care, it can be argued that the welfare state has even a double commodifying function. The arrangements for taking care of small children result in two outcomes. First, nursery school teachers are employed to carry out the work in day care centres, which implies a process of commodification in accordance with what has just been said. Second, families use day care centres in order for the adult/s (the female spouse) to be able to work and therefore this is for them a matter of commodification.

It has been very much debated whether the process of pulling women into the labour market has played an emancipatory or an oppressive role for most women (see Hernes 1987a, 1987b; Pateman 1988; Sainsbury 1994, 1996). We have no intention to engage in these debates, because they are mainly political and therefore belong outside the ambitions of our book. Let us just underline that it is too simple to equate decommodification with emancipation and commodification with oppression.

The state's role in relation to the labour market is complex and cannot be reduced to one or the other of the three general functions mentioned previously. This is also exemplified in a study by Walter Korpi (2000) in which the author classifies various OECD countries in terms of their gender policies. Many countries – like Germany and France – provide general family support (child allowance, tax levies and care for children aged three years or more), but there is no effort to make it easier for women to enter the labour market. Other countries are instead oriented towards creating a dual-earner family by providing public care for the youngest children, paid parental leave and public care for the elderly. Denmark and Sweden are perhaps the prototypes of this kind of gender policy. For a third category of countries – including Canada and the United States – these issues have basically been left to the market.

This typology – that distinguishes between general family support, dual-earner support and market-oriented policies – is then used for explaining, among other things, differences between various categories of men and women in labour force participation (Korpi 2000: 154–61). There is no perfect fit between the typology and the empirical outcome, but the general pattern is rather clear. The countries with the dual-earner model (including Denmark and Sweden) have the smallest gender differences and the countries providing general family support have the largest ones, with the market-oriented models (including Canada and the United States) somewhere in between. We would like to emphasise one point here: It is the combination of the different roles of the state that produces the outcome. Both redistribution (child allowance, paid parental leave) and service production (childcare, care for the elderly) are involved; moreover, behind these arrangements there is – as always in matters like these – a legal framework too.

Labour market policy

Unemployment is a main target for labour market policy and the reason is of course that individuals generally have trouble supporting themselves if they do not have jobs. In most advanced countries, therefore, the state intervenes in different ways, on the one hand, by providing for the unemployed, and on the other hand, by helping them find jobs. However, unemployment is not the only problem dealt with by labour market policy. Employers too may have difficulties in the labour market; they may not, for example, find the workers they are looking for ('bottleneck problems'). Labour market policy is to some extent also oriented towards helping employers through placement services, training programmes, etc. Whether active and passive programmes meet with success in handling different labour market problems is very much a matter of their co-ordination or integration with general economic policies.

The simplest way of intervening in favour of the unemployed is to provide financial support. Cash benefits do have consequences for the functioning of the labour market, but because they are not really aimed at attacking unemployment *per se*, they are commonly referred to as 'passive' measures. In most of the advanced countries the state does more than supporting the unemployed. When labour market policies are oriented towards finding people work, they are usually labelled 'active'. According to an OECD definition, active policies are measures 'aiming at improving access to the labour market and jobs, job-related skills and labour market functioning' (OECD 1993: 39). To achieve this there are several measures that can be used, such as placement services, labour market training and job creation programmes.

Passive measures include cash benefits to the unemployed, usually provided through the unemployment insurance that exists in all the countries studied. There are also passive measures that do not require the individual to be available to the labour market. Sometimes the state buys people out from the labour market as a strategy to reduce the supply of labour power. In several countries, there are early retirement programmes for labour market reasons. Early retirement for medical reasons may fulfil the same function. When it is difficult for an older worker to find a job and he or she has some health problem, it may be an easy solution to offer paid exit from the labour market.

As stated above, active measures are aimed at bringing people (back) to the work force either immediately or in a longer time perspective (as is the case when training is involved). This can be done in several ways, and there are different classifications of active policies (see Casey and Bruche 1985; OECD 1993: ch. 2). Roughly, these measures can be oriented to influence the supply and demand for labour (e.g., through training programmes and job creation respectively) or to make the labour market function smoother (e.g., through placement services).

Issues of labour market policy

Because – in the advanced Western countries – labour markets, employment and unemployment are crucial for people's lives and their standard of living, labour market policy is often subjected to rather intense discussions. It is, for example, debated what impact various measures have on unemployment and on people's chances of securing a job. There are also large differences between countries in terms of what role labour market policies – and in particular active programmes – are given.

Our four countries differ greatly with respect to their commitment to labour market policies. Neither Canada nor the United States can be said to have ever been very strongly committed to full employment (Campbell 1991; Gera 1991; Weir 1992; Wise 1988). It has not been considered a goal that is possible to achieve. The North American labour market policies have also had a weak connection to economic policy and – as we shall see – the resources spent on active programmes have been very limited, especially in the United States.

The efforts to achieve full employment have been much stronger in Scandinavia. Although Denmark pursued a rather Keynesian economic policy after World War II, it took some time before active labour market policies obtained any significant role in the country (Boje and Åberg 1999). In Sweden, the trade union economists Gösta Rehn and Rudolf Meidner outlined their model for labour market policy in the late 1940s and early 1950s (see Martin 1979, 1984). It was later adopted by the Swedish government and served as a guide for policy. In the Rehn-Meidner programme, a restrictive financial policy, a wage policy oriented towards solidarity with low-paid workers, and an active labour market policy were supposed to function together. Full employment was considered the most important goal for the labour movement. In terms of labour market policy, this meant that the work principle was assigned a decisive role – jobs or training programmes were given priority compared to cash benefits.

Labour market policies – and especially active policies – can be regarded as the result of a commitment of organised interest groups to avoid unemployment. Because labour movements have generally been most interested in full employment, it might be expected that countries with strong labour parties and unions would be particularly ambitious in developing programmes to fight unemployment. Douglas Hibbs's study (1977) of macroeconomic policies shows a considerable left-party effect on full employment policies and a corresponding conservative party tendency to favour price stability.

While Hibbs paid attention only to political parties, later research has emphasised the role of trade unions and employers' organisations. There was also a problem in explaining why nations with strong conservative orientation like Japan and Switzerland had such a good employment performance, while for example Denmark, with its strong social democratic party, was unable to avoid mass unemployment. The ambition to secure full employment has obviously not been confined to nations with strong labour movements. In Göran Therborn's analysis (1986), the most successful countries in avoiding unemployment are shown to be those that have institutionalised the goal of full employment, no matter whether this is the result of the efforts of strong labour movements or of the bourgeoisie's ambition to maintain social stability.

Analysing unemployment levels in various countries, Walter Korpi (1991) starts out from his power resources model focusing on long-term distribution and mobilisation of power in society (see also Korpi 1983). Institutional variables are basically seen as the outcome of a combination of relations of political strength and constitutional form, i.e., products of how conflicts of class and other interests have been regulated. Korpi makes a distinction between three forms of conflict regulation in Western nations: societal bargaining, pluralism and state-led capitalism.

Societal bargaining has been developed in nations where left-wing parties have had a strong position for a long time and gained political power (e.g., Austria, Norway and Sweden). However, societal bargaining can also be found in nations with weak labour movements, but the prerequisite is then that constitutional conditions give minority groups a pivotal role in political decision-making (e.g., Finland and Switzerland). Pluralism is characterised by Korpi as relationships where no long-term co-operation has been established between the state and the parties in the labour market such as in North America, Denmark and most central European nations. State-led capitalism, finally, is a special constellation where the ties between employers and the state are very close and unions are rather marginalised as in Japan. It is above all nations with societal bargaining or state-led capitalism that have been able to avoid high levels of unemployment.

In his study of the labour market policies in the United States and Germany, Thomas Janoski (1990: 9–36) argues that policy outcomes have to be understood as an interaction between organised interests and constitutional conditions in a long-term historical perspective, where external events such as wars and economic crises also have an impact. According to this author, Germany's relatively ambitious active labour market policies can mainly be explained in terms of strong social demands from the trade unions and the social democratic party, while the support for such policies in the United States is weaker because of divisions across class and status groups (blacks, women, etc.). State formation factors are therefore more important in understanding the American development: 'The cross-cutting action of class and status groups often left a social policy vacuum that third-party bureaucrats and "social welfare intellectuals" could fill' (Janoski 1990: 266).

Turning to the more direct effects of labour market policies, the main concern is of course with unemployment. To the extent that passive programmes allow people to turn down job offers, they can be regarded as having a decommodifying function (Esping-Andersen 1990: 35 ff.). Early retirement for labour market reasons definitely has this function – people are simply withdrawn from the labour force – but the effects of unemployment benefits are more debatable. If benefits are close to what people can get in the labour market, we might expect their reservation wage – i.e., the lowest pay that they are willing to work for – to increase. In other words, all other things being equal, unemployment may last longer than necessary. A similar conclusion might be drawn with respect to the duration of benefits. It should be added that these mechanisms might also affect the general wage level in a given society.

Much research has been carried out on the relationship between unemployment levels and the generosity (replacement rates, duration) of benefit systems (see Layard, Nickell and Jackman 1991: 254–6; Martin 2000; Nickell and Layard 1999: 3070–1; OECD 1994c: ch. 8). One conclusion seems to be that the more generous the benefit system, the greater the risk that people remain unemployed longer, which in turn means higher levels of unemployment.

However, there are certain complications to this conclusion (for an overview, see Reissert and Schmid 1994: 110–16). One is the above-mentioned 'entitlement' effect, identified by Hamermesh (1979, 1980). The assumption is that higher unemployment benefits give people an incentive to be part of the labour force. Another aspect is that unemployment benefit systems usually maintain some requirement that benefit recipients be available to the labour market, i.e., there is some work test involved. A crucial aspect is then the amount of pressure that is put upon the individual to take the jobs at hand. There is a Danish study on this topic claiming that Sweden has the most restrictive system among the four countries, the United States comes second, Canada third, and Denmark is the most liberal (Ministry of Finance 1998; see Chapter 8, this volume). Stricter work tests can be expected to modify the positive correlation between the generosity of unemployment benefits and unemployment levels (Nickell and Layard 1999: 3070–1).

Active labour market policies are oriented towards commodification or recommodification of labour power, i.e., the ambition is to make it possible for individuals to secure a job (see Offe 1984; Furåker 1989). It is an open question, however, whether they really accomplish what they are set out to do. There are many evaluations concerning active measures and, to say the least, they present us with a rather mixed picture (see Johannesson and Wadensjö 1995; Martin 2000; Nickell and Layard 1999; OECD 1993: ch. 2; Schmid 1994b).

Sometimes active programmes are referred to as 'make-work' and it has been pointed out that we know surprisingly little about their effects in spite of the fact that these measures are costly. They may of course affect participants' willingness or readiness to take jobs in the open market. Because people receive some type of financial support, it is likely that we find similar effects as with passive measures. Participants in active programmes may not have to look for jobs in the regular market – at least for some time and at least not very intensely. They are temporarily locked up in programmes and therefore not always immediately available when job openings emerge. If this is what happens, active measures can be considered to have a decommodifying function.

Unemployment insurance

The unemployment insurance systems in the four countries have different historical roots. In Scandinavia, voluntary funds evolved out of the early efforts of unions to secure income maintenance for its members in case of unemployment. Although these funds gradually became more subsidised, unified and integrated with government labour market policy, there is still a close administrative connection between the unions and the funds (the Ghent system). In contrast, the unemployment insurance system in North America came about as a result of government initiatives. With regard to financing of the unemployment insurance there are somewhat different solutions in Canada, the United States, Denmark and Sweden. The ones who pay for the benefits can be employers, employees, union members, governments or some mixture of them (see Schmid, Reissert and Bruche 1992).

Table 4.2 summarises a number of the main features of unemployment insurance in Canada, the United States, Denmark and Sweden. Although showing some variation across the four countries, work requirements for benefits can be regarded as strong in all of them. It should be mentioned that Sweden also has a low flat-rate unemployment benefit for people – mainly new entrants – who do not fulfil the requirements of the unemployment insurance. With respect to waiting periods, Canada has the toughest rule with a two-week delay, the United States has a one-week waiting period, Sweden five days and Denmark none at all.

The replacement rates in unemployment insurance are significantly higher in Scandinavia than in North America. In Denmark the unemployed can receive 90 per cent of their previous wage up to a ceiling (ceilings exist in all four countries), and the corresponding figure for Sweden is 80 per cent (somewhat lower after 100

Table 4.2 Main characteristics of unemployment insurance schemes in Canada, the United States, Denmark and Sweden in the 1990s

	Canada	United States	Denmark	Sweden
General qualifying conditions	10 to 20 weeks of employment in the last year (varies with regional unemployment rate). Minimum earnings	Previous employment history required. In most states minimum earnings in first 4 of last 5 quarters	Membership contributions of at least 1 year. 26 weeks of employment within last 3 years	Membership contributions of at least 1 year. 5 months of employment in the last year
Waiting period	2 weeks	In most states 1 week	None	5 days
Replacement rates (initial)	50–60% of gross wage up to a ceiling; taxable	Varies by state; usually 50% of gross wage; low ceiling; taxable	90% of gross wage up to a ceiling; taxable	80% of gross wage up to a ceiling; taxable
Net replacement rates (singles) % of APW[a] wage	% of previous income	Figures not available	% of previous income	% of previous income
75	56	–	80	80
100	56	–	63	70
150	44	–	46	52
Duration of benefits	35 up to 50 weeks	26 weeks in most states; longer if high unemployment state	2½ years; renewable up to 4 years for participants in labour market programmes	60 weeks; 90 weeks for persons aged over 57

Sources: Boje and Åberg 1999; Hansen 2000: 31; Storey and Neisner 1997: 599–651.

Note

a APW = average production worker.

days). Canada and the United States have replacement rates of approximately between 50 and 60 per cent, partly depending on the unemployment rate in the region.

With respect to net replacement rates, figures are related to the wage of an average production worker (APW). Data are calculated for singles and refer to 1997/8, but unfortunately we have no information for the United States. An individual with 75 per cent of the APW wage could get 56 per cent of his/her previous income in Canada and 80 per cent in the two Scandinavian countries. With an APW wage, net replacement rates were 56 per cent in Canada, 63 per cent in Denmark, and 70 per cent in Sweden. The lower rates in this case in the two Scandinavian countries are due to the ceiling in unemployment insurance. Such an effect also becomes visible for Canada when the previous income level is at 150 per cent of the APW wage.

The possible duration of benefit periods is one of the parameters displaying the most salient difference between North America and Scandinavia. In both Denmark and Sweden, the unemployment insurance and the labour market policy measures can be used alternately. In the 1980s, Denmark had the most generous model allowing people to have three benefit periods (two and a half years each) with two periods of job offer (*jobtilbud*) in between, adding up to a total of nine years. However, this was dramatically changed in the 1990s. Today people can receive unemployment benefits only for a period of two and a half years. Sweden used to have two different limits at 60 and 90 weeks (the latter for people aged 57 years or more), but this was changed in 2001 so that nobody can receive benefits for more than 60 weeks. The policy that the participation in labour market measures can help the unemployed person to re-qualify for additional periods has been tightened. Having a maximum duration of 50 weeks, Canada is less restrictive than the United States with its 26 weeks. However, the United States comes fairly close to the Canadian rules if federal-state and federal emergency benefits are considered.

It can be added that the percentage of unemployed receiving benefits in Canada in the 1990s decreased to about 40 (Mishra 1999: 48) and that the corresponding figure in the United States is about 35 (Nilsen 2001: 5). These figures are considerably lower than in the two Scandinavian countries. In both Denmark and Sweden about 80 per cent or more of the unemployed receive unemployment benefits (Aaberge *et al.* 2000: 85; SOU 2000: 3, 77).

There is thus no doubt that the unemployment insurance system is much more generous in Denmark and Sweden than in Canada and the United States. In particular, the two Scandinavian countries provide higher levels of compensation and benefits are supplied for longer periods of time. What these more generous benefit systems mean in relation to employment and unemployment is an empirical question that we will address in later chapters.

The size of active and passive measures

In this section, we will deal with public expenditures on labour market programmes in Canada, the United States, Denmark and Sweden. Some information will be given for other OECD nations as well. Table 4.3 shows a ranking of countries according to how much various countries spent on labour market policy (in total) as a percentage of GDP around 2000. We present separate columns for active and passive measures and, for comparison, figures are also provided for the mid-1980s.

Around 2000, in terms of total expenditures on labour market policies, Denmark had the top position, followed by Belgium, the Netherlands, Ireland, Finland, Germany, France and Sweden. Most of these countries scored relatively high on unemployment, but there is not always a very strong correlation in this respect. We can, for example, note that Spain – the country with the highest proportion of unemployed – is only ninth in the ranking. The relative costs in Spain were only about half the level of leading Denmark. Canada spent about one-third of what Denmark did but had higher unemployment. The United States is found at the bottom of the table.

Table 4.3 Public expenditures on labour market programmes in various OECD countries as a percentage of GDP, around 1985 and 2000 (ranked according to latest totals)

	Active measures		Passive measures		Totals	
	1985	2000	1985	2000	1985	2000
Denmark	1.09	1.54	3.90	2.96	5.00	4.51
Belgium	1.23	1.35	3.43	2.34	4.66	3.69
Netherlands	1.09	1.57	3.24	2.08	4.33	3.65
Ireland	1.58	1.54	3.69	1.90	5.27	3.44
Finland	0.91	1.22	1.34	2.32	2.25	3.53
Germany[a]	0.81	1.23	1.41	1.89	2.23	3.13
France	0.67	1.36	2.41	1.76	3.07	3.12
Sweden	2.11	1.38	0.87	1.34	2.97	2.72
Spain	0.34	0.98	2.89	1.34	3.23	2.32
New Zealand	0.84	0.55	0.65	1.62	1.48	2.17
Italy	0.45	1.12	1.04	0.71	1.49	1.83
Portugal	0.41	0.78	0.41	0.83	0.81	1.60
Austria	0.28	0.49	0.96	1.07	1.24	1.56
Australia	0.42	0.46	1.30	1.05	1.72	1.51
Canada	0.63	0.50	1.87	0.98	2.50	1.49
Norway	0.66	0.77	0.50	0.39	1.17	1.16
United Kingdom	0.74	0.37	2.11	0.58	2.85	0.94
Greece	0.21	0.34	0.43	0.48	0.64	0.83
Japan[b]	0.16	0.28	0.40	0.54	0.56	0.82
United States	0.28	0.15	0.57	0.23	0.84	0.38

Sources: OECD 1992: 92–103; 2001b: 24, 230–41.

Notes
a West Germany in 1985.
b 1987–88.

From the mid-1980s to 2000, less than half of the countries increased their expenditures on labour market policies as a proportion of GDP. Looking separately at active measures, however, we discover an increase in a majority of the cases. At the end of the period, nine countries spent more than 1 per cent on active measures –

compared to five countries in the beginning. The five reaching above 1 per cent at both points are Denmark, Sweden, Belgium, the Netherlands and Ireland. Canada and especially the United States score very low on active measures.

In contrast, most countries show a decrease from the mid-1980s to 2000 concerning passive measures. At the end of the period, we again find Denmark at the top with roughly 3 per cent of GDP devoted to passive measures, but the country had a clearly higher figure around 1985. Belgium, Finland and the Netherlands reached above 2 per cent around 2000, while Sweden was somewhat behind in spite of having made a great jump upward due to increased unemployment. Canada was close to the 1 per cent level and the United States again had a bottom position. Crudely, the North American percentages had been halved since the mid-1980s.

For most countries, the main part of the costs for labour market policy goes to income maintenance. However, in the mid-1980s, Sweden spent more than 70 per cent on active measures and no other country was close to that. Then things changed dramatically in Sweden during the recession in the 1990s, and in 2000 the share on active measures was just above half. Norway and Italy then had higher proportions with above 60 per cent. As regards Canada, the United States and Denmark, the costs of active programmes relative to the total expenditures on labour market policies have increased. In Canada and the United States this occurred notwithstanding that the proportion of GDP to active measures went down; in other words, the resources devoted to passive measures decreased even more.

While the costs for active policies are low in North America, the two Scandinavian countries have high such expenditures, among other things because they spend a lot more on labour market training, subsidised employment, and measures for the disabled. With respect to passive measures, we should observe one important difference between Denmark and the other three countries. Denmark has very high costs for early retirement for labour market reasons. Sweden used to have this kind of programme, but it was closed down in the early 1990s.

Let us end this section by considering labour market policy expenditures in the light of each country's level of unemployment. In Table 4.4 it has been calculated – for the same two years as above – how much Canada, the United States, Denmark and Sweden spent on active and passive measures for each percentage unit of unemployment they had.

Table 4.4 Public expenditures on labour market programmes (as a percentage of GDP) per percentage unit of unemployment (standardised). Canada, the United States, Denmark and Sweden around 1985 and 2000

	Active measures		*Passive measures*		*Totals*	
	1985	*2000*	*1985*	*2000*	*1985*	*2000*
Canada	0.06	0.06	0.18	0.12	0.25	0.19
United States	0.04	0.04	0.08	0.06	0.12	0.09
Denmark	0.20	0.33	0.72	0.63	0.93	0.96
Sweden	0.75	0.23	0.31	0.23	1.06	0.46

Sources: OECD 1992: 93–4, 101, 103; 2001a: 252, 2001b: 231–2, 240–1.

For the most recent year in the table, we find that Denmark has the highest scores – on both active and passive programmes. In the mid-1980s, Sweden was ahead as regards active policies and total expenditures. At that point in time, Denmark had much higher figures on passive measures, which is explained by its generous unemployment benefits and large expenditures on early retirement for labour market reasons. By 2000, both Scandinavian countries show somewhat lower figures for passive programmes. More importantly, Sweden's proportion on active policies had declined substantially, whereas Denmark recorded an increase in this respect. The explanations for these changes are simple. Active policies did not keep in step with the rise of unemployment in Sweden during the 1990s, while Denmark put increased emphasis on active programmes and succeeded in lowering unemployment.

There is not much to say about the figures for North America. As we can see in Table 4.4, both Canada and the United States score significantly lower than Denmark and Sweden – in the mid-1980s as well as in the late 1990s. This holds for totals and for active and passive programmes alike. We should, however, note one significant difference between the two North American cases; Canada is obviously more generous than the United States with respect to income maintenance for the unemployed.

Conclusion

What conclusions can be drawn from the presentation in this chapter? First, in terms of social security transfers our North American and Scandinavian cases clearly group in two clusters. Sweden and Denmark have much more generous social benefits than Canada and the United States. Second, there is a similar division concerning the government's role as an employer – what we have referred to as the producer state. Not counting public enterprises, in Denmark and Sweden public employment makes up almost one-third of total employment, while we find much lower proportions in North America. However, we also find a significant difference between Canada and the United States in that Canada clearly has a larger proportion of government employment. Third, with respect to labour market policy, the Scandinavian countries both have more generous passive measures and put much more effort into active measures than is the case in North America. The United States is doing the least for the unemployed.

A crucial point of departure for this book is the question whether or how different types of state intervention affect labour market outcomes. One issue is what social security transfers mean in relation to employment and unemployment patterns. Generous benefits may decrease people's willingness to work, but at the same time be conditional in a way that makes gainful employment attractive. Because our four countries represent (two) very different social security systems, they also offer good opportunities for comparisons.

The state does not only support people, it also appears as an employer in the labour market; it creates jobs to which people can be recruited. Of course, we cannot simply assume that an increase in the number of government jobs means an increase in total employment. A large public sector may perhaps be an obstacle to the growth of the private sector. Another possibility is that the two sectors represent alternative solutions, i.e., two countries may have similar proportions of employment in certain industries but very different combinations of private and public employment. We can thus expect to identify various post-industrial profiles. Given the differences between our four cases in terms of government employment, the empirical data to be presented in later chapters will provide interesting information.

Finally, a special type of state intervention in the labour market is labour market policy. It can be a matter of supporting people in case of unemployment, but it may also be an attempt to make the labour market function better – to avoid unemployment in the first place. There is a good deal of debate about the consequences of various active and passive measures and the knowledge about how these measures work is still rather limited. Because Canada, the United States, Denmark and Sweden represent different models in terms of labour market policy, the four cases are again well suited for empirical comparisons.

Part II

Labour market outcomes and welfare regimes

5 Labour force and employment

Age and gender differences

Thomas P. Boje

Introduction

The gap in employment rates between Europe and the United States has been debated intensively during the recent decades (Auer 1996; Blank and Freeman 1994; EC 1999).[1] Most studies comparing labour market development in Europe and the two other regions of the so-called world economic triad – the United States and Japan – find that the EU countries are characterised by significantly lower rates of employment and higher rates of unemployment than the two other regions (Appelbaum and Schettkat 1994; Cornitz 1988; EC 1999; Nickell 1997; Norwood 1988). Even more remarkable, the European overall rate of employment has declined radically over the last 25 years while it has increased in the United States. In the time period from the early 1970s to the mid-1990s, US non-farm employment expanded by more than 40 million people. In the same period Europe created slightly more than 6 million jobs (Auer 1995: 18).

The US employment rate has continued to grow in the 1990s and from 1988 to 1998 the employment increased by 20 million. In Europe, however, employment rates levelled off (BLS 1999a). In this book, we are comparing the United States and Canada with the two North European countries, Denmark and Sweden, which in many respects are performing markedly better than the Continental European countries, with respect to labour force participation, level of employment and rate of unemployment (Rubery, Smith and Fagan 1999).

A high level of employment is important for society as a whole for several reasons. First, a high level of employment means an important potential for economic growth beyond the economic prosperity created by increases in labour productivity. Second, high rates of employment reduce the economic burdens placed on public finances and the welfare systems by supporting non-employed people, a group that is growing and ageing. Third, it is important for the social cohesiveness of modern welfare societies that the large majority of the population have jobs and participate actively in society. Social inclusion and citizens' well-being are in Western economies closely related to the level of employment (see EC 1999; Coenen and Leisink 1993).

In this chapter, we primarily focus on the size and composition of employment.[2] However, we start our analysis with a short overview of the interrelationship between the growth in the working-age population, labour force and employment. Next, we describe some of the socio-demographic and institutional dimensions that influence the level of labour market involvement where we primarily focus on age and gender to explain the differences in employment in the four countries.

Growth in the working-age population, labour force and employment

Both labour force participation and employment are influenced by a variety of factors. Labour force participation, employment and consequently non-employment are determined by a complex interrelationship between trends in the economic cycle (demand for labour), the size and composition of the working-age population (potential and actual supply of labour), and a variety of institutional arrangements (the size of the public sector, the educational system, the content of economic as well as labour market policies, etc.). In analysing this relationship, we acknowledge the interdependency between demand and supply of labour as well as the need to separate the three dimensions in our analysis of labour market dynamics. In this chapter, we focus on the supply of labour (the composition of the employed labour force). In Chapters 6 and 7, we analyse the demand for labour (the distribution of the employed labour force for industries and occupations).

A closer look at the relationship between growth in the working-age population, labour force and employment in the four countries studied in this book highlights the differences between North America and the two European labour markets (Table 5.1).

The size and growth of the working-age population – age group 15 to 64 – are crucial for the development in both size and growth patterns of the labour force and employment. During the 1980s, roughly 85 per cent of growth in the overall labour force in the OECD countries could be explained by the growth in the working-age population (OECD 1994c: 23). Table 5. 1 shows that the four countries' levels of growth in the working-age population and in the labour force are closely related. During most of the analysed period, the annual rates of growth in the labour force are higher than for the working-age population for all four countries. The only exception to this pattern was in the early 1990s. Then, growth rates in the working population exceeded the growth rates in the labour force in Canada, Denmark and Sweden while the usual pattern remained in the United States. The high rates of growth in the overall labour force can be explained by a strong growth in the female labour force, which more than compensates for the decrease in the male labour force. During the analysed period, the working-age population has increased substantially more in Canada and the United States than in the two Scandinavian countries and this level of growth is similar to the pattern of growth in the labour force.

Looking at the growth rates of employment, we find a similar pattern: these rates are markedly higher in Canada and the United States than in Denmark and Sweden. This has been the case in all 5-year periods since 1970. Decline in employment has only happened in Denmark and Sweden. The relationship between

Table 5.1 Average annual rates of growth in the working-age population, labour force and employment in Canada, Denmark, Sweden and the United States from 1970 to 1999[a] (%)

	1970–74	1975–79	1980–84	1985–89	1990–94	1995–99
Average annual change in the working-age population 16–64 years[b]						
Canada	2.6	2.0	1.4	1.0	1.0	0.8
Denmark	0.2	0.4	0.6	0.3	0.3	0.2
Sweden	−0.1	0.2	0.4	0.3	−0.1	0.1
United States	1.7	1.7	1.2	0.6	0.7	0.6
Average annual change in labour force						
Canada	3.7	3.1	2.0	1.9	0.9	2.1
Denmark	0.9	1.4	0.7	1.1	0.0	1.2
Sweden	0.7	1.1	0.6	0.6	−1.2	0.7
United States	2.8	2.6	1.6	1.7	1.1	1.7
Average annual change in employment[c]						
Canada	4.1	2.6	1.2	2.8	0.3	1.6
Denmark	0.2	0.7	0.2	1.2	−0.8	0.6
Sweden	0.9	1.1	0.3	1.0	−2.5	0.1
United States	3.0	2.7	1.2	2.2	0.9	1.4

Source: OECD 1985: 19–21; 1997d: 20–1; 2000a: 16–17; 2001b: 14; 1994b; and BLS 1998.

Notes
a Five-year averages.
b The first time period differs from the others: 1973–74.
c Change in civilian employment.

growth in the labour force and employment has been stronger for Sweden and the United States than in Denmark and Canada. This has meant a relatively low level of unemployment in both Sweden and the United States during the 1970s and most of the 1980s (see Chapter 8 in this volume). In the early 1990s, the pattern changed fundamentally in Sweden. Then a severe economic crisis led to a strong decrease in employment growth and rapidly growing unemployment, which was followed by a significant decline in the Swedish labour force. In Denmark, growth in the labour force has been constantly higher than in employment while the relationship has been more mixed in Canada. In both countries, this means an increasing unemployment rate during the 1980s and early 1990s. For Denmark, however, the situation changed dramatically in the late 1990s with a significant decrease in unemployment. A similar decrease in unemployment started in Sweden a few years later than in Denmark (Boje and Åberg 1999; and Chapter 8 in this volume).

Socio-demographic and institutional factors that influence employment

A variety of socio-demographic as well as institutional factors help explain the development in employment and how it differs in the individual national labour markets. Here we give a short overview of some of the most crucial dimensions influencing the size and composition of the labour force/employment. Next, we analyse the importance of gender and age for the development of rates of employment in the four countries.

Migration

Immigration and emigration, may change the composition of a population and the labour force. Traditionally, migration is of greater importance for the size and composition of the labour force in North America than in most European countries. On the other hand, emigration, e.g., from Ireland and Italy, was important for the composition of the population and the labour force in these countries during the first decades of this century. Migration, however, has become important for several European countries during the most recent decade. The socio-political changes in the Central and Eastern European countries together with the civil war in the former Yugoslavia have caused tremendous growth in the number of immigrants and asylum-seekers in several European countries. Austria, Germany and Switzerland have been the principal destinations for immigrants from Central and Eastern Europe. Also Denmark and Sweden have experienced significant growth in the number of immigrants during the early 1990s.

A recent UN study calculated that the EU needs about 125 million immigrants to maintain the present size of the labour force during the next 25 years considering the present stagnation of the European populations because of decreased birth rates (Information 1999–12–28). A liberal but selective immigration policy has been the principal reason for a strong growth in the US population; the slow growth of the European population is, on the other hand, the result of decreasing birth rates combined with a highly restrictive immigration policy (Freeman 1999). Most Northern European societies are not accustomed to integrating immigrants, people with different ethnic backgrounds. Even in European countries with a progressive immigration policy – e.g., Sweden and the Netherlands – the institutional structure of the labour market makes it extremely difficult for most immigrants to be integrated into the labour force. Immigrants often lack the necessary language skills and have difficulties in getting their original qualifications accepted by the unions as well as the employers in the host country. Furthermore, immigrants usually do not have the social contacts and informal knowledge needed for accessing the permanent job positions in their new labour markets. Consequently, in all European countries ethnic immigrants have a significantly higher level of unemployment and their proportion of non-employment is markedly higher than for the natives.

Education and skills

In most studies, a close relationship is found between a worker's skills and his/her level of labour force involvement (Rubery *et al.* 1998). Individuals with a higher education have a higher level of labour force participation and more secure employment conditions compared to people with low or no vocational training. In all labour markets, higher education means higher employment rates, for all age groups, and for both men and women. Especially for women with small children the importance of education is crucial. In most countries, mothers without vocational training tend to have serious problems finding continuous employment while the employment situation for mothers with higher education does not differ radically from men in the same age groups (Rubery *et al.* 1998). (The relationship between the level of education and employment will be discussed in more detail in Chapter 7.) Generally, education means easier entry into the labour market for younger workers and it protects older workers against the risk of being unemployed for longer periods.

In all OECD countries, a growing proportion of each youth cohort gets vocational training and still more receive upper secondary or university degrees. This development has two consequences for their labour force participation and employment. First, today young people enter the labour market later than previous generations because of an extended period of school enrolment. Second, after finishing vocational training each youth cohort has a higher level of labour force participation and employment than the previous ones. Simultaneously, several studies analysing the connection between level of education and labour market performance show that workers without vocational training have more difficulties in managing the demand placed on them by the labour market (OECD 1997d). The differences in employment and wages between skilled and non-skilled workers are growing. Non-skilled workers have a markedly higher risk of being unemployed for longer periods of time and of being marginalised in the labour market than workers with vocational training are (see OECD 1994c: 116–25; Gallie *et al.* 2000). Education and vocational training are important conditions for gaining and maintaining continuous employment and re-qualification of the available labour force becomes even more important considering the large number of new entrants into the labour market (European Commission 1999; Carnoy and Castells 1997).

Welfare state

Welfare states create incentives and disincentives for people to enter the labour market. Welfare state intervention takes several different forms. Entry into the labour market is determined by educational credentials achieved in publicly financed training programmes and a variety of labour market policy measures have a large influence on job mobility, labour flexibility and labour market restructuring. Similarly, exit from the labour market is also influenced by welfare arrangements such as access to early retirement schemes, the generosity of the social benefits and the conditions for old-age pensions. Furthermore, the welfare state has to some extent taken over the responsibility for social reproduction in the household and in this respect the demand for social services and for public sector employment has increased. This development we find more clearly pronounced in Scandinavia than in the two North American countries. In the Scandianvian countries the welfare state thus accounts for the main part of employment growth in the service sector and this development has particularly increased women's labour force participation while the private service industries take a stronger position in creating jobs in the liberal market-dominated American economies (Esping-Andersen 1993 and 1999; and Chapter 6 in this volume).

The welfare state has a major impact on both the supply of, and demand for, female employees. Women's access to the labour market depends on the organisation of housework and childcare. In societies where the responsibility for housework and childcare is located in the home, women tend to do this work as unpaid work and this responsibility creates tremendous barriers for a woman's ability to find paid work. This is the situation in the so-called 'strong' male breadwinner societies where the welfare benefits are defined according to household-based assessments and benefits for women are calculated on their marital position and their spouse's income. Normally, the female rate of employment in this type of welfare system is low. The contrasting type of welfare system is the 'weak' male breadwinner or dual breadwinner system where taxation and benefits are individually based and the public policies try to facilitate the reconciliation of employment and unpaid work through comprehensive possibilities for paid leave and access to childcare and elderly care services. Here the majority of women are active in the labour market and usually find full-time employment (Sainsbury 1996; Rubery *et al.* 1998; Lewis 1992).

Also in other respects the welfare state has influenced women's growing entrance into the labour market. First, more women obtain higher education and a majority of these women want continuous employment. Studies show that the effects of education are especially positive for women with children, who have more than doubled their labour force participation in several European countries from 1970 to 1995 (Boje and Almqvist 2000). Second, the growing involvement of women in the labour market has caused childcare and elderly care responsibilities previously carried out in the family to be organised in collective and institutional forms either by the welfare state, through private organisations or by hiring a private nurse – which is the typical childcare arrangement in the United States. In this respect, changes in family patterns from a male breadwinner to a dual-earner model have thus in all four countries created a large number of new service jobs ready to be taken by those women who have entered the labour market (Lewis 1992; Fagan and Rubery 1999).

Changes in family patterns

Changes in family patterns are closely connected to the influx of women into the labour market. The size of the average family is smaller because greater social and geographical mobility has meant that different generations of family members live separately and because birth rates have decreased, compared to one or two generations ago. Changes in the family structure include an increase in single parent homes and non-married parent homes. For many families one of the major consequences of these changes has been that both parents are forced to work and to contribute in providing for the costs of living instead of the traditional stable male breadwinner family where the man was considered as the only or at least the primary income-earner.

The growing female labour market participation, however, depends on other women doing the unpaid care work women have traditionally done in relation to children, sick relatives and the elderly. Here the organisation and level of family-related measures such as child care and leave programmes play a significant role for women. Women's decision on being engaged in paid work, unpaid or care depend on the institutional and normative conditions prevailing in the specific society. In the more developed and highly regulated welfare states such as the Scandinavian countries this care work has been taken over by the welfare state or women have been paid for doing the care work within the family. Despite the fact that care work in the Scandinavian societies typically has been placed outside the individual households, it has still primarily remained women's work – now carried out as low-paid work in the public service sector. In the more restricted and market-oriented welfare states like the US system, substantial parts of the care work are provided in the individual households and the major responsibility for the care work rests with women and is unpaid – in spite of their growing involvement in paid work (Saraceno 1997).

In contemporary welfare states work and care have normally been constructed as mutually exclusive. For men this means that the concept of work is completely internalised in the male concept of citizenship, but for women it leads to a complicated dilemma between their caring work in the family and their searching for independence through wage labour (Knijn and Kremer 1997: 350). In solving this dilemma feminist researchers have proposed that the concept of decommod-ification must be supplemented by the concept of defamilialisation. Lister defines defamilialisation as a criterion for social rights by 'the degree to which individual adults can uphold a socially acceptable standard of living, independently of family relationships, either through paid work or through social security provisions' (Lister 1997: 173). In this context, the expansion of public facilities for childcare and elderly care as well as provision of well-paid jobs has been important for a woman's ability to reconcile work and obligations at home (Saraceno 1997). In Scandinavian countries, this development started in the 1970s. Then a growing number of women took up paid labour and today men and women have nearly the same rates of labour force participation. The same development has been under way especially in the United States during the 1980s and today in 42 per cent of US married couples both spouses work full-time compared to 24 per cent in 1969 (BLS 1999c). However, these families do not have a network of supportive state institutions to temper the stress induced by the individualisation of social and economic life which make the life of US families more troublesome and precarious (Carnoy and Castells 1997: 23)

Trends in employment by gender and age

Denmark, Sweden and the United States are among the OECD economies that have the highest rates of employment while Canada is lagging slightly behind the other three countries and is characterised by a pattern of labour market involvement more like Continental European countries (Table 5.2). Women in the two Scandinavian countries and the United States hold a top position in rates of employment among the OECD countries while the pattern is more mixed for men. Several other OECD countries have higher rates of male employment than both Canada and Sweden while Denmark and the United States hold the top positions. In the late 1990s, the only OECD countries that have higher overall labour force involvement than Denmark and the United States are the three small European countries, Iceland, Switzerland and Norway, which hold the top positions in employment rates (Auer 1996; OECD 2000a).[3]

In 2000, Denmark had the highest rate of overall employment among the four countries followed by Sweden and the United States. The male rate of employment was highest in Denmark and the United States while Sweden and Denmark hold the top position in women's rate of employment. Canada had the lowest rates of overall and female employment while Sweden was at the bottom for men. In Sweden, employment rates for men as well as for women decreased during the early 1990s and this downturn meant that it lost its previous top position among the four countries.

Historically, male employment rates have declined and female employment rates have increased. In the early 1970s, the difference between the male and female rates of employment in the United States and Canada were 35 and 38

Table 5.2 Employment rates by gender in Canada, Denmark, Sweden and the United States, 1973–2000 (%)

		1973	1979	1983	1990	1995	2000	Change 1973–2000 (%)
Canada	Total	63.1	68.0	66.4	70.5	67.5	71.1	+8.0
	Men	81.9	83.5	77.8	77.9	73.5	76.3	−5.6
	Women	44.1	52.4	55.0	62.7	61.7	65.8	+21.7
Denmark	Total	75.2	75.1	71.7	75.4	73.9	76.4	+1.2
	Men	89.0	85.9	78.3	80.1	80.7	80.7	−8.3
	Women	61.2	64.1	65.0	70.6	67.0	72.1	+10.9
Sweden	Total	73.6	78.8	78.5	83.1	72.2	74.2	+ 0.6
	Men	86.2	86.3	83.0	85.2	73.5	76.1	−10.1
	Women	60.8	71.1	73.9	81.0	70.8	72.3	+11.5
United States	Total	65.1	68.0	66.3	72.2	72.5	74.1	+9.0
	Men	82.8	81.4	76.5	80.7	79.5	80.6	−2.2
	Women	48.0	54.9	56.2	64.0	65.8	67.9	+19.9

Sources: OECD 1996c: 220–2;1999b: 203–5; 1999c.

Note
Employment rate is defined as the employment/population ratio for people between 15 and 64 years old.

percentage points, respectively. In Sweden and Denmark, the difference was 25 and 28 percentage points, respectively. This has changed radically and in 2000 the difference between the male and female rates of employment in percentage points decreased to 13 in the United States, 10 in Canada, 9 in Denmark and only 4 in Sweden.

The growth in employment rates in all four countries is caused by the increase in female employment rates. In the early 1960s, about 40 per cent of women were employed in all four countries. During the 1960s, Danish and Swedish women started entering the labour market in large numbers while in the United States and Canada female employment rates remained stable. Women in the United States and Canada first entered the labour market in large numbers during the late 1970s and throughout the 1980s. In 1990, the female rates of employment were 63 to 64 per cent in the United States and Canada while they were about 70 per cent in Denmark and 81 per cent in Sweden. In both Denmark and Sweden, the level of female employment decreased while it continued to grow in the United States and Canada throughout the 1990s but at a more restricted pace than in the previous decades.

The decrease or stagnation in Scandinavian female employment during the 1990s has several causes. Primarily, the decline is because of the economic recession and an overall decrease in the demand for female labour. Furthermore, both Scandinavian countries have experienced stagnation or decrease in public employment that has reduced the demand for female employees (see Chapter 6). This significantly increased the level of female unemployment and caused a growing number of older women to leave the labour market for early retirement while younger women have postponed their entry into the labour market and instead increased their enrolment in higher education. Since the mid-1980s, the increase of women enrolled in vocational training and university courses has markedly increased, especially in Sweden.

For men, growth in employment rates peaked in the early 1970s and since then these rates have been decreasing in Canada, Denmark and Sweden. As for women, this decrease has been particularly pronounced during the 1990s. In the United States, employment trends differ from the other countries. Men in the United States have had a nearly constant level of employment during the recent two decades. The decrease in male rates of employment has been most pronounced in Sweden where it declined by nearly 12 percentage points during the 1990s.

Denmark and Sweden have similar overall employment rates and are performing better than most other European countries in activating the working age population and in creating new jobs. This is simlar to the United States. On the other hand, the United States has clearly performed better than both the Scandinavian countries in job creation since the early 1970s. During the study period, Canada has remained in bottom position for overall employment rate but today is performing slightly better than Sweden when it comes to employment for men.

Employment by age and gender

Explaining the trends in labour market performance is complex and we have to include other variables in addition to gender in this analysis. Therefore, in the rest of this chapter we detail our analysis by looking at employment rates including both gender and age, the amount of work performed by men and women, and how it has developed in the four countries during recent decades. We start this analysis by looking at trends in rates of employment for men and women in different age groups during recent decades (Table 5.3).

Table 5.3 Employment/population ratio by age and gender in the period 1983–2000 for Canada, Denmark, Sweden and the United States

	1983	*1990*	*1994*	*1998*	*1999*	*2000*
Men aged 15–24						
Canada	54.3	61.5	53.2	53.0	55.4	56.7
Denmark	55.9	67.8	64.8	66.7	69.5	70.3
Sweden	60.6	64.2	40.0	42.4	44.8	46.7
United States	59.2	63.2	61.0	60.8	61.0	62.0
Men aged 25–54						
Canada	84.6	86.6	82.7	84.7	85.1	85.9
Denmark	87.1	87.4	85.7	88.9	89.3	88.3
Sweden	92.8	92.9	82.8	83.4	84.5	85.8
United States	86.1	89.2	87.2	88.8	89.0	89.0
Men aged 55–64						
Canada	66.4	60.9	54.6	55.5	56.9	57.7
Denmark	63.1	65.6	59.8	58.6	59.9	61.9
Sweden	73.9	74.0	64.5	65.8	67.1	67.8
United States	65.2	65.1	62.6	66.2	66.1	65.6
Women aged 15–24						
Canada	52.9	59.4	51.9	52.1	53.9	55.8
Denmark	49.9	62.2	59.1	66.0	62.8	64.0
Sweden	59.7	64.8	42.8	40.7	42.8	45.4
United States	52.2	56.4	55.3	57.2	57.0	57.6
Women aged 25–54						
Canada	59.1	70.0	68.9	71.8	73.2	74.0
Denmark	76.8	80.3	75.2	77.7	79.4	80.4
Sweden	84.9	89.4	81.0	79.1	80.6	81.7
United States	62.0	70.7	71.5	73.6	74.1	74.3
Women aged 55–64						
Canada	30.9	33.6	34.3	35.6	37.3	39.3
Denmark	39.1	42.4	40.2	41.3	41.8	46.2
Sweden	57.4	64.2	59.4	60.3	61.0	62.5
United States	39.4	44.0	47.0	50.0	50.1	50.5

Sources: OECD 1995; 1999b: 228–36; 2000a: 206–14; 2001b: 218–21.

For both men and women, the employment rates are highest in the prime-age group, 25–54 years. For this age group, we find marked similarities between the four countries in labour market involvement. From 1983 through 2000, the level of employment peaked in 1990, decreased until 1996–97 and then started increasing again during the most recent years. The United States deviates slightly from this pattern with only a minor decrease around 1990 and since then continuously increasing employment rates followed by stagnation and even a small decline among the elderly men in the late 1990s. Considering the high level of uniformity in prime-age employment, the differences registered in overall employment rates of the working-age population in the four countries have to be explained by the development among the young and the older age groups. Therefore, what follows is a more elaborated analysis for each of the three age groups shown in Table 5.3.

Youth in the labour market

Young people's rate of employment is different in the four countries. In 2000, Danish youth clearly had the highest level of employment; about two-thirds of youth between 15 and 24 were employed. Employment rates in the United States and Canada came next and at the bottom was Sweden with less than half of the youth employed. Between 1983 and 2000, the trend for most OECD countries has been a decline in labour force participation among young people because of high youth unemployment and thereby difficulties in getting a job. Young people tend to stay longer in initial education. Today most young people are first entering regular employment when they have finished upper secondary education or university studies in their mid-20s. Sweden has the largest decline in youth employment. Here the employment rates for both young men and women declined by more than one-third during the 1990s and are today among the lowest in Europe despite a slight increase in the late 1990s. For the other three countries, there was an increase in youth employment from 1983 to 2000. This was especially the case for Denmark where the rates of youth employment increased from 56 to 70 per cent for men and from 50 to 64 per cent for women in 1983 and 2000, respectively, whereas the rates in the United States have remained stable at a high level for young men and are slightly increasing for young women over the last 15 years. In both countries, a large number of young people combine educational activities with typically part-time employment. The differences in pattern of employment among young people in the four countries are reinforced when the employed are divided into full-time and part-time employment (Table 5.4)

In Canada, Denmark and the United States young employed women are nearly equally divided in the proportion working full-time and part-time while most young men work full-time. In Sweden, on the other hand, the large majority of both young women and men are employed part-time. Swedish youth who are employed are a minority of the age group 16 to 24. Few Swedish young people have left the educational system and are fully involved in gainful employment before they are in their mid-20s. Most of those who are employed combine work

Table 5.4 Proportion of employed people in the age group of 16–24 in full-time and part-time employment in Canada, Denmark, Sweden and the United States, 1998 (%)

	Canada	Denmark	Sweden	United States
Men				
Total	53.0	72.5	40.3	59.4
Full-time	33.0	45.6	8.3	36.5
Part-time	20.0	26.9	32.0	22.9
Women				
Total	52.1	65.0	38.9	55.7
Full-time	24.5	33.0	16.2	28.1
Part-time	27.6	32.0	22.7	27.6

Sources: Statistics Canada 1999; Statistics Denmark 1998; Statistics Sweden 1998; BLS 1998.

Note
Definition of part-time employment: persons who usually work less than 30 hours per week.

and education as is evidenced by the large number of part-time workers. Compared with Sweden significantly more Danish young people are employed and among Danish men the majority of those are employed full-time while employed young women are equally divided in full-time and part-time employment. Today, a substantial number of young Danish men are leaving the educational system before the age of 20 without finishing a higher education while young Danish women tend to stay longer in the school system (OECD 1998b).

In the last 15 to 20 years, employment of young women in the United States and Canada has declined compared with prime-age women while this ratio has been constant for men. The main reasons for this change are that young American women stay longer in the educational system combined with a growing number of prime-age women remaining employed during their child rearing period. In Canada, however, a large group of mothers are only employed on a part-time basis. More radical changes have happened in the ratio of employment between youth and prime-age people in Denmark and Sweden but in completely different directions. In Sweden, the employment rates for young people have declined markedly both numerically and relatively to the prime-age group. Today the rates of employment among youth are only half of the rates for people in the prime-age category. In Denmark, on the other hand, significant growth in employment rates for both young men and women have meant that their level of employment today is as high as 75 and 85 per cent, respectively, of the level for people in the prime-age group.

The difficulties for Swedish young people in entering the labour market grew significantly in the 1990s. Swedish youth unemployment skyrocketed in the early 1990s and many young Swedes have extended their time in education to avoid being unemployed. This is contrary to the Danish case where massive policy measures were introduced aimed at easing the transition process for teenagers from school to work. Since the early 1990s, all Danish teenagers who leave school and do not have a job are offered either government supported employment or access to vocational training. Consequently, the level of unemployment for young Danes has declined dramatically since the early 1990s.

Employment among prime-age people

For people in the prime-age group, the level of labour market involvement is high and has been growing for both men and women in Canada, Denmark and the United States during the last 15 years. For men in the prime-age category, however, the growth in employment rates is modest. In both Denmark and the United States, prime-age men have recovered from the employment crisis of the early 1990s. In the late 1990s, these countries are approaching 90 per cent employment while Canadian men are still slightly behind the 1990 level. In all three countries, the same picture can be registered for women but with markedly higher increase in the employment rates especially for Canadian and American women.

Again, we find a completely different picture in Sweden. Here the rates of employment for prime-age people – men as well as women – have declined. Since the rates peaked in 1990, they have declined about 10 percentage points for both men and women in 1997 when they reached the bottom of 83 per cent for men and 79 per cent for women (OECD 1999b: 233–6). During the last couple of years, the Swedish employment rates have, however, recovered slightly. On the other hand, in the early 1990s for both Swedish prime-age men and women the rates of employment were at record highs. In 1990, the rates were 93 per cent for men and nearly 90 per cent for women. The employment crisis of the 1990s hurt Sweden more than most other countries. From 1992 to 1993, more than 500,000 jobs – or nearly 15 per cent of the total employment – were lost and the recovery has been slow. This is mainly because it has taken place concurrently with a comprehensive restructuring of the economy and high rates of productivity growth (EC 1999: 13). It is important, however, to remember that Swedish women in the prime-age group still have one of the highest levels of employment in the OECD area whereas Swedish men's rate of employment – together with Canadian men – are far behind most other OECD countries and rank at a level with Spain and Italy (OECD 1999b).

Employment among old-age people – retiring from the labour market

The rate of employment for older people is different from the rest of the working population. In Sweden and the United States, men and especially women remain active in the labour market much longer than men and women in Denmark and Canada. In 2000, about two-thirds of Swedish and American men in the old-age group were employed while this is the case for 58 and 62 per cent of the Canadian and Danish men, respectively. The difference in employment pattern is even more striking for women: 63 per cent of older Swedish women and 51 per cent of American women are employed compared to 39 per cent and 46 per cent in Canada and Denmark, respectively.

The general trend among the OECD countries for older people is towards early retirement. Especially for men this tendency has led to a decline in employment rates in nearly all countries. The tendency towards earlier retirement among women has been equalised by higher employment rates in the cohorts of younger women entering the old-age cohort and consequently the employment rates of older women are still increasing in most OECD countries. We find nearly the same situation for the four countries included in this study. In Canada, Denmark and Sweden the male rate of employment decreased substantially during the last 15 years whereas it remained constant in the United States. Despite the fall in the rate of employment among older Swedish men it was still among the highest among the OECD countries together with the United States and Japan. Among older women, the rate of employment has increased in all four countries from 1983 to 2000. This increase has been more modest in Denmark and Sweden than in Canada and the United States. Older American women especially have experienced substantial increases in their rates of employment. Today, older American women together with Swedish women have the highest rate of employment within the OECD.

Gender differences in labour market involvement

Convergence of the gender rates of employment has taken place for all age groups in the four countries during the last two decades. The gender equality in labour market involvement is most obvious among youngsters aged 15 to 24 but has also improved for the other age groups (Table 5.5).

However, we still find substantial differences between male and female employment for the prime-age and older age groups in all countries except Sweden. In Sweden, the gender difference in rates of employment is about or less than 5 per cent for people in the prime-age groups and less than 10 per cent for the older age groups. This is clearly a higher level of gender equality than elsewhere. Especially among the older age groups, Sweden is far ahead of the other three countries. In the United States and Canada, the traditional gender differences in retirement patterns with women retiring earlier than men still exist. In Denmark, the early retirement reform of 1979 has especially favoured low-paid employees who want to withdraw from the labour market at an early age. This is an opportunity that has primarily been used by women who are employed in the public sector.

The gender equality in employment has particularly improved in Canada and the United States during the last two decades, especially in the prime-age and older age groups. In both age groups they were far behind the Scandinavian countries in emphasising female employment in the early 1980s but have now reached a level similar to at least the Danish situation, while Sweden despite some falling off in the early 1990s still holds a top position. Among the young age groups, the similarity between the four countries is higher than in the other age groups. Most of these young people have just started their labour market career. They are single or married with no children, which typically means a differentiation in male and female conditions for labour market involvement.

In all four countries, young women and unmarried women have always been in

Table 5.5 Employment/population ratio for women in relation to men in Canada, Denmark, Sweden and the United States by age and year, 1983–2000

	Young-age (15–24)	Prime-age (25–54)	Old-age (55–64)
Canada			
1983	0.97	0.70	0.47
1990	0.97	0.81	0.55
1994	0.98	0.83	0.63
1998	0.98	0.85	0.64
2000	0.98	0.86	0.68
Denmark			
1983	0.89	0.88	0.62
1990	0.92	0.92	0.65
1994	0.91	0.88	0.67
1998	0.92	0.87	0.70
2000	0.91	0.91	0.75
Sweden			
1983	0.99	0.92	0.78
1990	1.00	0.96	0.87
1994	1.07	0.98	0.92
1998	0.96	0.95	0.92
2000	0.97	0.95	0.92
United States			
1983	0.88	0.72	0.60
1990	0.88	0.79	0.67
1994	0.91	0.82	0.75
1998	0.94	0.83	0.76
2000	0.93	0.83	0.77

Sources: OECD 1997d, Table C; 1999b: 228–36; 2001b: 215–20.

the labour market in great numbers. They have done unskilled work in manufacturing industries and worked in low-paid jobs in personal services. During the recent two to three decades, a large number of women entering the labour market came from middle-class families and the strongest increase in labour market participation has taken place among women in the middle age groups. These new groups of female workers entering the labour market are primarily married women and younger women with higher education and they tend to be active in the labour market during most of their life, even during periods when raising young children (Rubery, Smith and Fagan 1999: ch. 8). Today more than 80 per cent of the Scandinavian mothers – married or cohabiting – are employed while this proportion is 70 per cent for single mothers. Both Canadian and American mothers have significantly lower rates of employment and this is primarily the case for married mothers, who had rates of employment of about 66 per cent in the mid-1990s (Bradshaw *et al.* 1996: 8).

In the 1970s and the early 1980s, the normal pattern of employment among

American and Canadian women aged 24 to 54 indicates that a large proportion left the labour market when they got married or became mothers (Dex and Shaw 1986). During the 1980s, this pattern, however, changed markedly and the female rates of employment have continually increased, especially for the North American women, but are still lower than for the comparable groups of Danish and Swedish women (Table 5.3). It is primarily among women with small children that the rate of participation is significantly higher in the Scandinavian countries.[4] Most of the Scandinavian married mothers with young children were previously employed in part-time jobs in order to reconcile work and childcare. Especially in Sweden the family policies for young mothers enable them to combine part-time work and childcare. Today still more mothers – married, cohabiting, or single – want, however, to utilise their education and have realised that long periods in part-time employment might negatively influence their labour market career. Therefore, they take up full-time work as soon as possible after childbirth and stay in full-time work throughout their labour market career (Abrahamson, Boje and Greve 2002).

In the United States, employed women with small children still have employment rates far below the average rate for American women generally. For most American mothers, it is difficult to combine work and care of their children because few public or private childcare facilities are available. Typically, American families have to find private solutions to their childcare problems, which are usually expensive. Therefore, most North American women with young children have to choose between leaving the labour market while the children are small or working full-time (see Dex and Shaw 1986). Both these solutions are mainly for educated and well-paid middle-class women. The unskilled and low-paid female workers are typically forced to stay in the labour market full-time and to organise private, often unpaid, care for their children.

Variations in labour market involvement

In the previous section, focus has been on gender and age in describing differences in labour market patterns between the four countries. Several other dimensions have to be taken into consideration – especially differences in how institutions influence the labour market behaviour of various social groups. In this section, we want to analyse how work time, hours worked during the year, etc. are fluctuating in the four countries.

Employment and working hours – the actual use of labour

Employment rates tell only a part of the truth about the development in employment and labour market involvement of different social groups. Rates of employment show how many persons are employed but nothing about how much they work and to what extent the potential resources of labour power are used. Here we need to look at other measures of labour market involvement. First, the proportion of employed people who work part-time, which again affects the number of annual working hours carried out by an average employee. Second, how variations in annual hours worked, and the proportion of employees working part-time, influence the level of overall employment in the four countries.

Patterns of part-time employment

The larger proportion of people working part-time is women. Therefore, the overall level of part-time employment is related to both women's need for reconciling work and family responsibilities and an economy's demand for part-time workers, which again depends on the industrial and occupational composition of the labour market. Jobs are more likely to be structured as part-time jobs if the demand is strong in the female-dominated industries or if the employers want to attract women, while overtime or shift work are typically used when the demand for labour concerns a male-dominated sector (O'Reilly and Fagan 1998: 7–11). Therefore, part-time employment tends to be more widespread in countries with large service industries, and the public service industries in particular are characterised by a high level of part-time jobs (Rosenfeld and Birkelund 1995: 116).

At an earlier stage of female integration in the labour market, growth in female labour market participation was highly correlated with an increase in part-time employment. However, since the late 1980s this connection has been weakened and several cross-national studies do not find any clear association between female employment and the level of part-time work in the 1990s (Gornick, Meyers and Ross 1997; and Rosenfeld and Birkelund 1995). This also holds for our four countries. The Scandinavian countries traditionally have had high levels of both female labour market participation and part-time employment but this relationship has also been weakened markedly since the 1980s and has more or less disappeared throughout the 1990s. For the United States, the relationship between level of female overall employment and part-time employment has always been weak. The United States has high levels of female employment but a relatively low proportion of women in part-time employment. Only in Canada might we find evidence of a relationship between growing overall and part-time employment for women (Table 5.6).

Table 5.6 shows the overall and gender-divided rates of part-time employment only for the period 1990–2000 because it is not possible to provide comparable figures for the previous decades. Before 1990, the figures for part-time employment were based on national definitions, which differ greatly among the countries meaning that we noted marked variations in the proportion working part-time in the individual labour markets.[5]

From 1990, OECD started calculating the proportion of part-time employment based on the same definition in all countries – persons who usually work less than 30 hours per week. Based on this definition the differences in the proportion of part-time jobs in the four countries are quite small. About 18 per cent of Canada's work force is working part-time; in Denmark and Sweden the proportion of the total employment working part-time is 16 and 14 per cent, respectively; and the United States has only 13 per cent in part-time employment. For women, we

Table 5.6 Size and composition of part-time employment in Canada, Denmark, Sweden and the United States, 1990–2000 (%)

	1990	*1995*	*2000*
Total part-time employment as a proportion of total employment			
Canada	17.0	18.6	18.1
Denmark	19.2	16.8	15.7
Sweden	14.5	15.1	14.0
United States	13.8	14.1	12.8
OECD Europe	13.2	13.7	14.9
Total OECD	13.4	14.1	15.3
Male part-time employment as a proportion of male employment			
Canada	9.1	10.6	10.3
Denmark	10.2	9.7	8.9
Sweden	5.3	6.8	7.3
United States	8.3	8.4	7.9
OECD Europe	4.4	4.9	5.9
Total OECD	6.0	6.7	7.6
Female part-time employment as a proportion of female employment			
Canada	26.8	28.2	27.3
Denmark	29.6	25.6	23.5
Sweden	24.5	24.1	21.4
United States	20.0	20.3	18.2
OECD Europe	26.8	26.5	27.5
Total OECD	23.6	24.2	25.7

Sources: OECD 1997d; 2001b: Table E.

Note
Definition of part-time employment: persons who usually work less than 30 hours per week.

find the same ranking with most working part-time less than 30 hours in Canada, least in the United States while Denmark and Sweden hold a position in between the two North American countries. For all countries except Canada the proportion of women in part-time employment has stagnated or declined during the 1990s. Still more women and especially married women in the prime-age group want full-time employment in Denmark, Sweden and the United States (BLS, 1999c; Boje 2002; SOU 1996).

There are many reasons for the variations in the proportion of employees working part-time. Differences in employment regulations, in rules for eligibility for social benefits, the size of the service sector – especially the amount of public employment – and emphasis on gender equality are all dimensions that have to be taken into account when explaining variation in the pattern of part-time employment. In the Scandinavian countries, the welfare state has been the principal creator of part-time jobs for women in the 1970s and 1980s. In the 1970s, these jobs were created to include married women and mothers more regularly in the labour market. Today, part-time jobs in Denmark are especially widespread among youth giving them the opportunity of combining education and work. In Sweden, part-time jobs are more equally represented in all age groups. Parents with children younger than 12 years have the right to reduce their working-time and many, primarily the mothers, reduced their weekly working hours, but not by more than 3 to 5 hours (Abrahamson, Boje and Greve 2002). Today most Scandinavian married women/mothers, however, want full-time jobs and want to combine labour force participation with comprehensive access to public child care facilities and parental leave during their children's first years. Strong commitment to gender equality both in family policy and in employment regulation makes it easier for women to shift between part-time and full-time jobs during their working life.

Working hours – the use of labour resources

Widespread part-time employment or other forms of reduced involvement in labour market activities – such as periodical unemployment or lay-off, absence because of sickness, holidays, etc. – have as a consequence lowered the average annual working hours even when a large proportion of the labour force is registered as employed. In Table 5.7 we have calculated a measure for the use of the labour resources in the four countries analysed in this book.

During the 1990s, the rates of employment have, as discussed earlier in the

Table 5.7 Mobilisation of potential labour resources for the population aged 15–64 in Canada, Denmark, Sweden and the United States in the 1990s

	1990	*1998*	*Difference 1990–98*
Employment/population ratio (%)			
Canada	70.5	67.9	−2.6
Denmark	75.4	75.4	0.0
Sweden	83.1	71.5	−11.6
United States	72.2	73.8	+1.6
Average annual working hours			
Canada	1790	1777	−13
Denmark	1579	1531	−48
Sweden	1480	1551	+71
United States	1943	1957	+14
Mobilisation of labour resources (%)			
Canada	60.7	58.0	−2.7
Denmark	57.2	55.5	−1.7
Sweden	59.1	53.3	−5.8
United States	67.4	69.4	+2.0

Sources: OECD 1999b: 225 and 241; and for Denmark: Ministry of Finance 1999, ADAM database.

Notes
Canada and Denmark: 1997 instead of 1998.
Denmark: Average annual working hours are only for manufacturing industries.
Mobilisation of labour resources defined as follows: employment/population rate x actual annual working hours/maximal annual working hours (2080 hours).

chapter, developed in different directions in the four countries. In 1990, Sweden had the highest overall rate of employment and Canada was placed at bottom position. In 1998, Canada still held the bottom position while Sweden had fallen below both Denmark and the United States. The Swedish rate of employment declined by nearly 12 percentage points from 1990 to 1998 while in the United States it had increased slightly.

Comparing the level of average annual working hours per employed person in the four countries gives another picture of how the potential labour force resources are used. The United States clearly has the highest level of annual working hours per employed person and it has been growing. Today the average working hours in the United States are close to the maximum annual working hours – calculated as 40 hours per week multiplied by 52 weeks per year = 2080 hours/year. The actual annual working hours in the United States reach 95 per cent of the maximum working hours while actual working hours in Denmark and Sweden cover only three-quarters of the maximum working hours.

Finally, in Table 5.7 we have calculated the level of mobilisation of labour resources: employment/population rate × actual annual working hours/maximal annual working hours (2080 hours) (See Nickell 1997). For Canada, Denmark and Sweden the use of labour resources has declined. The decline has been most pronounced in Sweden where it was about 6 percentage points, while the level of labour mobilisation increased in the United States during the 1990s. In both Denmark and Sweden only slightly more than half of the potential labour force resources in the population of working age (15–64 years) are used while this is the case for about 70 per cent of the potential labour force in the United States. Again, Canada holds a middle position with a level of mobilisation at 58 per cent.

There are different reasons for the variation in utilisation of the labour resources in the four countries. In Canada, the declining utilisation is caused by a decrease in both working hours and the rate of employment while in Denmark it is a decrease in the average annual working hours with a constant overall rate of employment. For Sweden the decrease in utilisation of labour resources is caused by a significant decrease in rate of employment while the annual working hours have been growing. The remarkable increase in annual working hours in Sweden is on account of the decrease in the number of people absent from work – sickness, parental leave, etc. – and the growing number of women working full-time (Table 5.6). Finally, the increasing utilisation of labour resources in the United States is a combination of growth in the overall rate of employment and increasing annual working hours for the employed persons (BLS 1999a).

The type of employment regulation implemented in each country is crucial in explaining the differences in working time patterns and in the use of labour resources. In both Denmark and Sweden, the working time is regulated and is implemented by the unions. During the past decade, there has been an intensive debate in favour of shorter working hours and this has primarily happened in Denmark. The decline in weekly working hours in Denmark has, however, partly been compensated for by more people working full-time (Table 5.6). Furthermore, in both countries the right to paid holidays is legally determined – 5–6 weeks per year – and parents have the right to paid leave because of childbirth and sickness that also lead to a reduction of the average annual working hours. This is in contrast to the situation in the United States where the working time is mainly unregulated and negotiated between the employer and the individual employee. Furthermore, American employees have a statutory right to holidays for only two weeks but with no payment, and a right to paid leave in connection with childbirth and benefits in case of sickness do not exist generally but can be part of the individual employment contract. This means that American employees are forced to work more than Scandinavian employees and to accept the conditions set by the employers (see Chapter 3 in this book).

Labour force participation and employment by gender and age – an OECD comparison

In the period from late 1970s to about 1990, the Scandinavian as well as the North American labour markets were characterised by a high level of employment for both men and women compared with the other OECD countries (EC 1999). In the late 1970s, Sweden and Denmark were front-runners for both male and female rates of employment while Canada and the United States combined a lower level of female employment with a medium level of male employment compared with other OECD countries (OECD 1997d). During the recent two decades, male employment rates have been levelling off or decreasing in the two Scandinavian countries while the female rates were increasing up until 1990 when they also began to decrease. The Danish labour market has recovered from the employment crisis of the early 1990s and has today higher employment rates for both men and women compared to 1990. The Swedish level of labour market involvement is, on the other hand, still far behind the record high level of 1990 and has only partly recovered from the dramatic employment crisis in the early 1990s. In both Canada and the United States, the rate of total employment has been growing during the last two decades. The increasing number of employed women primarily causes this growth in overall rates of employment whereas the male rate of employment has been stagnating in the United States and declining in Canada. This has placed the United States in a top position among the OECD countries together with Denmark and another Scandinavian country, Norway.

We want to end this description of trends in labour market involvement by analysing the relationship between male and female rates of employment in the major OECD countries from 1973 to 2000. Men have traditionally been more committed to active labour market participation than women and the employment conditions were previously outlined according to the male breadwinner model characterised by a clear division of labour in the family with the man as the main income provider and the woman as caretaker for the husband, children and sometimes also for elderly family members (Lewis 1992; Fagan and Rubery 1999). In the 1970s and part of the 1980s, this was still the employment pattern for a large number of families in most Continental European countries and especially in Southern Europe. Consequently, the female rates of employment were markedly lower than the male rates in these countries (Figure 5.1).

1973	Women – low < 40%	Women – medium 41–49%	Women – high 50% +
Men – high 90% +	Portugal, Spain		United Kingdom
Men– medium 81–89%	Belgium, Netherlands Greece, Ireland, Italy	Austria, Norway, Canada, United States, France, Germany OECD	Denmark, Japan, Sweden
Men – low < 80%			Finland

2000	Women – low < 50%	Women – medium 51–59%	Women – high 60% +
Men – high 80% +		Japan	Denmark, Netherlands, Norway, United States
Men – medium 71–79%	Greece, Spain	Austria, Germany, Ireland, OECD	Canada, Portugal, Sweden, United Kingdom
Men – low < 70%	Italy	Belgium, France	

Figure 5.1 Employment/population ratio for men and women in selected OECD countries, 1973 and 2000

Sources: OECD 1996c; 2001b.

Note
The three categories have been adjusted from 1973 through 2000. This adjustment is based on the changes in the average rates of employment for all OECD countries which in 1973 were 86 per cent and 46 per cent for men and women, respectively, and in 2000 the rates were 76 per cent and 57 per cent for men and women, respectively. Consequently, the male categories have been down-graded 10 percentage points and the female categories have been up-graded 10 percentage points.

In the early 1970s, most OECD countries were characterised by high rates of employment for men and low rates for women. The male breadwinner model was still the dominant pattern but it had started weakening in some countries. The differences among the OECD countries in the overall rates of employment were due primarily to differences in the female rates of employment. In the Southern European countries high rates of male employment were combined with extremely low rates for women while women in the liberal market economies and in the Scandinavian countries had started entering the labour market in large numbers.

In 2000 the picture was different. Greater diversity prevailed among the OECD countries in both the male and female levels of employment. Several trends can be registered. First, women's employment rates have increased markedly in nearly all countries while men's employment rates have declined. Second, a group of countries stands out from the rest with high rates of employment for both men and women – Denmark, Netherlands, Norway and the United States. Among these countries we find two different patterns of employment for women. In Denmark and the United States the large majority of women work full-time while part-time employment is dominant among Norwegian and Dutch women. Third, the Southern European countries are still the laggards – now for both the male and female level of employment. In these countries the male rates of employment have declined more than the average for the OECD countries. The only exception from this pattern is Portugal with an unusually high female rate of employment. Fourth, Sweden has lost its top position in levels of employment among the OECD countries. Today it is placed in the middle group for men but with relatively high female rates of employment together with Portugal, the United Kingdom and Canada. Sweden has thus fallen slightly behind the other Scandinavian countries – Norway and Denmark - while Canada has improved its position both compared with the OECD as a whole and with the other Anglo-American countries.

At the beginning of this chapter, we mentioned the employment policy debate emphasising the marked differences in labour market involvement of the working-age population in Europe and the United States. This debate does not, however, give a correct picture of the situation when we compare the United States with Denmark and Sweden. For all three countries, the overall rates of employment come close to each other. Canada is only slightly behind the other three countries primarily because of lower female rates of employment. Despite large differences in retirement patterns, employment policies, and in measures enabling women to combine work and family responsibilities the four countries have become more similar in labour market involvement of women and men in the prime-age groups during recent decades. Furthermore, the decline in employment rates for Scandinavians during the first part of the 1990s has partly been recovered and an up-turn has taken place during recent years. Since 1997, the rates of employment for both Danish men and women have increased significantly and have exceeded the levels before the latest employment crisis in 1990–92 and a similar development started in Sweden in 1999. In this respect, none of the Scandinavian labour markets can be characterised as 'sclerotic' but seem to have great capacity for creating new jobs in times of prosperity.

Conclusion

As we have pointed out several times in this chapter, one of the most remarkable trends in the labour market development for our four countries has been the convergence of male and female rates of employment during the last two to three decades. This convergence has been most obvious in Sweden. Today, Swedish men and women have nearly the same level of labour market activity while the convergence has been slower in Canada and the United States. In both North American countries, the difference between male and female rates of employment is still more than 10 percentage points despite a strong growth in the female labour market involvement. Traditionally, labour market involvement of women in Denmark has been lower than in Sweden but above the two North American labour markets. During the 1990s, this has changed and today the Danish rate of employment for women is at the same level as for Swedish women.

The demand for female labour is closely related to the growing demand for different kinds of services but has also been reinforced by the decline in supply of male labour in most Western countries. The influx of women has been of great importance for the transformation from an industrial goods-producing society to a service-producing one. On the one hand, this has facilitated the change in the labour market structure from employment in the male-dominated industries in agriculture, mining and manufacturing into employment in the fast-growing service industries by providing an adequately qualified supply of labour power. On the other hand, feminisation of the labour force has raised the demand for a variety of new service functions such as childcare, personal services and care for the elderly. This growth in services has again created many new jobs for women and thereby led to an additional increase in the female rates of employment.

The extent to which women are able to reconcile paid work with their traditional unpaid family responsibilities is crucial for female levels of labour force participation. In this respect, the availability of part-time jobs and comprehensive access to parental leave and later on to public childcare in the Scandinavian countries are of great importance for mothers to combine work and child rearing and for their prospects of remaining active in the labour market, possibilities which rarely exist in the United States.

Sweden

Each of the four countries included in this comparison has its own employment profile. Sweden has an extremely low youth employment and the youngsters tend to remain longer in the school system. Among those in education, a large group is combining education with different kinds of part-time jobs. The employment level is, on the other hand, high among people in the prime-age groups but for women in this age group it is often combined with extensive periods of reduced employment – parental leave or part-time employment. The Swedes remain active in the labour market longer than in any of the other three countries and this is especially the case for women. The Swedish labour market is characterised by a high level of gender equality. The male and female patterns of labour market involvement have been converging for all age groups during the recent decades and today Sweden has probably the most equal labour market among the OECD countries.

Denmark

Denmark represents another pattern of employment. Despite strong growth in women's rate of employment, the difference in male and female employment levels is still about 10 percentage points and this difference has been constant during the 1990s. Changes in rates of employment for Danish men and women have been surprisingly small for the prime-age groups during the last 15 years. The most profound changes have happened among youth; they have increased their labour market involvement and have the highest rates of employment among the four countries. Still more Danes work full-time and especially among women the level of part-time employment has declined during the last two decades. Part-time employment becomes still more concentrated among young people while people in the prime-age group pursue full-time jobs. Finally, the age of retirement has declined continuously in Denmark for both men and women during the last 20 years and the employment rates among the older age groups are close to the Canadian level that traditionally has been low.

United States

The United States is the only country where rates of employment have been growing for all age groups throughout the last 15 years. The US labour market is also characterised by a relatively high level of gender differences in both labour force participation and employment. This difference prevails despite a significant convergence during the last two decades. Traditionally, American women have had significantly lower rates of employment than women in Denmark and Sweden but this pattern has changed and today American women are approaching the Scandinavian level of employment. For American men, the employment rates are high and have been growing. US employees are clearly working more hours annually than employees in the other three countries and both the number of hours worked and the number of people in the labour market have increased in the United States during the 1990s.

Canada

Canada has the lowest overall rate of employment among the four countries and this is primarily because of a low female rate of employment. Like the Scandinavian countries, Canadian men have experienced a decrease in employment rates during the last two decades. While the decrease in labour market involvement in Sweden during the 1990s took place for both men and women in all age groups, it happened primarily for young and older Canadian men. This decrease combined with a low female rate of employment primarily among older Canadian women places Canada below the other three countries in rates of employment for women but slightly ahead of Sweden for men.

6 Towards a post-industrial service society

Thomas P. Boje

Introduction

The major sociological theories of the service or 'post-industrial' society were developed more than two decades ago (Bell 1976; Touraine 1969). These theories were formulated in a period when the present knowledge and information society was in its embryonic phase. Daniel Bell (1976), who has most coherently formulated a theory on the development towards a post-industrial society, combines three important trends to describe the development of this society. First, the impetus behind growth and productivity is to increase knowledge in all kinds of economic activities through the information process. Second, a shift in economic activities from goods production to service production occurs in all industrial societies. Third, a restructuring of the occupational structure is characterised by a development from manual to non-manual professional jobs requiring a large amount of scientific knowledge and information. Knowledge and technology have become even more important in determining economic and social structures. However, this theory and similar theories of the development of post-industrial service societies have been questioned by social scientists (see Chapter 1 in this volume).

The concept of service and the expansion of services have thus been criticised. For example, some theorists have postulated that growth in service jobs has been more modest than argued (Cohen and Zysman 1987; Gershuny 1978). Large amounts of the present service production were previously done either outside the formal economy as unpaid work in the households (Offe 1985: 108) or closely connected to the goods production taking place in companies (Gershuny 1978). Furthermore, a comprehensive externalisation or outsourcing of previous industrial jobs has taken place and increased the size of the service sector during the past couple of decades. According to Sayer and Walker (1992), this transition of the production from goods-producing into service-producing is primarily the result of a restructuring of the economic and social division of labour but has not fundamentally transformed the economic mechanisms of the industrial societies.

Recently, the discussion of post-industrial society has taken a new turn because of theories on the transition from an industrial society to an information society. According to Castells (1996), two major processes have transformed work and employment: the massive diffusion of new information technologies in the work place and the globalisation of the economy. Both processes have decreased the number of jobs in traditional industries – both goods-producing jobs and traditional service jobs; however, these processes have also created a significant number of new jobs based on the increased use of advanced information technology in factories and offices. Castells (1996: 171–2) argues that a new type of organisation has emerged: the network enterprise composed of several segments of autonomous systems of organisations each with specific goals. Communication within the network enterprise takes place using information technology and its main purpose is to transform information into commodities by processing knowledge. The main distinction in today's advanced economies is not between industrial and post-industrial societies, but between different forms of knowledge-based agricultural, manufacturing and service production.

A crucial aspect of the post-industrial revolution is thus the introduction of information technologies and their use in all types of social and economic activities. Instead of post-industrialism, Castells talks about informationalism, which means a production system organised 'around the principles of maximising knowledge-based productivity through the development and diffusion of information technologies' (Castells 1996: 204). The different theories of the post-industrial society have been presented in more detail in Chapter 1. In this chapter, I shall continue to analyse the different trajectories towards an information-based and knowledge-based service society.

The major indication of a shift from an industrial to a post-industrial economy is the transformation of the industrial and occupational structure. The different theories of post-industrialism argue that a new social structure is created based on service delivery, which emphasises information and knowledge. According to these theories, this development gives rise to a new social class of managers and professionals, but also a social differentiation based on educational credentials. The development towards a post-industrial social system means that industrial and occupational structures have been dominated by service production and information production; however, the path towards post-industrialism is by no means uniform. Significant historical variations can be seen among industrial countries as they move to post-industrialism depending on differences in organisational culture and institutional system (Castells 1996; Elfring 1988; Esping-Andersen 1993; Singelmann 1978a).

In all industrialised countries, the economic activities have shifted from the production of goods to the delivery of services. A decline in agricultural production and employment has been followed by a fall in manufacturing jobs. Many of the traditional companies in the automobile, construction and metal industries have been in the process of liquidation, and the labour force in these industries has been decreasing since the 1970s. The present labour market is a service labour market; half or more of the labour force is employed in private or public service industries. The more advanced and post-industrial an economy becomes, the more its production and employment is concentrated in services, and the less its production and employment is concentrated in agriculture and manufacturing (Castells and Aoyama 1994).

This is the empirical background for the classic thesis of post-industrialism;

however, some argue that many types of services are directly linked to manufacturing production or have been created in restructuring of manufacturing firms. These kinds of services depend on manufacturing; for example, Cohen and Zysman (1987) note that in the United States nearly one-quarter of the total gross national product (GNP) comes from value added by manufacturing production. Moreover, they note that in addition one-quarter comes from services directly linked to manufacturing, meaning that about half of the GNP still comes directly or indirectly from manufacturing. A similar result concerning the shift from manufacturing to service employment was found by the OECD (1994b) in a comprehensive study of job growth. The OECD study concluded that:

> a significant number of these temporary workers, classified as service sector workers, were hired by manufacturing firms who were trying to retain flexibility and cut costs. If these temporary workers working in manufacturing firms were counted as manufacturing workers, the loss of manufacturing jobs since 1991 would be cut by two-thirds.
>
> (OECD 1994b: 157–9)

The shift from manufacturing to services seems thus to be overestimated, which results in an inaccurate account of economic structures and employment structures.

This chapter will analyse the transformation process in the industrial structure using three different perspectives. First, I shall describe the overall employment restructuring between agriculture, manufacturing and services in the United States, Canada, Sweden and Denmark. This description will be detailed in an analysis of the restructuring of service employment focusing on the role of the different types of service industries in creating employment. Second, I will analyse the role of the welfare state in the restructuring of the labour market. In all advanced economies, there has been an increased demand for social services but different strategies have been used to organise how to provide these. In the social democratic Scandinavian countries the welfare state has been the major provider of social services and has played a crucial role in creating new service jobs. The liberal welfare systems, here represented by the United States and Canada, have instead given priority to market solutions. Therefore, the welfare state plays a markedly different and less intrusive role in creating new jobs and this difference is especially important in understanding the position of women in the labour market. Third, I will therefore analyse the gender composition of the labour force in the four countries. All four labour markets are sex-segregated: men primarily are employed in the goods-producing industries while women primarily are employed in the service industries. Consequently, the restructuring of the labour market with a growing emphasis on service production has different consequences for men and women.

Shifts in employment by industrial sector

In an analysis of the trends in employment growth from 1920 through 1970, Singelmann (1978b) found three distinctive patterns – employment patterns which still exist despite the globalisation of the national economies and a growing international division of both capital and labour enforced through the diffusion of information technologies and the network organisation. First, Singelmann noted a European pattern where the shift in employment from agriculture to manufacturing was followed by a progressive shift to service employment. In several of the major European labour markets – Italy, Germany and the United Kingdom – the manufacturing sector still provided more jobs than the service sector in the early 1970s (Castells 1996: 296–301). Second, there is a North American pattern with a higher proportion of people working in the service sector than in the manufacturing sector in the 1920s, but both sectors expanding their share of employment until the 1960s when manufacturing started to decline. In the 1970s, the proportion of service employees in the United States and Canada was more than twice the size of the manufacturing employees. Third, in Japan throughout the twentieth century the number employed in the manufacturing sector has been lower than in the service sector. Already by the 1920s, a decline in Japanese agricultural employment led to a significant increase in service employment and not in the manufacturing industries (Castells 1996: 282–302; Elfring 1988: 29; Singelmann 1978b: 110–12).

The structuring of the economy in three sectors – agriculture, manufacturing and services – is based on Clark's old division of economic activities into primary, secondary and tertiary production, respectively. This distinction gives an overview of the overall development in employment but might also be an obstacle in understanding the new information-based economy and its impact on social structure. The new information-based jobs can be found in all three sectors and the network enterprises combine the different types of production across the traditional sectors.[1] As illustrated in Table 6.1, the four countries included in this study had different starting points in their development into a post-industrial labour market but have converged towards an industry structure with 70 per cent or more employed in the service sector (Table 6.1).

The shifts in employment, as described by Singelmann and others, from agriculture and manufacturing to services have continued during the last several decades in all four countries. Singelmann's distinction between European and North American employment patterns has lessened during the last three decades

Table 6.1 Total employment by sectors in Canada, Denmark, Sweden and the United States, 1970–99 (%)

	Agriculture				Industry				Services			
	1970	1980	1990	1999	1970	1980	1990	1999	1970	1980	1990	1999
Canada	7.6	5.4	4.2	3.6	30.9	28.5	24.9	22.7	61.4	66.0	70.9	73.9
Denmark	11.5	7.1	5.6	3.3	37.8	30.4	27.5	26.7	50.7	62.4	66.9	70.0
Sweden	8.1	5.6	3.4	2.6	38.4	32.2	28.9	25.1	53.5	62.2	67.7	72.3
United States	4.5	3.6	2.9	2.6	34.4	30.5	26.2	23.1	61.1	65.9	70.9	74.4

Sources: OECD 1977b; 1999d; 2000a.

when comparing the United States and Canada with Denmark and Sweden. In the 1960s, the two North American economies had a larger service sector and a more restricted industrial sector compared to Denmark and Sweden. In the United States and Canada, industrial employment has never included more than one-third of the total labour force whereas industrial employment in Sweden at its height included about 45 per cent of the labour force (see OECD 1994c).

Among the OECD countries, Canada and the United States have been the front-runners in the shift from an industrial to a post-industrial service employment structure. If an economy with more than 50 per cent of the labour force employed in service industries is considered a post-industrial economy, then Canada and the United States have been post-industrial economies since the 1950s and Denmark and Sweden first reached this level of service employment in the late 1960s. In the early 1960s, Denmark still had a large proportion of the labour force employed in agriculture. In Sweden, the industrial sector was clearly more dominant than in any of the other countries. Since the late 1960s, the four countries' employment patterns have been dominated by the service industry. By the late 1990s, 70 per cent or more of the labour force was employed in the service economy in all four countries (OECD 2000a: 85). Denmark is lagging slightly behind the other countries mainly because the proportion employed in the industrial sector has remained relatively stable during the 1990s. Compared with the OECD average, the four countries included in this study clearly have a more service-dominated employment structure. On average, the OECD has a significantly higher proportion employed in agriculture (OECD 1994b: 5).

Transformation of the service labour market

Employment growth in all four countries is concentrated in the service industries and it can be expected that this growth pattern will continue. Therefore, to understand the variations in the labour market patterns in the four countries, it is of great importance to know how service employment is structured. The service industry is divided according to the different types of services produced. The typology chosen distinguishes between producer services, distributive services, personal services, and social services (Browing and Singelmann 1978). By using this classification I can elaborate on previous analyses done by Elfring (1988) and Castells (1996) and most recently the OECD has used this classification in assessing the development of employment in the service sector (OECD 2000a).

In applying this categorisation, the different types of services are divided according to the position they hold in the production chain, starting from the goods-producing process. A distinction is made between services purchased mainly by the companies and services purchased mainly by consumers. Producer services are typically services governed by decisions in companies and include a variety of services to business. Producer services are typically intermediate to the goods-producing process and can be carried out either by independent firms or within the company that wants the services. According to international industrial statistics, these services are in the first case classified as producer services and in the second case they are classified according to the main activity of the firm where they are carried out. These types of services typically have high information content. Distributive services include, on the one hand, the distribution of commodities and information and, on the other hand, the transportation of people. They concern all activities necessary for bringing commodities from the place of production to the place where they are used. Some of these services are for final consumption, but they are primarily subordinate to final consumption or production. Personal services are closely related to individual consumption and are determined by the demand of individual consumers and characterised by direct contact between the consumer and the service provider. Social services, which differ from the other forms of services in that they are typically non-market services such as health care, education and welfare, are most often provided by government activities or by non-profit private organisations. These services are for consumption by households (Browing and Singelmann 1978; Elfring 1988: 102–6).

In Table 6.2 (page 130), service employment in the four countries is divided into four groups according to the classification of the service industries described above.

In the literature on post-industrialism, producer services and social services represent the new economy with its emphasis on information and communication technology and professional care while personal services and especially distributive services are connected to the traditional economy and are associated with low-paying and low-skilled jobs (European Commission 1999). In all four countries, social services employ the largest proportion followed by distributive services with producer services and personal services far behind. Employment in producer services, however, has increased rapidly in all four economies and has doubled its proportion of total employment during the previous two decades. In the United States and Canada, producer services were large by the mid-1980s and they have been steadily growing in both countries. In Denmark and Sweden, producer services are catching up to the North American level with strong growth during the early 1990s. The expansion of producer services is closely related to the emergence of networking organisations in production and linked to the processes of vertical disintegration and outsourcing taking place in most companies (Chapter 9 in this volume).

Producer services include both financing and business services but it is primarily services offered to businesses that have expanded. In all four countries, business services have more than doubled their proportion of total employment while finance and insurance services have stalled (BLS 1998; and European Commission 1999). This strong growth in business services is, as mentioned above, mainly caused by an increase in contracting out of specific services in both manufacturing and service industries. The outsourcing of service activities include highly qualified services – marketing, financial and legal services, computing and design – as well as low-qualified services – cleaning and catering. In addition, the growing internationalisation of capital and goods has increased the need for financial services, marketing and commercial services as well as for electronic communication. All this has increased demand for employees educated and trained in different types of producer services (Carnoy 1994; Castells 1996; Noyelle 1987).

Table 6.2 Service employment by subsectors as a percentage of total employment in Canada, Denmark, Sweden and the United States, 1973–98 (%)

	Canada				Denmark				Sweden				United States			
	1971	1984	1994	1998	1974	1984	1994	1998	1973	1984	1994	1998	1970	1984	1994	1998
Producer services	6.6	13.0	15.1	16.5	6.2	7.8	11.3	11.4	5.1	6.4	11.4	12.2	8.2	13.0	14.9	15.8
Distributive services	20.8	20.4	19.6	19.4	20.5	21.3	20.5	21.1	19.8	18.3	19.0	19.4	22.4	21.5	21.2	21.2
Personal services	7.5	10.9	11.6	11.7	6.5	5.8	5.8	5.8	6.6	4.9	5.8	5.9	10.0	11.7	12.2	12.1
Social services	22.0	22.3	23.9	22.3	22.1	31.5	30.4	31.2	26.2	35.5	34.8	33.4	22.0	22.3	24.9	24.8
Total services	56.9	66.6	70.2	69.9	55.3	66.4	68.0	69.5	57.7	65.1	71.0	70.9	62.6	68.5	73.2	73.8

Sources: Canada: 1971, Castells and Aoyama 1994.
1984, 1994 and 1998, OECD 2000a: 122.
  Denmark: 1974, OECD 1991a.
1984, 1994 and 1998, OECD 2000a: 122.
  Sweden: 1973 and 1984, T. Elfring 1988: 201.
1994 and 1998, OECD 2000a: 122.
  United States: 1970, Castells and Aoyama 1994.
1984, 1994 and 1998, OECD 2000a: 122.

Notes
Producer services: financial institutions, insurance and business services.
Distributive services: trade, transport and communication.
Personal services: restaurants and hotels, recreational and cultural services, personal and household services.
Social services: social and related community services and producers of government services.

Despite the growing importance of producer services for the productivity of the information economy, this sector employs fewer workers than both distributive and social services in all four countries. Distributive services combine services such as information and communication that are crucial for the networking economy with trade and transport services that are typically considered as a type of service that dominates in less post-industrialised societies. These types of services have remained constant at about one-fifth of the total employed labour force in all four countries. Despite trade and transport including many low-productive and labour intensive jobs that could be automated by using information technology, the distributive services have employed a relatively stable proportion of the labour force during the last three decades. As the new information technologies increase, commercial transactions in both trade and transportation might be done using electronic networks and do not necessarily involve personal contacts. This might reduce the need for personnel in distributive services (European Commission 1998).

Personal services are usually considered as the most traditional and less qualified type of services, a remnant from less developed economies where domestic services were widespread. Personal services include both the traditional home domestic services, which have been in rapid decline, and the expanding leisure services such as hotels, holiday resorts and restaurants. Employment in leisure services has been growing slowly in all four countries. In Denmark and Sweden, personal services include only a minor proportion of the service employment; since the early 1970s, this type of service production has included a nearly constant proportion of the total employment in the two countries. Personal services in Canada and the United States, on the other hand, include significantly more workers and have been growing slightly as a proportion of the total labour force during the last two decades. The demand for services related to the 'leisure society' is obviously higher in North America than in Scandinavia. The proportion of persons employed in hotels and restaurants in the United States and Canada is more than twice the number employed in Denmark and Sweden (Table 6.3, page 133). Services in private households are rare in Scandinavia while North American middle-class families frequently use them (European Commission 1999). Traditionally, personal service jobs are low paying. The higher employment of personal services in Canada and the United States can be explained by the large group of high-income, middle-class families in North American societies who can afford to hire low-paid service workers and are more consumer-oriented than their Scandinavian counterpart (Esping-Andersen 1993). Furthermore, in Scandinavia the public sector has taken over a substantial proportion of the care services previously provided by households and thereby they are included in social services while a large majority of these services are marketed in the United States and Canada and thus are included in personal services.

In addition to producer services, social services characterise the new information economy. This sector includes the largest proportion of service workers in all four countries. However, the importance of social services differs in North America and Scandinavia. In both Denmark and Sweden, employment in social services represents a higher proportion of the total service sector employment than in Canada and the United States. The employment trends in social services are different in the four countries. In both Canada and the United States, the major increase in social services took place in the 1960s and was strongly affected by the civil rights movement's demand for better social protection for the poor and other vulnerable groups. However, its growth has been rather modest, if any at all, during the 1980s and the 1990s. In the two Scandinavian countries, the expansion of social services began later but on a much larger scale. The growth of employment in social services was primarily a result of growth in public sector employment. This sector reached its peak in the mid-1980s covering about – or in Sweden even more than – one-third of the total employment. Since then, public employment has declined slightly in relative terms in both Denmark and Sweden. The principal motives for this expansion of social services including education, health, social services and public administration were political rather than related to the expansion of the information society. In the late 1960s, Scandinavian left-wing parties, the women's movement, and other political movements demanded better and more comprehensive public services. In addition, the growing demand for social services is related to the reorganisation of the family structure and an enormous increase in the educational sector. The growing female labour market, which was largely motivated by the demand for labour in the public sector, re-created a demand for more services for children, the sick and the elderly (Saraceno 1997).

In all employment projections for the period from the mid-90s to the early 2000s, the large majority of new jobs are expected to be created in the service industries and within the service industries it is especially the post-industrial industries such as health services, business services and education that are expected to be the fastest growing industries (Little 1998; OECD 1994b). They are all, as argued by Castells, knowledge intensive industries, and part of the information network society (Castells 1996: 222–4). It is, however, not only industries with high-skilled jobs that are growing, but also industries with low-skilled and low-paid jobs have grown rapidly during the 1990s. It is especially in industries such as health care and in 'leisure' services where a strong growth in labour intensive, low-paid jobs is projected. Table 6.3 shows the growth rates for some of these post-industrial service industries in the four countries during the previous decade and the growth pattern confirms more or less the employment projections described above.[2]

In all four countries, business services have been the fastest growing industry among the knowledge-based industries and hotels and restaurants have the same position among the low-skilled service industries. In 1998, the proportion of the total labour force employed in business services was about the same in all four countries, although slightly higher in Sweden and the United States. In North America, leisure industries employ more than twice the proportion employed in Denmark and Sweden. The third post-industrial industry, health services, shows a more complex picture. In Denmark and Sweden, this industry has been declining since the mid-1980s while by the late 1980s it was rapidly growing in the United States. In all four countries, the health sector has been under comprehensive reorganisation with the purpose of reducing the fast growing health costs. These cost-containing efforts have obviously been more successful in the centralised

Table 6.3 Employment growth in selected post-industrial service industries in Canada, Denmark, Sweden and the United States, 1985–98 (%)

	Proportion of total employment 1998	*Annual growth 1985–91*	*Annual growth 1991–98*
Canada – total employment	100.0	1.4	1.1
Business services	7.2	6.0	4.9
Health services	7.3	–	0.5
Hotel, restaurants	6.4	3.1	1.6
Denmark – total employment	100.0	−0.5	0.9
Business services	7.2	–	4.4
Health services	5.3	−0.1	0.1
Hotel, restaurants	2.8	1.7	2.7
Sweden – total employment	100.0	0.3	−2.4
Business services	8.0	8.5	3.7
Health services	8.8	−0.6	−3.2
Hotel, restaurants	2.8	3.7	0.9
United States – total employment	100.0	1.7	1.5
Business services	8.8	2.7	8.5
Health services	8.9	4.6	2.7
Hotel, restaurants	7.3	4.2	5.9

Sources: Canada: Little 1998; Denmark: Statistics Denmark 1999; Sweden: Statistics Sweden 1998; and the United States: BLS (1999c).

publicly controlled Scandinavian health care sector than in the United States with its decentralised market-oriented health care system. From 1991 to 1998, two health industries – unclassified health services and residential care – were among the ten fastest growing industries in the United States and both these industries are dominated by low-skilled and low-paid 'female' jobs (BLS 1999b).

Employment trends in the service industries in the four countries are both converging and diverging as they move towards post-industrialisation. Today, the four countries represent some of the most developed service economies among the OECD countries. According to a recent OECD study, most OECD countries are following a common trajectory in growth of the total service sector employment while considerable differences prevail in the composition of service sector employment. The overall number of people employed in the service sector has become more uniform since the mid-1980s. This is also the case for employment in three of the analysed subsectors – producer, distributive and personal services – while the national differences for social services still remain considerable (OECD 2000a: 87–9). This pattern holds true comparing North America and Scandinavia.

The North American path towards post-industrialism includes a highly developed service economy and growth in the 'post-industrial' service industries – producer services and social services – combined with a continuously high and relatively stable employment in the traditional service sectors. Employment in personal services has also increased. From the early 1970s to the late 1990s, employment in the post-industrial service industries increased in Canada from 29 per cent to 39 per cent and increased in the United States from 30 per cent to 41 per cent of the total employment. The major part of this increase was in producer services while social services have changed very little.

The Scandinavian path toward a post-industrial service economy started later and was primarily focused on growth in social services initiated by the welfare state. During the early 1990s, producer services began growing and in Sweden this sector has rapidly increased and reached the North American level in 2000 (SCB 2000). From the early 1970s to the late 1990s, employment in post-industrial service industries increased in Denmark from 28 per cent to 43 per cent and increased in Sweden from 31 per cent to 46 per cent. Both countries thus have surpassed the US level of post-industrial service employment and the growth patterns of the post-industrial sector have become more similar. In the 1990s, the expansion of post-industrial services in both Scandinavian countries was primarily caused by growth in producer services while the social services have lost momentum and stagnated in recent years. The main reason for this change is a virtual hiring freeze in public service employment in the Scandinavian countries since the early 1990s.

According to the OECD study mentioned earlier, the international differences in the level and composition of service employment are caused by a variety of structural and institutional variables. The most important variables seem to be the level of income, the employment pattern for women, and the size of the welfare state. Income level here measured by GDP per capita has a positive effect on the size of all four service subsectors. This relationship, however, is especially strong for producer and social services indicating the higher demand for business and professional services as well as caring services in the more developed economies. Furthermore, a positive correlation exists between social service jobs and the size of the welfare state. In Scandinavia, the high number of social service jobs reflects a political priority that supports public provision for social services. Moreover, the growth in social services, especially in the United States, is primarily market-driven and related to the high level of service consumption in the well-off middle class. Finally, the size of the total service sector is correlated with the size of the female labour force. For producer services, personal services, and especially social services, a clear positive relationship exists between female employment and the size of these sectors. (see OECD 2000a: 97–105). In the remainder of this chapter the impact of the welfare state on service industry employment and the relationship between service employment and the female pattern of employment will be analysed.

The welfare state and the service labour market

It is in the composition of social services – health, education, social welfare – that we found the most profound differences between the OECD economies. These differences are primarily related to the role of the welfare state in each country. Since the late 1950s, most OECD economies have witnessed a continuous growth in the proportion of total economic resources channelled through the public sector. These economic resources primarily have been used to meet the welfare obligations of the society. The obligations are mainly related to health care, education, and social welfare of the population and the economic resources are allocated partly to finance social caring services, and partly used as income supplements for the sick, elderly and unemployed.

The modern welfare states differ in both type and scope of the intervention in the labour markets and the individual households. A variety of welfare typologies have been developed in order to characterise the relationship between the welfare state and the labour market in different countries. In nearly all typologies, the two North American welfare systems represent a liberal market-regulated type and the two Scandinavian welfare systems represent a social democratic political-regulated type (Castles and Mitchell 1990; Esping-Andersen 1990 and 1999; Korpi and Palme 1998; Lewis 1992; Sainsbury 1996). In the liberal welfare system, the market plays a crucial role in determining the employment conditions while the welfare state has been mainly passive in creating new jobs. The public expenditures in the liberal welfare regimes are restricted and this type of welfare system relies on more privately organised welfare than the other types of welfare systems. Consequently, most of the job growth related to social services takes place in the private service sector. In the social democratic welfare regime, on the other hand, new jobs have traditionally been created within public services. According to the typologies, this type of welfare state has fundamentally transformed the labour market and creation of jobs is thus more dependent on the fiscal policy of the government than motivated by market-related profitability. Moreover, in the social democratic welfare regimes employment regulation is primarily determined through negotiation in tripartite bargaining institutions rather than by market forces (Esping-Andersen 1993).

The private–public mix of service employment thus is an important indicator differentiating the two types of market systems included in this study. During the 1970s and the early 1980s, the welfare state was the major job machine in both Denmark and Sweden while it played a minor role in job creation in Canada and the United States. In Canada and the United States, it was the private service industries that caused the increase of service employment (Table 6.4).

In the late 1980s and the early 1990s, public consumption stalled in the two Scandinavian countries (see Chapter 4 in this volume) and this changed the growth pattern in service employment. In both Denmark and Sweden, the public sector lost its momentum and the private service industries created most of the job opportunities. During the same period, in Canada and the United States, the proportion employed in the public services has been constant or even in decline in the United States.

In 1997, the public sector in Denmark and Sweden employed slightly more than 30 per cent of the total labour force while only 13 per cent of the United States labour force was employed in the public sector. Canada held a middle position with about one-fifth of the labour force employed in the public sector. Despite the stagnation or even decrease in the number of public employees, Denmark

Table 6.4 The private–public employment mix in service industries in Canada, Denmark, Sweden and the United States, 1960–97 (%)

	1960	1975	1980	1985	1990	1994	1997
Canada							
Total services	54.1	64.6	66.0	69.5	71.1	73.3	74.0
Private services	41.5	44.3	47.2	49.6	51.7	52.9	55.1
Public services	12.6	20.3	18.8	19.9	19.4	20.4	18.9
Denmark							
Total services	44.8	58.0	62.4	65.2	66.9	68.1	69.5
Private services	32.7	35.2	34.1	35.5	36.5	37.1	38.6
Public services	12.1	23.6	28.3	29.7	30.4	31.0	30.9
Sweden							
Total services	44.0	57.1	62.2	65.3	67.3	71.6	71.3
Private services	31.2	31.6	31.5	31.6	35.7	39.6	40.6
Public services	12.8	25.5	30.7	32.7	31.6	32.0	30.7
United States							
Total services	56.2	65.3	65.9	68.8	70.9	73.1	73.4
Private services	41.4	47.5	49.4	54.0	56.3	58.6	60.2
Public services	14.8	17.8	16.5	14.8	14.6	14.5	13.2

Source: OECD 1999c.

and Sweden still have the largest proportion of public employees among the OECD countries. The United States, on the other hand, is one of the OECD countries with the lowest proportion of public employees (OECD 1998a). This picture was different three decades ago. Then, the public sector was nearly the same size in all four countries as a proportion of the total employed labour force. In the early 1960s, the public sector included about 12 per cent of the labour force in Canada, Sweden and Denmark and even more in the United States, and all four countries were among the OECD countries with the highest proportion of public employees (OECD 1999c).

The difference among the countries in the private–public mix of service employment emerged during the late 1970s. Here the public sector in Denmark and Sweden experienced a tremendous growth and reached today's high level of employment by the mid-1980s. This growth in public employment occurred simultaneously with the relative stagnation in employment in the private service sectors. In 1985, the Swedish public sector included even more employees than the private service sector.

In Canada and the United States, the composition of the service sector in private and public employment was almost identical in the late 1960s. Since then, US public employment has been declining as a proportion of the total employment and by 1997 was less than one-fifth of the total service employment. In Canada most service jobs have also been created in private service industries. In the early 1970s, public sector employment in Canada increased nearly at the same rate as in the Scandinavian countries. However, this increase stopped after a few years and the Canadian level of public employment remained at about 20 per cent of total employment throughout most of the 1980s and 1990s.

The impact of the welfare state on the share of service employment is especially strong for social services (OECD 2000: 103). Inside the social service industries – including public administration, health, education and welfare services – marked differences can also be found in the public–private mix of employment between the two welfare systems examined in this book. The difference between the two welfare systems in the composition of the labour force in social services is illustrated for Denmark, Sweden and the United States in Table 6.5.

As already noted, the total service industries in Denmark, Sweden and the United States make up almost the same proportion of the employed labour force – about 70 per cent by the late 1990s. Furthermore, the overall proportion of people employed in public administration, education and health in Sweden and the United States is similar. Denmark differs slightly from the other two countries with a higher proportion of people employed in public administration and a lower proportion of people employed in health services. The Danish health sector has been restructured and severe cutbacks including reductions in the number of employees took place during the late 1980s and most of the 1990s. As far as employment in welfare services is concerned, however, the three countries differ markedly. The proportion of employees working in Danish and Swedish welfare services is five times higher than in the United States. In both the Scandinavian countries, public services for children and the elderly are more comprehensive than in the United States and more people are employed in different types of municipal social services that support vulnerable social groups – unemployed, handicapped, broken families, etc.

Except for welfare services, the relative size of employment in the social service industries is thus similar in the two welfare systems. It is in the public–private

Table 6.5 The private–public mix in composition of the labour force in the social service industries in Denmark, Sweden and the United States, 1998 (%)

	Proportion of total employment			Proportion in public employment of total employment in the subsectors		
	Denmark	*Sweden*	*United States*	*Denmark*	*Sweden*	*United States*
Total employment	100.0	100.0	100.0	37.8	36.8	15.1
All services	69.5	70.9	73.8	50.9	49.2	19.9
Public adm.	6.6	4.3	5.1	96.1	98.9	100.0
Education	7.9	8.9	8.9	98.9	87.0	80.6
Health	5.6	8.8	8.6	84.6	90.2	11.5
Welfare service	12.2	12.5	2.2	98.5	92.1	12.1

Sources: Statistics Sweden 1998, BLS Employment and Earnings 1998; Statistics Denmark, Arbejdsmarked, 1999: 9; OECD 2000a: 122.

composition of the labour force in the four social service industries that we find the explanation for the significantly larger public employment in Scandinavian countries. Furthermore, it is primarily in the public–private mix of health and welfare services that the two systems differ while the proportion of public employees is nearly the same in public administration and education.[3] In both health and welfare services, more than 88 per cent of the US labour force is privately employed whereas this figure is only 10–15 per cent in Denmark and Sweden – and even less for Danish welfare services.

In the early 1960s, public sector employment had nearly the same proportion in the liberal welfare systems as in the social democratic welfare systems (Table 6.5). Political considerations changed, however, and consequently so did the welfare systems' labour force by the mid-1970s. The primary motive behind the tremendous expansion of public sector employment in the social democratic welfare systems was an increasing social commitment to create an egalitarian and universal welfare system with a high level of social benefits and equal access to education, care and health services. During the late 1980s and early 1990s, the conditions for the social democratic welfare systems changed again. The economic globalisation and the establishment of the EU monetary system have led to a decrease in Scandinavian welfare system spending and have changed the role of the public sector in the labour market. In Denmark, expansion of the public sector stopped in the mid-1980s and in Sweden, expansion of the public sector stopped in the early 1990s. In both cases, the cuts in public spending were part of the EU harmonisation and it resulted in a stagnation or decrease in the public sector's proportion of the total employment as private entrepreneurs grew in importance in providing social services.

Employment pattern by industries for men and women

During the past 20 to 30 years, still more women have entered the labour force and this has changed the gender composition of the labour market from being male dominated to being more balanced between men and women. Women have become more integrated in all the advanced industrial labour markets and several studies have shown that sex segregation is decreasing and this has been particularly pronounced during the last two decades (Charles 1992; Jacobs and Lim 1992; Jonung 1996; Nermo 1999). The increasing service sector has been a principal impetus behind the growth in female employment. Social services and to some extent producer services have driven this development (OECD 2000a: 104). In this section, I shall briefly analyse how the industrial restructuring of the four labour markets included in the study has influenced the number of women and men in the work force.

In 1997–98, the proportion of women employed was 45 to 46 per cent in Canada, Denmark and the United States and 48 per cent in Sweden. As discussed in Chapter 5, the level of female and male employment has converged. With the expansion of the post-industrial economy, significantly more women are employed not only in the traditional female service industries but also in previously male-dominated industries in both goods and service production. (Table 6.6).

Table 6.6 The proportion of women employed in major industrial sectors in Canada, Denmark, Sweden and the United States, 1980 and 1997 (%)

	Canada		Denmark		Sweden		United States	
	1980	1997	1981	1997	1980	1997	1980	1997
Agriculture	22.9	28.5	26.7	22.2	24.9	24.8	19.5	24.7
Mining	11.9	14.7	16.0	13.9	6.7	12.5	13.7	14.5
Manufacturing	26.9	28.2	31.0	31.5	26.9	26.6	31.5	32.1
Utilities	15.5	24.3	18.8	22.2	16.2	24.2	19.8	21.9
Construction	8.7	11.0	10.6	9.6	9.1	7.8	8.0	9.4
Wholesale, retail, and hotel and restaurant	47.0	48.0	45.8	42.9	51.6	46.2	47.3	47.6
Transport/comm	21.7	26.2	23.3	27.0	27.5	30.3	26.6	29.9
Finance/business	51.8	51.1	47.8	45.9	45.2	42.4	54.5	52.5
Community, social and personal Services	56.4	63.4	64.9	67.1	69.8	73.2	58.1	62.1
All activities	39.6	45.1	44.5	45.6	45.0	47.9	42.4	46.2

Sources: OECD 1999c; and for Denmark: Statistics Denmark 1994: 3; 1998: 31.

In all four countries, traditional employment patterns still exist. Men dominate in agriculture, manufacturing and construction while women are overrepresented in community, social and personal services. The concentration of women in the service industries is highest in Sweden while it is lowest in Canada and the United States with Denmark placed in a middle position. Looking at the development over the last two decades, the proportion of women has increased in all major industrial sectors in the Canadian and the US labour markets except for finance and business services. It is also in Canada and the United States that overall female employment has increased the most among the four countries. For both Denmark and Sweden, the proportion of women employed in community, social and personal services – primarily the public sector – has increased, while their representation has declined in wholesale, retail, hotel and restaurant work and in finance and business. The proportion of women employed in the goods-producing industries in the two Scandinavian countries has not changed much from 1980 to 1997. In both countries, however, overall female employment was already high by the early 1980s.

Sex composition of the employment in the industrial sectors is, at a more detailed level, even more diverse and no clear conclusions can be drawn (Table 6.7). The goods-producing industries are male-dominated. Here Swedish women represent only 22 per cent of the labour force while their proportion in the other three countries is about one-fourth and even more in Denmark. The high proportion of women working in Danish and US manufacturing industries can be explained by an over-representation of food producing and textile industries in these two countries. These industries traditionally have a large proportion of female employees.

Table 6.7 The proportion of women employed in industrial sectors in Canada, Denmark, Sweden and the United States in 1998 (%)

	Canada	Denmark	Sweden	United States
Agriculture	31.2	23.5	29.8	24.9
Other primary industries	13.9	8.7	9.3	14.4
Good-producing industries	24.0	27.2	22.4	25.2
Utilities	24.2	20.9	21.4	–
Manufacturing	28.2	33.8	26.5	32.1
Construction	11.0	9.6	8.4	9.4
Service-producing industries	52.9	54.5	57.7	54.0
Transport and Communication	26.2	27.0	29.1	28.8
Wholesale	28.6	30.3	29.3	29.6
Retail trade	49.7	46.5	51.3	51.2
Finance and insurance	68.2	52.3	57.0	58.4
Real estate	45.0	33.7	32.2	–
Business Services	43.3	45.4	39.8	37.2
Educational Services	62.4	59.3	65.9	63.7
Health and Welfare Services	78.6	83.7	86.6	78.7
Food and accommodation	59.0	51.9	52.8	49.0
Other Services	58.3	53.8	77.2	68.9
Public administration	43.6	47.3	49.5	44.5
All activities	45.1	45.7	47.8	46.2

Sources: Statistics Canada 1997; Statistics Denmark 1999; Statistics Sweden, 1998. For the United States: Bureau of Labor Statistics 2000: 421; and my own calculations.

Note
The industrial classification for the United States is slightly different from the other countries. Utilities are included in Transport and Communication and real estate is included in Finance and Insurance. Note that the Canadian and the US figures are from 1997.

Women are overrepresented in the service-producing sector in all four countries but most of all in Sweden where about 58 per cent of the employees in the service sector are women compared with 53–55 per cent in Denmark, the United States and Canada. Inside the service sector, women are overrepresented in social services – educational, health and welfare service – and in part of personal services – cleaning, domestic services, etc. Men dominate transportation, wholesale and real estate employment. In the remaining part of the service sector, employment is distributed equally among men and women.

In all countries, the most female-dominated industries are health and welfare services. In Sweden, women represent 87 per cent of the labour force in health and welfare services. In Denmark, women represent 84 per cent of the labour force in health and welfare services. In Canada and the United States, women make up about 79 per cent of the labour force in these industries. Among the other service industries, the picture is more complex. In Sweden and the United States, women are overrepresented in educational services and personal services (other services). In Canada, women are overrepresented in finance and insurance.

In the fast growing business services, on the other hand, women are underrepresented and this is particularly the case in Sweden and the United States – the two countries where this industry has been especially dynamic during the 1990s (see Table 6.3).

Women's employment and the public sector

Comparing the gender composition of the labour force and the growth pattern in industrial employment illustrates how the male and female workforces have been differently affected by employment restructuring.[4] The decline of employment in agriculture and manufacturing industries has decreased the possibility for employment for men whereas the expansion of the service sector has increased the possibility of employment for women. The entry of women into the labour market took place simultaneously with a strong growth in the service industries and with a declining male labour force. Women were recruited in large numbers to the new service jobs and this has continued throughout the 1990s as described in the previous section. The expansion of the service sector increased female employment but it also created a labour market clearly more structured by sex (Nermo 1999: 108).

In this respect, the expansion of the public sector has a significant importance for the growing involvement of women in paid labour by providing jobs for women and by taking over some of the informal care obligations previously fulfilled by women. The expansion of the public sector is thus important in order to understand the female patterns of employment. The relationship between women's rate of employment and the size of the public sector among the OECD countries is illustrated in Figure 6.1.

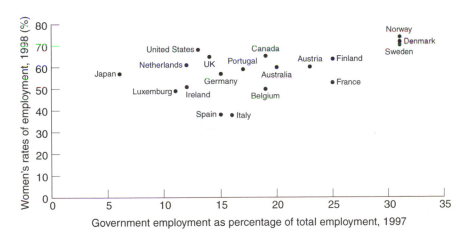

Figure 6.1 The relationship between women's rates of employment and government employment as a percentage of total employment among OECD countries, late 1990s

The levels of government employment and female employment are related but not strongly correlated. The level of public employment is only one of several dimensions explaining a high female rate of employment. In some countries with a low level of female employment – Spain, Italy, Ireland, Luxembourg – there is a low level of public employment as expected. Other European countries – Germany, Portugal, Austria – hold a middle position for both female rates of employment and levels of government employment. In the Scandinavian countries, a high level of female employment is associated with a large public sector. In the United States, the United Kingdom, the Netherlands and to some extent Canada, however, this is not the case: a relatively high level of female employment is combined with a low level of government employment. The proportion of women employed in the US labour market is nearly the same as in the Scandinavian countries and this is the case for the service industries as well. In the United States, most services are carried out by private firms and consequently the larger part of the female labour force is employed in the private sector while a majority of service workers in Scandinavia are public employees (Table 6.4). Therefore, in the Scandinavian countries the welfare state has played a significant role in creating jobs for women. In the liberal market-oriented countries, on the other hand, jobs for women have been created primarily in the private service industries.

Industrial structure and sex segregation

Measured as a proportion of men and women employed in the goods-producing and service-producing industries, Denmark – with the exception of the large proportion of women in health and welfare services – is the most sex equitable labour market of the four countries and Sweden is the most segregated labour market (Table 6.7). For Denmark, this result is contrary to the results of most studies analysing sex-segregation cross-nationally. According to these studies, the Danish and Swedish labour markets tend to be more sex segregated than Canada and the United States (Charles 1992; Esping-Andersen 1993; Rosenfeld and Kalleberg 1991).

Generally, these studies find that most industrial labour markets are still highly segregated by sex and that the level of sex segregation tends to be highest in labour markets with a high level of female participation. In a study of 12 industrial countries, Roos (1985) found that Japan had the lowest level of sex segregation while Sweden had the highest level. Others have confirmed this result and found that Greece, Japan and Portugal have low levels of sex segregation. These countries are characterised by relatively small service sectors, a large proportion of self-employed, and low rates of female employment. The countries with high levels of sex segregation – Scandinavia, the Netherlands and Austria – are characterised by highly centralised industrial relations systems and/or large service sectors with a high concentration of female employment (Charles 1992: 497–8). The variation in sex segregation between national labour markets seems thus to be related to specific institutional characteristics of the post-industrial economies – the size of the service sector, how the welfare states are organised, and the type of regulation of industrial relations (Nermo 1999). These characteristics tend to counteract the integrative factor of a high level of female labour force participation and in Scandinavian countries the impact of their 'women-friendly' welfare policies and egalitarian culture.

From previous research, it is possible to conclude that women have been more integrated into the labour market but their entry into the labour force has been concentrated in relatively few industries and occupational categories and it has therefore not changed the level of sex segregation to a great degree. This result has been confirmed in a recent analysis done by OECD (2000a) (see Table 6.8).

Table 6.8 shows that the Danish and Swedish labour markets are clearly more segregated than the two North American labour markets. Among the 27 OECD countries included in the ranking, Canada and the United States have the least sex-segregated labour market next to Japan.[5] Denmark holds a middle position while Sweden, Finland, Norway and Spain have relatively high sex segregation. It is difficult to explain these differences. According to OECD (2000a: 95), neither the size of the total service sector nor the female rates of employment seem to have any explanatory value. Several countries – the United States, Canada, Australia and France – are characterised by a low level of sex segregation in combination with a large service sector and relatively high rates of female employment (Figure 6.1). Charles argues that the United States has been able to overcome the sex-segregation effects of a large service sector and high rates of women's labour force participation because of its 'egalitarian ideological climate and a highly pluralist form of interest intermediation' (Charles 1992: 498). The size of the public sector seems to be an important factor when explaining levels of sex segregation. Among the OECD countries, a clear correlation exists between the size of government employment and the level of sex segregation (Figure 6.2, page 144).

This relationship is most obvious in Scandinavian countries where high sex segregation is combined with a high level of public employment and in Japan where low sex segregation and a low level of public employment co-exist. Also in the

Table 6.8 The level of sex segregation in Canada, Denmark, Sweden and the United States measured by distribution of employment of sectors in 1998 (dissimilarity indices[a])

Country	Index values	Rank among OECD countries[b]
Canada	14.8	2
Denmark	18.6	17
Sweden	20.6	21
United States	15.3	3

Source: OECD 2000a: 95.

Notes

a The dissimilarity index indicates the percentage of the specified group who have to change industrial sector in order to equalise the employment of men and women in a sector.

b The countries are ranked from the least segregated (first) to the most segregated (twenty-seventh) among the included 27 OECD countries.

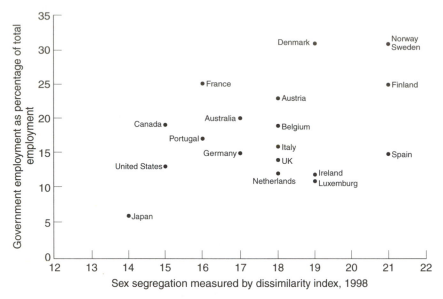

Figure 6.2 The relationship between sex segregation and government employment as percentage of total employment among the OECD countries, late 1990s

Sources: OECD 1999c; 2000a: 95.

United States, low sex segregation and a low level of public employment exist. Canada, however, has been able to combine a medium-size public sector with low sex segregation. In addition, Denmark deviates from the pattern by combining a high level of public employment with a medium level of sex segregation. The Danish level of sex segregation is more in line with Continental European countries than with the other Scandinavian countries. The larger proportion of Danish women employed in the manufacturing industries might be one explanation. The decrease in employment growth in the Danish public sector since the mid-1980s, which has forced women to find other employment alternatives (these alternatives primarily are found in private service industries), might also explain the lower Danish level of sex segregation.

Conclusion

Canada and the United States on the one hand, and Denmark and Sweden on the other hand, represent two different welfare regimes and institutional systems for regulating labour markets. Nevertheless, the overall trends in transformation of the labour market structure are in many ways the same for all four countries: employment in the service industries has increased and employment in agriculture and manufacturing has decreased. Employment declined both absolutely and relatively for agriculture in all countries while the development in employment for manufacturing industries showed a more complex pattern. In both Canada and the United States, the level of employment in manufacturing industries has been stable, but with respect to the rapidly growing service industries, it has relatively declined (OECD 1994b). In Denmark and Sweden, employment in the manufacturing industries has declined both in number and relatively from 1970 through 1998 and most dramatically in Sweden in the early 1990s (OECD 1999d, 1999e).

Today all four countries are post-industrial. This has been the case for Canada and the United States since 1970 and Denmark and Sweden have rapidly approached the North American level during the 1970s and early 1980s. Despite the convergence in the composition of the labour force in the four countries, significant differences still exist. In the Scandinavian countries, social services have a more dominant position than in the two North American economies whereas the situation is reversed for producer and personal services. The private–public mix in service employment is markedly different in the two types of labour market systems with the public sector in a more dominant position in the two Scandinavian service labour markets than in the US and Canadian service sectors. Finally, the two American labour markets are some of the least sex segregated among the OECD countries with high female rates of employment while the Scandinavian countries are more sex segregated.

The registered variations between the four countries in patterns of employment for men and women have several explanations. First, there has been significantly higher job growth in the North American than in the Scandinavian service sector throughout the entire period from 1970 to 2000. Even during the most serious downturns in the early 1990s, both the Canadian and the US economy created new jobs in the service industries while service employment in Scandinavia was in decline. In a period where large numbers of women have entered the labour force, this high overall growth in employment has created more jobs for women in nearly all types of services in the United States and Canada compared with the two Scandinavian countries.

Second, the service sector employment is different in each country. Here the private–public mix of employment seems to be the most important factor. In the social democratic welfare systems in Denmark and Sweden, employment growth was concentrated in the public service sector up to the mid-1980s when it stopped and the private service industries began creating new service jobs, but at a significantly lower level. From the mid-1960s to the mid-1980s, the public sector accounted for more than 75 per cent of all new jobs for women. A broader range of jobs for Scandinavian women in the private service economy first appeared in the 1990s. During the same period, the US public sector accounted for only 20 per cent of the new jobs for women (Esping-Andersen 1990; OECD 1989b). For American women, it has meant that they have been forced to penetrate a broader variety of industries and occupations (Esping-Andersen 1990; Noyelle 1987).

The US and Canadian service labour markets seem to be more open to mobility and career advancement for female employees than the Scandinavian labour markets. Some studies argue that women in Scandinavian countries have been forced into narrow job positions in the public sector with restricted possibilities for labour market mobility and career advancement (see Esping-Andersen 1990: 212; Rosenfeld and Kalleberg 1991). On the other hand, the large public sector in Scandinavian countries might indicate that social services have been given high political priority because the government provides these services instead of the market. Social service jobs are suited for women because they are often part-time jobs, which make it easier for women to reconcile work with caring obligations in the family.

The higher level of sex segregation in Scandinavia might be seen as a consequence of the comprehensive build-up of the public sector, but this development has, on the other hand, radically strengthened the economic, social and political position of women in society. Furthermore, a high level of sex segregation in the labour market does not necessarily mean a high level of sex inequality. Rosenfeld and Kalleberg (1991: 214) found in a study of sex inequality in highly industrialised countries that sex segregation and income equality between men and women are positively correlated. Some of the more sex-segregated labour markets – the Scandinavian countries – have greater gender equality in income than the less sex-segregated labour markets such as the United States and Canada. One explanation for this relationship, according to Rosenfeld and Kalleberg, is that these countries are characterised by a large female-dominated public sector where income equality is more pronounced than in the private service sector. Another explanation might be that the Scandinavian countries have the most comprehensive collective bargaining systems and strong labour unions. These unions aggressively fight for equal wage distribution between men and women (Chapter 2).

7 Occupational changes and education

Lars H. Hansen

Introduction

In the preceding two chapters the employment and industrial structures of Canada, Denmark, Sweden and the United States were examined. In this chapter, the analysis will be continued by an examination of the countries' occupational structures and overall levels of educational attainment. However, in order to prepare the ground for the coming empirical analyses a few pages will be devoted to a discussion of the possible development towards a post-industrial occupational structure.

Essentially, the occupational structure is an indicator of society's division of labour. It represents the distribution of persons in jobs, that is, each job's proportion of total employment. Since there are thousands of different jobs an occupation is in most cases defined as a bundle of jobs with similar tasks (e.g., engineer, nurse, secretary), and the occupational structure is mostly described by aggregating occupations into occupational groups (e.g., professionals, clerks). Provided that we have a notion of what kind of jobs are to be regarded as, for instance, post-industrial, the occupational structure can be used to compare countries concerning their level of economic development.

One major argument of the post-industrial theorists is that occupations based on theoretical knowledge will become more and more common concomitantly with a decrease in the number of workers in traditional manual occupations. Daniel Bell, for instance, argues that the advent of a post-industrial society will mean a growing demand for advanced services provided by professional workers:

> If an industrial society is defined by the quantity of goods as marking a standard of living, the post-industrial society is defined by the quality of life as measured by the services and amenities – health, education, recreation, and the arts – which are now deemed desirable and possible for everyone.
>
> (Bell 1976: 127)

More recently Harold Perkin (1996: 1) has declared that the '. . . modern world is the world of the professional expert. Just as pre-industrial society was dominated by landlords and industrial society by capitalists, so post-industrial society is dominated by professionals'. Assertions such as those by Bell and Perkin need, however, some clarification. For instance, who are the professionals? Can they be regarded as a specific class in modern society? And, further, what does domination mean in this context? According to Perkin the concept of professional expertise must be widened to include such positions as bureaucrats and managers besides professional workers such as doctors and lawyers. Conceived of this way, professional experts undoubtedly make up the most influential occupational group in modern society. Whether this group can be conceived of as a class remains, however, open to question.

Manuel Castells (1996: 243) argues that a new division of labour will characterise what he calls '. . . the emerging informational paradigm'. In this new division of labour Castells identifies six worker categories: commanders (strategic decision-makers), researchers, designers, integrators (middle management), operators, and the 'operated'.[1] Taken together, the first four categories can more or less be regarded as the equivalent of Perkin's professional expertise. The operators are workers who execute tasks under their own initiative, while the 'operated' are mere human robots who execute pre-programmed tasks. Hence, also here we find an image of a society in which highly skilled and highly educated workers will be dominating the division of labour.

That occupations based on theoretical knowledge will be dominating post-industrial society is maybe the most frequent prediction by the post-industrial theorists. However, we also find those who argue that lower-level categories will grow quite substantially. Castells (1996: 229), for instance, contends that even though more and more occupations will require higher skills and advanced education there will also be a growth among the low-skill occupations. Further, there are forecasts of an even greater growth in the number of low-skilled and low-paying service jobs. Bluestone and Harrison (1988: 72), for instance, contend that '. . . the reality of the new service economy entails a great many low-paying jobs and a much smaller layer of high-paying ones'. Therefore, we can conjure up a picture of a post-industrial occupational structure consisting primarily of 'good' jobs and 'bad' jobs. Logically, the simultaneous increase in good and bad jobs must lead to a reduction in the proportion of 'average' jobs (this development has sometimes been called the 'declining middle' or an 'hourglass economy'). The most obvious problem with this picture is the arbitrary choice of which jobs are to be designated as good or bad respectively. The total quality or desirability of a job is a compound of a number of elements: payment, benefits, employment security, kind of work, risk of injuries, opportunities for advancement and interaction with co-workers and supervisors (Meisenheimer 1998: 23). To this, we can add status or prestige as a significant feature of a job's quality. Even if we had access to data on the characteristics of different jobs (which we in most cases do not), it is nevertheless very difficult to give individual jobs a good/bad rating since a given job's desirability to a great extent depends upon individual preferences. Also, a person's family situation (e.g., parents of young children) can have an impact on whether a job is perceived as good or bad. Therefore, it seems wise to avoid the good versus bad jobs distinction altogether, and use occupational titles without any attached subjective judgements whatsoever.[2]

A comprehensive system for higher formal education is a prerequisite for a continual growth of occupations based on theoretical knowledge, and a large number of today's occupations are only accessible via the possession of specific types of diploma, something which has been labelled professionalism or credentialism (Abbott 1988; Brint 1993; Collins 1979). Consequently, such occupations are called professions (sometimes also a group of less professionalised occupations are called semi-professions).[3] Most observers of the highly educated occupations agree specifically on one point, that is, that they have been growing rather dramatically during the last decades (Brint 1994: 3). However, this growth is not necessarily merely the result of an increasing demand for highly educated people. Partly, it is the consequence of a prolongation of the required length of schooling for some occupations (e.g., primary school teachers and nurses), and, also, a result of the growth of the educational system itself, that is, that an increased output of people with higher education is expected to generate a high growth rate of businesses that primarily employ people with higher education (Sohlman 1996: 28ff.).

As indicated above, on the other side of the coin we find the projected growth of service occupations that do not require any specific education. Of course, this is a very extensive group of occupations that covers a wide array of different activities. Restaurants, hotels, shops, petrol-stations and cinemas are all establishments within which we find these kinds of job, but also such tasks as caring for children and the elderly belong to the category. Many of these services are undoubtedly low-pay and low-status without possibilities for advancement. Part-time work is also a common denominator and women are overrepresented in many of these occupations. It is, however, in line with earlier arguments, too simplistic to equate these kinds of service with bad jobs. Child care, for instance, can be organised in many ways, either by using unskilled (e.g., private childminders) or skilled personnel (e.g., public pre-primary school teachers). Also, many jobs in this category are performed by people who are self-employed (e.g., hairdressers and shop salespersons), something which – for many people – is rather desirable.

The coexistence of sometimes contradictory views regarding the evolution of a post-industrial occupational structure can be understood if we take into account that different occupational categories can be subject to vastly different forces and constraints. A couple of examples will clarify this argument. First, we have those occupations that commonly are labelled professions. By virtue of their monopoly of a specific field of knowledge they can control who has the right to perform a certain kind of work. Therefore, professionals do not have to compete for jobs with those who do not have the proper credentials. For instance, the labour market for medical doctors is restricted to medical doctors only. However, a profession can be challenged by the sudden rise of an occupation that lays claim to some of the tasks previously performed by the professionals (e.g., chiropractors). Whether a profession chooses to defend or let go of its privilege depends on a number of factors. For example, if there is a shortage of medical doctors on the labour market, then the medical profession will have great trouble defending its monopoly concerning tasks that can be performed by registered nurses (e.g., giving injections or carrying out the initial screening of patients). Such a situation can result in quite considerable changes in the occupational structure in a rather short period of time.

Second, at the other end of the job hierarchy we find a large collection of occupations that are totally open to competition since they do not require any specific education whatsoever. In this group there are jobs both within manufacturing (e.g., assemblers) and services (e.g., cleaners). The growth or reduction of these kinds of job is clearly subject to other forces than is the case among the professional groups. For instance, whether a manufacturing firm chooses to employ manual assembly workers or invest in highly automated machinery has to do with the wage level, the type of production, and the supply of either unskilled labour or technicians and engineers. Thus, it is possible to argue that different types of social mechanisms affect different strata in the occupational structure, which means that several processes (e.g., shedding of manual labour and specialisation) can be active at the same time on the same labour market but affecting different occupational categories.

We should expect not only differentiation within national labour markets though, but also, according to Gøsta Esping-Andersen (1990: 192), '. . . that nations are following distinctly different 'post-industrial' trajectories; that, indeed, we confront a variety of future employment-scenarios'. Thus, following the country clustering devised by Esping-Andersen (see Chapter 1) the occupational structures of Canada and the United States should differ from those of the Scandinavian countries. The North American countries are expected to have large proportions of managers and low-skill private sector service workers, while Denmark and Sweden's occupational structures should be biased towards public sector professionals and personal service workers. Following this line of thought, the notion of a declining middle is especially applicable to the American case.

Overall, the picture of a post-industrial occupational structure is manifold. It is supposed to be dominated by occupations based on theoretical knowledge, but also to display a rather large proportion of unskilled service occupations. Traditional industrial production work is supposed to be quite meagre since production facilities are being either automated or moved to low-wage countries. Among countries that can be regarded as post-industrial we may, however, find distinctly different occupational structures depending on institutional and cultural factors. In order to try out these propositions this chapter will present an in-depth picture of the four countries' occupational structures. Since two of the main features of a post-industrial development are women's increased labour force participation and the growth of higher education, special attention will be given to the way in which women are distributed in the occupational structure and the levels of educational attainment.

The occupational structure

If one adopts the more optimistic picture of the post-industrial change process, that is, that repetitive manual labour is becoming more and more rare and is gradually being replaced by a whole set of highly skilled occupations based on theoretical knowledge, this ought to be reflected in both the development of the occupational structure and in the level of educational attainment. In this section, to begin with, we will describe, compare, analyse and discuss the occupational structures of our four countries. We start at a rather crude level of analysis using data from the LABORSTA database of the ILO.[4] Table 7.1 shows the development of the distribution of employment among seven major occupational groups from the mid-1980s to the mid-1990s. Overall, the development in the four countries during this period seems to confirm the proposition of a continual growth in the professional and technical occupations together with a concomitant decrease in agricultural and manual occupations.

Manual jobs in the traditional high-volume enterprises have been decreasing in most OECD countries since the 1960s, and our four countries do not deviate from that pattern. Production and transport occupations have a downward tendency in all four countries, and in the mid-1990s they constitute approximately one-fourth of all occupations. Also, agricultural occupations have continued to diminish their share of employment. In Canada, Denmark and the United States clerical occupations have had approximately the same proportion of employment during the period in question (the Swedish data are not fully comparable to those of the other countries). Also sales occupations display a rather stable proportion of employment – about 10 per cent in all countries – in the mid-1990s. The difference between Denmark, which has the lowest share, and the United States, with the highest share, is only 4 percentage points. Furthermore, in Canada, Denmark and the United States service occupations are of almost equal size and have not changed at all since the mid-1980s. Here, Sweden is clearly a deviant case with a reduction in service occupations' share of employment by 5 percentage points, which has led to a somewhat lower proportion of service occupations than in the other three countries. Part of this change can quite possibly be explained by a significant shift in public sector employment where low-skill personnel (e.g., assistant nurses and childcare workers) have been replaced by workers with considerably higher education (e.g., registered nurses and pre-primary school teachers) (SCB 1996a).

Table 7.1 Employment by occupation in Canada, Denmark, Sweden and the United States, 1980s and 1990s (%)

ISCO-68 occupations	Canada		USA		Denmark		Sweden	
	1983	*1993*	*1983*	*1995*	*1984*	*1993*	*1983*	*1995*
Professionals and technicians	17	19	16	18	22	25	28	36
Managers and administrators	6	14	11	14	4	5	2	–
Clerical	17	16	16	15	18	18	12	17[a]
Sales	11	10	12	12	7	8	8	10
Service	14	14	14	14	12	12	14	9
Agriculture	6	4	4	3	6	5	6	3
Production and transport	27	24	28	25	31	26	30	26

Source: ILO LABORSTA database.

Note
a Includes administrative and managerial workers.

So far, what we have found is more a pattern of in-country stability and cross-country similarity than a pattern of divergence between different welfare regimes and rapid changes in the occupational structure.[5] In the mid-1990s, non-managerial and non-professional occupations account for roughly 65 to 70 per cent of employment, figures which have been decreasing by about 5 percentage points since the mid-1980s. The significant differences are to be found among the managerial and professional categories. First, we find a conspicuous difference between, on the one hand, Canada and the United States and, on the other hand, Denmark and Sweden regarding managerial occupations. Judging from these data, it seems as if the two North American economies are considerably more 'managed' than their Scandinavian counterparts. Also, both Canada and the United States have experienced a marked growth in managerial occupations since the mid-1980s, while we can only observe a minor increase in Denmark (no data on managerial occupations were available for Sweden in 1995). Second, Sweden experienced a quite remarkable growth (almost 10 percentage points) in professional and technical occupations during the period, while the other countries saw a rather modest increase. So in the mid-1990s these occupations account for more than one-third of employment in Sweden, a quarter in Denmark and approximately one-fifth in the North American countries. Again, the extraordinary growth in Sweden might partly be explained by an upward shift in skill levels in the Swedish public sector. Also, during the recession in the beginning of the 1990s a great many manual jobs within manufacturing were lost, while the numbers of technicians were not affected to the same extent.

However, it must be noted that clerical, sales and service workers are still more numerous than those in the upper part of the job hierarchy. Consequently, even if these data give some support to the notion of a post-industrial process of professionalisation, non-professional non-manual jobs constitute roughly 40 per cent of employment in all countries.

So, these data (crude as they admittedly are) seem to fit the welfare regime hypothesis quite well regarding professional/technical and managerial/administrative occupations. Also, the post-industrialists' notion of a growth in the highly educated occupations receive some support. On the other hand, the data for the other major occupational groups do not fit especially well with any of the propositions in the discussion above. Except, of course, the general tendency of a decrease in agricultural and manufacturing occupations.

This, then, is the big picture. It has provided us with an initial overview of the overall trends in occupational development during the last decade. However, a comprehensive understanding requires a considerably more detailed examination, which can be accomplished only with the use of less aggregated occupational data. Therefore, instead of seven major occupational groups we will use a selection of the 27 sub-major occupational groups of the classification ISCO-88(COM).[6] Unfortunately, it is practically impossible to construct comparable cross-national time-series using such detailed data. Hence, we will have to content ourselves with a snapshot of the four countries' occupational structures from the latter half of the 1990s (Sweden and the United States 1999, Denmark 1998 and Canada 1996).

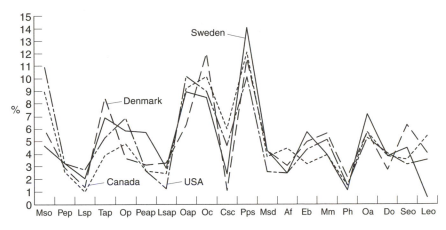

Figure 7.1 Employment by occupation in Canada, Denmark, Sweden and the United States, late 1990s

Sources: Statistics Canada 2000; Statistics Denmark 1998; Statistics Sweden 1999; BLS 2002.

Notes
Mso = Managers and senior officials; Pep = Physical, mathematical and engineering science professionals; Lsp = Life science and health professionals; Tap = Teaching and associate teaching professionals; Op = Other professionals; Peap = Physical and engineering science associate professionals; Lsap = Life science and health associate professionals; Oap = Other associate professionals; OC = Office clerks; Csc = Customer services clerks; Pps = Personal and protective services workers; Msd = Models, salespersons and demonstrators; Af = Agricultural and fishery workers; Eb = Extraction and building trades workers; Mm = Metal, machinery and related trades workers; Ph = Precision and handicraft workers; Oa = Operators and assemblers; Do = Drivers and mobile-plant operators; Seo = Sales and services elementary occupations; Leo = Labourers in mining, construction, manufacturing and transport.

Figure 7.1 presents a graphic representation of the proportion of people employed in 20 occupational groups.[7]

On first inspection the occupational structures of the four countries seem fairly alike in their overall patterns. Of course, there are a number of noticeable differences regarding each occupational group's share of employment in the four countries, but this does not, however, take away the overall impression of similarity. In the following the most interesting aspects and differences of these patterns will be commented upon and analysed.

To begin with, as noted above, it seems that Canada and the United States have significantly more people employed in managerial occupations (Mso) than Denmark and Sweden. The observation of a rather heavily managed working life in the two North American countries is far from new and supports earlier research (e.g., Esping-Andersen 1990: 202f; Castells 1996: 216ff.). Esping-Andersen presents several possible explanations as to why the US economy is 'overmanaged'. First, it could actually be a statistical chimera since it is common in the United States to label even low-grade supervisors as managers. The second explanation is in fact a group of explanations, which all take their departure in such phenomena as technology, bureaucracy and class struggle. The third explanation builds on the fact that the US economy lacks certain features. A want of publicly provided social services makes many fringe benefits (e.g., health insurance and pension plans) important in collective bargaining, which calls for managers. Also, US firms must exercise control by the use of managers since the unions (via comprehensive agreements) cannot be counted on to control their members. Further, the huge American labour market has no equivalent to the more comprehensive Scandinavian system of labour exchanges and worker-training institutions, which forces firms to be more or less self-servicing on these accounts with talent scouts, educators and very large personnel departments.

This type of institutional explanation receives some support from the fact that the country with the most regulated labour market and the most powerful unions is also the one with the smallest proportion of managers. Sweden has less than 5 per cent managers, which is more than 6 percentage points less than the United States. Actually, Sweden and the United States constitute two terminal points on a scale of unionisation. In Sweden, the absolute majority of the workforce is unionised while the workers in the United States for the most part are unorganised (see Chapters 2 and 3). The proportion of managers in Canada and Denmark fits quite well with the notion of an institutional basis for the management situation in an economy. The Danish labour market is somewhat less regulated than the Swedish and the level of unionisation is a bit lower, which, consequently, results in a higher proportion of managers. Canada follows the pattern of the other countries with a proportion of managers that reflects the Canadian institutional labour market arrangements.

However, another differentiating aspect of the Scandinavian and North American labour markets might also help to explain the large proportion of managers in Canada and the United States. Denmark and Sweden have a considerably larger share of people working in the public sector (see Chapter 6), which can affect the occupational structure since it is probable that those employed in the public sector are classified as professionals or technical workers while their privately employed counterparts tend to be classified as managerial or clerical workers (van den Berg, Furåker and Johansson 1997: 66).

To be sure, the way in which organisations arrange their control structures is one of the most interesting objects of study in today's quickly changing economy. For instance, will managers become fewer when the number of professionals increases? On the other hand, is it conceivable that some management occupations will begin a process of professionalisation, and thereby secure a position in tomorrow's organisations? Such questions are very difficult to answer at this point in time. Esping-Andersen's idea that the control structure of organisations is partly determined by a country's way of arranging its labour relations is intriguing, and would certainly be worth more in-depth studies. However, let it suffice here to conclude that there seems to be a correspondence between institutional arrangements and the proportion of managers in a country.

In the introduction it was noted that a frequent claim by many post-industrial theorists is that occupations based on theoretical knowledge will dominate post-industrial society. In ISCO-88(COM) such occupations are gathered under the labels professionals and associate professionals, which in Figure 7.1 are split into seven occupational groups. Even if the majority of jobs in these occupational groups have their basis in theoretical knowledge, they are nevertheless a very diverse category regarding what tasks are actually performed.

First, there are two occupational groups that above all consist of jobs that have to do with a theoretical understanding of the material world. That is, physical, mathematical and engineering science professionals (Pep), and physical and engineering associate professionals (Peap). The former is made up of occupations which require a university education that lasts at least three years (e.g., physicists, chemists, architects and engineers), while the latter group comprises occupations that require somewhat less theoretical schooling (e.g., technicians, pilots, air traffic controllers, ships' engineers and quality inspectors). While the proportion of employment in the first group is rather similar across the four countries, Sweden stands out in the second group with almost 6 per cent of employment. This is nearly twice as many as in Denmark and Canada, and close to four times the proportion in the United States. These figures are to some extent correlated to the industrial employment structures of the countries. Denmark and Sweden both have about 19 per cent employment in manufacturing, while the rates for Canada and the United States are approximately 4 percentage points lower (ILO 2001). Sweden's extraordinarily high rate is probably explained by its many large high-tech transnational corporations (e.g., Astra-Zeneca, Ericsson, Asea Brown Boveri, Volvo, Electrolux) with a large focus on R&D, while Denmark is characterised by many small manufacturing companies primarily production oriented (OECD 1996a). If we take both groups together, we find that Sweden clearly deviates with a proportion of employment of over 9 per cent, while the other countries have between 5.5 and 6 per cent.

Second, life science and health professionals (Lsp), life science and health associate professionals (Lsap), together with teaching and teaching associate professionals (Tap) are occupational groups intimately connected to the workings of the modern welfare state. Incumbents of these occupations are responsible for most of those tasks that are the epitome of the very concept welfare state itself. Examples of occupations in the first group are medical doctors, dentists, biologists and veterinarians, while the second group comprise such occupations as hygienists, dieticians, opticians, dental assistants, physiotherapists, pharmaceutical assistants and, above all, nurses. Taken together, these occupations have approximately the same proportion of employment (about 5 per cent) in Denmark, Sweden and the United States, while Canada has roughly one percentage point less. Denmark and Sweden have significantly more teachers than Canada and the United States. This difference is almost completely due to the high incidence of pre-primary school teachers in Denmark and Sweden, which is a consequence of a legislation in these countries that has established childcare as a right for all children up to the age of six (Gornick, Meyers and Ross 1997: 58).

Third, there are two – what can be called – 'residual' groups among the 'theoretical knowledge occupations', which both consist of a large number of very diverse jobs. The group other professionals (Op) is made up of such jobs as accountants, lawyers, judges, economists, sociologists, psychologists, writers and priests, while other associate professionals (Oap) comprise jobs such as police inspectors, social workers, trade brokers, insurance representatives, musicians and clowns. Among the four countries the United States has the highest and Denmark the lowest proportion of employment in both groups. One reason for the high incidence of many of these occupations in the United States is probably its high proportion of producer services (see Chapter 5). It is also conceivable that the US economy (being the dominating media producer in the world) harbours a larger proportion of creative artists with associated occupations than do other countries. All in all, these residual occupational groups make up as much as 17 per cent of employment in the United States, 15 per cent in Sweden, 14 per cent in Canada and only 10 per cent in Denmark.

One important thing to note regarding all the 'theoretical knowledge occupations' is their extremely heterogeneous character (their only common trait is the considerable length of education that prospective incumbents have to go through). Therefore, it is quite difficult to analyse and discuss cross-country similarities and differences. It seems, however, possible to argue that there are rather few country specificities that are attributable to either the Scandinavian or the North American way of organising society.

Clerical occupations are to be found within all sorts of industries and their relative size in the occupational structure seems to be rather stable over time (see Table 7.1). ISCO-88(COM) distinguishes between office clerks (Oc) and customer services clerks (Csc) and the main difference between them is that the latter category deals directly with customers. This distinction is not all that clear cut and it is quite possible that the same type of job can be regarded as either one of the two categories depending on classificatory practices. So, taken together clerical occupations make up 11 per cent of employment in Sweden, 13 per cent in Denmark, 14 per cent in the United States and 16 per cent in Canada. The two North American countries have a larger share of customer services clerks, which quite possibly reflects these countries relatively large share of employment within consumer-oriented services (i.e., retail trade, restaurants and hotels). The rather large difference between Denmark and Sweden regarding office clerks can possibly be accounted for by differences in establishment size. It is conceivable that large organisations need proportionally fewer office clerks since they can rationalise by centralising certain administrative tasks and invest in expensive data processing equipment. Establishment size data seem to support this notion. Denmark has the highest proportion of office clerks but the lowest proportion of large establishments, while for Sweden it is the other way around (OECD 1996a).

Personal and protective services workers (Pps) exceed 10 per cent of employment in all countries and particularly so in Sweden where they stand for as much as 14 per cent. This group of occupations provide personal and protective services (e.g., hairdressers, cooks, waiters, childcare workers and fire-fighters) and – considering the notion of a post-industrial labour market consisting to a great extent of non-professional service workers – it definitely constitutes one of the most interesting occupational categories. The reason why Sweden has such a large proportion of workers in this category is its very high incidence of care workers, which, of course, is a consequence of Sweden's comprehensive welfare system. It is interesting to note that the United States has the smallest proportion of employment in both this and the other group of service workers (Msd). This certainly does not correspond especially well with the idea of the United States as a forerunner in a development towards a service society.

Above, it was shown that the proportion of those occupational groups that – using a traditional terminology – can be called manual or blue-collar occupations has been decreasing, but, at the same time, that they still constitute approximately one-fourth of employment in all four countries. Therefore, it is indeed too early to write them off as the last and quickly vanishing remnants of a soon to be foregone industrial era. Actually, it is possible to identify a number of manual occupations that – by virtue of their specific characteristics – do not run the risk of imminent extinction.

First, the two occupational groups extraction and building trades workers (Eb) and metal, machinery and related trades workers (Mm) are to a large extent made up of jobs that require quite extensive vocational schooling and/or long periods of apprenticeship (in a few cases the time required to be regarded as a fully trained worker can in fact be equivalent to the time spent to receive a college diploma). Carpenters, electricians, welders plumbers, painters, tool-makers and machinery mechanics are but a few examples of such occupations. Second, precision and handicraft workers (Ph) is a category that in many cases can be compared to artistic jobs, sharing with them all the rather specific problems that come from belonging to the artistic labour markets (Menger 1999). Potters, glass engravers, musical-instrument makers, cabinetmakers and tailors are examples of occupations that belong to this somewhat special category. However, common to all these manual occupations is that they are relatively safeguarded from threats of automation or competition from cheap labour abroad. Taken together, they constitute 13 per cent of employment in Denmark and the United States, 11 per cent in Sweden and close to 9 per cent in Canada. These differences – which are almost wholly to be found within the first two categories (Eb and Mm) – are probably explained by differences in the countries' industrial structures and shifts in the business cycle. Another rather 'secure' occupational group is drivers and mobile-plant operators (Do). It consists of drivers of taxis, vans, motorcycles, buses, lifting-trucks, heavy trucks, etc., but also of ships' deck crews. Thus, all occupations in this group are connected to the activity of transporting either people or goods. In Canada, Sweden and the United States these kinds of jobs account for 4 per cent of employment, while in Denmark they make up one percentage point less. The specific features of today's economy (e.g., networking firms and just-in-time production) make a large reduction in transport jobs quite unlikely.

A group of manual occupations that holds a much more precarious position in the more advanced economies than the above occupations is operators and assemblers (Oa). Even though much work in this category calls for a fair amount of on-the-job training, no specific education is normally needed (ILO 1990). These occupations are almost exclusively to be found within the manufacturing sector and in many respects they can be regarded as the archetypal occupations of the industrial era (e.g., assembly-line workers). With slightly above 7 per cent of employment Sweden clearly has the largest share of these occupations among the four countries. The United States deviates in the other direction with approximately 3.5 per cent, while Denmark and Canada both have roughly 5.5 per cent of their labour force engaged in this type of work. As was noted in the introduction, if the cost for this type of manual labour increases, there is a risk that employers might either automate the production process or move the establishment to a low-wage country. The rather low incidence of operators and assemblers in the United States can possibly reflect a more advanced state in the restructuring of manufacturing than in the other countries.

Before concluding this first analysis we must consider two more occupational groups: sales and services elementary occupations (Seo) and labourers in mining, construction, manufacturing and transport (Leo). Both groups are made up of jobs that do not require any schooling above the primary level and, at the most, a few weeks on-the-job training. Examples of jobs in the first group are cleaners, hand-launderers, porters, messengers and garbage collectors. Comparing the four countries we can see that Denmark has the highest proportion of employment in this group with 6.5 per cent, which is roughly 2 percentage points more than Canada and Sweden and 3 percentage points more than the United States. The second group is composed of such jobs as building construction labourers, freight handlers, packers and movers. Our countries differ quite considerably regarding these occupations' share of employment with Sweden at a low 0.5 per cent and Canada at a high 5.5 per cent and the United States and Denmark with 2.5 and 4 per cent respectively.

The rather large differences between the countries regarding these elementary occupations' share of employment is difficult to account for. Since we do not have access to comparable data on a more detailed level we can only make some tentative suggestions. First, it is possible that different classifying practices place the same jobs in different categories. For instance, it seems a bit odd that Sweden (with a total of 23 per cent in manual occupations) has no more than 0.5 per cent labourers, something which might indicate that manual labour in Sweden generally is regarded as being more skilled than in some other countries. If we, on the other hand, accept these data as good approximations of the real world of work there must exist some real world facts that can account for the differences. Then the extremely low incidence of labourers in Sweden could be an effect of the massive lay-offs by manufacturing firms during the crisis in the beginning of the 1990s. More than 20 per cent of the blue-collar workforce (mostly unskilled) was dismissed between 1990 and 1995 (SCB 1996a). Also, the demands by the powerful Swedish metal workers union for better working conditions, more on-the-job training, job rotation and extended responsibilities for their members may have been beneficial in reducing the number of unskilled jobs. Canada's larger share of labourers – compared to the United States – can possibly be attributed to the fact that the

United States has a considerably larger share of high-tech companies and Denmark's high proportion might be a consequence of employment practices among its many small firms.

So, what have we learnt after this in-depth study of the four countries' occupational structures? First, compared to other less economically advanced OECD countries (e.g., Mexico and Turkey) our four countries must be regarded as having rather similar occupational structures. Second, high-skill occupations seem to be growing more rapidly than other occupations, thereby confirming one of the most important propositions by the post-industrial theorists. On the other hand, it has not been possible to discern an occupational polarisation as proposed by some scholars. Third, among the managerial, professional and personal service occupations we find some support for the impact of welfare regimes on the occupational structure, but there is no clear overall pattern that distinguishes the liberal from the social democratic welfare regime. Castells contends that

> while there are certainly signs of social and economic polarisation in advanced societies, they do not take the form of divergent paths in the occupational structure, but of different positions of similar occupations across sectors and between firms. Sectoral, territorial, firm-specific and gender/ethnic/age characteristics are clearer sources of social polarisation than occupational differentiation per se.
>
> (Castells 1996: 220)

Moreover, he argues (as have many others before him, e.g., Block 1990; Esping–Andersen 1990) that the major difference between the labour markets of twenty years ago and today is the massive incorporation of women into paid work. Also, the data presented in Chapters 5 and 6 show clearly the importance of women's changing labour market behaviour. Therefore, we will now move on to examine how women are distributed in the occupational structure of the four countries.

Occupational sex segregation

Whether or not women engage in paid labour is essential for the occupational structure. If they choose paid labour instead of unpaid labour at home the demand for services will increase, which, in turn, will increase the share of service workers in the occupational structure (Esping-Andersen 1999: 57ff.). The existence of, and easy access to, services will induce more women to take up paid labour, thus creating a virtuous circle for women's employment. This virtuous circle can, however, have the side-effect of locking women into certain occupations, especially in the Scandinavian countries with their large public service sectors (Esping-Andersen 1993: 237). Or, as Rosen (1996: 734f.) puts it: 'In Sweden a large fraction of women take care of the children of women who work in the public sector to care for the parents of the women who are looking after their children.' In the North American welfare states, on the other hand, another process might be at work, namely that the '. . . elite corps of professional and managerial women, whose ranks have expanded so dramatically in recent years, can now purchase on the market much of the labour of social reproduction traditionally relegated to them as wives and mothers' (Milkman, Reese and Roth 1998: 485). In Chapter 5 we saw that women's employment has been converging in the four countries, so that today women's employment rates are roughly between 66 and 70 per cent. We should, therefore, following the line of argument above, also expect a convergence in the countries' occupational structures, but, at the same time, quite distinct differences between Denmark and Sweden on the one hand, and Canada and the United States on the other hand. Danish and Swedish women ought to be more concentrated in social service jobs than women in North America.

To begin with, the same major occupational groups that were analysed in the previous section will be utilised in order to get a first view of women's position in the occupational structure. In Table 7.2 we can see that the proportion of women has increased in most major occupational groups in all four countries since the mid-1980s. Actually, in the mid-1990s women dominate in three out of seven occupational groups, that is, professional/technical, clerical and service occupations. However, we also find a clear male dominance in agricultural and production/transport occupations. In all four countries women constitute less than one-fifth of those in production/transport occupations and (especially in Denmark) their share has been in decline during the period.

Again, we find the most interesting changes among the professional and managerial occupations. In both Denmark and Sweden the female proportion among professional/technical occupations has increased to almost two-thirds. The North American countries have considerably lower female shares among the professionals, which undoubtedly is due to the high incidence of female dominated welfare

Table 7.2 Women's share of major occupational groups in Canada, Denmark, Sweden and the United States, 1980s and 1990s (%)

ISCO–68 occupations	Canada		USA		Denmark		Sweden	
	1983	*1993*	*1983*	*1995*	*1984*	*1993*	*1983*	*1995*
Professionals and technicians	51	56	48	53	60	63	54	64
Managers and administrators	30	42	32	43	17	20	20	–
Clerical	78	80	80	80	63	63	81	61[a]
Sales	41	45	48	50	50	52	47	48
Service	54	56	60	60	74	71	75	61
Agriculture	21	24	16	20	7	19	24	24
Production and transport	14	13	19	18	23	17	18	17
Total labour force	42	45	44	46	45	46	47	48

Source: ILO LABORSTA database.

Note
a Includes administrative and managerial workers.

occupations in the Nordic countries. On the other hand, Canada and the United States have experienced a remarkable growth (more than 10 percentage points) of women in managerial/administrative occupations during the period. This can simply be an effect of the increase in the proportion of managers generally, but it is also possible that the opportunities for women to advance hierarchically are greater in North America than in Scandinavia.[8] We should, however, remember that the cross-national similarities are greater than the differences regarding sex segregation, which implies the existence of a rather general pattern of occupational sex segregation.

In order to get a more comprehensive picture of women's occupational patterns it is, again, necessary to move on to a more detailed level since it has been shown that '... the more aggregated the categories across which segregation is measured, the less segregation we will capture' (Reskin 1993: 243). So, the equality in some occupational groups that was identified above (i.e., professional/technical and sales occupations) might actually be nothing but a chimera hiding considerably more segregated labour markets and also greater (or lesser) cross-country variations. Figure 7.2 shows the proportion of women in the 20 ISCO-88(COM) occupational groups.

Of course, the first thing to notice is the conspicuous agreement among the four countries' proportion of men and women in different occupational groups. It is also

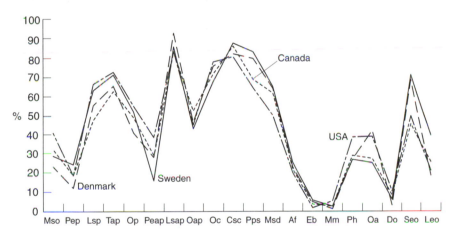

Figure 7.2 Women's share of occupational groups in Canada, Denmark, Sweden and the United States, late 1990s

Sources: Statistics Canada 2000; Statistics Denmark 1998; Statistics Sweden 1999; BLS 2002.

Note

Mso = Managers and senior officials; Pep = Physical, mathematical and engineering science professionals; Lsp = Life science and health professionals; Tap = Teaching and associate teaching professionals; Op = Other professionals; Peap = Physical and engineering science associate professionals; Lsap = Life science and health associate professionals; Oap = Other associate professionals; OC = Office clerks; Csc = Customer services clerks; Pps = Personal and protective services workers; Msd = Models, salespersons and demonstrators; Af = Agricultural and fishery workers; Eb = Extraction and building trades workers; Mm = Metal, machinery and related trades workers; Ph = Precision and handicraft workers; Oa = Operators and assemblers; Do = Drivers and mobile-plant operators; Seo = Sales and services elementary occupations; Leo = Labourers in mining, construction, manufacturing and transport.

easy to observe that the more aggregated categories in Table 7.2 did indeed hide a considerable sex segregation. The physical, mathematical and engineering occupations (Pep/Peap) are male dominated, while the teaching occupations (Tap) are dominated by women. Also, the life science and health associate occupations (Lsap) are to a large extent a female group of occupations, which is not especially surprising since nursing is one of the jobs included in this category. The incidence of women is almost negligible in the extraction and building (Eb) and metal and machinery occupations (Mm) and also very low among drivers and mobile-plant operators (Do). However, we find a fair number of women within the precision and handicraft occupations (Ph), among operators and assemblers (Oa) and within the labouring occupations (Leo), even though men are in a clear majority in most countries. Concerning the sales and services elementary occupations (Seo) the picture is twofold with a female dominance in the Scandinavian countries and close to equality in the North American countries.

This striking similarity in cross-national segregation profiles has been observed before and for other countries (e.g., Nermo 1999) and it seems as if differences in welfare regimes (at least between the liberal and social democratic types) do not produce any clear-cut differences in patterns of occupational sex segregation. Regarding Sweden and the United States Nermo (1999: 143) observes that in spite of all efforts in Sweden '. . . for gender-neutral legislation and less focusing on women as primarily mothers and wives, the two countries demonstrate similar patterns and trends in levels of horizontal sex segregation'.

Notwithstanding the overall impression of similarity, we can nonetheless notice some minor differences between the countries. The two most interesting occupational groups in this respect are personal and protective services workers (Pps) together with sales and services elementary occupations (Seo). In Denmark and Sweden women have a clear dominance in both categories and particularly so in the first one which has more than 80 per cent women in both countries. In Canada and the United States the jobs within the elementary services category are equally distributed between men and women and the personal and protective services occupations have a considerably lower female proportion than the Scandinavian countries, even though women still account for two-thirds of that category. Actually, these are the only occupational groups that seem to follow the welfare regime typology. As noted above, personal and protective services occupations include those care jobs that in many ways exemplify the social democratic welfare regime (i.e., personal care workers). It is therefore not surprising that this group is so heavily female biased in the Scandinavian countries (in Sweden close to one-fourth of all women in paid work have jobs within this group of occupations, while the corresponding figure for the United States is less than 15 per cent). Also the elementary sales and services occupations are heavily female dominated in the Nordic countries, which can be taken as a sign of a more gendered opportunity structure.

Thus, what we have found are patterns that confirm the impression of national labour markets in which one of the most important divisions is that between male and female jobs. It is rather difficult, however, to compare the extent of sex segregation in the four countries only by looking at the proportion of women in each occupational group. In addition we need some summary measures of overall occupational sex segregation. There exists a number of more or less elaborated measures (see Nermo 1999: 18ff. for a comprehensive overview), but here we will only make use of two quite simple and easily interpreted measures. The first one (S) measures the proportion of segregated occupations, that is, the share of occupations that consist of more than two-thirds of either men or women. The second one is the most widely used measure of segregation, namely the index of dissimilarity (D). This index measures the distribution of two groups within a set of categories. Most probably, its popularity is due to its uncomplicated interpretation, that is, that '. . . it represents the proportion of women or men that would, without replacement, have to change occupations in order to receive an equal distribution of all occupations in the labour market' (Nermo 1999: 22).

In Table 7.3 we can see that the proportion of sex-segregated occupations (S) is larger in the Scandinavian than the North American countries. With more than 70 per cent segregated occupations Sweden and Denmark seem to be considerably more segregated than Canada and the United States which both have about 60 per cent segregated occupations. The dissimilarity index (D) tells a similar story. In the Scandinavian countries half of all women or men would have to change occupations to bring about a perfectly sex-integrated labour market, while in the North American countries a sex-integrated labour market would be achieved if only 41 per cent should change occupations. These figures seem to suggest that the Scandinavian type of welfare state gives rise to a higher level of sex segregation than the regimes in North America. However, it is possible that these differences are highly concentrated to a limited number of occupations, which, consequently, would imply that the overall pattern of occupational sex segregation is almost

Table 7.3 Occupational sex segregation (%)

	S	D
Canada	62	41
United States	58	41
Denmark	71	50
Sweden	75	51

Sources: Statistics Canada 2000; Statistics Denmark 1998; Statistics Sweden 1999; BLS 2002.

Notes
S = the proportion of sex segregated occupations.
D = the index of dissimilarity.
Both S and D are based on calculations using 24 occupational groups. It is to be noted that the level of sex segregation tends to increase with the number of occupations used in the calculations, i.e., the labour market appears to be more segregated on more detailed levels of analysis (Jonung 1993: 69). D is defined as

$$D = \frac{1}{2} \sum_{i=1}^{n} \left| \frac{F_i}{F} - \frac{M_i}{M} \right|$$

where F_i refers to the number of women in an occupation, F to the number of all employed women, M_i to the number of men in an occupation, M to the number of all employed men and n the total number of occupations.

identical. Figure 7.2 is partly a confirmation of this notion, since we find the largest differences between the North American and Scandinavian countries in two occupational groups that comprise many of those care jobs that are publicly provided for by the Danish and Swedish welfare states.

Educational attainment

Above we noted that the proportion of occupations that require some kind of higher education has been growing in all our countries. All post-industrialists are in agreement that higher education is a significant aspect of the 'new' society. Bell (1976: 232), for instance, argues that the '. . . major problem for the post-industrial society will be adequate numbers of trained persons of professional and technical caliber'. Further, it has been claimed that a nation's or region's ability to attract employers will depend increasingly upon the skills and educational level of its population (Reich 1991; OECD 1994b, 1999c). The argument is that in an open economy firms can easily move to those regions where they have a good supply of well-educated and highly productive workers. Thus, in a post-industrial society the primary asset for both individuals and nations is the 'human capital'. Consequently, education is a key variable when trying to understand differences or similarities between countries in their post-industrial change process. A high proportion of well-educated people in the labour force can be thought to accelerate the shift towards a post-industrial labour market, while a dominance of low-educated people can have the opposite effect.

Table 7.4 shows the level of educational attainment for 25- to 64-year-olds, that is, those among the population who have supposedly finished their education and are economically active. Before proceeding it must be noted that the educational systems vary considerably among the four countries, which means that the figures in the following tables need to be treated with some caution.[9] The tripartite division of educational levels in Table 7.4 is relevant in that the three levels correspond quite well with the dominant need of schooling in different time periods. Until the 1970s lower secondary education (i.e., up till 10–11 years in school) or lower education was all that was required for the great majority of jobs. During the 1970s and 1980s upper secondary education (i.e., 12–14 years of schooling) became the norm for access to more and more jobs and the development through the 1990s has meant that post-secondary or tertiary education (i.e., college and university levels) has become more and more of a standard requirement for a great many occupations.

According to Table 7.4 the proportion of the population that has attained less than upper secondary education is less than one-fourth in all countries and at least one-fourth has attained tertiary education. There is, however, a higher overall level of educational attainment in the North American countries. This difference can be due to a number of factors. For example, strong incentives for education (higher wages for higher educated people), differences in the educational systems and a high demand for well-educated labour generated by an earlier shift towards post-industrial activities in North America.

Table 7.4 Distribution of the population 25 to 64 years of age by level of educational attainment, 1998 (%)

	Below upper secondary education	Upper secondary education	Tertiary education	Total
Canada	20	41	39	100
United States	14	51	35	100
Denmark	22	53	25	100
Sweden	24	48	28	100

Source: OECD Database.

Table 7.5 Percentage of the population that has attained a specific level of education, by age group, 1998 (%)

	At least upper secondary education				At least tertiary education			
	Age 25–34	Age 35–44	Age 45–54	Age 55–64	Age 25–34	Age 35–44	Age 45–54	Age 55–64
Canada	87	83	77	65	46	39	37	28
United States	88	88	87	80	36	36	37	27
Denmark	85	80	78	67	27	27	27	19
Sweden	87	80	73	60	31	31	29	20

Source: OECD Database.

By comparing age groups and their level of educational attainment we get an indication of whether the population is becoming more or less educated, which is displayed in Table 7.5. Most young people have attained at least upper secondary education and the figures are almost identical for our four countries. This clearly strengthens the conception of upper secondary education as having become the 'normal' educational level in economically advanced countries. Differences are appearing in the higher age groups and it is clear that the United States has been a forerunner in the development towards a more or less compulsory upper secondary educational level. The proportion attaining tertiary education shows some interesting differences between both age groups and countries. In all countries tertiary education has become more common, but there is a conspicuous difference between the Scandinavian and the North American countries. This concerns especially the youngest age group within which almost half of the Canadian and more than one-third of the US population has completed tertiary education. In contrast, in Denmark only slightly more than one-fourth of this age group has moved beyond upper secondary education and in Sweden the proportion is still below one-third.

It was shown above that the labour markets of our four countries are heavily gendered and that all display a similar pattern of occupational sex segregation, but, at the same time, with a somewhat higher segregation rate in the Scandinavian countries. It is a more or less common feature among the OECD countries that women have increased their educational activity and in many countries young women in fact spend more years in education than do young men

(OECD 1996b: 38f.). It seems as if these countries are in the middle of a process of a 'feminisation' of higher education, which can partly be the result of an upgrading of the educational requirements for a number of jobs in the health and personal services sectors. Also, today it appears as if many (maybe most) young women finish their education before marrying and settling down. Further, it might be that the equal level of educational attainment between young men and women marks the end of a long process of convergence and that the sexes from now on will exhibit similar educational trajectories, at least regarding the length of education.

The gender differences are illuminated in Table 7.6 where the labour force participation of groups with differing levels of educational attainment is displayed. Two distinct patterns of labour force participation emerge, one Scandinavian and one North American. The labour force participation rate rises with higher education in all countries, but in particular among women in Canada and the United States. The differences between the countries are most striking within the lowest educational strata, where the participation rates of women in the North American countries are below 50 per cent. Sweden has the highest participation rate for both men and women in the lowest educational strata and Denmark falls somewhere in between. In the Scandinavian countries we find very small differences between men and women in the higher educational groups, while in both Canada and the United States women have approximately 10 percentage points lower participation rates. In this respect, the more extensive scope of the Scandinavian countries' welfare systems seems to be beneficial for women's labour force participation, especially for those with low education.

Table 7.6 Labour force participation rates by level of educational attainment and gender for the population 25 to 64 years of age, 1996 (%)

	Below upper secondary education	Upper secondary education	Non-university tertiary education	University-level education	All levels of education
Canada					
Men	74	89	90	92	86
Women	47	72	79	85	70
United States					
Men	74	88	93	93	88
Women	46	72	81	82	72
Denmark					
Men	77	89	93	94	87
Women	64	83	91	91	78
Sweden					
Men	82	90	90	94	88
Women	71	85	89	92	83

Source: OECD 1998b.

The figures presented above show that educational attainment and labour market position are closely connected. To anyone interested in such matters this is no novelty. Of considerably greater interest is an interpretation of these figures. Generally, the labour force has a higher level of educational attainment than the population at large. This overall picture is not surprising since labour force participation to an increasing extent is based on education in post-industrial societies. Further, since a growing proportion of the work force has attained at least secondary education, the labour market possibilities for those with less schooling will undoubtedly deteriorate.

The divergences between the four countries have also to be commented upon. The figures show that a higher proportion of the low-educated stratum is economically active in the two Scandinavian countries (especially Sweden). A plausible interpretation for this is that the more regulated labour markets in the Scandinavian countries have 'sheltered' those with a low education. Thus, it is the institutional arrangements of two different welfare state types that these differences emanate from. Another explanation is that it has to do with the level of unemployment. In a situation with high unemployment it can be expected that individuals with low education exit the labour force (e.g., by early retirement) to a greater extent than those with higher education. When people with low education experience unemployment they are not as likely as those with higher education to find new jobs in connection with a growth period in the economy. The difference between Denmark and Sweden – where Sweden has a higher proportion of low-educated in the labour force than Denmark – can be attributed to the fact that it is quite recently that Sweden has experienced high levels of unemployment and a decreasing demand for labour.

The higher level of educational attainment in the two North American countries can be interpreted in several ways. It is possible that a less regulated and more market driven economy gives incentive for people to invest in higher education. Also, a high education is, in these countries, more connected to the actual welfare of individuals since the state does not have the same overarching responsibility for individuals as the Scandinavian countries. Another aspect is that the restructuring of the labour market towards a domination of service jobs took place earlier in the North American countries, thereby creating a demand for a higher educated labour force. The convergence in labour market structure will quite possibly also mean a convergence in educational attainment between the four countries. Today we can observe that the absolute majority of young people completes upper secondary education and that a sizeable proportion also obtains some kind of tertiary education.

Conclusion

Overall, the findings in this chapter confirm the proposition of a movement towards a labour market with a high incidence of professional and managerial occupations. Together, managerial and professional occupations account for between 35 and 43 per cent of employment in the four countries: 43 per cent in the United States, 41 in Sweden and 36 and 35 per cent in Canada and Denmark respectively. On the other hand, it has not been possible to identify a concomitant growth of low-skill service occupations in any of these countries. Further, manual or blue-collar occupations still constitute one fourth of employment in all our countries. So, the picture of a post-industrial labour market consisting primarily of, on the one hand, a large group of high-skill occupations and, on the other hand, an equally large group of unskilled service workers is not consistent with the data presented in this chapter. Despite rather far-reaching changes in these countries' economic structural conditions their occupational structures do not display changes of a similar magnitude.

The four countries in this study are different in a number of ways. The two Scandinavian and the two North American countries represent in many respects two different welfare regimes. In spite of these differences the occupational structures of the four countries do not deviate that much from each other and, clearly, the similarities are much greater than the differences. There does not seem to exist distinctly different occupational structures that can be connected to different welfare regimes. Even more similar are the patterns of occupational sex segregation. Women and men dominate in the same jobs in all four countries, even though they display a higher concentration in some occupations in the Scandinavian countries.

A rising educational level is a significant indicator of a movement towards a labour market where formal education is the prime factor concerning the possibility of both getting a job and for upward mobility. The level of educational attainment has been rising in all four countries. Today, most young people have completed at least upper secondary education, which can be considered as the lowest level for getting access to qualified jobs. In Canada and the United States a larger proportion of the population has attained tertiary education compared to Denmark and Sweden. That education is an important factor for labour market possibilities can be seen by the fact that those with lower education also have a lower labour force participation rate.

So, occupation and education are two features of society that are intimately connected to each other. And, judging from the data presented in this chapter, it seems quite safe to conclude that occupations which are accessible only via the acquisition of certain educational credentials have indeed – in concord with many predictions – become central to today's labour markets. However, in my view it is premature to argue that what we have been witnessing during the last decades signals the advent of a post-industrial era in which the occupations of the industrial epoch are quickly becoming obsolete. That four of arguably the most economically and technologically advanced countries in the world still harbour a respectable 25 per cent of employment in occupations which can be called 'industrial' is indicative that a possible shift to a post-industrial labour market is farther away than is sometimes presumed.

8 Patterns of unemployment

Bengt Furåker

The subject matter of this chapter is the unemployment patterns in Canada, the United States, Denmark and Sweden since the early 1980s. A crucial question is whether these patterns can be accounted for in terms of economic cycles, institutional arrangements, or other factors. Given the overall theme of this book, differences in national institutions – such as labour legislation, unemployment insurance systems and active labour market policies – deserve particular attention. It will also be asked to what extent existing theoretical perspectives can help us explain levels and distributions of unemployment.

To start with, I shall spell out some ideas concerning the possible significance of national institutions for unemployment patterns. This discussion will be tied to different theoretical approaches to the issue. As has been shown in several of the previous chapters, the four countries represent separate models with regard to, among other things, social protection and labour market policy. The question is what impact such differences have on patterns of unemployment.

After having presented some theoretical foundation for the following analysis, I will turn to some of the available statistical data. An empirical picture will be given of the phenomenon of unemployment, covering not only its general level and development but also its distribution across social categories. It is common to find significant differences related to, for example, gender, age, socio-economic status, education and citizenship. Moreover, involuntary joblessness is presumably a more serious social problem if the period is drawn out and not just temporary. Attention will therefore be paid to the duration of unemployment that of course also affects the general unemployment rates.

The reason for providing these descriptions is that important national differences may remain hidden if we content ourselves with the general levels only. We need to examine whether the four countries – with respect to unemployment patterns – show any distinctive character or peculiarities. Such information may help us explain differences in the overall unemployment rate or at least help us avoid the most erroneous or irrelevant theoretical assumptions in the field. In the concluding section of the chapter, various explanations will be discussed and evaluated.

Unemployment and its possible determinants

North America and Scandinavia differ substantially from each other concerning social protection, no matter whether people have gainful employment or not. A significant factor behind the existing differences is the strength of the labour movements. In the Scandinavian countries, for a long time strong labour unions and strong social democratic parties have to a large extent shaped both workplace and political decisions, whereas such organisations have had little say in North America. However, it is worth repeating that there are also differences between Canada and the United States on the one side, and between Denmark and Sweden on the other. On the assumption that we can establish an ordinal scale ranging from the most 'social democratic' to the most 'liberal' model – to borrow the labels used by Gøsta Esping-Andersen (1990) – the rank order between the four countries would be: Sweden, Denmark, Canada and the United States.

In the social science literature there are many explanations given for the occurrence of (high) unemployment. Although perhaps simplifying a complex issue somewhat too much, we can make a distinction between two main theoretical approaches: the 'sclerosis' and the 'full-employment commitment' perspectives (see Esping-Andersen 1990, 1999; Esping-Andersen and Regini 2000; Hibbs 1977; Korpi 1991; Lindbeck 1992; Lindbeck and Snower 1988; Nickell 1997; Nickell and Layard 1999; Scarpetta 1996; Schmid 1994b; Therborn 1986; see also the discussion in Chapter 4). The principal idea behind the first approach is that high unemployment has to do with labour market rigidities, e.g., wage inflexibility and strict employment protection legislation. In the second perspective, low unemployment levels are associated with the institutionalised ambitions to achieve full employment, often but not always assumed to emanate from strong labour movements.

The sclerosis view tends to treat union and welfare state interventions as obstacles to the free and proper functioning of the labour market. When unions are strong they can keep up minimum wages, but with the consequence that some individuals run the risk of being priced out of the market. Generous unemployment benefits is another mechanism that may contribute to wage inflexibility by raising the reservation wage, i.e., the lowest wage at which people accept a job offer. There are studies indicating that generous unemployment compensation has the effect of prolonging unemployment periods (Layard, Nickell and Jackman 1991; Martin 2000; Nickell 1997; Nickell and Layard 1999; cf. also Esping-Andersen 1999: 124–5; Esping-Andersen and Regini 2000). Undoubtedly, other welfare benefits may affect the reservation wage in a similar way.

Scandinavia has clearly smaller earnings differentials than North America (see Chapter 10; see also Freeman and Katz 1994; OECD 1996c: ch. 3; Korpi 2000). In addition, even though there is a similar trend in many countries, the growth of earnings inequality during the 1980s and the 1990s has been remarkable in the United States. The wage flexibility argument says that if the price of labour increases, employers become more likely to refrain from hiring workers. In particular, this mechanism is supposed to hit workers with low qualifications. It has thus been argued that a downward wage adjustment is needed in order for these categories to avoid unemployment (OECD 1994c: 51–2).

Compared to North America, the two Scandinavian countries have more generous unemployment benefit schemes as well as more generous welfare systems in a number of other respects (see Chapter 4). Denmark has for a long time provided munificent compensation for the unemployed. A significant reorientation was made in the 1990s towards active labour market policies and towards a more restrictive provision of unemployment benefits, but on international comparison the system is still very generous. The Swedish unemployment insurance is similarly liberal, in spite of certain recent changes in the opposite direction. Among other things, the replacement rate has been lowered in the 1990s and benefits are today reduced after 100 days of payment.

Taken in their entirety (i.e., considering replacement rates, ceilings, qualification rules, duration, etc.) the Danish and the Swedish unemployment benefit systems are both much more favourable for the possible recipients than are the schemes in Canada and the United States. Without going into the details here, we must again emphasise the differences between Scandinavia and North America in terms of other social benefits (sickness insurance, paid parental leave, etc.). Such measures may also affect the reservation wage.

There is, however, one other aspect to be brought up in relation to the unemployment insurance, namely the pressure put upon people to take available jobs. Strict work tests may be important to shorten unemployment spells (see, e.g., Nickell and Layard 1999: 3070–1). In a study by the ministry of finance in Denmark (1998), an attempt is made to judge the strictness of availability criteria in 19 OECD countries. Several indicators are used: demands on job search activity; availability during participation in active labour market programmes; demands on occupational and geographical mobility; extent of valid reasons for refusal of job offers; and benefit sanctions in case of self-induced resignation, refusals without valid reasons and repeated refusals. On each of these dimensions, the 19 countries were given 1–5 points according to the strictness of rules and there was also some weighting procedure involved. The actual total score ranges from a high of 25.25 (most restrictive system: Luxembourg) to a low of 11.25 (Ireland). Among the four countries in our study, Sweden was considered to have the strictest rules and it was placed third in the total ranking (with 23.5 points). The United States came sixth (21.25 points), Canada tenth (18.25 points) and Denmark eleventh (18 points).

To make realistic judgements about availability criteria is fraught with many problems, but we should not therefore refrain from paying attention to such rules. Still, the most crucial questions remain unanswered. Although admitting that 'it will be difficult to construct a much better index for the relative "strictness" of the criteria as they appear in legislation', the OECD (2000a: 138) has been very critical of the analysis done by the Danish Ministry of Finance. The main argument is that the report does not tell us whether – or to what extent – formal rules are implemented. An in-depth analysis of actual implementation practices would, however, require a kind of study that is very difficult, time-consuming and expensive to carry out. Before such a study is done, it is better to have information about the rules than to have nothing. It is a reasonable hypothesis that generally formal availability criteria are at least to some extent reflected in how the system works.

Another way of protecting people in the labour market is through employment protection legislation (cf. Chapter 3). Again, of course, having knowledge about formal rules does not mean that we know whether or how they are implemented. It is nevertheless often assumed that severe employment protection legislation makes employers hesitate about recruiting new workers, because it can then be rather costly to get rid of them if necessary (see, e.g., Giersch 1985). There are different methods of classification, but the United States is usually regarded as having the least restrictive employment protection legislation among all the OECD countries, both in the late 1980s and the late 1990s (OECD 1999b: 66–7). Canada is also counted among the least restrictive nations. Sweden, on the other hand, is ranked above the middle, but still with quite a few countries – mainly south European ones – behind her. Denmark is in fact not very far away from the North American model (it is eighth in the latest OECD ranking), although similar solutions as in Sweden are to some extent reached through collective agreements. Still, we must conclude that there is no homogeneous Scandinavian model in terms of employment protection legislation.

It has been difficult, however, to demonstrate any clear effects of restrictive employment protection legislation on general unemployment levels. In a recent report, the OECD (1999b: 88) concludes that employment protection regulation seems to have very little or even no effect at all on overall unemployment. These results are also consistent with what has been found in previous studies (see Nickell and Layard 1999). Now, one qualification can be added: the composition of the unemployed may be affected (see also Esping-Andersen and Regini 2000). There is some evidence suggesting that stricter rules lower unemployment rates among prime-age males and that other groups, in particular young people, therefore have higher rates.

The welfare state may also intervene in the labour market through active labour market policies. Such programmes usually express political ambitions to achieve full employment. The common purpose behind active measures is to get people without jobs (back) into work – through employment services, labour market training or job creation programmes. As shown in Chapter 4, Sweden and Denmark belong to those countries that spend most on active labour market policies relative to GDP, whereas Canada and above all the United States score low on international comparison. However, the success of active labour market policies must imply a commitment 'also to effective management of' such programmes and not only 'just to spending' on them (OECD 1994c: 108). In this context, Sweden has been mentioned as an example of a success story during the 1970s and the 1980s.

Moreover, active labour market policies cannot in themselves be the only remedy; full-employment commitment must mean more than implementing active programmes. Even if these programmes are effectively managed, in the end people will have to become employed in the regular labour market. A key issue is then whether there are macroeconomic policies stimulating demand for labour and whether active measures are co-ordinated with these policies. Measures that fit well in a recession may not be the best in periods of economic upturn and vice versa (OECD 1994c: 108). In addition, the benefits or wages paid in connection with training and job creation programmes may of course also affect the reservation wage, thus perhaps prolonging unemployment periods. We must thus be aware of the risk of counterproductive elements in these policies.

Behind the full-employment commitment approach there is often the assumption that labour movements are particularly interested in fighting unemployment (see, e.g., Hibbs 1977). Göran Therborn (1986) has however pointed out that there can also be another political background to full-employment commitment, namely the 'bourgeois' need for stability. Also, right-wing politicians may be concerned over unemployment and adopt the view that it can be a threat to the stability of the economy and the social order. Therefore, they sometimes also become strongly committed to the full-employment goal. The main examples in Therborn's analysis are Japan and Switzerland.

It should be underlined that doubts have been growing in recent years as to whether active labour market policies really accomplish what they are set up to accomplish. There is now a large body of literature indicating that the positive effects of such policies are rather limited (for an overview, see Martin and Grubb 2001). However, certain programmes turn out to be helpful at least for some categories. Among other things, it seems that women re-entrants gain from various types of labour market training, but it is then important that these programmes meet labour market needs. Most unemployed are likely to be helped by job-search assistance and long-term unemployed individuals and women re-entrants appear to benefit from subsidies to employment. Another aspect is the relationship between the size of programmes and their efficiency; it is difficult to avoid diminishing utility when the number of participants grows above a certain level.

After these introductory paragraphs three empirical sections will follow. To begin with, I shall provide an overview regarding the general development of unemployment rates in the four countries. Second, the distribution of unemployment across social categories will be focused. The final empirical section deals with the duration of unemployment spells. At the end of the chapter it will be asked how the patterns presented can be accounted for.

The development of unemployment rates

Figure 8.1 shows the development of standardised unemployment rates[1] in Canada, the United States and Sweden from 1980, while the Danish curve starts from 1982 because standardised figures are not available for Denmark before that. As we can see, unemployment levels have varied with economic cycles. Western economies have experienced two major recessions in these two decades. The first one occurred in the early 1980s when unemployment rose substantially in our four countries. Canada obviously had the highest rates, with more than 11 per cent in 1982–84 (nearly 12 per cent in 1983). The United States never reached the two-figure level but was close to it in 1982–83. Although the full picture is not visible due to lack of comparable data for 1980–81, we can imagine something similar for Denmark in the early 1980s. Sweden also had an increase, but its highest figure during this period – 3.7 per cent in 1983 – is still below the lowest level of all the other countries in the whole figure.

The economic recovery during the later half of the 1980s led to decreasing unemployment rates in the four countries. In 1989 Sweden had 1.5 per cent, which is the lowest rate of all those registered in Figure 8.1. The second international recession came in the early 1990s and unemployment then turned upward again. Compared to the previous economic trough the most significant difference is the sky-rocketing development in Sweden. The Swedish unemployment rate crossed the 9 per cent level in 1993 and peaked in 1997 with 9.9 per cent after which it began to fall back. The other three countries also had high unemployment levels at the beginning of the 1990s. For Canada we find two-digit figures from 1991 through 1994 and somewhat lower rates after that. The annual average in Denmark exceeded 10 per cent in 1993, but has since then declined more than in any of the other countries. Although, to begin with, the United States also experienced rising unemployment, the increase was modest and figures soon turned downwards. By 2000, the American unemployment rate was down at 4 per cent, the lowest level in the country since the early 1970s.

One reservation needs to be added. Standardised unemployment rates do not include all participants in active labour market programmes. It is an open question whether participants in such programmes should be treated as unemployed, but if we did do so we would get higher unemployment rates in all four countries. However, there are large cross-national differences in this respect. Although no comparable statistics are available, we know that Denmark and Sweden have had much larger numbers of participants in active programmes than North America (cf. the figures on

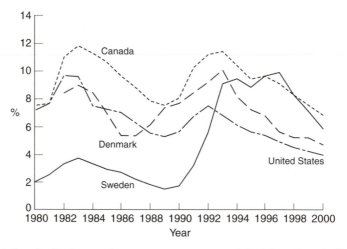

Figure 8.1 Standardised unemployment as a percentage of the labour force in Canada, the United States, Denmark and Sweden, 1980–2000

Sources: OECD 1999a: 216; 2001a: 252.

costs for active programmes in Chapter 4) and these participants are only partly included in the standardised unemployment rates. On the other hand, the United States has a much larger prison (male) population than any of the other countries and this is also an aspect that might be taken into account (cf. Western and Beckett 1999).

To summarise, Canada shows the highest unemployment rates, above or close to the two-digit level for some years in both the early 1980s and the early 1990s and somewhat lower in between. Danish unemployment has also been very high, but it has more recently declined in a remarkable way. The United States is not very different; it had a peak in 1982–83 – with close to two-figure numbers – and a strong improvement later on. During most of the 1990s it had the lowest unemployment rates in this four-country comparison. Unemployment in Sweden was by far the lowest all through the 1980s, but in the early 1990s it rose dramatically and even passed that of the other three countries. By the turn of the millennium, however, the Swedish unemployment rate had come down substantially – and below the Canadian level – although it was still clearly above what Sweden had in the 1980s.

Differences between social categories

Unemployment is not equally distributed across social categories. There are many national and international studies that describe the differences between various categories (see Gallie, Marsh and Vogler 1994; Gallie and Paugam 2000; Layard, Nickell and Jackman 1991: 286–300; OECD 1994b: ch. 1). In the following I will inspect some information on the distribution of unemployment in Canada, the United States, Denmark and Sweden, because it may help us understand at least parts of the cross-national variation. The data used in this section are based on national definitions of unemployment rates (in contrast to the previous section that is based on standardised rates).

Table 8.1 shows gender and age-category ratios of unemployment for a number of years since the beginning of the 1980s. Both 1983 and 1994 were characterised by recessions, while the demand for labour during the remaining three years was stronger or even much stronger. The table also includes data for the OECD European member states as well as for all the OECD members.

Starting with the female/male ratios, we can observe that the figures across both OECD columns clearly exceed 1, i.e., female unemployment rates have been higher. Among our four cases, this gender pattern consistently applies only to Denmark. The two North American countries score close to 1, with Canada below 1 for all five years. In the United States women's unemployment rates were lower than those for men in the first three years in the table, but for the remaining two years this pattern is reversed. In Sweden, it is rather the other way around. The reason for this is that the recession in the 1990s above all hit male-dominated industries and men's unemployment thus soon exceeded that of women.

With respect to age categories, a similar way of calculating ratios has been used. Regarding the relationship between youth and the prime-age population, the numerator consists of unemployment rates of youth (15/16–24 years of age) and the denominator of the rates of the prime-age category (25–54 years of age). In the

Table 8.1 Gender and age-category ratios of unemployment rates in Canada, the United
States, Denmark and Sweden, comparison with OECD averages, selected years
1983–2000

	Canada	United States	Denmark	Sweden	OECD Europe	OECD total
Female/male labour force						
1983	0.95	0.93	1.13	1.06	1.36	1.14
1990	0.98	0.98	1.13	1.00	1.60	1.50
1994	0.91	0.98	1.23	0.74	1.22	1.14
1997	0.95	1.04	1.41	0.92	1.31	1.34
2000	0.96	1.08	1.25	0.86	1.36	1.34
Youth/prime-age labour force						
1983	2.01	2.15	2.36	3.33	2.84	2.65
1990	1.70	2.43	1.46	3.46	2.35	2.42
1994	1.77	2.50	1.31	2.42	2.16	2.17
1997	2.08	2.90	1.69	2.33	2.21	2.23
2000	2.21	3.00	1.63	2.43	2.17	2.23
Older/prime-age labour force						
1983	0.83	0.71	0.78	1.63	0.90	0.86
1990	0.82	0.72	0.77	1.15	0.89	0.85
1994	0.97	0.82	0.83	0.94	0.82	0.82
1997	0.97	0.74	1.06	0.91	0.98	0.90
2000	0.95	0.81	0.98	1.24	1.07	1.04

Sources: OECD 1997d: 164–8; 1998a: 194–6; 1999b: 225–6; 2001b: 210–14.

two OECD columns we find youth unemployment to be between two and three
times higher than prime-age unemployment. Our four countries are sometimes
close to this pattern, but not always. One difference is that – except for 1983 –
Denmark has had relatively low ratios. Two of the Canadian scores are also rather
low. Both the United States and Sweden show ratios above 2 and even above 3, but
while the American ratios have increased over time, the Swedish figures have
decreased (although we can register an upward turn in 2000).

Thus, youth unemployment seems to be a greater problem relative to that of the
prime-age labour force in the United States and Sweden than in the other two
countries. It is sometimes argued that strict employment protection legislation
makes it difficult for entrants from outside – 'outsiders' who to a large extent consist of young persons – to be let into jobs. Now, it turns out that the United States
does not avoid the problem with youth unemployment, in spite of its weak legislation concerning employment protection.

Table 8.1 also shows the ratios between unemployment among the older (those
aged 55–64) and the prime-age labour force. For every year included in the table
we can register scores below 1 for Canada and the United States. In four out of the
five years the same holds for Denmark, OECD Europe and OECD total, whereas

the Swedish ratios show more variation. If we look at men and women separately, we discover that male ratios are generally higher than the female ones (not shown), although this pattern is consistent only for the United States and the OECD European member states.

Unemployment among the older labour force is not very different from that among the prime-age category. Most often figures are lower for the older category. There are few exceptions to this pattern and they are above all found for Sweden. Generally, it seems that unemployment is less of an issue for the older labour force than for the young. One reason for this is of course the implementation of early retirement schemes.

Historically unemployment has above all been a working-class phenomenon, although in recent decades it has become more prevalent among white-collar workers too. As shown in two OECD comparisons covering a number of countries (but not Denmark) over a number of years from 1980 through 1993, Canada, the United States and Sweden are no exceptions to that rule (OECD 1992: 15; 1994a: 15, 18). In the three countries, blue-collar workers usually have had somewhat less but sometimes more than twice the unemployment rates of white-collar workers.

Educational attainment is another indicator of social stratification and we shall therefore take a look at the unemployment rates for individuals with different schooling backgrounds. Table 8.2 displays data for five years in the period 1994–99. It refers to people aged 25–64, thus excluding the youngest age category of which many are still in school. Two calculations are presented. First, the unemployment rates for individuals with less than upper secondary education are divided

Table 8.2 Higher/lower education ratios of unemployment among individuals aged 25–64 in Canada, the United States, Denmark and Sweden, comparison with OECD averages, 1994–96 and 1998–99

	Canada	United States	Denmark	Sweden	OECD Europe	OECD total
Less than upper secondary/tertiary						
1994	1.96	3.94	3.26	2.44	–	–
1995	2.00	3.70	3.17	2.24	2.44	2.93
1996	2.00	4.54	3.03	2.25	2.21	2.78
1998	2.35	4.05	2.12	2.89	1.75	2.37
1999	2.52	3.67	2.33	2.31	2.26	2.17
Upper secondary/tertiary						
1994	1.23	1.94	1.89	2.11	–	–
1995	1.32	1.85	1.80	1.93	1.40	1.55
1996	1.33	2.13	1.79	2.00	1.40	1.63
1998	1.50	2.10	1.39	2.00	1.49	1.74
1999	1.57	1.76	1.37	1.67	1.65	1.62

Sources: OECD 1997d: 175–6; 1998a: 203–5; 1999b: 237–9; 2000a: 215–7; 2001b: 221–3.

by the figures for those with tertiary schooling. Second, the figures in the numerator are replaced by the unemployment rates among people with upper secondary education and another series of ratios is calculated.

A first and obvious conclusion is that people with compulsory education only (less than secondary education) have much higher unemployment than individuals with tertiary education. This is particularly accentuated in the United States, but we also find a few rather high ratios for Denmark. For the last two years in the table, however, Denmark shows among the lowest scores. The Canadian ratios were around 2 in the first three years but thereafter increased. For Sweden there is no clear trend.

The calculations on upper secondary versus tertiary education end up in substantially lower ratios and the country differences are smaller. In this case, there are no major or consistent differences between the United States and the other three countries. However, the United States and Sweden alternate with the highest ratios, whereas both Canada and Denmark score lower in each of the five comparisons.

There are also other dimensions such as race, ethnic belonging and citizenship to consider. Cross-country comparisons along these dimensions would require a more careful analysis (of the composition of the populations and of the underlying historic circumstances) than can be done here, so I will just give a few illustrations. During the whole period since the late 1970s, the annual average unemployment rates among blacks in the United States have been more than twice the level of the white population (US Department of Labor 1999: 206). American Hispanics have also had very high figures not so far from those of blacks. Another example can be taken from the Swedish labour force surveys that provide information on citizenship. In 2000, the average unemployment rates among non-Nordic citizens and Nordic non-Swedish citizens were 16.9 and 6.7 per cent respectively compared to 4.2 per cent among 'Swedes' (SCB 2001).

To conclude so far, Canada, the United States, Denmark and Sweden resemble each other a great deal – although not in all respects – concerning differences in unemployment levels across social categories. In all four cases the gender differences are relatively small. We have seen higher female than male unemployment rates in Denmark, whereas it has often been the other way around in the other three countries. Considering age, we find youth everywhere to be relatively more often unemployed than prime-age workers. The strongest differences in this respect are found in the United States and Sweden. For the older/prime-age labour force, the relationship appears most commonly to be the opposite, i.e., the older labour force has lower unemployment rates.

Our measures of social class and educational attainment indicate rather strong similarities between Canada, the United States, Denmark and Sweden. Blue-collar workers and people with only mandatory schooling run much higher risks of becoming unemployed than do white-collar workers and people with higher schooling. However, educational differences play a particularly important role in the United States, where low education increases the likelihood of becoming unemployed.

Coming back to the main question of this chapter, i.e., how to explain the differences in unemployment levels between the four countries, we must conclude that the descriptions given do not change the general picture very much. At the same time, we now know that the general differences can hardly be explained with reference to the composition of the unemployed, although some interesting differences exist. Consider, for example, the fact that youth unemployment has been relatively high both in Sweden and in the United States, although during different periods (higher in Sweden in 1983 and 1990 and lower in 1994, 1997 and 2000, and vice versa in the United States). I will make some further comments on this pattern in the concluding section.

Duration of unemployment

The general level of unemployment is the result of the flows into and out of it, and of its duration. It will be high if the number of individuals who become unemployed is large and these individuals on average stay jobless for long. If many become unemployed but are able to find employment quickly, the unemployment rate can still be kept rather low. The individual consequences of involuntary joblessness are no doubt related to its duration. Being unemployed for a short period of time does not have to mean very much to the individual; if he or she can find a suitable and rather stable job after such a period, there is little reason to worry. It is long-term unemployment that creates most problems or, rather, the most serious problems, in terms of both financial situation and psychosocial well-being.

In this section I will pay attention to these dynamic aspects of unemployment. The data available for comparative purposes are limited, but two types of information will be presented. They measure proportions of long-term unemployment and duration of unemployment. I shall examine the differences and similarities on these dimensions between the four countries.

Research publications dealing with labour market issues commonly report data on the proportion of the unemployed that are long-term unemployed. For example, the OECD presents such figures in each issue of its annual *Employment Outlook*. Surprisingly enough, it seems to be less common to find information on the proportions of the *labour force* that are long-term unemployed, although this measure has the advantage of not being dependent upon the general level of unemployment. In the present chapter it is the latter measure that will be used.

Figures 8.2a and 8.2b thus give us curves describing long-term unemployment as percentages of the labour force in Canada, the United States, Denmark and Sweden. They both cover the 18-year period 1983–2000. In the first case, long-term unemployment is defined as at least six months of continuous unemployment. The demarcation line in the second case is drawn at 12 months or more.

The two figures show basically the same picture. In 1983, Canada and the United States had substantially higher long-term unemployment rates than Sweden, but the Danish figures were in turn much above the North American ones. By 1990, when most Western economies were booming, the scores were lower in all four countries, although Denmark had had even lower levels some years earlier. At the beginning of the 1990s, the four curves moved upward – above all

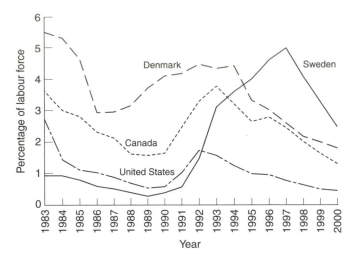

Figure 8.2a Long-term unemployment, ≥ 6 months, as a percentage of the labour force in Canada, the United States, Denmark and Sweden, 1983–2000

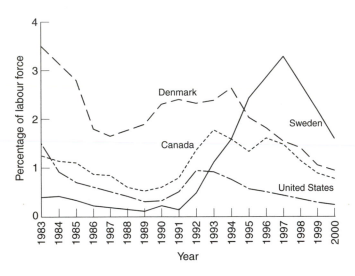

Figure 8.2b Long-term unemployment ≥ 12 months, as a percentage of the labour force in Canada, the United States, Denmark and Sweden, 1983–2000.

Sources: OECD 1989b: 217; 1990: 203; 1991b: 259; 1993: 196; 1994c: 206; 1996c: 202; 1998a: 208; 1999b: 242; 2000a: 220; 2001a: 252; 2001b: 227.

in Sweden – and then turned downward again after a longer or shorter period of time. The United States soon clearly had the lowest figures, whereas Sweden eventually scored higher than both Canada and Denmark.

Another relevant piece of information is the average duration of ongoing unemployment. This information is not available for Denmark, but only for Canada, the United States and Sweden. People defined as unemployed in the labour force surveys have been asked how long they have been without a job. Table 8.3 shows the duration of unemployment – in average number of weeks – for the three countries for which we have data.

Apparently, there were no great differences between Canada, the United States and Sweden in 1983. Since then a gap has emerged between the United States and the others, indicating more flexibility in the former country. The patterns for Canada and Sweden are rather similar, but Canada has higher figures for three of the four years in the table. However, Sweden passed Canada towards the end of the 1990s and the gap was then larger than before.

A few words can also be mentioned about flows into and out of unemployment. An OECD comparison (1995: 27–8) – covering a number of years from 1979 through 1994 (for Denmark only 1985 and 1993) – shows that inflows used to be much higher in North America than in the two Scandinavian countries, but in the early 1990s this gap diminished substantially or even disappeared. Unfortunately, there is no information as to whether the unemployed have found a job or left the labour force. With respect to outflows, the United States had the highest rates, which is not surprising given its high inflows and the information provided in Table 8.3. For a long time Canada and Sweden seemed to be on about the same level, but in the 1990s we find much lower figures for Sweden. Denmark had very low outflow rates in both 1985 and 1993, although in the latter case higher than in Sweden.

Table 8.3 Average duration of unemployment in Canada, the United States and Sweden, selected years, 1983–98 (weeks)

	Canada	US	Sweden
1983	21.8	20.0	20.7
1990	16.8	12.0	14.7
1993	25.1	18.1	23.4
1998	24.1	15.8	29.0[a]

Sources: Statistics Canada (various years); SCB (various years); US Department of Labor 1999: 207.

Note
a 1997.

How do we account for existing patterns?

Summarising the picture of unemployment patterns in Canada, the United States, Denmark and Sweden presented above, a few features can be stressed:

1   There are rather large variations – across countries and time – in terms of unemployment levels. Economic cycles are certainly a most important explanatory factor behind the variation over time, but they can hardly explain all the country differences. The most striking of the latter differences is that between Sweden and the other three countries in the 1980s. Sweden then had very low unemployment rates and all the others much higher figures. Moreover, the most striking change in the period covered by this analysis is the dramatic rise in the Swedish unemployment level in the 1990s. Another important change is the declining figures in all four countries during the last years.

2   We have found relatively little variation across countries with respect to sub-group unemployment rates, but there are certain differences to be observed. In Denmark, women show clearly higher unemployment rates than men. This pattern does not appear in the other three countries, where generally speaking gender differences are smaller and often to men's disadvantage. Moreover, the ratios of youth/prime-age unemployment turn out to be higher in the United States and Sweden than in Canada and Denmark, indicating that lacking a job is relatively more of a youth problem in the first two countries. When comparing the older labour force in the same way with the prime-age category, we see that unemployment is commonly lower among the former, although it used to be the other way round in Sweden. Another aspect is that there are substantial differences with respect to education. The general pattern in all four countries is that people with low education are much more likely to become unemployed than are the highly educated. Relatively speaking they are, however, worse off in the United States than in the other three cases.

3   Finally, our data reveal some significant differences in long-term unemployment, in flows and duration. It is above all the United States that shows shorter spells of unemployment and larger flows in and out of it. Most of the time, Denmark has had the least flexible labour market in these respects, although considerable improvement has occurred in the last few years. Canada is relatively close to the American pattern and for a long time this was also true for Sweden, but in the recession of the 1990s it had a huge increase in the proportion of people in long-term unemployment.

We may then ask how these patterns are to be explained. The advocates of the sclerosis perspective often take the declining unemployment figures in the United States in the 1990s as evidence of the accuracy of their arguments. Still, these figures are not that low. It can be added that in the last quarter of a century the average annual unemployment rate in the United States has never been below 4 per cent and in the early 1980s it almost reached 10 per cent. Moreover, much of the American institutional framework (in terms of employment protection legislation, unemployment benefits, active labour market policies, etc.) has been relatively stable for a rather long time. Obviously this institutional framework is compatible with both low and high unemployment rates. Now, some significant changes have taken place since the early 1980s in the United States. Union density has declined and wage differentials have increased. These developments may of course be significant factors behind the fall in unemployment.

For those who argue that unemployment can be successfully combated only through macro-economic policies and active labour market measures oriented towards full employment, i.e., through a full-employment commitment, the United States may appear as something like an anomaly. Or, to be more precise, its development in the 1990s seems difficult to explain. Why has unemployment declined the way it has, although American governments have never been very interested in giving priority to full employment? There must be some other factors in operation and we can hardly avoid the suspicion that the increasing wage flexibility – or, more precisely, the increasing wage differentials – in the American labour market have something to do with the declining unemployment level.

Another issue is the sclerosis perspective on employment protection legislation. It is assumed that restrictions of this kind prevent young people from being recruited to jobs, since employers are reluctant to recruit new workers as it is costly to get rid of them again if necessary. As a consequence we must expect young people more often to become unemployed. The United States is characterised by the least restrictive regulation among all the OECD countries and it should therefore be expected to have comparatively low youth/prime-age unemployment ratios. However, although American employers have little to risk by taking on young people, youth unemployment is still a relatively severe problem in the United States. In this respect, not much support for the sclerosis explanation can be found in the American experience.

There are also other problems facing the sclerosis perspective. It can hardly be proved by the fact that one country – for a limited period of time – shows declining unemployment. There has been too much focus on the United States as a model to look up to. But why does, for example, Canada have such a poor unemployment record? It is after all also rather far from the Scandinavian systems. All through the 1980s and the 1990s, Canada has been less 'rigid' in terms of employment protection, wage differentials, welfare benefits, etc., than Denmark and Sweden. Nonetheless its level of unemployment has all the time been higher than that in at least one – and very often both – of these two countries. The full-employment commitment approach would in this case claim that Canadian governments have never cared very much about full employment and that the country has therefore proceeded as a society with high unemployment.

The changes that have taken place in Denmark represent another analytical problem. Can the declining Danish unemployment rates in the 1990s be explained in terms of deregulation and diminishing rigidities? The answer to that question is evidently no. Denmark's employment protection has been rather weak all the time and cannot possibly explain the declining unemployment level. The possibilities of being supported by unemployment insurance have been limited in recent years, but the benefit system is still one of the most generous in the West. Of course, the reservation wage may have decreased for many categories due to stricter rules in the unemployment insurance and other welfare systems, but wage differentials have remained very much the same. One of the most significant institutional changes that have taken place in Denmark imply a more active profile in its labour market policy and these changes indicate that the government's commitment to fight unemployment is important.

With regard to Sweden, it can be assumed that if nothing had happened in the 1990s one explanation would have presented itself immediately, namely that a strong commitment to full employment leads to low unemployment. During most of the post-World War II period up to the 1990s Sweden was perhaps the best example of how a strong labour movement oriented towards full employment could be successful in its efforts. But how do we account for what has happened in the 1990s? The high unemployment levels in the last decade cannot easily be explained in terms of the sclerosis perspective. For this approach to be relevant, the rapid increase in the Swedish unemployment level would need to have something to do with increased rigidities.

However, the significant changes that have taken place all go in the opposite direction. There have, for example, been some changes in employment protection legislation, making it somewhat less strict. It has become possible to organise private employment services and temporary work agencies. Temporary employment contracts are also more common today than in the beginning of the 1990s (Storrie 2002). Moreover, wage differentials have become larger, not by much but still larger. Full employment has been given less priority since 1991, when price stability was emphasised as a crucial goal for economic policy. Social benefits, including unemployment benefits, have been cut. A number of deregulations have been carried out in other areas; finance and credit markets have become deregulated, public monopolies have been broken, etc.

By far the most important change that Sweden has gone through in the 1990s is that it has become a member of the European Union (EU). Many of the changes mentioned above represent adjustments to this new situation, no matter whether they occurred before or after the membership came into force. This is not to say that unemployment would now be lower in Sweden had the country remained outside the EU. There is simply no way of knowing what would have happened then; counter-factual questions have no ready answers. We can however be sure that the process of internationalisation of the economy would have taken place anyway, although in somewhat different forms. Now, over the last decade Sweden has become a rather normal European country. The EU as a whole has long since been characterised by very high unemployment and Sweden – with its dramatic increase of unemployment in the 1990s – is no longer very far from the average. We can recall that when Denmark joined the EU in 1973 its unemployment rate rose quite substantially, but it should be emphasised that this coincided with the first oil crisis.

To repeat, the recent international debate has been very much centred on the differences between Europe and the United States (hence the expression

'Eurosclerosis'; see Chapter 1). However, Europe is not homogeneous. It has had a very high average unemployment level for many years, but some European countries fall or at least have fallen clearly short of this level, e.g., Austria, Norway, Sweden and today also Denmark. The sclerosis argument is, furthermore, too much based upon the case of the United States. It is assumed that the type of flexibility that characterises the American labour market can explain why unemployment is low and that it can be a model for other countries to follow. But the question is whether lack of regulation is the main explanation for the recent, successful employment development in the United States. There are also other factors that may provide explanations for this development, for example the role played by 'the world's largest integrated economy' (Esping-Andersen 1999: 141) and the rapid and successful expansion of information technology.

The decline of unemployment in the United States during the 1990s is no doubt related to the remarkable growth of the economy. It is impossible or at least difficult to find any support for the various prophesies of 'jobless growth' that have been brought forward in the public debate. The expanding American economy has created a strong demand for labour and therefore both increasing employment and decreasing unemployment. In relation to the issues discussed here it must then be asked whether or to what extent the economic growth in the United States is due to its relatively unregulated labour market. The lack of regulation may have had some role to play, but the market position (at home and abroad) of American companies and their lead in developing technology – especially information technology – are probably more important.

Another aspect to consider is of course that in the late 1990s unemployment also went down in other countries with more regulated labour markets and very different institutional set-ups. In particular, the Danish development in the late 1990s suggests some complications here. Furthermore, why was unemployment during the 1980s clearly lower in Sweden which was then much more 'rigid' in terms of employment protection, wage differentials, social benefits, etc.? And, if North American flexibility is the answer, why does Canada – which also has a relatively unregulated labour market although not as unregulated as the United States – have such a high level of unemployment?

Let us for the sake of the argument assume that Denmark should take some steps towards the model represented by the United States. It does not seem very likely that Denmark would quickly go all the way to this very market-oriented type of society, but we can – with some creativity – imagine that it would end up in a position similar to that of Canada in terms of wage inequality, employment protection, welfare state generosity, etc. The question is then what unemployment rates should we expect to get. Given what Denmark now has, would it get higher unemployment as in Canada or lower as in the United States? This rhetorical question puts the finger on some of the difficulties experienced with too simple answers.

9 Flexibility and employment insecurity

Thomas P. Boje and Anne Grönlund

Introduction

During the last decade, flexibility is frequently mentioned when characterising the ongoing transformation of work organisation and employment patterns, as well as in regulation of the labour market. Flexibility is seen as a main instrument in reducing labour costs, boosting employment, and increasing productivity. Consequently, the need for flexibility in work and employment is emphasised by both politicians and employers as a necessity to adjust the national labour markets to the intensified competition following from globalisation, new forms of technology, and changing consumer patterns and family relations. Seen from the employer's perspective, introduction of labour flexibility is a convenient instrument for helping firms cope with the growing uncertainty in the market and in giving the employers the possibility of transferring this uncertainty on to their employees. For the employees, the introduction of flexible work organisations and employment contracts are more dubious. On the one hand, it might release the employees from the most rigid forms of organising the work process and thereby give them greater possibilities of combining work and family responsibilities. On the other hand, it typically also means more insecurity and irregularity of employment contracts and consequently greater vulnerability in their position in the labour market (Benoit 2000; Carnoy, Castells and Brenner 1997; Castells 1996; Dex and McCulloch 1997; O'Reilly and Fagan 1998; Rubery *et al.* 1998).

In the labour market literature, flexibility is generally defined as the capacity of firms and workers to adjust to changes (Meulders and Wilkin 1987: 50; OECD 1989a: 13). This general definition of flexibility does not specify the different types of flexibility and how to accomplish them. Most theories on labour market flexibility distinguish, however, between two main types of flexibility – numerical and functional flexibility (Atkinson 1987: 90–2). In the following analysis, we want to elaborate on this distinction. In addition to functional flexibility we distinguish between numerical flexibility related to change in the number of workers and work time flexibility related to change in the number of working hours. The three forms of flexibility discussed here are defined as follows. *Numerical flexibility* refers to measures used by a firm to adapt the volume of labour to the demand for labour by adjusting the number of workers. *Work time flexibility* is accomplished by a firm changing the number of working hours and the distribution of working hours during the day without modifying the number of employees (see below for a more detailed operationalisation of these two types of flexibility). *Functional flexibility* indicates the capability of a firm to adapt the work organisation and the present work force to changes in product, technology and consumer demands without changes in the volume of labour. Typically, this takes place by reallocation of the labour force through job rotations or shifts of occupation in the firm-internal labour market and includes retraining of the employees.

An additional type of flexibility, wage flexibility, is often included in the definition of flexibility. This type of flexibility means, among other things, a firm's attempt to adjust the labour costs to the company's needs by replacing 'across-the-board pay structures by some form of performance-linked system' (OECD 1989a: 169). Wage flexibility is often seen as a means by which employers can raise productivity and as a mechanism by which they can initiate other types of flexibility. Wage flexibility will not be included in this chapter but will be dealt with in Chapter 10 in this volume

The literature defines labour flexibility as a highly complex concept with a variety of strategies primarily used by employers to accommodate the size and costs of labour to shifting demands. The trends towards flexibility in work and employment practices are driven by intensified market competition and information technologies. Moreover, the institutional framework for regulation of the labour market and the social organisation of the work process is also crucial in determining the type and extent of labour flexibility imposed on workers (see also Chapter 3 in this volume).

In understanding labour flexibility, we have to take into consideration the complex set of social and economic institutions surrounding the work process and labour relations. Rubery (1989) has identified a framework that structures the relationship between the employment system and labour flexibility. She identifies the following four components: the system of labour market regulation including the legal system of industrial relations as well as the voluntary collective bargaining system; the labour market system consisting of labour market flows, forms of employment, the vocational training system, and the labour supply and demand; the industrial system covering the structuring of industries and occupations, the firm organisation as well as the employer strategies for competitiveness and implementing of new technologies; and finally the system of social reproduction, which includes the systems for income maintenance, how childcare and the care of the elderly is provided as well as the structuring of families.

In this chapter, we will concentrate our analysis of labour flexibility on two specific elements of the labour market system: type of employment relations and work patterns used by employers in our four countries. The chapter is organised in the following way. First, we discuss some of the theories describing the development of flexibility in labour as well as in the organisational structure of businesses. Second, we elaborate the concept of flexibility and operationalise the two forms of flexibility dealt with in this chapter – numerical and work time flexibility. Third, we analyse the extent to which employment relations and the work schedule standards have become more diverse in the four countries included in this study.

The new labour market: flexibility, externalisation and individualisation

The market conditions of all Western economies are characterised by growing instability and unpredictability. The internationalisation of product markets has intensified competition and the pace of technological innovations in society as well as in the work place has increased tremendously. This development has caused a strong pressure for cost reductions of labour through a more flexible use of labour and a flexible organisation of firms. The economic restructuring has led to a variety of organisational changes in the work processes as well as in the employment system. Changes where the primary goal has been to cope with the uncertainty caused by changes in the economic and technological environment of the firms. Castells mentioned a variety of organisational changes aimed at redefining work organisation and employment processes. The most important changes addressing labour flexibility are: the transition from mass production to flexible production; the introduction of new methods of management or the development from 'Fordism' to 'Toyotism' defined as 'just-in-time' production, team work, decentralisation and a flat management hierarchy; inter-firm networking either through a system of networks developed by small and medium-size firms or through licensing-subcontracting by large corporations using subproductions (Castells 1996: 153–6). Castells concludes his analysis by saying that the traditional form of work based on full-time employment and career pattern over the lifecycle is being slowly but surely eroded (Castells 1996: 268).

Instead, it is argued that different types of non-standard employment contracts have been introduced. Contracts characterised by insecure, tenuous or indirect relations between employee and employer. The non-standard employment relationship is typically framed by contingency or transient work and can be characterised by two fundamental characteristics: lack of continuous employment and variability and unpredictability in work schedule (Polivka and Nardone 1989). In his analysis of part-time work, Tilly (1996) advocates another definition of contingency. He classifies a job as contingent if it has a low level of skill and responsibility, offers low pay, involves high rates of turnover and tends to be a job that does not provide advancement. The definition of non-standard contracts is closely related to flexible employment and the principle forms of flexible work usually include temporary work, contract work, part-time employment, certain categories of self-employed persons, subcontracted work and work at home (Belous 1989; Carnoy, Castells and Brenner 1997; Tilly 1996). In this chapter, we analyse the flexibility of the four labour markets by focusing on trends in employment tenure, temporary work, job turnover and the pattern of work schedules.

From labour market segmentation to the flexible firm

In the early 1970s, theories that described the labour market as divided into different segments were developed among primarily American institutional economists and sociologists in opposition to neo-classic labour market theories.

According to the original dual labour market theory, the labour force was divided into two distinct segments acting differently and with restricted inter-segment mobility; a primary segment characterised by firms with stable and well-paying jobs and opportunities for advancement and a secondary segment characterised by firms with unstable employment and low-paying and dead-end jobs (Doeringer and Piore 1971; Gordon, Edwards and Reich 1982). This division corresponds to a division of the industrial structure in a sector with large firms producing for large and predictable markets and a sector with small firms producing for more competitive and casual market segments.

During the 1970s, the dual labour market theory was developed into a more complex theory of labour market segmentation operating with diverse segments and several explanatory variables (Boje 1987). Both the primary and secondary segments were divided into subsegments. The primary segment was divided into an upper segment including professional and managerial positions in the firms and a lower segment that includes the firm-specific qualified core workers who have long tenure and are promoted through an internal career organisation. The secondary segment was divided into subgroups based on ethnicity, gender and region. In the early 1980s, it was obvious that the mode of production began to change, the labour market became more unpredictable and the emerging post-industrial work organisation was more complex and dynamic than described by the segmentation theories. Intensified global competition and new technology caused this change in labour market organisation but it does not mean that the labour market was not divided. Instead, the segments became more varied than predicted in the segmented labour market theories (Rosenberg 1989).

In one of the first descriptions of the new condition operating in work organisations and labour markets, Piore and Sabel (1984) formulated the thesis of 'flexible specialisation'. They identified a second industrial divide and contrasted mass and flexible production or Fordist and post-Fordist types of production instead of the previous division between mass production for a regulated and for an unregulated commodity market. They argued that the increasingly unpredictable and fragmented commodity market required firms to abandon the 'Fordist' combination of mass production and narrowly qualified workers and replace it with small-batch production and broadly qualified workers. Piore and Sabel's flexible specialisation theory has many similarities with the dual labour market theory developed more than a decade earlier by Piore (1975), just adapted to the flexible work organisation of the 1980s (Fine 1995). While Piore and Sabel (1984) focus primarily on the trends towards developing a more skilled labour force, other labour market researchers talk about a new labour market characterised by a growing number of contingent workers, a decline in employment protection and an increased division within the labour force (Boyer 1987; Christopherson and Stroper 1989; Rosenberg 1989). They argue that the move towards greater flexibility in work organisation and in use of labour has led to a more differentiated employment pattern.

The diffusion of information technologies has mixed consequences for both the work processes and the workers. In the work process, the implementation of information technology has led to a replacement of routine and repetitive work, which through automation has been programmed into machines and thereby many unskilled and semi-skilled workers have been replaced. Furthermore, it has enriched the remaining work by giving the workers at the shop floor level more control over the work process and consequently this led to an increase in skills of many of the remaining workers (Castells 1996: 242). The implementation of the information technologies has also caused different trends for the employees. On the one hand, an increase in skills takes place among the workers handling the new information technologies and the variety of highly specialised professional jobs – a growing demand for symbolic analysts according to Reich (1992). On the other hand, many of the traditional skilled crafts jobs in goods-producing industries have disappeared and a significant number of the new service jobs are low-skilled and contingent jobs, which are created especially in personal and social services. Of these two trends, the dominant trend in a given labour market depends on the institutional arrangements surrounding the work organisation and the strictness of employment regulation. In countries with strict regulation of employment relations, internal task flexibility and ongoing skills training, stable employment relations seem to prevail while a growth in external job flexibility, individualised employment relations and casual jobs seem to be the dominant trend in countries with a deregulated labour market (Pollard 1995: 123).

In the segmentation theories the firms were seen as stable and homogeneous units while the flexible firm is described as internally divided and can thus be considered a hybrid including highly qualified, well-paid and permanent jobs as well as low-qualified, low-paid and temporary jobs. Atkinson (1987) describes this new type of work organisation as 'the flexible firm'. Atkinson's work is probably one of the most influential models that explains how employers develop flexibility in the use of labour and in organising the work processes (Atkinson 1987: 94). According to Atkinson, flexibility is optimised by dividing a firm's labour force into different subgroups of workers, with very different employment relations to the firm. First, there is a core group of workers who perform what a firm considers the most important job functions. These workers have long-term employment contracts, are well paid and are mainly men. Another subgroup is composed of several peripheral groups of workers who perform routine and repetitive tasks. They are often part-time or temporary employees, receive lower pay than the core group and are typically women. The third subgroup consists of external groups of workers such as agency temps, self-employed service workers or subcontractors. The different kinds of jobs included in this third subgroup range from highly specialised tasks – designing, engineering and accounting – to very simple tasks – cleaning, repairing and policing. These workers perform the simple tasks and are not considered as part of a firm's labour force but as an external group of flexible labour.

Both men and women are exposed to flexibility but in different ways. The typical male type of flexibility is contractual work, overtime work or shift work, which is better compensated than female forms of flexibility, which typically are part-time, temporary jobs, or work at home (Bettio and Rosenberg 1999: 277; Burchall and Diana 1999: 454). On the other hand, the trend towards growing precariousness in employment relations seems to have worsened male positions in the labour market and this is especially the case for men employed in the traditional industries and primarily in unskilled jobs.

Externalisation and networking

The theories of flexibility have argued that the large corporations are in crisis and the small and medium-sized firms have taken over innovation and job growth (Piore and Sabel 1984). This thesis is highly contested and as shown by Harrison (1994) large corporations still dominate the European and American commodity markets and their share of employment has not declined during the recent decades. Instead, we have seen a decline of large vertically integrated firms as an organisational model. By adapting information technologies, large corporations have been able to create a more flexible organisation. Through a network organisation, the different parts of the total production process can be placed at different sites and can be controlled from a central position. This makes it possible for the company to localise subproductions in regional areas with a cheap and adequately qualified labour force and to locate the administrative headquarters and research departments in the urban business centres optimal for its commercial purposes and where highly qualified labour is located.

The large corporations have been restructured. A vertically integrated organisation has been replaced by a horizontal organisation where significant parts of the production are externalised. Pfeffer and Baron (1988) distinguish between three different types of externalisation. The first type is externalisation of the workplace – working at home and telecommuting. This type of work is made possible primarily by information technology, can be the result of a lack of adequate labour and the search for cheaper labour, and is especially popular for office work and professional employment. The second type of externalisation takes place by hiring the workers for a limited time of employment. Typically, it concerns temporary jobs or contract work on specific projects. Traditionally, this type of externalisation has been widespread in the construction industries and for seasonal work but today it is common in most industries and especially growing in business and social services. Finally, externalisation occurs when work is contracted out or when employees are leased. These arrangements mean that the employers assign work tasks to be done by companies or individuals who are not connected with the firm by an employment contract but are expected to deliver products or services (Brunhes 1989: 14–15). The last type of externalisation aims primarily at solving sudden demands for labour or specific defined work functions peripheral to the core tasks of the firms.

We find several trends indicating an increasing externalisation in the labour market; one trend is the growth of business services, temporary employment agencies and consulting firms, and another is the large corporations' outsourcing or subcontracting of parts of their production to external suppliers. This externalisation of work and workers makes it easier for the individual firm to accommodate to growing market competition (Hirschhorn 1997; Carnoy 1994 and Chapter 6 in this volume). For the individual employee, subcontracted labour does not need to be a contingent job. Often the contracted employees perform a job previously held by employees employed directly by the firm. The work contract has changed from the core firm to a subcontractor and this change often means insecure employment and lower payment, but not necessarily. If the subcontracting firms have high independence and a large number of clients, then they are able to provide their employees permanent fulltime employment contracts (Carnoy, Castells and Brenner 1997).

Flexibility – an empirical reality?

The theories of flexibility are primarily abstract constructions. They have been criticised for being fiction rather than fact and for being far too one-dimensional in their analysis of the transformation from a 'Fordist' protective production system and work organisation to a more competitive and vulnerable system. It is unclear to what extent these changes in Western labour markets are a dominant trend. Many researchers (Bettio and Rosenberg 1999; Fine 1995; Pollert 1988 and 1991; Wood 1989) have questioned the assumption that a flexible production regime will replace the Fordist mass production regime.

The high unemployment, relocation of subproduction on to the newly industrialised countries and growth in the volatile informational companies have for many employees made their employment conditions insecure, reduced their bargaining power and consequently worsened their social protection. However, this development is highly dependent on the institutional structure of the regional labour market as well as the type of production discussed. In the United States and the United Kingdom, where neo-liberal ideology prevails, labour flexibility together with other policy measures have worsened the conditions of labour while flexibility has not had these consequences in countries with the more regulated employment relations and universal social protection that exist in Scandinavian countries (Pollard 1995; 123).

Finally, several studies criticising the thesis of labour flexibility argue that its development is contradictory. The first and probably the most serious critique, addresses the extent of labour flexibility. In most studies, flexibility is documented by cases taken from regional labour markets, which obviously have been difficult to generalise; in some cases, labour flexibility appears to be a temporary phenomenon.[1] The second critique states that a high level of flexibility and deregulation might be devastating for the stability and competitiveness of the individual firms if it implies high labour turnover and an increasing number of short-term employees. In the expanding informational sector, most firms depend on firm-specific skills and investments in production of those skills that are poorly suited for high levels of labour turnover. Therefore, too much flexibility might destabilise a firm's organisation and create potential problems in controlling labour by breaking up the collective labour structures (Peck 1994; and Pollard 1995). Castells (1996), who has closely reviewed the literature on flexibility, finds that the transformation of work means an individualisation of labour and a restructuring of the labour force into two opposite groups: a core labour force of qualified workers that handle -

information-based production technologies and a variety of disposable labour forces that 'can be automated and/or hired/offshored'. Which one of these two groups is dominant largely depends on the composition of specific national labour markets and their institutional surroundings (Castells 1996: 272).

The concept of flexibility – how to measure it?

We want to end this theoretical section by giving a short description of the different types of flexibility used in our empirical analysis. In this context, it is important to remember that we are analysing flexibility from the point of view of the employer. Including the employee's perspective in an analysis of flexibility is extremely important but would make it even more complex and therefore we will not do this in this chapter (see Meulders and Wilkin 1987; OECD 1989a).

Numerical flexibility means adjusting the volume of labour in firms to the demand for labour conditioned by the structural and economic variations in production and demand for goods (Meulders and Wilkin 1987: 7). This type of flexibility can take several forms:

- Variation in the volume of labour by employer-initiated moves of workers into and out of the firms. This job mobility, to some extent, can be measured by job turnover and employer tenure. Increased numerical flexibility means a growth in job turnover and shorter job tenure.
- Temporary employment refers to employment contracts between employer and worker, which from the outset have a specified end date.
- Externalisation of work refers to replacement of firm-based employment contracts by commercial labour contracts through subcontractors or temporary employment agencies.

Work time flexibility is achieved by modifying working hours without changing the number of workers. This is primarily accomplished by varying the number of working hours during the day, week and year an employee works or by reorganising a worker's schedule. We can distinguish between different forms:

- Part-time employment is often seen as a way for employers to balance the labour force in periods with strong fluctuations in demands for labour.
- Overtime work, shift work and annualisation of hours. All different types of adaptation of work time to seasonal and cyclical fluctuations in demand for work.
- Variable work hours is defined as work time arrangements such as work outside the normal working hours – work on weekends or nights – and finally flex-time. Flex-time means that the individual workers can decide when the working day starts and ends within certain limits set up by the firms.

The theories often assume that the employers are applying different types of flexibility to different groups of workers. Numerical flexibility is primarily used to organise the peripheral groups of workers who conduct the routine and mechanical job functions and are employed on temporary or part-time contracts through subcontractors or temporary employment agencies. Functional flexibility is expected from the core groups of workers, i.e., those who have permanent jobs and qualifications which are valuable to a firm. These workers are continuously retrained and relocated within the firm as the demand for labour in different parts of the production process changes (Atkinson 1987; Hakim 1990; Rodgers and Rodgers 1989: 11). Traditionally, work time flexibility has been used to organise the peripheral work force but has become common in all types of job functions. This is caused by a firm's need to adjust the production process to the demands of the product market and by increasing pressure on the workers to reconcile work and family obligations (O'Reilly and Fagan 1998).

Flexibility – empirical trends in North America and Scandinavia

Although flexibility has been a popular concept in labour market research for over a decade, the theories described in the previous section have been confronted with surprisingly little empirical research. In this section, we will look at data from national and international sources[2] in order to find out whether employment relations and work time standards are in fact becoming more diverse in our four countries and whether this will lead to increasing differences in working conditions between different groups.

Increased employment instability?

Tenure

A widely used measure of employment stability is employer tenure, i.e., the number of years a person has been with his or her current employer. In this respect, Sweden stands out from the other countries. In 1998, the average tenure in Sweden was 11.4 years, which was several years more than in the other three countries. The shortest average tenure, 6.6 years, was found in the United States, while Denmark and Canada had an average tenure of about 8 years (Table 9.1).

The differences between the countries could have several explanations. First, demographic factors, such as age and gender, may play a part. Naturally, tenure increases with age and consequently, an ageing population could increase the average tenure. The Swedish population is older than the population of the other countries, but since tenure in Sweden is longer in all age groups, the age factor seems less important (Table 9.2).

In Canada, Denmark and the United States, tenure is very similar in the younger age groups, but differs in the group aged 45 or more, indicating that the different age structure of the countries cannot fully explain the difference in average tenure (OECD 1997ad, 1997b). Gender, on the other hand, seems to be important. Swedish men and women have the same average tenure, but in the

Table 9.1 Average employee tenure: development over time in Canada, Denmark, Sweden and the United States (years)

	1976	1980	1985	1990	1995	1998
United States						
Total	–	6.6	6.5	6.7	6.7	6.6
Men	–	7.7	7.4	7.5	7.3	7.1
Women	–	5.4	5.5	5.9	6.1	6.1
Canada						
Total	7.0	7.0	7.3	7.2	7.9	8.0
Men	8.2	8.2	8.6	8.3	8.8	8.8
Women	5.0	5.1	5.8	5.8	6.9	7.2
Sweden						
Total	8.5	9.2	–	10.1	10.9	11.4
Men	10.0	10.2	–	10.1	11.2	11.3
Women	6.8	8.1	–	9.7	10.6	11.5
Denmark						
Total	7.0	6.7	7.6	8.2	7.9	–
Men	7.9	7.7	7.9	8.8	8.3	–
Women	5.7	5.4	7.2	7.7	7.5	–

Sources: CPS (USA); CLFS (Canada); Engelund 1992: 82 (Denmark 1974–90); OECD 1997d (Denmark 1995). The Swedish data (1975–91) are from Holmlund and Vejsiu 1998: 24 and special calculations done by Vejsiu and data for 1996–98 are from the SLFS.

Notes
We have not been able to find data for the same years for all countries, therefore, the following years differ from the years indicated in the head of the table:
Data for the USA are from 1983, 1987, 1991 and 1996. Data from 1996 and 1998 are not strictly comparable to earlier data, due to a change in definition. Data cover workers aged 16 and over.
Data for Sweden are for 1974, 1981, 1991 and 1996. Data from 1974–91 cover workers aged 20–64 years, while the data for 1996 and 1998 cover workers 16–64 years.
Data for Denmark are for 1976 and 1979 and cover workers 20–64 years.
Data for Canada cover all employed aged 15 and over.

Table 9. 2 Average employee tenure by age in Canada, Denmark, Sweden and the United States in 1995 (years)

Age groups	United States	Canada	Denmark	Sweden
15–24	1.6	1.6	1.5	2.2
25–44	6.2	6.5	6.3	8.2
45–	12.4	13.8	14.5	15.9

Source: OECD 1997d: 139.

Note
The US data are for 1996.

other countries, female tenure is 0.8–1.9 years shorter than that of men (Table 9.1). In addition, female employment rates differ between the countries and both these factors, which can be seen as a result of the different labour market and welfare regimes, will obviously influence tenure data. Employment protection legislation – another manifestation of the different labour market regime – could have some impact too. According to the Swedish Employment Protection Act, dismissals must follow the seniority principle of 'last in – first out',[3] whereas in North America, the employer is more or less free to pick and chose among the employees. Even in Denmark, where the labour market regime bears many similarities to Sweden's labour market, employment protection provisions are much less strict (Bruun *et al.* 1990; OECD 1999b; see also Chapter 3 in this volume).

Part of the difference in average tenure within Scandinavia may also be explained by the fact that the Danish labour market is dominated by small and medium-sized enterprises, which offer less career opportunities than larger Swedish companies. Although there is no clear dividing line between Scandinavia and North America, the longer average tenure in Sweden leads us to believe that the difference in labour market regimes does have an impact on average tenure; however, other factors should be considered.

Since the mid-1970s, average tenure has increased slightly in Canada and Denmark and rather markedly in Sweden (Table 9.1). In the United States, there has been no change since 1983, when the data series begins. From our data, it is also clear that the trends for men and women are quite different. Among women, tenure has increased in all four countries, most dramatically in Sweden. Male tenure has increased in Sweden and to some extent in Denmark and Canada, but not as much as female tenure. Although tenure has fallen slightly for American men, our tenure data do not support the hypothesis of increasing employment instability.

The tenure difference between Sweden and the other countries has increased over the years, a fact that strengthens the impression that labour market regimes do make a difference. For example, the large-scale entry of women into the labour market took place much earlier in Sweden than in North America, much as a result of Swedish welfare policy. This policy, which included a tax reform favouring dual-earner couples, a rapid expansion of public childcare and the introduction of a generous parental leave[4] (Sundström 1991; Anxo 1995), has enabled Swedish women to work continuously throughout their childbearing years and by the early 1990s, they had achieved an average tenure equal to that of men (Table 9.1). Similarly, in Denmark welfare policy has encouraged female labour market participation, but again, there are differences between the two Scandinavian countries. For example, parental leave is not as generous in Denmark as in Sweden (OECD 1995; Boje and Almqvist 2000). In addition, it is reasonable to assume that the introduction of the Swedish Employment Protection Act in 1974 has contributed to an increase in tenure, especially during recessions when the law protects long-tenured workers against dismissals.[5] However, other factors could be important. For example, employment has grown much faster in North America than in Scandinavia, keeping average tenure down (OECD 1997b).

In the theories of flexibilisation, a company's search for flexibility is often assumed to lead to increasing differences in job stability between men and women or between groups with different education levels. The tenure difference between the young and the old, on the other hand, would be expected to decrease because a dismantling of internal labour markets would primarily affect the tenure of middle-aged and older people. However, neither of these hypotheses can be confirmed by our tenure data. First, there is no clear relation between tenure and education. In Denmark, tenure clearly increases with education, but in the United States, workers with a university education have a shorter tenure than workers with a secondary education. In Sweden and Canada, the group with only primary education has the longest average tenure (OECD 1997d). Second, the gap in average tenure between men and women has narrowed considerably since the 1970s in all four countries, reflecting an increase in female employment rates. Third, the tenure difference between the young and the old has not decreased. Quite to the contrary, this difference has increased among women in all four countries due to a slight fall in tenure among young women, but mainly due to the sharp increase in tenure among middle-aged and older women.[6] This development has been most obvious in Sweden. Among men in Scandinavia, there is a similar trend (Engelund 1992; SLFS Holmlund and Vejsiu 1998). Only among men in North America is the development in line with the hypothesis. In both Canada and the United States, male tenure has fallen in all age groups since the mid-1980s; therefore, the aforementioned increase in average tenure among Canadian men can probably be attributed to the ageing of the population. In absolute terms, the sharpest decrease has occurred among middle-aged and older men. This could be an indication of the dismantling of internal labour markets and the development of more 'flexible' employment relations at least for men in North America.

It should be pointed out that average tenure is a far from perfect measure of employment stability. As we have already seen, it is influenced by demographic factors and it is affected by the economic cycle. For example, average tenure may rise in a recession, as people cling to their jobs and decline when the economy improves and there are more jobs available. In addition, we should be cautious in using tenure as an indicator of an employer's search for numerical flexibility, as we do not know whether employers or employees end employment contracts.

Temporary employment

A seemingly more reliable indicator is temporary employment.[7] Here the United States stands out with a very low share of temporary workers: less than 2 per cent of all workers, compared to about 11–15 per cent in the other three countries (Table 9.3).

However, the level of temporary employment can be difficult to compare since employment protection provisions differ considerably among the countries. In Sweden, laws protect permanent jobs. In order to end such a contract, the employer has to present a just cause, negotiate with the union, observe certain

Table 9.3 Incidence of temporary employment (percentages of total number of employees) in Canada, Denmark, Sweden and the United States, 1987–97

	1987	1989	1991	1993	1995	1997
United States					2.2	1.9
Canada					12.0	
Sweden	11.7	10.7	9.9	11.5	14.1	14.6
Denmark	12.3	10.8	11.9	12.0	11.2	11.1

Sources: Storrie 1997 (Sweden);, CPS (USA);, Statistics Canada 1998 (Canada); European Commission 1999 (Denmark).

Notes
All data are for workers, but the definitions of temporary employment vary as follows:
The United States: workers who expect their job to last for an additional year or less and who have had their job for a year or less.
Canada: workers on a job that will end on a predetermined date or when a specific project is completed.
Sweden: workers on different kinds of limited duration contracts specified in the law (leave replacements, project work, probationary work, on-call, seasonal work, holiday work, work experience, relief work).
Denmark: fixed-term contracts.

periods of notice, etc. In the United States, on the other hand, all employment relations may be ended promptly and without any notice and therefore the distinction between 'permanent' and 'temporary' jobs is not obvious (Holmlund 1995).

Nevertheless, temporary employment is a phenomenon that has attracted much attention in recent years, especially in Sweden where it has increased. To many observers this is a striking sign of labour market 'flexibilisation', while others see it mainly as a result of the deep recession in the early 1990s or as a shift in employment regulations (Holmlund 1995; Storrie 1997). A problem is that data are collected over a short time, which makes it difficult to draw viable conclusions about or identify trends in any country. However, it should be pointed out that young people are heavily overrepresented in temporary employment. For example, people aged 20 to 24 comprise a quarter of the temporary work force in both the United States (CPS) and Sweden (SLFS). In Scandinavia, especially in Sweden, temporary employment is very common among young people. In 1997, 43 per cent of Swedish employees aged 20 to 24 and 65 per cent of Swedish employees aged 16 to 19 had a temporary job (SLFS). This gives us reason to believe that temporary employment, at least to some extent, is a result of normal 'job-hopping' among young people trying to gain work experience and make career decisions. Thus, temporary jobs may serve as a stepping stone to permanent employment (Gallie *et al.* 1998: 178–9; Holmlund 1995). However, the high level of temporary employment also reflects the difficulties young people experience in finding a permanent job and may indicate that the process of finding a job takes longer than before. Also, some people, such as women in the public sector in Scandinavia, run the risk of being trapped in 'permanent temporariness', moving between unemployment, education activities and different temporary jobs (Gonäs 1995: 156). In a US survey, half of the contingent workers came from other jobs, some of which had been 'permanent' (Polivka 1996b).

Job turnover

Another indicator of labour market flexibility is job turnover, defined as the sum of job gains and job losses during a year. In the late 1980s and early 1990s, job turnover was higher in the two Scandinavian countries than in North America (Table 9.4).

In addition, the composition of the turnover was different. For example, the United States has a larger share of openings and closures of new establishments compared to the other countries, where a greater part of the turnover resulted from expansions and contractions in firms. This is hardly in line with the economic theories arguing that the employment protection legislation in Scandinavia makes it difficult for employers to hire and fire. Instead, the US labour market appears to be turbulent, with many short-lived companies. However, we should remember that the data only cover the private sector, a fact that may affect the comparison since job turnover is often presumed to be lower in the public sector and since both Scandinavian countries have large public sectors. In addition, there is some doubt as to the quality and comparability of the data. The US data seem to overestimate openings and closures and in Canada job turnover might be underestimated, as the data refer to firms and not establishments (OECD 1996c and 1994a). Bearing this

Table 9.4 Job gains and job losses. Average annual rates as a percentage of employment in the private sector in Canada, Denmark, Sweden and the United States

	USA 1984–91	Canada 1983–91	Sweden 1985–92	Denmark 1983–89 –A	Denmark 1981–93 –B
Gross job gains	13.0	14.5	14.5	16.0	12.4
Openings	8.4	3.2	6.5	6.1	3.9
Expansions	4.6	11.2	8.0	9.9	8.5
Gross job losses	10.4	11.9	14.6	13.8	11.8
Closures	7.3	3.1	5.0	5.0	4.2
Contractions	3.1	8.8	9.6	8.8	7.5
Net employment change	2.6	2.6	-0.1	2.2	0.5
Job turnover	23.4	26.3	29.1	29.8	24.2
Job turnover in continuous establishments only	7.7	20.0	17.6	18.7	16.0

Sources: OECD: 1996c: 163. For B, OECD: 1999e, Denmark.

Notes
Data cover employees in the private sector. The public administration and establishments providing non-market services have been excluded, as well as the primary sector except mining and quarrying.
Data for Canada refer to firms, whereas data for the other countries refer to establishments.
In addition, the OECD warns that the US data are problematic, as they seem to overestimate openings and closures (OECD 1994a: 108 and Annex 3A).

in mind, the overall impression is that job turnover is high in all four countries, with two to three out of ten private sector jobs being exchanged over a year.

Employment security

As we have seen, the stability of employment relations, measured by standard measures such as tenure or job turnover, has not been eroded. Yet, an increasing number of people seem to feel that their job is not secure. During the 1990s, perceived job security has decreased in all four countries included in this study, as well as in the rest of the OECD. Of our four countries, the United States had the lowest reported level of job security in 1996, when only 48 per cent of Americans felt that their job was secure (Table 9.5).

This may seem surprising, considering the low and declining level of unemployment, but it might be explained by the lack of employment protection and lack of economic security when unemployment occurs. On the other hand, the level of perceived job security is lower in Sweden than in Canada and Denmark, despite stricter employment protection. The severe economic crisis that hit Sweden in 1992 and peaked in the mid-1990s, resulted in large dismissals and growing unemployment. This most certainly could be part of the explanation. As the OECD points out, job insecurity is likely to reflect both the risk of losing one's job and the

Table 9.5 Employee opinions on job security in Canada, Denmark, Sweden and the United States in 1992 and 1996 identified as a percentage

	Canada		Denmark		Sweden		USA	
	1992	*1996*	*1992*	*1996*	*1992*	*1996*	*1992*	*1996*
Not worried about the future of their company	71	61	71	68	66	60	60	52
Saying that the company offers job security as good as or better than other companies	61	56	70	69	61	59	58	55
Sure of a job with the company as long as they perform well	49	45	54	52	46	44	46	38
Satisfied with their job security	60	56	62	58	49	49	57	47
Level of overall job security	61	55	64	62	56	53	55	48

Source: OECD (1997d): 135.

Note
Employees have been asked: (1) whether they are frequently worried about the future of their company; (2) whether the level of job security offered by their company is as good as, or better than, that of other companies in the industry; (3) whether they can be sure of a job with the company as long as they perform well; and (4) how satisfied they are with their job security. The overall index of employment security is a composed measure of the four questions mentioned above (OECD 1997d).

consequences of such a loss. Employment protection legislation, union coverage, unemployment levels and the generosity of unemployment benefits must be considered if we are to understand the spreading feelings of insecurity (OECD 1997d). In Denmark a high level of job turnover and low employment protection in combination with a comprehensive safety net provided by a generous system of unemployment benefits might explain the high level of experienced job security (Madsen 1999: 17).

Employment stability – more similar than different?

The similarities between the four countries are striking, considering the difference in labour market regimes. For example, job turnover is as high in Scandinavia as in North America. If we compare the job turnover resulting from changes in existing establishments with that resulting from the opening and closing of establishments, we find that in Sweden the share of job gains occurring through expansions of existing establishments is lower than in Canada and Denmark. This could indicate that Swedish employers are, in fact, more wary of hiring. On the other hand, the share of job losses occurring through contractions in existing establishments is higher in both Canada and Sweden than in Denmark, despite the difference in employment protection. Also, the fact that there was a 'fast and sharp fall' in employment among workers with permanent contracts during the recession of the early 1990s (Holmlund and Vejsiu 1998: 3) strengthens the impression that Swedish employers do not face any serious obstacles in reducing their staff.

In any case, it is interesting to note that in terms of flexibility – as it is measured here by tenure, turnover and temporary employment – Scandinavia (especially Denmark) seems to be closer to North America than to the rest of Europe. Average tenure in OECD Europe is just about the same as in Sweden and much longer than in Denmark (OECD 1997d: 138). Temporary jobs are slightly more common,[8] job turnover is higher and long-term unemployment (see Chapter 8 in this volume) lower in Scandinavia than in Continental Europe. A possible explanation for this could be the role of the Scandinavian trade unions. Compared to other European countries, the Scandinavian trade unions show much higher membership figures and they play an influential role in society. They are an integrated part of the 'associative democracy' prevailing in both Denmark and Sweden (see Chapter 2 in this volume). In both countries we find an extensive labour market regulation, which in Sweden is enforced by legal measures while in Denmark it is based on collective agreements. In both countries the labour market regulation is subject to negotiation and in these negotiations, the trade unions in Denmark as well as Sweden have chosen a strategy of co-operation rather than confrontation (Bruun *et al.* 1990). Through their position and strategy, the Scandinavian trade unions have in many ways facilitated structural rationalisation and labour market adjustment to economic realities. Thus, numerical flexibility can be achieved in different ways and under different labour market regimes.

Diversification of work time?

Actual work hours and part-time work

During the 1980s and 1990s, the long-term decline in actual work hours per person has slowed in many OECD countries including Canada, and in Sweden and the United States the trend has even been reversed. Denmark stands out from this pattern because its work time decreased even during the 1980s and early 1990s (OECD 1998a; and Chapter 5 in this volume). Over the last two decades, the difference in actual work time between Sweden and Canada has diminished, while the gap between Canada and the United States has widened. Still, actual work time is considerably shorter in Scandinavia than in North America. In 1998, the average American employee spent almost 400 hours more at work than the average Dane or Swede (OECD 1998a) (Table 9.6).

To some extent, the different trends can be explained by changes in statutory work time. In Sweden, radical reforms were carried out during the 1970s, shortening the workweek, increasing the number of paid holidays, introducing parental leave, etc. Since the early 1980s, there has been no statutory work time reduction in Sweden, apart from lengthening parental leave. In Denmark, however, reductions have continued to a point where the full-time workweek is only 37 hours (Anxo 1995; Schönemann-Paul, Körmendi and Gelting 1992; SOU 1989).[9] In Canada, the reduction of work time has not been as dramatic, although reforms have been carried out in some provinces (Bellamare and Poulin 1994; OECD 1998a). In the United States, neither trade unions nor politicians have had work time reductions on their agenda (Christopherson 1991; Rosenberg 1994).

The number of hours actually worked per person is also influenced by other factors, such as absence from work and overtime work. Especially in the United States, but to some extent also in Sweden, the increase in working hours is largely due to full-time workers working more hours (Anxo 1995; OECD 1998a). Another important factor is the share of part-time workers. From the early 1970s to the late 1980s, part-time work has grown considerably, mainly because of increasing female employment

Table 9.6 Average annual hours actually worked per employed person in Canada, Denmark, Sweden and the United States

	1979	*1983*	*1990*	*1993*	*1996*	*1998*
United States	1,905	1,882	1,943	1,946	1,951	1,957
Canada	1,802	1,731	1,738	1,718	1,787	1,777
Denmark	1,640	1,653	1,579	1,574	1,521	1,531
Sweden	1,451	1,453	1,480	1,501	1,554	1,551

Sources: ADAM database (Denmark); OECD 1998a and 1999b (other countries).

Note
Danish data are for workers in manufacturing only, whereas data for the other countries cover all employed.

rates. In the 1990s, however, women started working longer hours and increasingly turning to full-time work in Denmark, Sweden and the United States (Anxo 1995; Bellamare and Poulin 1994; Boje 1987; Christopherson 1991; SOU 1989). It is thus only in Canada that part-time work has grown between 1990 and 1998. Regarding the incidence of part-time work, there is no clear dividing line between North America and Scandinavia (OECD 2000a; see also Chapter 5 in this volume).

In the debate on flexibility, the rise in part-time work has caused much concern. Companies are assumed to use part-time workers as a 'buffer' when demand for products or services changes; these jobs are often seen as inherently precarious. There are several reasons why part-time workers could provide employers with a source of flexibility. Part-time schedules can more easily be changed than full-time schedules to adapt to peaks in the workload and part-time workers are cheaper to use for overtime work. Traditionally, there has also been less regulation protecting the employment and working conditions for part-time workers, but today, there is regulation in Europe forbidding discrimination against part-time workers (OECD 1999b). Above all, we would like to emphasise that the question whether part-time work is precarious or not, is really a question of empirical analysis (Polivka 1996b; Polivka and Nardone 1989; Tilly 1996; Wood 1989). Our data suggest that conditions of part-time workers differ between countries. For example, about one in five Canadian women work less than 20 hours a week while such short hours are relatively uncommon in Sweden. In fact, almost 20 per cent of Swedish women are regarded as part-time workers, although they work 30 hours or more every week (OECD 1997c). In Sweden, part-time work is not classified as unstable work. For example, many Swedish women work part-time only when their children are young and then go back to full-time (OECD 1999b; Sundström 1991). In addition, there is no difference in tenure between part-time and full-time workers in Sweden, while this is the case in North America (Vejsiu 1997 and other computations by Vejsiu, CLFS, CPS, OECD 1999b). In all four countries, however, part-time work is associated with lower wages and fewer benefits, as well as a lower degree of unionisation and a higher incidence of temporary employment (Bellamare and Poulin 1994; Lipsett and Reesor 1997; Nätti 1994; OECD 1999b; Peterson 1993; Rothstein 1996; Tilly 1996). At the same time, involuntary part-time workers, defined as people working part-time because they cannot find a full-time job, seem to be more common in Sweden and Canada than in Denmark and, especially, the United States In all countries, however, most part-time work seems to be voluntary (Eurostat 1996; OECD 1995, 1999b).

Diversity of hours and schedules

Although the increase in part-time work seems to have slowed down, there is a trend towards more diversity in working hours. The 40-hour workweek is still the most frequently reported usual work schedule among men in Sweden and Canada, but it is much less prevalent than in the 1970s (OECD 1998a). Considering the impact the 40-hour week has had, and still has, as a universal norm, it is interesting to note that it is only among Swedish men that a bare majority still has a 40-hour week (Table 9.7).

Table 9.7 Diversity of work hours. Proportion of all employed with a normal working
week of 40 hours in Canada, Sweden and the United States and 37 hours in
Denmark

	1990			1996		
	1–39 hours	*40 hours*	*41+ hours*	*1–39 hours*	*40 hours*	*41+ hours*
United States						
Total	30.6	39.9	29.5	32.8	35.5	31.6
Men	21.3	40.6	38.1	23.9	36.2	40.3
Women	42.4	38.8	18.8	44.0	34.7	21.3
Canada						
Total	41.1	40.5	18.4	42.9	37.6	19.5
Men	25.2	48.8	26.0	26.8	45.5	27.7
Women	61.0	30.2	9.0	62.4	28.0	9.6
Sweden						
Total	35.1	49.2	15.6	35.4	48.6	16.0
Men	16.6	61.0	22.4	18.8	58.6	22.6
Women	54.3	37.2	8.5	53.3	37.8	8.8
	1991			1996		
	1–36 hours	*37 hours*	*38+ hours*	*1–36 hours*	*37 hours*	*38+ hours*
Denmark						
Total	27.2	53.4	19.5	26.7	51.4	22.0
Men	12.9	60.0	27.1	13.6	55.9	30.5
Women	43.7	45.7	10.6	42.5	45.8	11.7

Sources: LFS (Denmark), CLFS (Canada), SLFS (Sweden), CPS (USA).

Notes
The data for Denmark are for the years 1991 and 1996. In Denmark, the most frequent work time was
37 hours in both 1991 and 1996. Data are for all employed in Denmark, Sweden and Canada. The US
data includes non-farm employees.
The US data refer to hours at work during survey reference week. Other countries report usual work
hours.

During the first half of the 1990s, there has been an increase in both shorter
(1–39 hours) and longer (41 or more hours) workweeks in North America.[10] This
is true for men as well as women, although the main tendency among Canadian
women is towards shorter hours. In Sweden, the dominant trend is that men are
working shorter and women are working longer hours. Denmark is a special case,
as the most frequent work time is no longer 40 but 37 hours. If we look at the share
of Danish workers with a 37-hour week, we find that since 1991 it has decreased
among men while both shorter and longer hours have increased. Among women,
there has, on the other hand, been a slight trend towards longer hours (Table 9.7).

Regarding scheduling, there is no unequivocal trend towards more diversity, but
we should point out that the data cover a short period. In Sweden, Canada and
Denmark non-standard schedules, i.e., schedules other than daytime work, have

Table 9.8 Percentage of employees with regular daytime schedules in Canada, Denmark, Sweden and the United States, 1985–97

	1985	1990	1991	1992	1995	1996	1997
United States	78		77				80
Canada			70		68		
Denmark	82		80			77	70
Sweden	70	65		64			

Sources: SCB 1989 and 1992 (Sweden), CPS (USA), Statistics Canada 1998 (Canada), Schönemann-Paul, Körmendi and Gelting 1992 (Denmark 1988 and 1991), DLFS (Denmark 1996 and 1997).

Notes
The Danish data are for 1988 instead of 1985. The Swedish data are for the years 1982 and 1988 instead of 1985 and 1990, respectively, and include the self-employed (for workers only the 1992 figure is 66 per cent).
In Denmark and the United States, regular daytime is defined as anytime between 6: 00 a.m. and 6: 00 p.m., in Sweden it is anytime between 6: 45 a.m. and 5: 45 p.m. The Canadian definition is work that begins in the morning and ends in the afternoon.

become more common, but in the United States daytime work has increased (CPS; SCB 1994; Statistics Canada 1998). Nevertheless, workers on non-standard schedules form a substantial group, about 20 per cent of the employees in the United States and about one-third of the employees in Canada and Sweden (Table 9.8).

The fact that such schedules are more common among part-time workers may indicate that part-timers are to some extent 'flexible' labour. However, we have to remember that part-time work is more common in health care and other services where much work has to be carried out at nights and weekends. In addition, the difference in schedules between part-time and full-time workers is not necessarily growing. For example, the incidence of regular daytime schedules has increased substantially among part-time workers in the United States (SCB 1989 and 1994; CPS; Schönemann-Paul, Körmendi and Gelting 1992).

The most conspicuous change in recent years is the increase in flex-time in all four countries. It is most common in Sweden where 43 per cent of employees have the option of choosing when to start and end the working day (SCB 1994; Schönemann-Paul, Körmendi and Gelting 1992; Statistics Canada 1998; CPS) (Table 9.9).

An increase in the use of overtime – a traditional way for employers to achieve flexibility – has been a trend in manufacturing in Sweden and the United States since the 1970s, whereas in Canada the pattern is more cyclical. (Agnarsson and Anxo 1996; OECD 1998a).

Working time and flexibility – how it goes together

As with employment protection legislation, there are important differences in the regulation of work time between Scandinavia and North America, with Sweden and the United States at the opposite extremes. Swedish legislation has a number of detailed rules specifying a minimum of daily and weekly rest, minimum holidays, maximum workweek, maximum overtime hours, etc. The United States,

Table 9.9 Percentage of employed persons with flex-time working schedule in Canada, Denmark, Sweden and the United States from 1985 to 1997

	1985	1991	1995	1997
United States	14	16		30
Canada		17	24	
Denmark	23	26		
Sweden		38	43	

Sources: SCB 1992 and 1994 (Sweden), CPS (USA), Statistics Canada 1998 (Canada), Schönemann-Paul, Körmendi and Gelting 1992 (Denmark).

Notes
The Swedish data are for 1992 and 1994 instead of 1991 and 1995, respectively.
The Danish data are for 1988 instead of 1985. All data are for workers, but the definition of flex-time varies somewhat. In the United States, it is defined as the possibility for workers to vary or make changes in the time they begin or end work. Canada: to choose their times within limits established by the employer. Sweden: to decide, within certain limits, when the working day starts or ends. Denmark: regular flex-time or working time by own choice (no regular meeting time).

however, has few regulations regarding working schedules (Bosch, Dawkings and Michon 1994; Rosenberg 1994). This weak regulation, combined with the low level of unionisation and the highly decentralised negotiations, seems to provide employers in North America with the ability to pursue work time flexibility. Judging from our data, there seems to be more diversity in working hours in North America than in Scandinavia.

This must be seen as a result of more regulation and stronger trade unions. In Sweden, the Working-Time Act has made the 40-hour workweek the norm for full-time work and in Denmark, the 37-hour workweek is standard and has been set in collective agreements covering most of the labour market.[11] Of course, this norm does not apply to a large minority of Scandinavian women who are working part-time. Nevertheless, working hours are less diverse among Scandinavian women than among American women. The lack of regulation in the United States means that the normal working week for full-time workers can be much longer than 40 hours. Having said this, we would like to point out that the regulation on work time also could provide flexibility, especially for the individual. The Scandinavians are entitled to long holidays and have the opportunity to take a long leave of absence (in most cases with some income compensation) to take care of children or pursue training (Holt and Thaulow 1996). In Canada, the province of Quebec recently introduced a reform granting parental leave of 52 weeks with a compensation of 75 per cent of wages (Benoit 2000), but otherwise there seems to be substantial differences between North America and Scandinavia in this respect.

Studying the development over time, we find that the standard working week has given way to a greater diversity. In North America and among Danish men, there has been a polarisation, meaning that both short and long work hours have become more common. In addition, in three of the four countries, more people seem to be working on non-standard schedules. This increase in diversity could be a result of employers attempting to adjust work hours to changes in the market situation.

During the 1990s, the regulatory framework has become weaker in many countries, including Denmark and Sweden, where many decisions, including many of those regarding work time issues, have been decentralised and the employers, fervently and with some success, have argued for the 'annualisation' of work time. That is, it is possible to vary the length of the normal workweek from one period to another, subject to a fixed number of annual hours. What these changes will mean to the employees remains to be seen. On one hand, the standardisation of work time has strengthened the position of the workers by reducing the competition between employees and establishing a boundary between an employer's time and a worker's time. On the other hand, it can be argued that the criteria for this standardisation have been negotiated by unions representing male, skilled, full-time workers in manufacturing (Hinrichs, Roche and Sirianni 1991). As the service sector and female employment have grown, work time preferences have become more diverse (Meulders, Plasman and Plasman 1997). Seen from this perspective, an individualisation of working hours and greater flexibility could make it easier to combine work with family responsibilities and leisure activities. However, there is also a risk that this may lead to an increased stratification of the labour force where especially women and young people may be trapped in insecure and low-paid part-time and temporary jobs (Beechey and Perkins 1987; Christopherson 1991; Presser 1995).

Flexibility and labour market regulation – conclusion

The responses from employers and employees to the demand for greater flexibility differ markedly between the individual countries, depending on the type of industrial relations and the institutional framework for employment regulation. The US labour market, with its market-driven industrial relations and scarce regulations on employment conditions, has often been seen as the ideal model for an adaptable and flexible labour market and this has led to strong demands for deregulation of the European labour markets (Blank 1994; EC 1994; Freeman 1999). Deregulation of employment conditions and flexibility are, however, by no means interchangeable as often it is stated in labour market literature.

In previous chapters of this book, we have analysed the main differences and similarities between the four countries in labour laws, industrial relations and employment regulation. Let us in this concluding section take a closer look at the relationship between flexibility and labour market regulation. In the neo-classical labour market approach, it is argued that comprehensive employment regulation restrains the economic decisions of employers and prevents an appropriate adjustment of the labour force and the employment conditions to economic demands. The neo-classical theories claim that the employees will seek as much protection as possible against the competitive pressure to adapt to the changing economic and technological conditions and they are assumed to have a fairly strong aversion to changes in their employment situation. Their possibilities for turning this opposition into effective resistance are, according to the theories, obviously much better in the highly unionised and regulated Scandinavian countries than in the open and competitive North American labour markets. On the other hand, when the regulation of employment is relatively modest as in the United States and Canada, employers do not have strong incentives to change their types of employment into non-standard forms (Robinson 2000; and OECD 1999b).

Contrary to the neo-classical assumption, the institutional approach argues that attitudes of the employees towards changes vary depending on the level of labour market security. Employees who consider their employment situation as relatively secure might not be afraid of becoming unemployed or shifting to another job position and will generally be more positive towards changes in their working conditions. On the other hand, employees who are insecure in their labour market position tend to oppose changes in technology and work conditions and reject moves to other job positions. Therefore, according to the institutional approach, legislation on employment protection and work conditions might constitute an important element in the social protection of employees and is crucial for the functioning of the labour market. When employees feel a certain amount of security in their labour market position, they can afford to co-operate with the employers in implementing organisational measures that increase labour market flexibility (van den Berg, Furåker and Johansson 1997: 93–7).

We have measured the level of flexibility by employer tenure, temporary employment and job turnover. The empirical evidence examined in this chapter provides mixed support to the theories arguing that strong employment protection is detrimental to labour market flexibility. Instead, we may conclude that the relationship between flexibility and different types of labour market systems is highly complex. This result is confirmed by a recent OECD study. In the OCED study overall employment protection is defined by 12 indicators referring to three elements of employment protection: (1) strictness of dismissal for permanent workers; (2) regulation of fixed-term contracts and temporary agency work; and (3) strictness of collective dismissal regulation (OECD 1999b: 54) . According to this study the United States had the lowest level of overall employment protection while Denmark was ranked closer to Canada than to Sweden and Sweden is characterised by the most strict overall employment protection among the four countries analysed in this book (OECD 1999b: 55).

Looking at the three indicators of flexibility separately we find in our empirical analysis that labour markets with strict employment protections tend to have longer average employer tenure (Figure 9.1).

The countries with the least employment protection – the Anglo-American labour markets and Denmark – also have the lowest average employer tenure. The Southern European countries, on the other hand, are characterised by a high level of employment protection with heavy restrictions on hiring and firing of permanent workers. This results in long average employer tenure. Sweden, with its comprehensive protection of employees, holds a position in between the two extremes together with other countries characterised by a highly developed industrial relations system – Finland, France, Belgium and Germany.

The longer employer tenure in Sweden, could imply less numerical flexibility than in the other countries included in our study, but on the other hand, the share

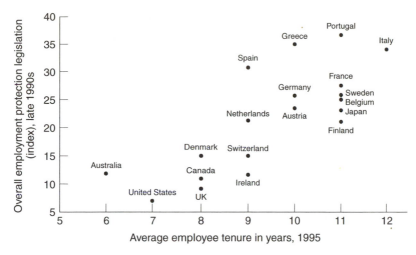

Figure 9.1 The relationship between average employee tenure and overall employment protection legislation among the OECD countries, late 1990s

Sources: OECD 1997d: 139; 1999b: 66.

of temporary employment is relatively high in Sweden. This is not necessarily a
contradiction. In fact, a high level of temporary employment is often seen as a
result of strict employment protection legislation, as the restrictions on dismissals
are assumed to make employers reluctant to hire workers on permanent contracts.
This is the case for some countries looking at the relationship between overall
employment protection and level of temporary employment (Figure 9.2).

However, there exists no obvious relationship between temporary employment
and overall employment protection neither in our data, nor in the OECD study.
Apart from Spain, the countries with high levels of employment protection – Italy,
Portugal and Greece – are not characterised by a large proportion of temporary
workers. Instead, these countries have initiated flexibility by a high frequency of
self-employment or a large number of illegal immigrant workers (OECD 2000a).
On the other hand, we find low levels of temporary employment in the countries
with the least restrictive legislation in employment protection – the United States,
the United Kingdom and Canada. Here there is no need for creating temporary
jobs because the costs of hiring and firing in permanent jobs are typically low.
Denmark does not easily fit into the pattern but holds a middle position on both
employment protection and amount of temporary employment. In Denmark legislation on employment protection is limited but several unions have made special
agreements strengthening the employment protection for their members. In this
respect Denmark looks more like several other European countries – Germany,
France, the Netherlands and Sweden – and less like the market-regulated Anglo-
American countries. In both Denmark and Sweden employment regulation
distinguishes clearly between permanent and temporary work and the use of
temporary workers become still more liberal (Edin and Holmlund 1993). This

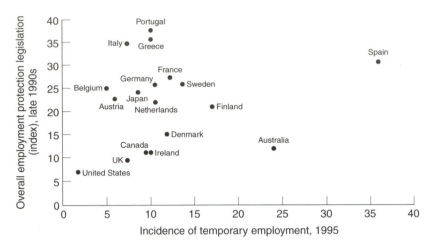

Figure 9.2 The relationship between incidence of temporary employment and overall employment protection legislation among the OECD countries, late 1990s

Sources: OECD 1996c: 8; 1999b: 66.

makes it possible to combine strictness in employment protection for permanent workers with high numerical flexibility among the temporary workers.

Scandinavian labour market regimes appear just as flexible and adaptable as the American labour market regimes and international comparisons confirm this picture (OECD 1999b). The labour markets in all four countries are flexible but different flexible employment regimes are evident. Sweden is characterised by long employment tenure, but has a relatively large proportion of the labour force employed on temporary contracts. The United States is characterised by short tenure and extremely few employees on temporary employment contracts. Employment tenure and the proportion of workers on temporary contracts in Canada and Denmark are positioned in between the two extremes. The overall level of job turnover, another indicator for flexibility, is higher in the two Scandinavian countries than in the United States while Canada again is positioned in the middle (OECD 1996c: 164). The composition of job turnover is also markedly different between the four countries. As noted above, in the United States most job shifts take place with closings and openings of firms while job shifts in Scandinavia more frequently take place in relation to expansion and contraction of existing firms. This does not necessarily mean low labour market flexibility. According to the OECD study, industrial relations systems which facilitate negotiations between employers and employees typically are combined with greater use of work practices aiming at functional flexibility. Workplaces in the Nordic countries are thus often organised to create flexibility, through job rotation, team working, etc. (OECD 1999b).

These variations between the countries in how flexible employment conditions are achieved indicate that the capability of individuals and firms to adapt to changing markets and organisations is highly dependent on the industrial relations and the balance of power between employers and employees. Flexibility becomes a matter of social control in the labour market and of organisational control in the labour–management relations inside the firms. In this context it is important to notice that primarily we have analysed flexibility from the employers' perspective. Seen from the perspective of the employees flexibility becomes more an issue of control over their work schedule and working hours and an issue of reconciling work and family obligations. In this respect we found that the pattern of work schedules becomes still more variable for both men and women in all four countries. A growing number of employees are working flex-time and the pattern of work schedules has become more diverse with more employees working long or short work hours and a decline in employees working the normal weekly hours (40 or 37 hours).

The demand for flexibility in the work processes and among the employees has induced different forms of contingent employment, influenced the patterns of job turnover and created greater variation in work schedules. However, the much debated flexibility theories of Atkinson and others do not gain much support based on the empirical results shown in this chapter. This does not mean that the concept of flexibility has to be rejected, but the implications are certainly less clear-cut than the theories suggest. For example, one important aspect of flexibility is the tendency of companies to purchase services instead of hiring employees, which is illustrated by the rapid growth in licensing/subcontracting of productions and in business services such as data consultants, personnel and accounting services (see Chapter 6 for more details concerning the growth in business services).

While this trend certainly will increase flexibility for companies, it does not necessarily mean that all jobs with temporary employment agencies or contract jobs are 'bad' jobs. For example, in the United States independent contractors earned more than workers in traditional arrangements and were largely satisfied with their jobs while workers in temporary jobs earned less and a majority of them would have preferred a traditional job (Polivka 1996a). The growing incidence of outsourcing means that *all* jobs are increasingly exposed to external market competition, which may affect work conditions and employment security even for those with 'permanent' jobs.

Appendix

The empirical analysis of flexibility draws mainly on data from the following sources:

Denmark

Labour Force Survey (DLFS) published in Statistics Denmark: 'Arbejdsmarked' (serial publication) 1986: 6; 1988: 8; 1990: 16; 1996: 1; 1998: 17; 1997: 31; 1999: 26; 1991: 23; 1998: 5.

The tenure data 1976–90 are from Engelund (1992) which draws on four different surveys: Survey of Living Conditions 1976; Unemployment Survey 1979;

Mobility Survey 1985; and Survey of Working-time 1990. Tenure data are from OECD 1997d.

The figures on annual actual working hours are from the ADAM database, Ministry of Finance.

Sweden

Labour Force Survey (SLFS), published in Statistics Sweden: 'Arbets-kraftsundersökningen', annual averages for the years 1988–98; and in Storrie (1997); and special tabulations provided by Statistics Sweden.

Some tenure data are from the Level of Living Surveys 1974, 1981 and 1991, published in Vejsiu (1997); Holmlund and Vejsiu (1998); and from special tabulations by Vejsiu.

Canada

Labour Force Survey (CLFS) 1976–98, data supplied by Statistics Canada.

Data on working time and temporary employment are from the Survey of Work Arrangements, carried out in 1991 and 1995 as a supplement to the CLFS. The data are published in Statistics Canada (1998); and Lipsett and Reesor (1997).

The United States

Current Population Survey (CPS) January 1983, January 1987, January 1991, February 1990, February 1996, and February 1998 partly supplied by the Bureau of Labor Statistics (BLS), US Department of Labor, and partly published at the BLS web site.

10 Wage formation, institutions and unemployment

Thomas P. Boje and Per Kongshøj Madsen

Introduction

This chapter has three purposes. First, we will give an overview of aggregate wage formation analysing the pattern of wage growth and wage differentiation in the four countries included in this study. Second, the relationship between earnings inequality, earnings mobility and low pay is analysed in order to evaluate the consequences of low pay. Does taking a low-paid job give access to a better paid job later on or is it a trap leading to poverty? Third and finally, clarify how labour market institutions affect the pattern of wage growth. This will be done by analysing the relationship between unemployment and wage growth applying the Phillips curve argument, which in its classic version documents an inverse relationship between nominal-wage growth and unemployment. How does this relationship hold for our four countries and how can variations in the relationship be explained historically and nationally ?

Wage dispersion as well as earnings mobility are frequently considered as central dimensions in the debate on labour market flexibility and creation of new jobs. A low wage dispersion is often mentioned as an important reason for a high level of unemployment and the argument is that low wage dispersion and high minimum wage standards reduce the capability of the economies in creating jobs for groups with low human capital – young people, unskilled workers, ethnic minorities, etc. – thereby being the main reason for high unemployment among these groups (Westergaard-Nielsen 1999) A similar type of argumentation holds for the relationship between earnings mobility and job creation. More earnings flexibility, it is argued, can be accomplished by removing the minimum wage standards, replacing the collective with individual wage setting practices and by reducing the generosity of social benefits. All three measures would force the unemployed to look harder for work and to accept low-paid jobs. The crucial point in this argumentation for job creation through increased wage dispersion and earnings mobility is that the low-paid entry jobs 'provide the unemployed with a stepping-stone into the labour market and onto the ladder of economic mobility' but this strategy may also imply that a growing number of workers with a low level of human capital end up in poverty with their benefits taken away and not able to remain in even a low-paid job. A large proportion of low-paid workers are thus employed in contingent jobs and move frequently between low-paid jobs and unemployment. If these groups are not eligible for reasonable benefits, a majority end up in poverty and risk being completely excluded from the ordinary labour market (Marx and Verbist 1997: 6).

This discussion on the relationship between wage formation, earnings mobility and job creation was one of the major issues in the OECD job study from 1994 and in much of the subsequent debate on the European 'job deficit' focus has been on how far the poor record in job growth in Europe, compared with the United States, could be explained by a compressed wage distribution and low trade-off between wages and employment, which, it is argued, characterises economies with a low wage flexibility. In a comprehensive overview of the most frequently discussed explanations for the job deficit among the EU countries the American economist R. Freeman mentions two dimensions related to wage formation and income distribution. First, it is argued that real wages in the EU have increased from a level below the United States to the US level while the rates of employment have moved in the opposite direction (Freeman 1999: 27) and, second, during the 1980s and 1990s, the dispersion of wages was high and growing in the US labour market simultaneously with a strong increase in new jobs. According to Freeman, it has been the opposite among the EU countries where both the wage dispersion and the capacity of creating new jobs have been low and declining (Freeman 1999: 21). The extent to which this relationship holds for our four countries will be scrutinised in this chapter.

The overall relationship between employment/unemployment and nominal-wage changes is probably the most debated issue in the labour market literature. Since the British economist A. W. Phillips in 1958 documented empirically an inverse relationship between nominal-wage changes and unemployment for the United Kingdom a long-standing and comprehensive debate on this relationship has taken place and the 'Phillips curve' strongly influenced the economic policy of the 1960s and 1970s. The original Phillips curve, however, fell in dispute during the 1970s. The combination of rising unemployment and rising inflation, characterised as 'stagflation', shattered the empirical foundations of the traditional Phillips curve. Instead, a widespread acceptance of the monetarist's idea of a vertical long-run trade-off between unemployment and inflation became the dominant economic wisdom, followed by the important assumption of a natural rate of unemployment (see Chapter 8 in this volume).

Since the fall of the traditional Phillips curve in the early 1970s researchers have followed many different roads in their attempts to understand the interplay between wage inflation and the dynamics of the macro-economic development. One research strategy is the econometric approach, which has primarily aimed at refining statistical methods in analysing the wage equations. Here special popularity has been gained by various versions of the so-called insider–outsider model, which explores the different roles of employed and unemployed in the wage formation process. Holmlund (1991) concludes, based on a study conducted for the OECD, that higher unemployment in general reduces real wages. Furthermore, his study indicates a weak downward pressure on wages exerted by long-term unemployment while the more extreme version of the insider–outsider thesis arguing that no pressure on real wages can be noticed from changes in unemployment has to be rejected according to the Holmlund study. This position is supported by several more recent studies (see Elmeskov 1993; OECD 1997d; Locking 1995).

A second approach in analysing the relationship between wage inflation and unemployment has been taken by those researchers who aimed at relating the processes of wage inflation to a more comprehensive political and economical institutional framework of the national and international economy. This approach is closely related to the broader comparative analysis of the interrelations between the institutional characteristics of the labour market and of economic development in general (Boyer 1993; Golden 1993; Henley and Tsakalotos 1991). Central to this work is the hypothesis that various institutional characteristics of the national labour market and the political system are decisive in explaining the wage equations. These institutional characteristics are among others: level of industrial conflict, unionisation, pattern of collective bargaining, level of job security, income policies and labour market policies. It is not possible to go into details with this literature in this chapter but two examples might be illustrative for the debate. In discussing the relationship between institutional characteristics of the labour market and economic performance the liberal economists of the 1980s assume a linear relationship meaning that labour markets with weak unions and decentralised wage bargaining perform better than labour markets with strong unions and centralised bargaining procedures. This assumption has been challenged by Calmfors and Driffill (1988) who argue that the relationship is non-linear. The relationship between economic performance and labour market institutions is instead 'U-shaped' meaning that both labour markets with centralised and decentralised collective bargaining systems are likely to outperform countries with intermediate sectoral bargaining system. The centralised and decentralised countries tend to have higher wage flexibility and lower levels of unemployment while the worst off labour markets are characterised by a medium level of centralisation. The argument goes that decentralised bargaining systems tend to externalise the costs of higher wages, because those who receive the benefits are usually only a small minority of those who are harmed by the bargained higher wages while a centralised bargaining system with strong unions typically will internalise the macroeconomic consequences of raising wages either by combining lower real wages with improved social protection or by recognising that there are no outsider groups to which the negative effects can be shifted (see OECD 1997d: 65)

Another important study testing the institutional approach was done by Heylen (1993) who illustrated how a large number of the institutional variables discussed above could be integrated into a more general comparative study. This study has been replicated and up-dated by Madsen (1995). The theoretical framework for Heylen's study is the conventional insider–outsider model and he identifies four factors that are assumed to reduce the impact of unemployment on wages: the relative preference of 'insiders' for wages over employment, union density, the generosity of the unemployment benefit system and the frequency of temporary lay-off procedures. Heylen's approach is unusual in that it is based on eight earlier empirical studies of the relationship between changes in nominal wages and unemployment and from these studies he constructs an average of the estimates found in the literature. The empirical data included in the Heylen study covers the 1960s and 1970s. The Madsen study, on the other hand, calculates its own estimates for the explanatory variables determining wage flexibility and the main data source is the OECD's time series for the years 1960–92. In estimating the elasticity of nominal wages to unemployment for the individual OECD countries the two studies come out with nearly the same results for most countries. Sweden, according to the two studies, is placed in the group with very high wage flexibility together with Japan and Italy while the United States is found at the opposite end of the scale in a group of countries with very low wage responsiveness to changes in unemployment together with Spain and the United Kingdom. Canada holds a position characterised by low to medium wage flexibility. The two studies disagree on the ranking of Denmark, which is placed in a group of countries characterised by very low wage flexibility in the Heylen study while Madsen places Denmark in a group characterised by medium to high wage responsiveness to unemployment together with Finland and Norway. This disagreement seems, according to Madsen, to be caused by different data sets in the two studies. In the 1960s and 1970s covered by Heylen Denmark was characterised by low elasticity in relation to changes in unemployment while in the 1980s a high level of unemployment was combined with low wage growth indicating relatively high wage flexibility (see Heylen 1993, table 3, and Madsen 1995: 22–3).

Looking at the determinants of wage flexibility both studies find that the level of centralisation in wage bargaining is positively correlated with wage flexibility, which runs contrary to the Calmfors-Driffill hypothesis mentioned above. This hypothesis, however, has been questioned in several studies arguing that some countries that have been labelled as decentralised because the formal negotiations take place at the firm level, are characterised by strong employers' organisations or tripartite institutions, which have a co-ordinating function in the wage setting. Consequently, the bargaining may well be co-ordinated even when it is decentralised – see Soskice (1990), OECD (1997d) and Turner and Seghezza (1999). Another institutional variable showing a significant effect on wage flexibility is a variable which measures the institutional flexibility of the national political system. This variable shows significant negative correlation to wage flexibility and we find the same for the duration of unemployment benefits implying that long duration periods might diminish wage flexibility. The effects of other institutional variables such as level of unionisation and the level of government expenditure on active labour market policy are more doubtful. The insignificant relationship between unionisation and wage flexibility probably indicates different types of responses from workers depending on the strength of unions. In strongly unionised labour markets the unions might consider the 'outsiders' as part of their membership core in negotiating wages and therefore take into consideration the harmful effects a strong rise in wages may have for the employment of these groups. In labour markets with weak unionisation the 'insiders' tend to control the wage bargaining at the firm level as a substitute for union control and may in this way be able to externalise the negative effects of higher wages (see Madsen 1995: 25; Leisink *et al.* 1996). A preliminary conclusion to be drawn from the various studies of wage flexibility is that the huge variation prevailing in the relationship between wage growth and change in unemployment among the OECD countries depends primarily on the institutional framework of the individual countries and in this respect our four countries represent markedly different institutional models for wage flexibility and earnings mobility

The rest of the chapter is structured as follows: we will start with a short overview of the wage inflation pattern in the four countries in the period 1960 to 2001 followed by a description of trends in wage differentiation and mobility. Then comes an analysis of flexibility in wage formation and wage mobility followed by a section analysing the relationship between wage growth and unemployment – 'the 'Phillips curve' revisited'. Included in this section is also a discuss of the possible factors which explain the wage responsiveness to changes in unemployment in the individual countries.

Trends in wage and income

The aggregate pattern of wages and prices

Here we shall give an overview of the differences in wage growth and wage differentiation in our four countries. First, an overview of wage inflation in the period 1960 to 2001 is presented (Figure 10.1).[1]

Some preliminary conclusions can be drawn from Figure 10.1. First, in all four countries the general pattern of wage growth is nearly the same. Wage growth increased during the 1960s and early 1970s, peaked in the mid-1970s and had

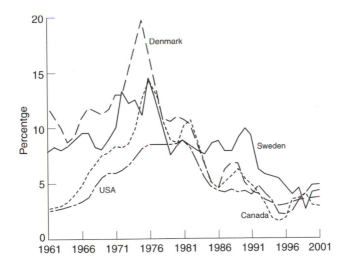

Figure 10.1 Nominal wage growth in the private sector, 1961–2001

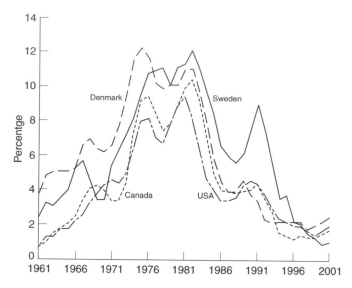

Figure 10.2 Growth in consumer prices, 1961–2001

another minor peak around 1980. This was the time period where most economies were characterised by a combination of high inflation, stagnating economic growth and falling employment – mentioned as 'stagflation'. During the 1980s the level of wage growth declined slowly in all four countries – with the exception of the sudden jump around 1990 in Sweden caused by a combinated of hyperinflation and large public debt. In the 1990s, wage growth has stabilised in all the four countries around or below 5 per cent. Second, the level of wage growth has tended to be higher in the two Scandinavian countries than in Canada and the United States during most of the years. It was especially the case in the 1970s and during the late 1980s.

In most respects the development of consumer prices has followed a similar pattern, cf. Figure 10.2. Again we note the change from relative low, but rising, rates of inflation in the 1960s and early 1970s, to the familiar patterns of the first and the second oil crisis in the 1970s. For Sweden one can also observe the effect of the outburst of inflation in the late 1980s and the large devaluation in 1992.

Finally, Figure 10.3 shows the development in real wages resulting from the combined effects of wage growth and changing consumer prices. Again we can note both similarities and dissimilarities among the four countries. It is interesting to observe that apart from the 1960s, the pattern of real wage growth is rather close for the two Scandinavian countries and Canada. All three countries show strong changes in the level of real wage growth. By contrast, the rate of growth for the United States is more stable. In all four countries, the growth rate of real wages increased during the 1990s because of a strong fall in the consumer prices throughout the decade, in spite of the lowering of the growth rates in nominal wages noted

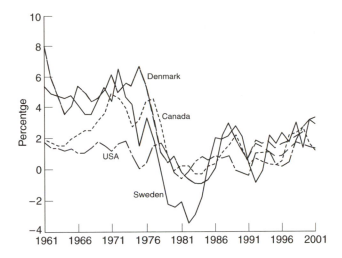

Figure 10.3 Growth in real wages, 1961–2001

above. This unusually low level of inflation in all four countries was caused by a restrictive fiscal policy with low interest rates and enforced balances in public budgets. We shall return below to a closer analysis of the patterns of nominal wages including the interrelationship between wage growth and unemployment.

To analyse in more detail the earnings development in the individual countries, the overall growth rates in real wages have to be divided (see OECD 1996c: 67). Then we find a highly differentiated pattern with marked variation in real wage growth for low-paid and high-paid workers in the four countries. Looking at the development from the mid-1980s to the mid-1990s we find the most diversified growth pattern in the United States. Here real wages have declined for low- and medium-paid workers while it has increased for the high-paid and especially for American women.[2] In Sweden, also, the earnings differentiation has increased. The real wages have been growing for all three categories of Swedish employees but most for the high-paid employees and slightly more for men than for women during the late 1980s and early 1990s. Finally, Canada represents the only country among our four where the earnings differentiation has declined. The low-paid Canadian employees have had significantly higher growth in real earnings than employees in both the medium- and high-paid deciles and women in all three categories have experienced stronger growth in real wages than men (OECD 1996c).

Earnings dispersion

The earnings dispersion has historically been significantly higher in Canada and the United States than in Denmark and Sweden (Table 10. 1). In an OECD context Canada and the United States have some of the highest levels of earnings dispersion. In both countries the earnings dispersion is highest among the lower earnings categories (D5/D1). In Canada employees in the lowest decile earn 2.3–2.4 times less than employees placed in the middle decile while the ratio between the top and middle deciles is about 1.8. In the United States the differences in earnings between the middle and the top and the bottom, respectively, are nearly the same – slightly more than 2 times – in the mid-1990s. The level of earnings dispersion has, however, developed in different directions in the two countries. In Canada the earnings dispersion was high and increasing until the mid-1980s. Since then it has been more or less constant but has remained at a high level compared with the European level. Canada has the highest overall level of earnings dispersion among the four countries analysed here and next comes the United States. In the United States the earnings dispersion has been constantly growing during the last decade and in the mid-1990s the US earnings dispersion was the highest for the upper half of the earnings hierarchy both among our four countries as well as for the OECD as a whole, while the earnings dispersion for the lower echelon of the earnings hierarchy was lower than the Canadian but significantly above the Scandinavian level.

Both Denmark and Sweden are, on the other hand, characterised by a low level of earnings dispersion and it is the lowest among the OECD countries. The earnings differences have been constantly low during the whole period 1980 to 1995 despite significant fluctuations in the economic cycle and in the level of unemployment for both Denmark and Sweden. In both countries, but especially in Sweden, the dispersion in earnings has been highest among employees in the upper half of the earnings hierarchy and has increased during the 1990s.

Looking at the earnings dispersion for male and female employees we find slightly higher dispersion among the American men compared with women while the opposite is the case for Canada but the growth in wage dispersion among US employees has been nearly the same for men and women. In Sweden – for Denmark no data is available – the earnings dispersion is constantly lower for female employees than for men and this is especially the case in the upper earnings hierarchy. Most Swedish women are employed in the public sector where the earnings profile is more equal than in the private sector which is highly dominated by men. Among Swedish men employed in the private sector the wage growth has been high, especially in the higher deciles of the wage hierarchy.

Furthermore, the OECD has calculated the earnings dispersion between the highest (D9) and lowest decile (D1). The United States and Canada also have here the highest earnings differentiation among all the OECD countries. The highest paid decile earns about four times more than the lowest decile for both countries in the mid-1990s. In the United States the dispersion has been constantly growing for both men and women during the period 1980–95 while it peaked in Canada in 1986–87 and then started falling slowly. In Sweden the dispersion in earnings between D9 and D1 is two times for men and 1.7 for women. These levels have been stable for the whole period 1975 to 1995 and they are the lowest among the major OECD countries (OECD 1996c: 64–5).

Table 10.1 Trends in earnings dispersion among full-time year-round employees, 1980–95

Canada

	1981	1986	1990	1994
Total employees				
D9 / D5	1.79	1.83	1.85	1.84
D5 / D1	2.24	2.43	2.38	2.28
Male employees				
D9 / D5	1.67	1.68	1.75	1.73
D5 / D1	2.07	2.40	2.28	2.18
Female employees				
D9 / D5	1.76	1.76	1.75	1.78
D5 / D1	2.12	2.41	2.28	2.25

Denmark

	1980	1985	1990	
Total Employees				
D9 / D5	1.52	1.54	1.57	–
D9 / D1	1.41	1.41	1.38	–

Sweden

	1980	1985	1990	1993
Total Employees				
D9 / D5	1.57	1.59	1.52	1.59
D5/ D1	1.30	1.30	1.32	1.34
Male employees				
D9 / D5	1.61	1.58	1.56	1.62
D5 / D1	1.31	1.35	1.33	1.36
Female employees				
D9 / D5	1.32	1.36	1.40	1.40
D5 / D1	1.25	1.28	1.22	1.30

United States

	1980	1985	1990	1995
Total employees				
D9 / D5	–	–	–	2.10
D5 / D1	–	–	–	2.09
Male employees	–	–	–	
D9 / D5	1.76	1.84	1.96	2.04
D5 / D1	1.85	2.03	2.02	2.13
Female employees				
D9 / D5	1.76	1.80	1.92	2.03
D5 / D1	1.66	1.86	1.91	1.95

Source: OECD 1996c: 61–2.

In addition to gender, educational level is probably the most important dimension in understanding the wage inequality among different countries. The level of human capital is crucial in determining the bargaining power of the individual employees as well as their unions. In Table 10.2 (page 223) we have calculated the earnings differences between employees in different educational categories. Again we find that the biggest differentiation in wages is in the United States and Canada and in both countries these differences have increased during the 1980s and 1990s. The wage differentiation is, not surprisingly, especially pronounced between highest (level E) and lowest (level A) educational categories. During the recent two decades the wage ratio between these educational categories has increased markedly for both the Canadian and US labour market while inequality in wages has only grown slightly among employees in the lower end of the educational hierarchy (level D and level A). The wage differentiation is higher for US male employees than for women while it is the opposite in Canada.

For both Denmark and Sweden earnings differences between various educational categories are small and lower than for any other OECD countries. Employees with university education (level E) earn on average about 50 per cent more than employees with only compulsory education (Level A) and in both countries the earnings inequality between these two categories was nearly constant during the last two decades. Between employees with post-secondary education (level D) and compulsory education (level A) we find nearly no earnings differences in Denmark and Sweden – except for Danish men who have had a traditionally strong position in the labour market through their occupation-based trade unions (see Chapter 2 in this volume). In Sweden a fall has happened in both wage ratios and this fall has been most obvious among female employees while the male ratios have fluctuated a great deal between the two decades analysed. The Danish wage differentiation between educational categories has been constant except for the ratio between women with high and no vocational education, which has declined. The solidaristic wage policy still enforced by the unions in both Scandinavian countries combined with a low growth rate for earnings in the public sector are the main factors explaining the wage pattern among educational groups.

Summing-up this section we find that the earnings inequality rose markedly in the United States as well as Canada during the 1980s and peaked in the late 1980s. Then the trajectory differed with a continuous rise in earnings inequality in the United States while the inequality has been slowly falling in Canada during the 1990s. More recent studies for the United States show that earnings have increased most for the highest and lowest earnings groups while earnings have been nearly unchanged for the middle-income groups during the period 1989–99. This has meant that no general rise in earnings dispersion can be discerned during the 1990s. Only within the US occupations with the highest earnings can a growing dispersion be registered during the 1990s (Ilg and Haugen 2000: 31). Denmark and Sweden are placed at the other end of the scale with the lowest level of earnings inequality and in both countries the overall level of inequality has been stable despite profound changes in the economic cycle. The low level of wage dispersion and earnings inequality found in the Scandinavian countries is caused by a combination of the solidaristic wage policy enforced by all the institutional partners in the labour market and a centralised system of wage bargaining where the peak organisations are more or less controlling the wage setting at regional and firm level.

Table 10.2 Earnings differentiation by educational level and gender from the early 1970s to the early 1990s

	Early 1970s	*Early 1980s*	*Early 1990s*	*Five years' change in the 1980s–90s*
Canada				
Men				
Level E / Level A	2.09	1.90	2.08	+0.16
Level E / Level D	1.49	1.52	1.51	+0.05
Women				
Level E / Level A	2.44	2.22	2.23	+0.10
Level E / Level D	1.42	1.59	1.53	+0.05
Denmark				
Men				
Level E / Level A		1.58	1.61	+0.02
Level E / Level D		1.32	1.34	+0.01
Women				
Level E / Level A		1.46	1.36	−0.06
Level E / Level D		1.15	1.15	−0.00
Sweden				
Men				
Level E / Level A	1.68	1.37	1.55	+0.09
Level E / Level D	1.27	1.55	1.13	−0.21
Women				
Level E / Level A	1.76	1.49	1.51	+0.01
Level E / Level D	1.31	1.24	1.16	−0.04
United States				
Men				
Level E / Level A	1.92	2.33	2.47	+0.20
Level E / Level D	1.36	1.48	1.58	+0.07
Women				
Levell E / Level A	1.85	2.15	2.32	+0.21
Level E / Level D	1.29	1.36	1.46	+0.07

Source: OECD 1994c: 160–1.

Note
Educational classifications and definitions of population:
Canada: Level A = 0 to 8 years of education
           Level D = Some post-secondary or post-secondary diploma
           Level E = University degree
           Annual gross earnings of full-time workers – including self-employment income
Denmark: Level A = Basic elementary, pre-vocational education
           Level D = Short post-secondary education
           Level E = University degree or medium length of post-secondary
           Mean yearly gross earning for those working more than 30 hours per week.
Sweden: Level A = Old compulsory schooling (6 – 8 years) or new compulsory shooling (9 years)
           Level D = High school degree and at least one year of post-secondary education
           Level E = University degree
           All workers on full-time based on data from level of living surveys
USA: Level A = less than 4 years of high scool
           Level D = less than 4 years of college or university
           Level E = At least 4 years of college or university
           Mean gross annual earnings for full-time, full-year workers aged 18 and over – including income from self-employment

Low pay and earnings inequality

The frequency of low pay is, as expected, strongly correlated with a high level of earnings inequality and poverty. By looking at the incidence of low pay and earnings inequality in the early 1990s among the OECD countries we find that the United States and Canada have the highest number of low-paid employees and are among the countries with the highest level of poverty (see Figure 10.4).[3]

Sweden – and Denmark – on the other hand, has the lowest proportion of low-paid employees among the OECD countries and a fairly low level of earnings inequality. Concerning the last indicator Sweden has a position close to several other European countries such as Finland, Belgium and the Netherlands – all countries with a relatively comprehensive level of income redistribution through taxation and income transfers (see OECD 1997e). Several dimensions have to be considered in understanding the high proportion of low-paid jobs. Work experience, tenure and gender are probably the most important dimensions. Young employees and women are more likely to be in low-paid jobs than men and older employees. Furthermore the level of low-paid employment is generally higher in the service industries than in manufacturing but with large variations in the service sector. It is especially in trade, hotels and restaurants and personal services we find the low-paid jobs while communication, transport and producer services have relatively few low-paid jobs (OECD 1996c: 70–1).

In addition to the demographic, educational and industrial characteristics of

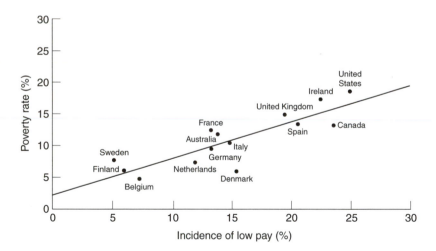

Figure 10.4 The relationship between low pay and poverty among OECD countries in the early 1990s

Source: OECD 1996c; 1997e; Marx and Verbist 1997.

Note
Low pay refers to the proportion of full-time workers earning less than two-thirds of median earnings. The poverty rate refers to the proportion of all individual aged 16–64 living in households with total income less than 50 per cent of the average household income – adjusted for the size of the household.

employees earnings inequality and incidence of low pay are determined by a variety of institutional and structural dimensions such as the level of unionisation, the coverage of collective bargaining, trends in employment and non-employment, etc. For the 15 countries for which detailed data on low pay and earnings inequality are available the OECD (1996c: 75) has calculated the correlation between these variables, a number of institutional dimensions and labour market outcomes. According to this analysis low pay and earnings inequality are strongly correlated with coverage of collective bargaining and union density but also with the replacement rates of unemployment benefits. High coverage of bargaining and high unionisation mean low frequency of low pay (Blau and Kahn 1996; Mishel and Bernstein 1995; OECD 1996c: 71). These two institutional factors prevent creation of low-paid jobs by establishing a wage floor and favouring solidaristic wage formation. The level of unemployment benefits might in a similar way create a floor below which workers will not accept payment in an offered job. The variables measuring labour market outcome – rates of employment and unemployment – do not in the same way correlate strongly with incidence of low pay. There is a positive correlation between the level of employment for young and female workers – which tend to be overrepresented among workers with low pay – and the overall incidence of low payment but this is a weak relation. Also the relation between rates of unemployment and incidence of low pay is weak although in the right direction. Consequently, we might conclude that it is not possible to find substantial evidence for a strong connection between employment among the precarious groups of employees and level of payment. Low earning inequality and few low-paid jobs do not necessarily mean higher unemployment nor lower employment for groups with low human capital resources – young people, women and the unskilled (OECD 1996c: 76). Looking at the labour market development among the European OECD countries during the recent decades seems to support this conclusion. In several of these countries – e.g., Sweden, Finland and Germany – unemployment has risen substantially for both young people and women while the level of real earnings among these groups has remained relatively stable or even been falling. The vast majority of the rise in overall unemployment as well as for specific groups of employees is thus due to other factors than high wages and comprehensive wage equality.

Low-paid work, earnings mobility and poverty

In order to evaluate the consequences of earnings inequality it is necessary to supplement the analysis of earnings dispersion with knowledge on how earnings inequality develops over time. If low-paid work tends to be concentrated amongst the same workers over extended periods, then the risk of poverty is high while this risk is reduced in labour markets with high earnings mobility meaning that the position of the workers within the earnings distribution changes substantially over time. Recent studies from OECD, however, suggest that mobility out of low-paid work is limited and this is especially the case in countries where low-paid work is most widespread (OECD 1997e). The mobility among low-paid workers is greater between unemployment, non-employment and low-paid jobs than between low-paid and well-paid employment. Data on earnings mobility can thus enrich our understanding of trends in earnings inequality. For an overview we have shown in Table 10.3 the earnings mobility in a 5-year period for the two Scandinavian countries and the United States.

Looking at the earnings mobility based on changes in income quintile we see that approximately half of the employees have remained in the same quintile in the earnings distribution and 14–16 per cent of the employees have moved two or more quintiles in all three countries over the time period 1986–91. The stability in the earnings structure seems highest in Sweden and lowest in Denmark but with small variations. The size of earnings mobility is sensitive to the type of measure used. Mobility measures derived from transitions between quintiles are purely relative. In a country with a low level of cross-sectional earnings inequality, a modest increase in earnings could cause a large change in the relative position of the individual worker – typically the situation for many low-paid workers in Scandinavia. The same rate of quintile transition in another country, with the high cross-sectional inequality that we find in the United States, would require a large percentage increase in earnings. The same level of earnings mobility in two countries thus indicates similar relative mobility but means more volatility in the earnings of the individual workers in the country with the highest cross-sectional earnings inequality. In Denmark and Sweden the distance between the quintiles is smaller than in the United States, which means that it is easier to move between the quintiles in the two Scandinavian countries. Considering the nearly similar pattern of wage mobility between the different quintiles in the three countries, but a significantly greater earnings dispersion in the United States, we might conclude that the overall earnings mobility is highest in the United States and lowest in Sweden, with Denmark in a middle position (OECD 1996c: 78–83).

The previous analysis informs us about the level of earnings mobility and thereby

Table 10.3 Five-year earnings mobility for full-time wage and salary workers in Denmark, Sweden and the United States, 1986–91 (%)

	Denmark	Sweden	USA
D9/D1 Earnings dispersion 1991	2.15	2.11	3.66
Mobility between 1986 and 1991, transition among quintiles			
Stayed in the same quintile	47.6	52.7	48.8
Moved up or down one quintile	35.6	33.8	35.5
Moved two or more quintiles	16.8	13.5	15.7

Source: OECD 1996c: 81.

Notes
Quintiles are calculated by dividing the total group of employees in 5 groups of equal size from the lowest to the highest earnings.
Population is full-time wage and salary workers in both 1986 and 1991.
Earnings are calculated based on gross monthly/weekly earnings.

about the flexibility in the wage/earnings structure but nothing about the persistence of being in low-paid work for the individual employee. Therefore, we need to go further analysing the frequency of movement out of low-paid jobs which will indicate the probability of low-paid employees improving their earnings capacity. In Table 10.4 we have shown the pattern of earnings mobility among low-paid employees in the period 1989–91 again based on figures calculated by the OECD (1996c).

Calculated for quintiles, the proportion of Danish employees moving upward between 1986 and 1991 from a low-paid job position in 1986 is higher than in any of the other OECD countries included in this study.[4] About one-third of the low-paid employees in 1986 are still in the bottom quintile in 1991 in all three countries – slightly more for Sweden and less for the United States – but significantly more employees have moved upward in Denmark compared with the United States – 41 per cent and 28 per cent, respectively. On the other hand, more than 40 per cent of the US employees who were low-paid in 1986 are no longer in full-time employment in 1991. The typical low-paid US workers are young workers who have shifted from employment to education, women who have shifted from full-time to part-time, and finally many low-paid US employees are moving in and out of employment. In cross-country comparisons we find no correlations between the rates of employment for youth, women and unskilled workers, and the incidence of low-paid employment and consequently reduced wages does not seem to improve the chances of these groups being integrated in the labour market. The high concentration of low-paid employment among these groups might instead indicate that regulation of low earnings through a legal minimum wage is not

Table 10.4 Five-year earnings mobility among low-paid workers in Denmark, Sweden and the United States in the period, 1986–91 (%)

The earnings status in 1991 of workers who were low-paid in 1986	*Denmark*	*Sweden*	*USA*
Low-payment defined as bottom quintile			
Share of low-paid in 1986	20.0	20.0	20.0
No longer employed full-time	26.7	27.6	41.4
Still in the bottom quintile	32.1	35.5	30.6
Moved to second quintile	20.5	18.4	16.7
Moved to the 3rd–5th quintile	20.7	18.4	11.3
Low-payment defined as below 0.65 of median earnings			
Share of low-paid in 1986	6.5	5.0	27.5
No longer employed in full-time	25.7	31.6	39.2
Still below 0.65 of the median	6.0	10.5	33.9
Moved to the band 0.65–0.95 of the median	43.1	34.2	17.2
Moved to bands above 0.95 of the median	25.2	23.7	9.7

Source: OECD 1996c: 97.

adversely affecting the overall possibilities of finding employment for low-skilled or inexperienced workers, but might if anything ensure that those who get a job are paid enough to maintain a decent standard of living.

Looking at earnings mobility calculated for low-payment defined as below 0.65 of the median earnings the ranking order between the three countries remains the same. But a substantially larger number of the US employees in low-paid jobs in 1986 were also in this job position in 1991 and the total number of US employees in low-paid jobs calculated for low-payment below 0.65 of the median earnings are significantly higher than in the Scandinavian countries. The small group of low-paid workers in the two Scandinavian countries have for the large majority left their low-paid position during the 5-year period 1986–91. The US employees, as we have shown earlier in this chapter, are more frequently moving between the different earnings bands but those who have ended in the lowest band have significantly more difficulty improving their earnings and in coming out of their low-paid job position, which has as a consequence that their risk of ending up in poverty is markedly higher (OECD 1996c: 97).

The lower mobility out of low-paid work among the US workers thus means that a higher percentage of the US workers are living in poverty generally, even if they are in employment or have full-year, full-time (FYFT) work – see Table 10.5, where the rates of poverty are calculated based on household income. There are striking differences in rates of poverty for the working-age populations in our four countries. The United States has nearly five times and Canada 3 times higher rates of poverty than Denmark, with the lowest rate among the four countries. The Scandinavian countries – Sweden and Denmark as well as Norway and Finland – have some of the lowest rates of poverty among the OECD countries but also the highest rates of employment. This indicates that there is no direct trade-off between work and poverty. It is other dimensions

Table 10.5 Poverty rates for working-age population, for those in work and for low-paid, full-year, full-time workers, by gender, in the early 1990s

	Working-age population	Individuals in work			Low-paid full-year, full-time (FYFT) workers		
	All	All	Men	Women	All	Men	Women
Canada	12.3	7.6	6.9	8.5	11.5	13.7	9.8
Denmark	4.0	2.8	2.5	3.1	–	–	–
Sweden	6.6	5.2	4.8	5.6	5.5	10.8	2.2
USA	19.1	13.8	13.3	14.4	24.0	32.2	18.3

Source: Marx and Verbist 1997: 9, 12 and 18.

Note
Definition of poverty: The poverty threshold is defined based on household income and a household is said to be in poverty if the total disposable household income, adjusted for family size, is less than 50 per cent of average equivalent income.

which are determining both employment and poverty (Cantillon 1997: 127–9; Marx and Verbist 1997: 8).

We find as shown in Figure 10.4 (page 224) a close relationship between the incidence of low-paid work and the rate of poverty. For all in work the poverty rate in the United States is 14 per cent while about a quarter of the low-paid US workers in FYFT-employment have earnings below the poverty threshold. The figures for Canada are about 8 per cent in poverty among all workers and 11.5 per cent of the FYFT low-paid workers below the poverty line. The figures are much lower among Scandinavian workers and here we find only small differences in poverty rates for all workers and for low-paid workers. The legal minimum wages in these countries are fixed at a level which ensures most individuals in work receive an income sufficient to avoid living in poverty.

Poverty has a gender dimension. In the total working-age population women more frequently live in poverty than men and this is also the case among individuals in work. Women have poorer wages, are more frequently employed in contingent jobs and have lower work experiences than men, which altogether means that they earn less than men. On the other hand, the poverty rates for low-paid men are significantly higher than for women in low-paid jobs. Most low-paid workers live in multi-earner households and this is especially the case for low-paid women, while low-paid men often live alone or are the only breadwinner in the household (Cantillon 1997).

Looking at the relationship between earnings mobility, low-paid work and poverty we found nearly the same earnings mobility in our four countries, and considering the broader earnings dispersion in the United States we might conclude that earnings mobility was slightly higher here than in the Scandinavian countries. On the other hand, the probability of moving out of low-paid work was significantly higher in Scandinavia than in the United States and this has as a consequence that more US workers were living in poverty even if they have a full-year, full-time job because as many as 26 per cent of these workers are low paid and many of these low-paid jobs are paid below the poverty threshold. This is opposite to the Scandinavian countries where the rate of escape from low-paid work is significantly higher (Cantillon 1997). In some sense there seems to be a marked inverse relationship between incidence of poverty and the rate of escape from low pay and poverty not because of a high earnings mobility but owing to regulated wage setting, legal minimum wages and generous income protection or income supplements for those who are not able to earn sufficient in regular employment.

Flexibility of average nominal and real-wage growth

As discussed above, there are a number of arguments which can support the idea that 'institutions matter' in the sense that the response to the business cycle of real and nominal wages will depend on the institutional framework of the labour market.

In the present section these differences are studied applying the theory of the traditional Phillips curve in order to identify different patterns in the relationship between unemployment and nominal-wage growth. This focus on nominal wages is based on two lines of reasoning (cf. Madsen 1995).

First, the approach taken is based on the Keynesian belief that nominal variables like wages and prices are to be considered independently and in nominal terms. As argued by Mitchell, wage nominalism is inherent in a monetary economy:

> It would be peculiar in a monetary economy if wage nominalism did not exist. Elaborate explanations about wage relativities, decentralized bargaining, risk aversion, menu costs, and the like are at best supplementary explanations. Money as a value standard is the basis of wage (and price) nominalism.
>
> (Mitchell 1993: 26)

Basically the argument is that the individual and collective actors on the labour market (and elsewhere in a monetary economy) will react to changes in nominal variables. This, of course, does not deny that the interplay between nominal variables may be important – as for instance the effect of price inflation on the purchasing power of money. But to reduce this interplay by focusing directly on the statistical artefact of a real wage would be a misinterpretation of the actual behaviour of employers, employees, labour market organisations and political actors. If one aims at understanding the actual economic behaviour of economic agents, one must focus on variables which are empirically observable to these agents – that is, nominal and not real variables.

The second argument for focusing on the traditional short-run Phillips curve is based on a rejection of the concepts of long-run parameters and equilibria in relation to empirical work. One cannot deny that the distinction between short-run and long-run equilibria for certain purposes can be a useful analytical distinction in theoretical work. But when dealing with empirical analysis, one should always be aware of the difference between *analytical time* as used in theoretical modelling and *historical time*, which is the only relevant concept in empirical work. In historical time, economic variables are never in a state of long-run equilibrium. The value of any economic variable at any point of historical time is the result of a complex set of dynamic processes – and thus influenced both by more recent events and by events dating further back in history. We might be able to uncover some of these dynamic relationships by econometric time-series analysis. But we shall not be able to deduce the relevant specification of these functional relationships from theoretical models of long-run equilibria.

The data

Therefore, we now take a closer look at unemployment and nominal-wage growth in the four countries from 1961 to 2001.

First, Figure 10.5 presents the time-series for unemployment rates. The patterns are remarkably different. The United States and Canada show a rather high level

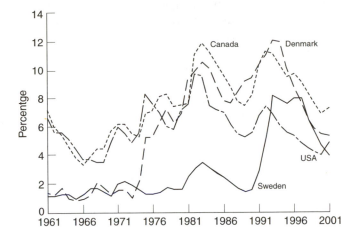

Figure 10.5 Unemployment rates, 1961–2001

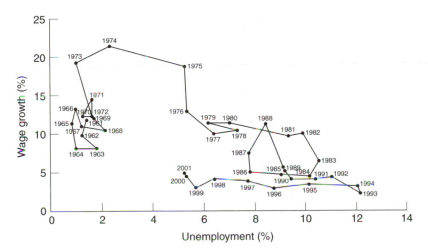

Figure 10.6 Denmark: unemployment and nominal-wage growth, 1961–2001

of unemployment of 4–6 per cent even during the 'full-employment period' of the 1960. The level increases for both countries to between 5 and 12 per cent in the following decades, higher for Canada. From the early 1990s unemployment then drops again to between 5 and 8 per cent, still higher in Canada.

The two Scandinavian countries share a low level of unemployment until 1973. Then Denmark takes off and soon reaches a level of unemployment very similar to that of Canada. Sweden keeps a remarkably low unemployment level until the crisis in 1990, when unemployment rises steeply to about 8 per cent. The four countries show some convergence in unemployment rates in recent years with the two Scandinavian countries and the United States having levels of unemployment between 4 and 6 per cent. Canada, however, still has a rather high level of unemployment of around 8 per cent (the development in unemployment and its composition is analysed in more detail in Chapter 8, in this volume.)

Figures 10.6 to 10.9 depict the Phillips curves for our four countries based on data for nominal-wage growth and unemployment rates for the period 1961 to 2001.

Looking first at Denmark in Figure 10.6 (page 231), the pattern of wages inflation and unemployment in the years from 1961 to 2001 can be divided into four distinct subperiods. Phase 1 from 1961 to 1971 is a period with a low level of unemployment and a tendency for wage inflation to slowly increase from the first to the second half of the decade, but still being below 15 per cent. During phase 2 from 1972 to 1975, the level of wage increase rises to around 20 per cent per year, while the unemployment rate at the same time increases from 2 to 6 per cent.

An important institutional factor behind this development was the automatic indexation of wages based on price inflation, which was then part of the Danish wage agreements. Thus, the outburst of inflation related to the first oil crisis automatically spilled over into rising nominal wages. The automatic indexation of wages was restricted somewhat in 1975 and finally suspended in 1983.

The third phase can be identified from 1975 to 1994. Here one sees what can be interpreted as a new, rather stable, Phillips curve where the wage increases during the upswing from 1984 to 1988 tend to reach the levels seen at the same level of unemployment around 1980.

Finally, the fourth phase is represented by the observations from 1993 to 2001. During this period open unemployment in Denmark was cut by half compared with the previous period. This was mainly due to a sharp increase in effective demand, while the level of wage inflation was below 5 per cent during the entire period. In the literature several explanations are given for this exceptional development. One explanation focuses on a changed climate in wage negotiation with the organisations on both sides being increasingly aware of the potential damages for employment caused by high nominal wages in a situation where the Danish currency had been firmly linked first to the German Mark and then to the Euro. Another explanation points to the contribution of the Danish labour market reform of 1994 in reducing imbalances in the labour market during the upswing (Madsen 1999). Finally, some researchers focus on the artificial reduction in registered unemployment caused by the rising number of people in labour market programmes and leave schemes. However, though there was an increase in the take-up of such programmes in 1994–95, the fall in unemployment since then cannot be attributed to such 'book-keeping effects' (cf. Madsen 1999: ch. 3).

Sweden also shows a configuration of unemployment and wage-inflation, which during some subperiods may be interpreted along the lines of a traditional Phillips curve, cf. Figure 10.7 (page 233). Most of the observations from the first 30 years – the period 1961–91 – are located in a cluster, where the rate of unemployment is in the interval from 1 to 3 per cent and wages increase by between 7 and 11 per cent per year. The main exceptions are again found in the early 1970s where the

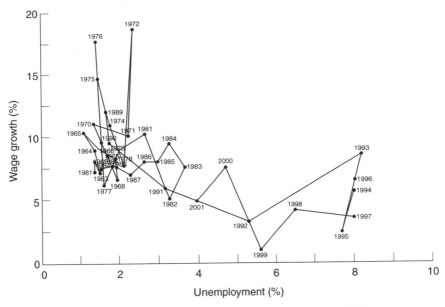

Figure 10.7 Sweden: unemployment and nominal-wage growth, 1961–2001

inflationary push of the first oil crisis made Swedish wages grow by up to 19 per cent per year. Apart from that, it is tempting to interpret these three decades as the golden years of the Swedish model, where low unemployment and moderate wage inflation went hand in hand. This unusual combination of low unemployment and low wage inflation is caused by a mix of several institutional traits. The wage bargaining took place in highly centralised and stable forms and was combined with a strong commitment enforcing a solidaristic wage policy from both unions, employers and the state. During most of the 1960s and 1970s these two institutional features of the wage bargaining were, in Sweden but not in Denmark, co-ordinated with an active labour market policy characterised by a comprehensive occupational and industrial labour mobility and large-scale retraining/up-skilling of the labour force (Iversen 1996)

After this long first phase, a second period can be identified covering the 1990s. Here unemployment rapidly increased to 8 per cent. At the same time wage growth declined to a level of 3 to 6 per cent per year. Especially, one notes that the recent Swedish recovery, which has lowered unemployment to around 5–6 per cent has not yet been accompanied by a new rise in wage inflation. For Sweden – and also for Denmark as noted above – this presents a remarkable change in the pattern of nominal-wage formation. Also in Sweden the climate in wage negotiation has changed and job creation has been given priority instead of nominal-wage growth. This in combination with a restrictive monetary policy linking the Swedish currency closely to the European low-inflation policy has led to low nominal-wage growth but increasing real wages (see Figure 10.3, page 219).

Turning then to the two countries from the North American continent, Figure 10.8 shows the pattern of unemployment and wage inflation for Canada. With some exceptions, there is a remarkable similarity to the Danish case. For Canada we can also identify four phases during the four decades depicted in the figure. A first phase from 1961 to 1973 shows a gradual upward drift in the yearly wage increases from the level of 3–5 per cent in the first half of the 1960s to between 6 and 9 per cent in the following 5 to 7 years. Then follows a second phase (1974–76), where wage inflation and unemployment both rose significantly, followed by a third phase lasting until around 1990. The third phase mainly shows downward sloping combinations of unemployment and wage increases, however, with some shifts in the pattern between the subperiods of 1976–83 and 1984–93. The fourth and final phase depicts a combination of falling unemployment and rather stable wage inflation, with wages increasing by between 1 and 3 per cent per year.

Finally, in Figure 10.9, we turn to the Phillips curve for the USA, which is in many respects the most complicated. For the 1960s there is some similarity with the other three countries, especially with Canada. Wage inflation gradually increases until 1971 and then shoots off to a high level during the years 1973 to 1975, while at the same time unemployment rises from 5 per cent to around 8 per cent. But then during the subsequent period until 1981, there is a remarkable stability in wage inflation at the level of 8 to 9 per cent in spite of rather large fluctuations in unemployment between 5.5 and 8.5 per cent. Finally, in 1982–83 unemployment increases to around 9.5 per cent and wage growth dampens to around 5 per cent per year. This level acts as a new 'plateau' for wage growth until the early 1990s where wage growth drops to levels around 3 per cent per year while unemployment has settled around 6 per cent, a configuration almost like the 1960s. The circle is

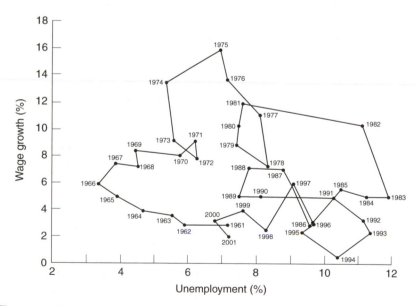

Figure 10.8 Canada: unemployment and nominal-wage growth, 1961–2001

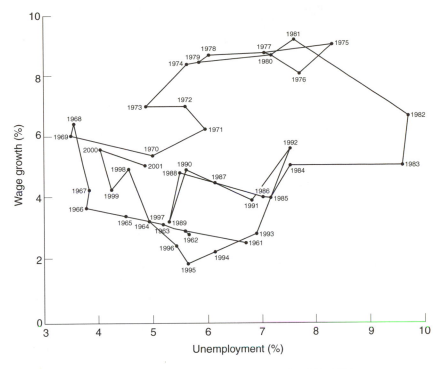

Figure 10.9 USA: unemployment and nominal-wage growth, 1961–2001

completed in the sense that the configuration of unemployment and nominal-wage growth observed in the late 1990s is very close to the situation of the early 1960s.

Based on the four national Phillips curves just studied, some general observations can be made:

- As exemplified by the two oil crises, in all countries external price shocks are important explanations for sudden outbursts of high wage increases in combination with rising unemployment (stagflation). This is also illustrated by the Swedish experience following the large devaluation in 1993.
- Over long periods, a significant decline in wage inflation can be seen at the same time as a sharp upward shift in the level of open unemployment, thus supporting the traditional idea of a dampening effect of wage inflation from high unemployment. This observation can be made in Denmark from the early 1970s to the early 1990s, in Sweden from the early 1980s to the early 1990s, in Canada from the early 1970s to the early 1990s and in the United States from the mid-1970s to the early 1980s. However, this pattern is clearly more pronounced for some countries (Denmark and Canada) than for others.
- In all countries, a significant fall in unemployment has been observed in recent years without a subsequent rise in wage inflation. This pattern is very distinct

for Denmark, but may also be observed for Sweden and Canada. On the other hand, in the United States the reduction in unemployment since the mid-1990s has been accompanied by some *increase* in nominal-wage inflation.

Especially for Denmark and Sweden, but to some extent also for Canada, there is a need to look for possible explanations for the apparent change in wage setting mechanisms, which might account for the change from a downward sloping to an almost horizontal Phillips curve in recent years.

Thus, in the Danish case the following set of interrelated explanations have been offered (Madsen 1999):

    I.   The positive effects on the functioning of the labour market caused by extensive labour market reforms in the second half of the 1990s.

    II. The changing attitudes of the dominant trade unions towards a larger emphasis on stable growth in employment and real wages – instead of short-term gains in nominal wages.

   III. The ongoing internationalisation of the economy, which has been intensified due to membership of the EU and the development of the Single Market. The changing attitudes of the trade unions could be seen in this light.

   IV. The dampening effects on wage claims from the increase in real incomes that has been accompanying the Danish economic upswing since the mid-1990s.

Some of these explanations may also be valid for Sweden, where we also observe an increased focus on labour market reforms, new attitudes of social partners, a more international economy and rising real wages. The condition for the well-known Swedish model of labour market regulation changed dramatically in the late 1980s and the early 1990s. A highly centralised system of wage bargaining was abandoned in the mid-1980s, the increasing internationalisation of product and services markets undermined the unions' possibilities of pursuing militant wage strategies and instead they tried to prioritise protection of jobs. This in combination with Sweden's membership of the European Union led to a change of policy priorities from redistributive fiscal policy to restrictive monetary policy characterised by low inflation, lower taxation and tightening of the fiscal policies as part of the intended harmonisation between the EU Member States.

For the United States also, one should note that a significant dampening of nominal-wage increases has taken place in recent years. If one shifts the focus on compensation per employee to hourly wages, one would find an even stronger reduction in nominal-wage growth in the United States due to the fact that working hours per employee have increased in recent years. Thus, from 1990 to 2001, the average annual hours actually worked in the Unites States increased by 2.9 per cent, while the average annual working hours were almost stable in Sweden and Canada (OECD 2001b: 225).

Since neither labour market reforms, nor new attitudes of social partners seem to be relevant explanations in the case of the downward pressure on wages in recent years in the United States, the analysis should also stress that the same outcome – a lower level of nominal-wage growth at a given level of unemployment – may arise from different causes. Thus, in the case of the United States one may, instead of institutional labour market reforms, point to the effects of rising working hours and the permanent inflow of new – partly illegal – workers to the labour market. Thus, strong capacity effects seem to have been present in the US labour market implying that the rate of open unemployment becomes a less reliable measure of the balance of power between workers and employers in the negotiations over wages.

The extent to which the changes in institutions and in the behaviour of actors on the labour market has shifted the Phillips curve to the left allowing for further reductions in unemployment without creating an upward drift in nominal wages still remains to be seen. The main lesson from the analysis above is that the concept of a certain fixed level of 'structural unemployment', which acts as a solid barrier to rapid decreases in unemployment, has proved to be fragile. In all four countries analysed in the present study we have observed recent subperiods of strong reductions in unemployment without outbursts of wage inflation in situations where certain configurations of institutional change make this possible.

Conclusion

The purpose of this chapter has been to explore the pattern of wage formation and wage dispersion in our four countries which, as shown in Chapters 2–4 of this volume, are characterised by markedly different institutional configurations of the labour market in respect to centralisation and co-ordination of wage bargaining between the institutional actors and in the level of state intervention in labour market issues. Not surprisingly, we thus found clear differences between North America and Scandinavia in both wage formation and wage dispersion. The wage dispersion and consequently the earnings inequality were significantly higher in the United States and Canada than in Denmark and Sweden. Looking at the earnings mobility we do not find strong differences between our four countries. About half of the employees stay in the same earnings quintile during a five-year period in the early 1990s but the proportion of low-paid workers was markedly higher in the United States than in both Denmark and Sweden. Furthermore, among those employed in low-paid jobs it seems significantly more difficult to move out of these low-paid jobs in the United States than in the two Scandinavian countries, and the lower mobility out of low-paid work among the US workers combined with the high level of wage inequality thus means that a higher proportion of the US workers are living permanently in poverty.

High wage dispersion as well as high earnings mobility is considered to speed up job creation in the economy. In this study we have not found any clear relationship between wage formation, earnings mobility and job creation. Furthermore, we find no evidence for a trade-off between wage and employment in the sense that low wage flexibility and a compressed wage structure cause low job growth. Likewise, the so-called labour market rigidities, such as strict employment protection, generous levels of employment benefits and high levels of unionisation, do not necessarily mean either low earnings mobility or slow job growth if these measures are combined with an active and interventionist labour market policy as we have seen is the case in the Scandinavian countries during the 1990s. Denmark especially, but also Sweden during the late 1990s, has experienced strong job growth and a declining level of unemployment in combination with remarkable stability in wage inflation without giving up its solidaristic and strongly regulated wage policy, thus highlighting the fragile character of the traditional concepts of 'structural' or 'natural' rates of unemployment.

In a recent comparative study of the ILO analysing the role of policies and institutions in four successful small internationalised European economies – including Denmark – it is similarly concluded that the outcome of the functioning of the labour market related to stable employment and inflation must be attributed to a number of institutional factors such as those suggested by Auer (2001: 2):

- macroeconomic policy and macroeconomic conditions in general, which provide the necessary framework for a sound development of the labour market;
- flexibility in employment relations, which can easily be combined with high social protection;
- equal opportunities, which is important for obtaining high employment; and
- a labour market governance system based on a developed social dialogue between the social partners and the government is considered to be conducive to labour market success in relation to both wage stability and job creation.

The findings thus run contrary to the traditional conception of regulated European labour markets as being less successful and flexible than the more liberal model for market regulation found in the United States.

Part III

Comparisons with other OECD countries

11 Post-industrial profiles

North American, Scandinavian and other Western labour markets

Bengt Furåker

In the last decades, the world economy has undergone significant transformations, with undeniable consequences for national socio-economic conditions. The countries in our study – Canada, the United States, Denmark and Sweden – represent separate societal models and we have asked whether their labour markets develop along separate routes due to their divergent institutional set-ups. Or do the four labour markets tend to converge – no matter what institutional differences have been established – because they are subjected to similar pressures from strong social, economic and technological forces, the intensified international competition and the general shift toward post-industrialism?

My aim with this final chapter is more systematically to place Canada, the United States, Denmark and Sweden in a wider international context. The labour markets in the four countries will be compared with those in a number of other OECD member states. It can still only be a matter of comparing them from a few – but hopefully important – angles. To put it very briefly, in one section of the chapter, the distribution and the amount of paid work will be focused. Two sets of questions guide this part of the analysis: first, to what extent is the population engaged in gainful employment? Are there country-specific patterns that can be related to differences in institutional arrangements? Second, how much work is actually carried out in various countries? This question implies paying attention not only to employment rates but also – and simultaneously – to hours worked. The issue is to what degree a given country's work potential is made use of. Again, it will be asked whether the variation – if there is any – can be understood in terms of institutional models.

Another part of the chapter will be devoted to the social division of labour. There are also in this case two principal questions that guide the analysis. The first one focuses on how the occupational structure in post-industrial societies is to be characterised. To what extent do countries differ from each other in terms of socio-economic structures and to what extent are existing differences associated with the size of the service sector? The second question concerns the role of the public sector in the organisation of services. What is the relationship between the degree of post-industrialism and the size of public service production?

In the following pages, besides the size of the service sector, differences in terms of welfare or social protection arrangements are taken as a crucial background against which some of the labour market outcomes will be analysed. Therefore, it seems appropriate to begin by giving a summary outline of how various countries differ from each other in this respect.

Social protection arrangements

Several of the previous chapters in this book have described the social protection systems in Canada, the United States, Denmark and Sweden. It should thus by now be evident that there are fundamental differences between these systems and that the differences have existed for quite a long time. We have certainly witnessed many changes over the past two or three decades, but the general models have continued to be markedly separate. The social protection arrangements in the four countries will now be compared with those in other countries. In order not to drown the presentation with details, a few key dimensions are to be focused; this obviously means a simplification of matters, but hopefully not an oversimplification. Five dimensions or indicators will be considered: union density, employment protection legislation, social security transfers, government employment and active labour market policies.

Every country is classified as 'high', 'high medium', 'low medium', or 'low' on each of these indicators. Moreover, figures are assigned to each of the labels, ranging from 4 (high) to 1 (low). By doing so, we can calculate a 'social protection score'. The results are displayed in Table 11.1. It must be admitted that this is a crude way of classifying protection systems – involving a certain amount of arbitrariness as to where the dividing lines are being drawn between labels. Nevertheless, the picture presented is pretty much in line with what we would expect. Let us take a closer look at the components behind the index.

Chapter 2 dealt with industrial relations and it showed that Canadian, American, Danish and Swedish unions clearly differ from each other in terms of power and strength. The first dimension in Table 11.1 is based on unionisation rates or union density among employees. Data ideally refer to 1998, but sometimes to 1997 and for a number of countries to previous points in time (Kjellberg 2001: 27; OECD 1997d: 71; 1994a: 184). Both Sweden and Denmark score 'high' on this dimension. Union density for these two countries in 1998 has been set at 81 and 76 per cent, respectively (Kjellberg 2001: 27). For the same year Canada is classified as 'low medium' (with 33 per cent) and the United States as 'low' (with 14 per cent). The United States is one of three countries with figures below 20 per cent; the other two are France and Spain.

The second dimension in Table 11.1 is employment protection legislation, previously analysed in Chapter 3. I simply make use of the employment protection score (version 2) for the late 1990s given by the OECD (1999b: 66). At that time, as well as in the mid-1980s, the United States was assigned the lowest score of all (0.7) and Portugal the highest (3.7). Among our four nations Sweden received the highest figure (2.6), i.e., still much below that of Portugal (and other southern European countries). Sweden is therefore classified as 'high medium'. Denmark and Canada score close to each other with 1.5 and 1.1, respectively, which means

Table 11.1 Social protection characteristics in various OECD countries in the late 1990s (ranking according to total score)

	Unionisation rate	Employment protection score	% of GDP on social security transfers	Government employment as % of total	% of GDP on active labour market policies	Total score
Sweden	H	HM	H	H	H	19
Denmark	H	LM	H	H	H	18
Finland	H	HM	H	HM	HM	17
Belgium	HM	HM	H	LM	HM	15
Norway	HM	HM	LM	H	LM	14
France	L	HM	H	HM	HM	14
Italy	LM	H	HM	LM	HM	14
Austria	LM	HM	H	HM	L	13
Germany	LM	HM	HM	LM	HM	13
Netherlands	L	HM	H	L	H	13
Portugal	LM	H	LM	LM	LM	12
Spain	L	H	LM	LM	LM	11
Ireland	HM	LM	L	L	H	11
Canada	LM	LM	L	HM	LM	10
Greece	LM	H	LM	L	L	10
Australia	LM	LM	L	LM	L	8
NZ	LM	L	–	L	LM	7.5
Japan	L	HM	L	L	L	7
UK	LM	L	LM	L	L	7
USA	L	L	L	LM	L	6

Sources: See text.

Note
H = High (4); HM = High medium (3); LM = Low medium (2); L= Low (1).

that in both cases the distance to the United States is shorter than to Sweden. They have been counted as 'low medium' and the United States – of course – as 'low'.

The third column is based on one of the tables presented in Chapter 4 (Table 4.1). It presents a classification of social security transfers in 1996 or 1997 (or for some countries even earlier than that) as a proportion of GDP. Denmark and Sweden have been classified as 'high', but we should note that there are quite a few other countries with similar or higher scores. Again, Canada is included in the 'low medium' category and the United States is labelled 'low'.

Next we find information on the proportion of government employment of total employment (the underlying percentages refer to 1998 and are taken from the OECD database). The two Scandinavian neighbours are both assigned the label 'high'. Together with Norway they are the only countries reaching up to or above the 30 per cent level. This time, however, North America is somewhat higher than on the other dimensions: Canada just exceeds the minimum level for 'high medium' and the United States surpasses the 'low medium' limit.

Finally, there is a column classifying expenditures for active labour market policy as a proportion of GDP. The data again come from the OECD (2001b: 24, 230–41) and they mainly refer to 1998. It should be noted that this information is partly included in other columns, i.e., those for social security transfers and government employment. In other words, the index contains an element of weighting. Both Denmark and Sweden are great spenders on active measures, while Canada and in particular the United States do not spend much at all. This means 'high' for the Scandinavian cases and 'low' for the North American ones.

Adding up the scores on each dimension of union protection and welfare state arrangements, we find Sweden and Denmark at the top, with a slight lead for Sweden. The United States comes last of all countries in Table 11.1, indicating that market mechanisms are allowed plenty of scope. Canada is relatively close to the United States but some steps higher up in the ranking. In other words, if there are differences in labour market performance due to the degree to which the market can operate freely without the intervention of the state and the unions, we no doubt have four cases that are well suited for comparison.

The distribution and amount of paid work

The key question to be addressed in this section is whether Canada, the United States, Denmark and Sweden in comparison with other economically advanced countries can be characterised as 'work societies'. We may find it difficult to agree upon the meaning of such a label, but it is used only to indicate how much paid work – in relation to the active population and the potential it represents – is carried out in a given society. It is not meant to deny or hide that people toil without pay in the so-called informal sector or in societies where money has no or little role to play. The focus is the modern labour market in which employment basically equals paid work. Accordingly, we shall examine the scope and distribution of gainful employment in different countries and the quantities of work actually carried out.

The distribution of paid work

A first aspect to be considered is the relationship between male and female employment rates. Presenting data for various OECD countries in 2000, Figure 11.1 shows that the two measures are clearly positively correlated. Female employment rates are not high because male rates are low or vice versa; instead the two go together. Denmark and the United States appear in the upper right-hand corner together with Norway and the Netherlands. Canada and Sweden are somewhat further away, due to their relatively low male employment rates. The countries tending towards the opposite corner are above all south European ones (but Portugal is an exception).

Gainful employment is common among both men and women in Canada, the United States, Denmark and Sweden and more so than in many other countries, although similar patterns also appear elsewhere. Next, we will turn to the distribution of paid work among age categories. As a first step, employment rates for youth (15/16–24 years of age) and the prime-age population (25–54) are related to each other (Figure 11.2a, page 246). In a second step, the youth category is substituted for the older working-age population (55–64) and the same procedure is repeated (Figure 11.2b, page 246).

Looking first at the relationship between youth and prime-age employment rates, we must comment upon a few things. As we can see, there is some positive correlation between the two variables. The category aged 25–54 has high employment rates in our four countries, but youth score lower in Sweden than in Denmark and North America. Denmark, followed by Norway, the Netherlands, the United States and the United Kingdom, is located closest to the upper right-hand corner. Canada and particularly Sweden are somewhat further away. Besides Spain, Italy, and Greece, it can be observed that Belgium and France have very low youth employment rates.

The scatter plot for employment rates among the older and the prime-age populations (Figure 11.2b) tells us yet another story. Again, the two variables correlate positively with each other, but the location of our four cases is different. This time Sweden is found in the upper right-hand corner just behind Norway and somewhat ahead of Denmark and the United States. Canada has a lower employment rate among its older working-age population, but it is still higher than in most central and southern European countries.

Paid work is thus relatively widely distributed in the populations of Canada, the United States, Denmark and Sweden – in comparison with other countries. We have, however, noted certain differences between our four cases. Female employment rates are slightly lower in North America and especially in Canada than in

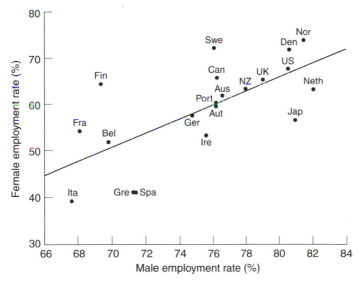

Figure 11.1 Male and female employment rates in various OECD countries, 2000
Source: OECD 2001b: 209–11.

Note
Aut = Austria; Aus = Australia.

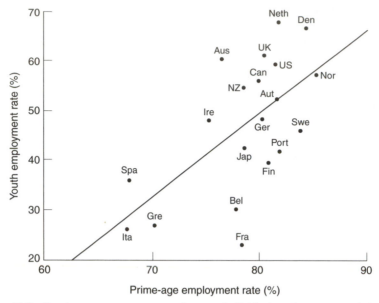

Figure 11.2a Employment rates among prime-age individuals and among youth in various
OECD countries, 2000

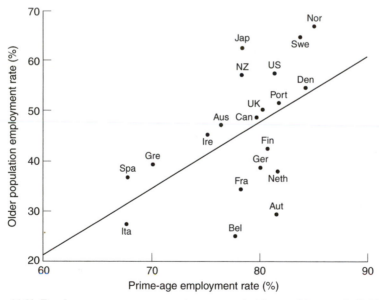

Figure 11.2b Employment rates among prime-age and older working-age individuals in
various OECD countries, 2000

Source: OECD 2001b: 209–11.

Note
Aut = Austria; Aus = Australia.

the two Scandinavian countries. With regard to age there are somewhat divergent patterns. Sweden has lower employment rates among youth than Denmark, the United States and Canada. As to the older working-age population, however, it is Sweden that has the highest employment rate.

Compared with most other Western nations, our four cases show rather high employment rates for most of the categories analysed. The main competitor is Norway – another Scandinavian country – but we find high scores also for the Netherlands, the United Kingdom and Japan. Among most central European countries, employment rates are middle level and frequently low in some respect. With the exception of Portugal, the countries in southern Europe turn out low on all the dimensions covered.

Since Canada, the United States, Denmark and Sweden are all highly post-industrial in the sense that they have a relatively large service sector, we may expect to find a positive relationship between the latter variable and employment rates. This is confirmed in Figure 11.3 where employment rates in 1998 are related to the proportions of service sector employment the same year.

Service employment proportions and employment rates are positively correlated with each other, but the observations are rather spread out in the figure. Our four countries are all found in the upper right-hand corner of the figure – with Norway, the United Kingdom, the Netherlands and Australia – implying that they score high on both variables. Again, there are a number of Mediterranean countries with low positions in the figure.

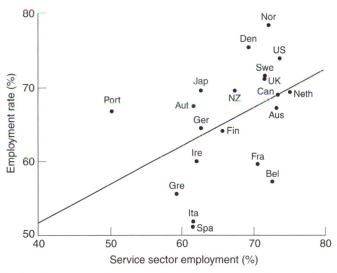

Figure 11.3 Service sector employment and employment rates in various OECD countries, 1998

Sources: OECD 2001b: 209; 2000b: 41.

Note
Aut = Austria; Aus = Australia.

One reason why there is a positive association between the relative size of the service sector and the proportion of people in paid work is that many women are employed in the service sector. At the same time, however, male employment rates are also positively correlated – although more weakly – with the proportion of services (not shown).

The analysis will now be pushed one step further with the help of the social protection score calculated in Table 11.1 (page 243). We can thus examine whether, and to what extent, institutional patterns are correlated with employment rates. Figure 11.4 presents the relationship between the social protection scores and the employment rates in 1998 for the same countries as before.

There is a U-shaped relationship between the two variables. However, it should be observed that countries with middle level social protection scores differ substantially from each other in terms of employment rates (cf., e.g., Norway and Italy). This time our four cases are quite far apart from each other. Denmark and Sweden are located in the upper right-hand corner and the United States in the upper left-hand corner, while Canada is more in the middle. Between the United States and Canada we find the United Kingdom, Japan, New Zealand and Australia. The countries that are closest to Denmark and Sweden – although not very close – are Norway and Finland. In conclusion, social protection is not negatively associated with employment rates. The latter can be high with both strong and weak institutional welfare arrangements.

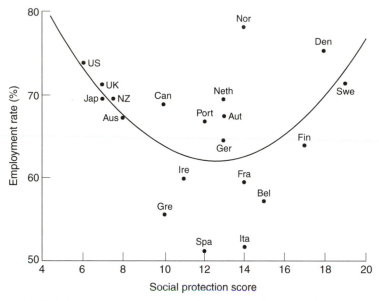

Figure 11.4 Social protection scores and employment rates in various OECD countries, late 1990s

Sources: See text related to Table 11.1; OECD 2001b: 209.

Note
Aut = Austria; Aus = Australia.

Low employment rates seem above all to be associated with weak female participation in the labour market. In Figure 11.3 this is illustrated by the position of Spain, Italy, Greece, Belgium, France and Ireland which all have low female employment rates. At the same time these countries mainly have middle level social protection scores, most likely related to the role played by the family in providing for people.

In other words, welfare state arrangements do not appear to be very important for employment rates. On the other hand, the mechanisms behind such high rates may differ between countries with, respectively, strong and weak social protection. In the first case, for example, people often need to have (had) gainful employment in order to be entitled to benefits, economic policies are perhaps characterised by a full employment commitment with active labour market policies, and the size of the public sector means a large demand for labour. In the second category of countries – where the social security net is weak – there may be no other way for people to provide for themselves than through finding a job in the labour market.

We must be aware that the category of employment is different from what can be referred to as work mobilisation. The latter concept also takes the number of hours worked into account. It is now time to include this dimension in the analysis.

Work mobilisation

As we have seen, Canada, the United States, Denmark and Sweden belong – more or less – to the same top category with respect to employment rates. However, gainfully employed individuals may carry out very different quantities of work. Some have part-time jobs with longer or shorter working hours. Others have full-time jobs, but full-time often does not mean the same across countries. Moreover, people may work overtime and they may be absent from work, because of sickness, vacation, parental leave, or other reasons. Countries differ from each other as to how welfare state arrangements and transfers make absence from work possible and not too punishing financially. In these respects, the Scandinavian welfare states are no doubt much more generous than their North American counterparts. From Chapter 5 we know that gainfully employed Scandinavians on average work less – in terms of annual hours – than gainfully employed North Americans (Table 5.7). Given that the employment rates do not differ that much between the four countries, it follows that the potential labour resources are utilised to a larger extent in North America. This was also shown in Table 5.7.

How, then, do Canada, the United States, Denmark and Sweden compare with other OECD countries regarding the amount of work actually carried out as a proportion of the potential? The measure to be used can be called the 'work mobilisation rate' and it is calculated in the way presented in Chapter 5 (see also Nickell 1997). It is based on the assumption that an individual might work a maximum of 40 hours per week during 52 weeks per year. We may of course question whether it is realistic to assume full-time work all year round. On the other hand, it really does not matter very much if another standard is chosen: 40 hours per week during 48 weeks, 35 hours per week during 50 weeks, or the like. No doubt, the measure is somewhat arbitrarily chosen, but it has no other purpose than to provide a standard for calculating the mobilisation of people for paid work. The percentage of gainfully employed is multiplied by the annual average of hours worked per employee and the outcome is divided by 2080 (40 × 52). For those countries that provide statistics on average annual working hours – unfortunately, in many cases no such data are available – work mobilisation rates are presented in Table 11.2.

The highest work mobilisation rate in the table is found for Japan in 1983. It has, however, decreased substantially between 1983 and 2000 – by more than 10 percentage points. By 2000, the United States had the highest score after a remarkable jump upward since the beginning of the period. Then there is a rather large gap down to New Zealand, Australia, Canada and Japan which all show figures somewhat over 60 per cent. Canada also belongs to those countries that have had a clear increase across time. Sweden and Denmark are located in the middle of the table (we should observe that the Danish data refer to 1998), but they score much higher than the countries at the bottom: Spain, Germany, France and Italy. None of the latter four reached the 50 per cent level in 1999 or 2000.

Thus, although their employment rates for various social categories are generally high, our four countries do not use their work potential to the same extent. In fact, the United States appears as much more of a work society than the other three, among which Canada comes first, Sweden second and Denmark third. We may now ask whether strong social protection is associated with work disincentives, i.e., whether it can be assumed to make people less prepared to work much. Figure

Table 11.2 Work mobilisation rates in various OECD countries, selected years, 1983–2000 (ranking according to latest figures available)

	1983	*1990*	*1996*	*2000*	*Difference 1990–2000*	*Difference 1983–2000*
US	59.1	63.1	64.4	66.9	+3.8	+7.8
New Zealand	–	58.9	62.8	61.8	+2.9	–
Australia	55.3	61.0	60.4	61.8	+1.0	+6.5
Canada	55.5	60.4	57.7	61.6	+1.2	+6.1
Japan	71.5	67.0	63.2	61.0[a]	−6.0	−10.5
UK	55.2	61.5	58.4	59.5	−2.0	+4.3
Sweden	58.5	61.8	55.9	57.9	−3.9	−0.6
Denmark	57.1	57.2	54.1	55.4[b]	−1.8	−1.7
Finland	63.7	62.8	53.2	55.4	−7.4	−8.3
Norway	55.2	50.3	50.9	51.5	+1.2	−3.7
Spain	45.5	44.8	41.9	48.9	+4.1	+3.4
Germany	49.6[c]	49.2	46.8	47.2	−2.0	–
France	51.0	47.7	45.8	44.9[a]	−2.8	−6.1
Italy	44.9	43.4	39.8	41.2[a]	−2.2	−3.7

Sources: OECD 2001b: 209, 225; 1997d: 163; Ministry of Finance (Denmark).

Note
a 1999; b 1998; c West Germany.

11.5 gives us the opportunity to examine how the two variables – social protection and work mobilisation – are related to each other.

Starting from the upper left-hand corner, we find countries with low social protection scores and high work mobilisation rates. The United States is closest to this corner, but Japan, New Zealand, the United Kingdom and Australia are not very far away – and then Canada follows. With increasing social protection the curve runs downward (indicating decreasing work mobilisation) to a point where it bends upwards. At the opposite pole we find Sweden and Denmark as well as Finland. Although Figure 11.5 reminds us of Figure 11.4, the rise of the curve – on the right-hand side – is more moderate. Behind this shape of the curve we can identify certain institutional arrangements limiting the number of hours worked in the Nordic countries: more part-time jobs (in this respect, however, Finland is an exception), better possibilities for taking study leave and parental leave, longer vacations, etc.

The rank order between three roughly defined categories of countries can be used to summarise the outcome in Figure 11.5. We find the highest degree of work mobilisation among the countries with low social protection; then come those with strong social protection and finally those in the middle. We must keep in mind, however, that there are few cases in the figure.

Viewed in an international perspective, the North American and Scandinavian countries qualify as work societies in the sense that paid work is fairly widely distributed among their populations. With respect to the total quantities of work carried out, however, it is clear that the United States has a strong lead ahead of –

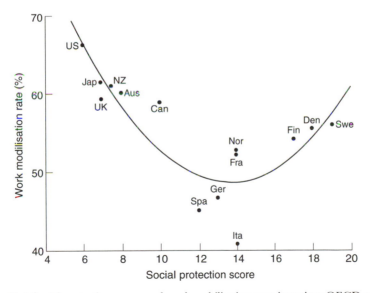

Figure 11.5 Social protection scores and work mobilisation rates in various OECD countries, late 1990s

Sources: See Tables 11.1 and 11.2.

among our four cases – Canada, Sweden and Denmark, in the order mentioned. Thus, the label work society is more relevant for the United States than for the other three countries and it is more relevant for North America than for Scandinavia.

The social division of labour

Chapter 6 tells us that the economically advanced world has become more post-industrial in recent decades and less agrarian and less industrial. The service sector has been in a process of steady expansion, while the industrial sector is generally declining and agricultural employment has shrunk dramatically. In some countries, like Japan and Portugal, we find rather small changes in manufacturing. As is also demonstrated in Chapter 6, Canada, the United States, Denmark and Sweden belong to those countries that have moved furthest along the post-industrial road. Some questions will now be asked about the relationship between the post-industrial development and the social division of labour. Three dimensions will be focused: (a) the occupational composition of the employed; (b) the development of self-employment; and (c) the role of the public sector in the production of services.

Occupational patterns

The introductory chapter mentioned that Daniel Bell (1976: 20) emphasised the role of knowledge and technology in post-industrial society. He predicted that – with the expansion of services – the need for theoretical knowledge would increase and significant changes would take place in the occupational structure. With the coming of post-industrial society a new class of professionals and technical intelligentsia could be expected to get a dominant position (Bell 1976: 358–9).

In his analysis of what he calls the 'informational' society, Manuel Castells (1996: 216ff.) summarises the predictions of general post-industrial theory with respect to occupational change in the following way. First of all, managerial, professional and technical positions will become more important. Second, there will be a decline in the number of workers in craft and operator occupations. Finally, an expansion is expected of the proportions of clerical and sales workers. Castells adds that there is also a 'left-wing' version of post-industrial theory assuming a growth of semi- and unskilled service occupations.

Examining developments in the so-called G-7 countries (Canada, France, Germany, Italy, Japan, the United Kingdom and the United States), Castells concludes that Japan and the United States represent two opposite poles. The United States fits well with the expectations – simply because post-industrial theory was modelled on its development – by replacing old occupations (craft industrial work) with new professions. Japan also shows an increase with regard to the new professions, but has kept a relatively large craft labour force. However, Castells observes a general trend in all seven countries towards an expansion of what we could call a 'professional-managerial' class (cf., e.g., Ehrenreich and Ehrenreich 1979). But he finds no support for the idea of an increased polarisation of the occupational structure; there is no simultaneous growth in both the top and the bottom of the occupational hierarchy.

There are many problems with the international statistics on occupational structures (for further discussion of these problems, see Chapter 7), but data are fairly comparable for at least a number of countries. We shall take a look at some of the available information. It refers to somewhat different years (1996–99) for different countries. Three figures (11.6a, 11.6b and 11.6c) present the relationships between the relative size of service employment and three broad occupational categories. Distinctions are made among 'professionals and managers', 'clerical, sales and service workers' (Castells uses a somewhat different classification due to the fact that his data are older), and 'craft workers, plant and machine operators, etc.'.

The three figures show two rather strong correlations. Obviously the relative size of the service sector is positively correlated with the proportion of managers and professionals and negatively correlated with the proportion of craft workers, machine operators, etc. These two results are in line with the assumptions made by post-industrial theory. In Figure 11.6a, the United States and Sweden are located high up in the right-hand corner – below the Netherlands but above Belgium. Canada and Denmark as well as Australia and New Zealand are not so far behind. Portugal is located in the opposite corner – with surprisingly low figures – and next to it come Greece, Spain, Austria and Ireland.

Jumping over Figure 11.6b for a while and instead turning first to Figure 11.6c, we find support for the assumption that the proportions of craft workers and plant and machine operators decrease with the coming of the post-industrial era. The

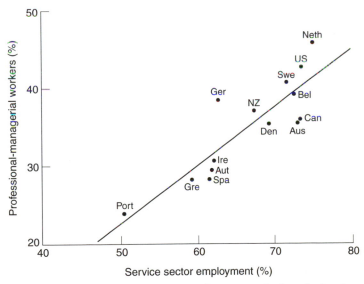

Figure 11.6a Proportions of service sector employment and of professional-managerial workers in various OECD countries, late 1990s

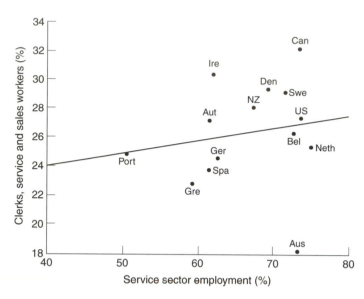

Figure 11.6b Proportions of service sector employment and of clerks, service and sales workers in various OECD countries, late 1990s

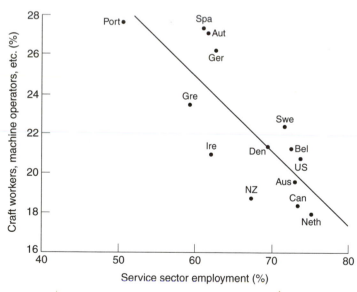

Figure 11.6c Proportions of service sector employment and of craft workers, machine operators, etc. in various OECD countries, late 1990s

Sources: OECD 2001b: 41; ILO database (LABORSTA).

Note
Aut = Austria; Aus = Australia.

relative size of these occupations is negatively related to the proportion of service employment. In Figure 11.6c the Netherlands appears closest to the lower right-hand corner, followed by Canada and – a few steps behind – by Australia, New Zealand and the United States. Sweden and Denmark are located more in the middle. The opposite pole is above all represented by Portugal, Spain, Austria and Germany.

Figure 11.6b presents a more complicated picture. There is some positive correlation between the relative size of the service sector and the proportion of clerical, service and sales workers, but it is weak indeed. Canada, the United States, Denmark and Sweden are relatively close to each other and to the upper right-hand corner of the figure. Portugal, Greece, Spain and Germany are the countries appearing closest to the opposite corner. However, it must be emphasised that we have to do with a very heterogeneous occupational category and that the observations are widely scattered in the diagram. We should therefore avoid drawing firm conclusions about the relationship between the two variables.

Self-employment

It is well known that self-employment is particularly common in the agrarian sector. The reason is that farming is very much a family-based business. With the decline of employment in agriculture we might expect the proportion of self-employment of total employment to decrease, and this also happened in most countries during the 1970s (OECD 2000a: 155). More recently, however, there has been a trend towards growing self-employment in non-agricultural sectors. In the 1990s, this growth has been larger than that of employment generally in the OECD area (OECD 2000a: 156–7).

Table 11.3 (page 256) displays some data on non-agricultural self-employment. Before turning to its contents, we need to comment upon a few definitional issues. To begin with, it should be pointed out that unpaid family workers are not included. They are certainly a separate category, although the boundary towards the self-employed is not always that clear.

A second issue, however, creates problems. It has to do with the fact that the classification of owner-managers of incorporated businesses differs from one country to the other. This category consists of 'workers who hold a job in an incorporated enterprise, in which they: (a) alone, or together with other members of their families or one or a few partners, hold controlling ownership of the enterprise; and (b) have the authority to act on its behalf as regards contracts with organisations and the hiring and dismissals of persons in the "paid employment" of the same organisation' (OECD 2000a: 191). The notes in Table 11.3 specify for each country how the self-employed have been defined. In Canada, owner-managers are included, in Denmark and Sweden most of them are included, and in the United States they are excluded.

In other words, the figures for the latter three countries – and above all the United States – would be higher, if the same definition as for Canada had been used. This also means that making cross-country comparisons is often impossible,

Table 11.3 Proportion of self-employed in non-agricultural employment in various
OECD countries, selected years 1983–98 (%)

	1983	1990	1997 or 1998	Difference 1983–98
Australia[a]	12.1	12.9	11.8	−0.3
Austria [b]	8.1	6.6	7.4	−0.7
Belgium[c]	12.3	12.9	13.9	+1.6
Canada [c]	11.4	12.3	16.0	+4.6
Denmark[d]	8.5	7.2	6.9	−1.6
Finland [d]	7.0	8.8	10.0	+3.0
France[d]	10.5	9.3	8.2	−2.3
Germany[d]	7.4 [e]	7.7	9.4	−
Greece[d]	27.9	27.4	27.0	−0.9
Ireland[d]	10.7	13.4	13.4	+2.7
Italy[b]	20.7	22.2	22.7	+2.0
Japan [a]	13.3	11.5	9.7	−3.6
Netherlands[d]	8.6	7.8	9.7	+1.1
New Zealand [b]	−	14.6	16.9	−
Norway [f]	6.8	6.1	5.4	−1.4
Portugal[b]	17.0	16.7	19.1	+2.1
Spain[c]	17.0	17.1	17.6	+0.6
Sweden[d]	4.8	7.3	9.0	+4.2
UK[d]	8.6	12.4	11.4	+2.8
US [a]	7.7	7.5	7.0	−0.7

Source: OECD 2000a: 158.

Note
a Excluding owner-managers in incorporated businesses.
b Classification of owner-managers in incorporated businesses unclear.
c Including owner-managers in incorporated businesses.
d Including most owner-managers in incorporated businesses.
e West Germany.
f Excluding most owner-managers in incorporated businesses.

and we have to be very careful with such undertakings. It is generally easier to compare figures for the one and same country across time. However, also in this respect
we may encounter certain difficulties. For example, when the labour force survey
questionnaire was revised in Sweden in 1987, it became easier for respondents to
be classified as self-employed (SCB 1996b: 3). Part of the Swedish increase
1983–98 is thus a statistical artefact, although not all of it.

   Ten of the countries for which the table allows us to calculate differences
between 1983 and 1998 had higher percentages at the latter point in time, while
eight had lower. The picture is thus divided, but growth is the dominant pattern.
In terms of change in percentage points, Canada shows the largest increase of all
countries. Sweden has also had a clear growth, but this is – as pointed out above –
to some extent due to a statistical redefinition. Both Denmark and the United
States had lower figures in 1998 than in 1983.

   Although it is difficult to make cross-country comparisons, we can be sure that
Greece, Italy, Portugal and Spain – that have the highest figures in Table 11.3 –

would be at the top also if the owner-manager category had been treated in the same way in all countries. There is simply no way that this definitional inconsistency could explain the whole gap down to the relatively low figures for many other countries – among them the United States, Denmark and Sweden. In other words, it is not the countries with the relatively largest service sector that have the largest proportions of self-employment of non-agricultural employment. We should keep in mind that Greece, Italy, Portugal and Spain all have a huge tourist industry, with hotels, restaurants, small shops, and other activities well suited for small-scale entrepreneurship.

It has been suggested that the expansion of the informational society – with its networking, flexibility, new technologies, etc. – will create new openings for entrepreneurship (Castells 1996: 220–1). This may be true, but we need to examine carefully in what service industries self-employment tends to expand. According to the OECD (2000a: 160), most of the growth in non-agricultural self-employment in the 1990s took place in 'financial mediation, real estate, renting and business . . . followed by community, social and personal services'. It is possible that this development will continue, but prognoses concerning such issues are often not very reliable.

Increasing non-agricultural self-employment is thus a feature that can be observed in many economically advanced countries, but we must not forget that in the main they are all wage-earner societies. Even in countries with extensive non-agricultural self-employment, the vast majority of the gainfully employed are wage earners. Whether this pattern will undergo more significant change remains to be seen.

The role of the public sector

Daniel Bell (1976: 336–7, 342–5) assumed that the possibility for social planning in various spheres would expand with the increasing significance of knowledge under post-industrialism. Thus, the door would be opened for the public sector to play a greater role. For a long time there was also a substantial growth of the government service sector in most advanced Western countries (see, e.g., Alestalo, Bislev and Furåker 1991; Rose 1985; Saunders and Klau 1985; and Chapter 6 in this book). Somewhat later, however, the tide turned. Part of the service production organised by the central state, regional or local authorities has been cut down or privatised (see, e.g., Kamerman and Kahn 1989; Martin 1993; Saunders and Harris 1994; Whitfield 1992). In these respects, considerable changes have taken place in many countries over the past few decades. Nevertheless, the public sector continues to play a highly significant societal role, especially in Scandinavia.

Figure 11.7 provides information on how the proportions of service and government employment were related to each other in various OECD countries in 1998. It gives us a picture of what the public sector means for the service sector. The definition of government employment is the rather narrow one used by the OECD, excluding employees in publicly owned enterprises.

There is some weak, positive correlation between the two variables, but several countries are far from the fit curve. Among the most post-industrial societies – i.e., those where service employment makes up around 70 per cent or more of total

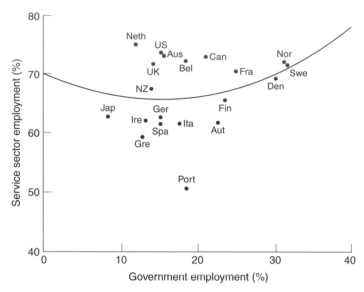

Figure 11.7 Government and service sector employment as a percentage of total employment in a number of OECD countries, about 1998

Sources: OECD database; OECD 2000b: 41.

Note
Aut = Austria; Aus = Australia.

employment – we may distinguish two 'ideal types', due to the role of the government sector. In one category of countries – mainly including Denmark, Sweden and Norway – a large proportion of the production of services is organised by the government. The opposite pole is above all represented by the Netherlands, the United States, the United Kingdom and Australia, where instead the private service sector is much larger. Canada is closer to the latter than to the former category but has an in-between position.

A main conclusion so far is that there are at least two roads to post-industrialism; the expansion of services can occur either through the public or through the private sector. We may then ask why the one or the other solution is selected. To throw further light on this issue, some of the results presented earlier in this book will be discussed. Let us go back to the analysis in Chapter 6, showing that the United States, Denmark and Sweden (Canada is not included in the analysis) differed from each other in 1998 concerning the relative sizes, and the government proportion of, educational, health and social services (see Table 6.5, page 137).

Two aspects will be emphasised. First, in Denmark and Sweden the majority of workers in all three sectors – education, health care and social care – are public employees. In the United States it is only in the educational system that public authorities are the major employer; in the health and social care sectors almost nine out of ten employees work for private organisations. Second, as regards the relative size of the three sectors there is in particular one remarkable difference among the three countries. Education has roughly the same proportion of total employment in the United States as in Denmark and Sweden, and the same could be said concerning health care had it not been for Denmark which here shows a lower proportion. This Danish divergence is, however, still of minor significance, whereas social care presents us with a fundamentally different pattern. Workers in the latter sector make up just above 2 per cent of total employment in the United States. Although this proportion may be somewhat underestimated (cf. Henrekson 1998: 143), it is very far from the Danish and Swedish figures that in both cases exceed 12 per cent, i.e., between five and six times more.

The question now is how we shall explain these patterns. Starting with education, we may be surprised that the public engagement is so dominant in all three cases, but there is hardly any machinery other than the political mechanism to ensure that all children and youth acquire a satisfactory depth of knowledge and skills. Countries with strong political ambitions that its citizens enjoy at least elementary education may find it convenient that central or local governments take the main responsibility. Not even in the United States has this task been left to the market. However, even if private organisations run educational activities, it might be possible to keep society's general goals as long as governments maintain an overriding control and provide the financial resources.

With respect to health care, the situation is somewhat different. If private alternatives are to be acceptable for most citizens and not just for those who can afford to pay for themselves, there are two possibilities. The first one is that just mentioned above concerning the educational sector, i.e., activities are controlled and paid for by public authorities, while private organisations produce the services. The other possibility is a private insurance system with some security net for people without the means to pay for themselves and this is the main solution in the United States (see, e.g., Ginsburg 1992: 127ff.). Although it is a costly system and large groups have no sickness insurance at all, it has long resisted every attempt to be reformed.

What, then, can be said about social care? A crucial problem is, again, that those who need these services may not be able to pay for them. Profit-oriented companies have no interest in furnishing services to people who cannot pay for themselves or are not paid for by others. It is also difficult to imagine that an insurance system would work. This makes pure market solutions less likely, and one alternative is that the government tries to fulfil people's needs. However, caring for children, the elderly and others is probably easily perceived of as a private – or rather a family – matter. Therefore, governments may in turn be less inclined to engage in these tasks than in education and health care. In the case where people have no family (or other close relatives) and there is no or little public sector engagement, the door is opened for charity. It is not surprising that charity organisations play a much greater role in the United States than in Scandinavia.

Moreover, it is also possible that certain services are not produced at all. People who do not have the resources to pay for the services themselves and who lack relatives to provide them may get no help at all. We may suspect that the low proportion of social care employment in the United States to some extent can be explained in this way. Some needs are not satisfied, simply because there is no mechanism to make this happen.

The post-industrial profiles of the United States on the one hand, and Denmark and Sweden on the other are markedly different as regards government employment. In quantitative terms Canada is closer to the United States, but is perhaps better characterised as having an in-between position. Focusing on the two opposite poles, there are especially two aspects to observe. The first one has to do with the way in which health care is organised. It may in the main be an insurance-based, private sector business as in the United States or an industry that is owned – or at least controlled and financed – by the government as in Scandinavia. In both cases, the health care sector can be of about the same relative size in terms of employment. The second aspect is that social care is to a much larger extent provided by the government in Denmark and Sweden than in the United States. More interestingly, however, in the American case there is not very much social care furnished by the private market sector either; unless the government gets involved it seems rather unlikely that these services will be delivered at all outside the informal sector, the family or charity organisations.

Post-industrial work and employment profiles

Canada, the United States, Denmark and Sweden can all be called work societies, if that concept is taken to refer to a society where large segments of the working-age population are involved in paid work. Compared with other countries they display similarities rather than differences in this respect. However, when we focus on the total quantities of work carried out, the four cases appear as rather different. The degree of work mobilisation is higher in the United States than in any of the other three countries, and it is higher in Canada than in Sweden and Denmark. This might suggest that it is inversely related to the social protection provided by governments and unions (high in Scandinavia and low in North America), but we have also found that levels of work mobilisation are even lower in a number of countries with middle level protection.

Looking at the post-industrial profiles in terms of occupational structures and government employment, we discover both similarities and differences. The occupational structures are relatively similar in Canada, the United States, Denmark and Sweden. They largely fit the typical post-industrial pattern with a low proportion of craft workers and machine operators and a high proportion of professional-managerial employees. Moreover, in many countries – although not everywhere – we have seen that non-agricultural self-employment tends to increase. Among the four countries under scrutiny here, we cannot unambiguously verify the assumption that post-industrialism leads to an expansion of self-employment, but this seems to hold for Canada and perhaps also for Sweden. It must be recalled that – due to definitional differences – it is difficult to make cross-national comparisons.

The service sector has expanded all over the economically advanced world, but its private–public mix differs substantially across countries. In terms of composition of industries, Canada, the United States, Denmark and Sweden are all post-industrial, roughly to about the same degree. The proportion of service sector employment is slightly higher in North America, but a more significant difference is that the two Scandinavian countries have much higher proportions of government employment. Public sector growth is thus something else than the development of post-industrial society. The post-industrial expansion in Canada and the United States has above all been a matter of an enlargement of the private sector, while in Denmark and Sweden it has been strongly associated with the public sector. It seems, however, that private services tend to become increasingly more important also in the two Scandinavian countries.

Obviously, the two North American labour markets have a different profile from the two Scandinavian ones. This becomes clearly visible in two simple observations. Whereas large shares of the employed in Denmark and Sweden are engaged in caring for children, the elderly, etc., Canada and the United States – more or less counterbalancing this – have relatively large proportions working in trade, hotels and restaurants. In other words, North America – and especially the United States – has a more 'commercial' post-industrial profile than Scandinavia's which in turn can be characterised as more 'social'. No doubt, this is one of the most significant single differences that appear in our comparisons. We may ask what will happen to it in the long run, under the pressure of the social, economic and technological forces that more or less all labour markets are subjected to. There is no self-evident answer to that question; the forces mentioned are no doubt strong, but so are national institutions and traditions.

Notes

2 Labour movement and industrial relations

1 The assaults from employers and government on the unions and their right to represent workers intensified as mentioned earlier from the late 1970s. The next two decades were a long period of organised opposition against union activities. 'Beginning in the 1970s in the US, unions saw the judicial arm of government chip away at these rights. The early 1980s saw the President of the United States fire striking air-traffic controllers. The 1990s saw the massive use of replacement workers (scabs) to break strikes at companies with long bargaining relationship and cooperation programs' (Moody 1997/2001: 122).

2 The fluctuation in rates of unionisation during the 1990s, however, is mainly artificial and depends more on a decrease in employment than an increase in union members. Rate of unionisation is normally defined as union members in proportion to the employed individuals and when the employment decreases as it did in the early 1990s, then the rate of unionisation will increase with a constant number of union members. This was precisely what happened in both Denmark and Sweden in the early 1990s.

4 The welfare state and labour market policies

1 The concept of welfare state is used in many different ways in the literature. Without entering into a discussion over definitions, we agree with Chikako Usui (1996: 272 n.1) in saying that the welfare state concept generally refers to 'a state in which the government promotes social welfare through the collection of resources and the distribution of goods and services to its citizens'.

2 Esping-Andersen has recognised these criticisms in his more recent work; see Esping-Andersen 1999.

5 Labour force and employment: age and gender differences

1 In Chapter 1 of this book, we discuss in more detail differences in the development of the labour market in Europe and the United States. In this debate the 'American employment miracle' has often been contrasted with 'Eurosclerosis' meaning few new jobs and high and sustained unemployment in the European labour markets (Cornitz 1988; Freeman 1999; Auer 1996). The institutional system and its importance for employment relations is discussed in more detail in Chapters 2 and 3 of this volume.

2 The rate of employment tells us more about the actual involvement of people in the labour market than the labour force participation rate, which includes both the employed and unemployed persons. The number of unemployed persons registered in the labour force surveys depends to some extent on the legal system regulating unemployment benefit – who are eligible for benefits and how long – and the type of labour market policy. In both cases there are huge variations between the countries and

consequently in how large a proportion of non-employed people are counted as unemployed. Comparing the employment/population ratio thus gives us a more exact measure of the actual labour market involvement.

3 For both Iceland and Switzerland the figures for labour force participation are dubious. In Iceland it is typical for a large group of employees to have two jobs and they are probably counted twice. In Switzerland the labour immigrants are included in the number of employed persons but not as part of the working population.

4 In both Denmark and Sweden public support in child rearing is comprehensive but organised completely differently. In Denmark the coverage of childcare is high for both small children aged 0–3 and children aged 3–6, which enables mothers with small children to remain in employment even on a full-time basis. Sweden has organised child rearing through extensive parental leave schemes making it possible for mothers (and fathers) to be out of employment for at least one, often two, years on paid leave (see Gornick, Meyers and Ross (1997).

5 According to national definitions, Canada defines part-time employment as less than 30 hours, in Sweden part-time is defined as less than 35 hours while the Danish figures rely on peoples' self-declarations in the annual labour force surveys. Based on these definitions significant differences exist between the four countries in levels of part-time employment for women while the pattern for male part-time employment is more similar (OECD 1995: 268). Denmark and Sweden have much higher proportions of women in part-time employment based on national definitions. In the 1970s and 1980s, more than 40 per cent of the Scandinavian women were employed in part-time jobs while it was the case for about one-quarter or less of the Canadian and the American women. The main reason for these marked variations in the proportion of women working part-time is that a substantial number of Scandinavian women have part-time jobs with more than 30 hours per week while most American women are employed in short part-time jobs working 20–25 hours per week.

6 Towards a post-industrial service society

1 When using this division of the labour force, it is important to note that the definitions of what activities are to be placed in different sectors can cause some confusion. Many activities that were formerly conducted in the agricultural sector have become either industrialised (e.g., dairies and slaughterhouses) or services (e.g., the transportation chain from farmer to grocery store). In addition, more activities are being outsourced from the industrial firms (e.g., accounting, marketing, cleaning). Both employment and economic activity are largely still connected to the agricultural and industrial sectors.

2 The three industries listed in Table 6.3 are included in the service subsectors that were analysed in Table 6.2. Business services are included in producer services; health services are part of social services; hotel, restaurants, etc. are part of personal services. These three industries are separated for a special analysis because they are considered fast growing industries.

3 The high proportion of public employees in Denmark in education and welfare services is partly an overestimation. In Denmark, a significant proportion of service production is organised in private non-profit co-operatives that are approved by the public authorities. These co-operatives are private, but receive substantial public subsidies and are strictly controlled by the public authorities. In this respect, they may be considered as public institutions despite being privately organised. The non-profit co-operative organisations employed 15.8 per cent of the labour force in health, education and welfare in 1998. These organisations are particularly common in education and welfare services where they represent 31.6 per cent and 22.1 per cent, respectively, of the labour force.

4 From the statistical sources on which Tables 6.7 and 6.8 are based, the growth pattern in employment for men and women can be calculated. These figures are not shown here

but are important for the discussion about the relationship between growth in industrial employment and growth in women and men' s employment.

5 Japan, in many respects, is a special case characterised by an extremely small public sector and low sex segregation, but it has a medium size in the level of service employment and in the level of female employment.

7 Occupational changes and education

1 Castells (1996: 244) combines this typology with two other typologies. One that distinguishes between the *networkers*, the *networked* and the *switched-off* workers, and another that differentiates between the *deciders*, the *participants* and the *executants*. According to Castells all three typologies are necessary to fully understand the new division of labour. However, since our aim here is to study the occupational structure we will only use the worker typology.

2 If we are interested in whether the post-industrial occupational structure primarily consists of good or bad jobs (or good and bad jobs together with few average jobs) we cannot be content with just occupational titles. Meisenheimer (who has made a comprehensive study of job quality in the United States) uses pay, employee benefits, job security, occupational structure and occupational safety as main indicators. He concludes that '. . . many industries within services equal or exceed manufacturing and other industries on measures of job quality, and some services industries could be viewed as less desirable by these measures. Thus, employment shifts away from manufacturing and toward services do not necessarily signal a deterioration in overall job quality in the United States' (Meisenheimer 1998: 45).

3 There exists no agreed upon definition of the concept 'profession' and, to be sure, no consensus regarding what occupations are to be defined as semi-professional either. However, in most cases occupational groups that have a considerable control over the acquisition, development and application of a certain type of abstract formal knowledge obtained at higher educational institutions are labelled professions (e.g., doctors and lawyers), while occupational groups that score somewhat less on these characteristics are called semi-professions (e.g., nurses and primary school teachers). In some occupational classifications (e.g., ISCO-88, which will be used in the empirical analyses) the distinction is between professions and associate professions. For a comprehensive outline of research on the professions, see Macdonald (1995).

4 LABORSTA is the International Labour Organisation's principal database. It consists of annual time-series that present data on a number of subjects (e.g., employment, unemployment and wages).

5 The observation of stability is confirmed for the United States by Gullason (2000) who – in spite of dramatic structural changes in the US economy during the 1990s – finds remarkably small change in the occupational structure.

6 ISCO-88 is the latest version of the International Standard Classification of Occupations, and it has quite recently replaced the classification of 1968 (ISCO-68). The comparability between the two classifications is rather limited since they are based on somewhat different principles. ISCO-88(COM) is the European Union variant of ISCO-88. It is very similar to ISCO-88 and should not be regarded as a different classification, but rather as an adaptation to the reality of the European labour markets. It has a hierarchical structure that consists of 10 major groups (1-digit), 27 sub-major groups (2-digit), 111 minor groups (3-digit) and 372 unit groups (4-digit). In the 1990s, both Denmark and Sweden have replaced their old classifications with standards that are national adaptations of ISCO-88(COM), for Denmark DISCO-88 and for Sweden SSYK96. The figures for Canada and the United States have been obtained by transforming detailed occupational data from these countries' Standard Occupational Classifications into ISCO-88(COM) sub-major groups.

7 The reduction in the number of sub-major occupational groups from 27 to 20 has

several causes. First, all military occupations were excluded since it was not possible to acquire comparable data for all countries. Second, all managerial occupations have been collapsed into one group since the managerial categories in the Canadian and the US occupational classifications did not allow for a transformation to the managerial sub-major groups of ISCO-88(COM). Third, all teaching occupations have been assigned to one category because of similar mapping problems as with the managerial occupations. Fourth, because of their relatively small size all agricultural and fishery occupations have been put in one and the same category. Fifth, for the same reason all handicraft occupations were put in the same category, and the same goes for all operators and assemblers.

8 Unfortunately, the highly aggregated level of these data make it impossible to determine whether the rising incidence of women is in the higher or lower echelons among the managerial/administrative occupations.

9 For a comprehensive overview of differences between countries' educational systems, see OECD 1996b.

8 Patterns of unemployment

1 The standardised unemployment rates to be used here derive from the OECD that has tried to bring data as close as possible to the ILO guidelines for international comparison of labour force statistics. Although standardisation of national unemployment figures is aimed at improving comparability between countries, there are still differences for which adjustments have not been made (for a detailed overview of these issues, see Sorrentino 2000).

9 Flexibility and employment insecurity

1 See Harrison's study of the Northern Italian case where he found that the major part of the small firms established in the 1970s were merged with larger corporations and have established inter-firm networks during the late 1980s and early 1990s (1994).

2 See Appendix to Chapter 9 for more information about the different data sources.

3 This is only applicable when the dismissals are due to redundancies. In addition, the employer and the trade union can agree on other principles.

4 Sweden was the first OECD country to introduce a statutory six-month parental leave in 1974. It has since been expanded to 15 months (Anxo 1995; OECD 1995).

5 The employment security of long-tenured workers in Sweden should not be exaggerated. Early retirement schemes are common and during the latest recession, such options were used frequently. In addition, it is common that employers and unions agree to exclude people with a special set of skills from the priority order set by the law.

6 The oldest women may be an exception. In Sweden, tenure has fallen among women over 60. In the United States, it has remained stable among women aged 55–64 and decreased among those 65 and over. In the data for the other countries, it is not possible to separate the oldest age groups.

7 Generally, temporary employment means that the job ends on a specified date or when a specific project is completed, but the US definition is somewhat different. In the Current Population Survey, there are three estimates of 'contingent work'. The one used here comprises workers who have tenure of one year or less and who expect their job to last for an additional year or less. In the widest definition, the share of contingent workers, is 4.4 per cent, but this estimate seems less comparable to that of the other countries. For example, self-employed and independent contractors are included (CPS).

8 Not counting Spain, where temporary employment is extremely high; about 33 per cent are employed as temporary workers.

9 In Denmark, the work time reductions have been established through collective bargaining, rather than legislation.

10   US data used here refer to hours at work (during the survey reference week) and are not strictly comparable with the data for the other countries, which report usual working hours.

11   According to the Swedish Working-Time Act, normal full-time work is 40 hours a week (or as an average over four weeks). Other limitations may be set in collective agreements. Traditionally, this possibility has mainly been used to cut work hours for certain categories such as shift workers, but in the last few years general cuts have been made for large groups such as metal workers (Johnsson and Malmberg 1998).

10 Wage formation, institutions and unemployment

1   Since our focus is on the long-term trends rather than on year-to-year fluctuations, all time series shown in this section have been smoothed by using 3-year moving averages. All data are from the OECD database.

2   The real wage index is defined by earnings deflated by the consumer price index and high-, medium- and low-paid workers are defined by the average earnings for workers in deciles 9, 5 and 1, respectively.

3   Low pay is defined as less than two-thirds of median full-time earnings and earnings inequality is calculated as D5:D1 – D5 as the median earnings and D1 as the top of the lowest decile.

4   The other countries covered by the study were Germany, France, Italy, Sweden, the United Kingdom and the United States.

References

Aaberge, R., A. Björklund, M. Jäntti, P. J. Pedersen, N. Smith and T. Wennemo (2000) 'Unemployment shocks and income distribution: How did the Nordic countries fare during their crises?', *Scandinavian Journal of Economics* 102: 77–99.

Abbott, A. (1988) *The System of Professions. An Essay on the Division of Expert Labor*, Chicago: The University of Chicago Press.

Abrahamsson, P. (1999) 'Activation and social policies: Comparing France and Scandinavia', in *Comparing Social Welfare Systems in Nordic Europe and France*. Copenhagen Conference 4, Paris: MiRe Drees.

Abrahamson, P., T. P. Boje and B. Greve (2002) *Welfare and Solidarity in Western Europe.* Forthcoming.

Adams, G. W. (1985) *Labour Law. A Comprehensive Text*, Aurora, Ontario: Canada Law Books Inc.

Adell, B. (1993) 'Workplace disciplinary rules and procedures in Canada', *International Labour Review* 132, 5–6: 583–604.

Agnarsson, S. and D. Anxo (1996) *Arbetstid och arbetsmarknadsekonomi*. Rapport till 1995 års arbetstidskommitté. Bilaga 8 i SOU 1996:145 *Arbetstid – längd, förläggning och inflytande*.

Alestalo, M., S. Bislev and B. Furåker (1991) 'Welfare state employment in Scandinavia', in J. E. Kolberg (ed.) *The Welfare State as Employer*, New York: M.E. Sharpe.

Åmark, K. (1986) *Facklig makt och fackligt medlemsskap*, Lund: Arkiv.

Amin, A. and D. Thomas (1996) 'The negotiated economy: State and civic institutions in Denmark', *Economy and Society* 25, 2: 255–81

Anxo, D. (1995) 'Working-time policy in Sweden', in R. Hoffmann and J. Lapeyre (eds) *A Time for Working, A Time for Living*, Documentation on the December 1994 Joint Conference of the European Trade Union Confederation (ETUC) and the European Trade Union Institute (ETUI), Brussels: ETUI.

Appelbaum E. and R. Schettkat (1994) *The Employment Problem in Industrialized Countries*, Washington, DC: Economic Policy Institute

Arthurs, H. W., D. D. Carter and H. J. Glasbeek (1988) *Labour Law and Industrial Relations in Canada*, 3rd edition, Scarborough, Ontario: Kluwer, Butterworths.

Atkinson, J. (1985) *Flexibility, Uncertainty and Manpower Management*, IMS Report No. 89, Institute of Manpower Studies, University of Sussex, Brighton.

Atkinson, J. (1987) 'Flexibility or fragmentation? The United Kingdom labour market in the eighties', *Labour and Society* 12, No. 1: 87–105.

Atkinson, J. and N. Meager (1986) *Changing Work Patterns: How Companies Achieve Flexibility to Meet New Needs*, Institute of Manpower Studies Report No. 121, Brighton: IMS.

Atkinson, M. M. and W. D. Coleman (1989) *The State, Business and Industrial Change in Canada*, Toronto: University of Toronto Press.

Auer, P. (1995) 'The American employment miracle', *Employment Observatory Policies* 49: 33–43.

Auer, P. (1996) 'Participation and employment rates in Europe: Convergence or Divergence?', *inforMISEP* 56: 25–35.

Auer, P. (ed.) (2001) *Changing Labour Markets in Europe. The Role of Institutions and Policies*, Geneva: ILO.

Bacchi, C. L. (1996) *The Politics of Affirmative Action. 'Women', Equality and Category Politics*, London: Sage.

Badham, R. (1986) *Theories of Industrial Society*, New York: St. Martin's Press.

Baglioni G. and C. Crouch (eds) (1990) *European Industrial Relations: The Challange of Flexibility*, Newbury Park: Sage.

Bamber, G. J. (1998) 'Employment relations and labour market indicators in ten industrialized market economies', *International Journal of Human Resource Management* 9, 2: 401–35.

Bamber, G. J. and R. D. Lansbury (1998) *International and Comparative Employment Relations. A Study of Developed Market Economies*, revised edition, Newsbury Park: Sage .

Beechey, V. and T. Perkins (1987) *A Matter of Hours*, Cambridge: Polity Press.

Bélanger, J., P. K. Edwards and L. Haiven (eds) (1994) *Workplace Industrial Relations and the Global Challenge*, Ithaca, NY: Cornell University Press.

Bell, D. (ed.) (1968) *Toward the Year 2000: Work in Progress*, Boston, MA: Daedalus.

Bell, D. (1976) *The Coming of Post-Industrial Society. A Venture in Social Forecasting*, New York: Basic Books.

Bellace, J. R. (1992) 'The United States', in Blanpain R. (ed.) *Bulletin of Comparative Labour Relations* 23: 241–53.

Bellemare, D. and S. L. Poulin (1994) 'Canada: The case of Quebec', in G. Bosch, P. Dawkins and F. Michon (1995) *Times Are Changing – Working Time in 14 Industrialised Countries*, Geneva: International Institute for Labour Studies.

Belous, R. S. (1989) 'How human resource systems adjust to the shift towards contingent workers', *Monthly Labour Review* March: 7–12.

Benoit, C. (2000) 'Gender, work and social rights. Canada, the United States and Sweden as case examples', in T. P. Boje and A. Leira (eds) *Gender, Welfare State and the Market*, London and Oxford: Routledge.

van den Berg, A., B. Furåker and L. Johansson (1997) *Labour Market Regimes and Patterns of Flexibility. A Sweden–Canada Comparison*, Lund: Arkiv Förlag.

Bernstein, I. (1960) 'Union growth and structural cycles', in W. Galenson and S. M. Lipset (eds) *Labor and Trade Unionism. An Interdisciplinary Reader*, New York: John Wiley and Sons Inc.

Bertola, G., T. Boeri and S. Caxes (2000) 'Employment protection in industrialized countries: The case for new indicators', *International Labour Review* 139, 1: 57–72. .

Bettio, F. and S. Rosenberg (1999) 'Labour markets and flexibility in the 1990s: The Europe–USA opposition revisited', *International Review of Applied Economics* 13, 3: 269–79.

Blank, R. (ed.) (1994) *Social Protection versus Economic Flexibility. Is there a Trade–off?*, Chicago and London: The University of Chicago Press.

Blank, R. and R. Freeman (1994) 'Evaluating the connection between social protection and economic flexibility', in R. Blank (ed.) *Social Protection versus Economic Flexibility*, Chicago and London: University of Chicago Press.

Blank, R. and M. Hanratty (1993). 'Responding to need: a comparison of social safety nets in the United States and Canada', in D. Card and R. B. Freeman (eds) *Small Differences That Matter: Labor Market and Income Maintenance in Canada and the United States*, Chicago: University of Chicago Press for NBER.

Blau, F. D. and L. M. Kahn (1996) 'Wage structure and gender earnings differentials: an international comparison', *Economica* 63, 250 (S): S29–S62.

Block, F. (1990) *Post–Industrial Possibilities: A Critique of Economic Discourse*, Berkeley: University of California Press.

Bluestone, B. and B. Harrison (1988) *The Great U-Turn. Corporate Restructuring and the Polarizing of America*, New York: Basic Books. .

Boje, T. P. (1987) *Mobilitets- og beskæftigelsesmønstre på det danske arbejdsmarked 1980–81* (Patterns of Mobility and Employment in the Danish Labour Market 1980–81), Copenhagen: Copenhagen Business School.

Boje, T. P. (1996) 'Gender work time and flexible employment', *Time & Society* 5, 3: 341–61.

Boje, T. P (2002) *Women Between Work and Family*, Roskilde University, Working Paper in progress.

Boje, T. P. and R. Åberg (1999) 'Den nya danska arbetsmarknadspolitiken – rättigheter såväl som skyldigheter', *Arbetsmarknad & Arbetsliv* 5: 5–26.

Boje, T. P. and P. Kongshøj Madsen (1994) 'Wage formation and income policy in Denmark in the 1980s', in R. Dore, R. Boyer and Z. Mars (eds) *The Return to Income Policy*, London: Pinter.

Boje, T. P. and A.-L. Almqvist (2000) 'Citizenship, family policy and women's pattern of employment', in T. P. Boje and A. Leira (eds) *Gender, Welfare State and the Market*, London and New York: Routledge.

Borch, S. (1996) 'Denmark', in R. Jeffers. and T. Cox (eds) *International Handbook of Contracts and Employment*, Boston, MA: Kluwer.

Bosch, G., P. Dawkins and F. Michon (1994) 'Overview', in G. Bosch, P. Dawkins and F. Michon (eds) *Times Are Changing – Working Time in 14 Industrialised Countries*, Geneva: International Institute for Labour Studies.

Boyer, R. (1987) 'Labour flexibilities: Many forms, uncertain effects', *Labour and Society* 12, 1, January, pp. 107–29.

Boyer, R. (ed.) (1988) *The Search for Labour Market Flexibility: The European Economies in Transition*, Oxford: Clarendon Press.

Boyer, R. (1993) 'Labour Institutions and Economic Growth: A Survey and a "Regulationist" Approach', *Labour* 7, 1: 109–29.

Bradshaw, J., S. Kennedy, M. Kilkey, S. Hutton, A. Corden, T. Eardley, H. Holmes and J. Neale (1996) *Policy and the Employment of Lone Parents in 20 Countries*, York: University of York, European Observatory on National Family Policies.

Brint, S. (1994) *In an Age of Experts. The Changing Role of Professionals in Politics and Public Life*, Princeton: Princeton University Press.

Bronfenbrenner, K. (1994) 'Employer behavior in certification elections and first-contract campaigns: Implications for Labor Law Reform', in S. Friedman, R. W. Hurd, R. A. Oswald and R. L. Seeber (eds) *Restoring the Promise of American Labor Law*, Ithaca, NY: ILR Press, 75–89.

Browing, H. and J. Singelmann (1978) 'The transformation of the U.S. labor force', *Politics and Society* 8, 3–4: 481–509.

Brunhes, B. (1989) *Labour Market Flexibility in Europe: A Comparative Analysis of Four Countries*. Working Paper for the OECD Working Party on Industrial Relations. Paris: OECD.

Bruun, N., B. Flodgren, M. Halvorsen, H. Hydén and R. Nielsen (1992) *The Nordic Labour Relations Model: Labour Law and the Trade Unions in the Nordic Countries Today and Tomorrow*, Dartmouth: Aldershot.

Buechtemann, C. F. (1989) 'More jobs through less employment protection? Evidence from West Germany', *Labour: Review of Labour Economics and Industrial Relations* 3, 3: 23–56.

Buechtemann, C. F. (ed.) (1993) *Employment Security and Labor Market Behavior: Interdisciplinary Approaches and International Evidence*, Ithaca, NY: ILR Press.

Burchall, B. J. and D. Diana (1999) *Job Insecurity and Work Intensification: Flexibility and the Changing Boundaries of Work*, York: York Publishing Services – Joseph Rowntree Foundation.

Bureau of Labor Statistics (BLS) (1998) *Earnings and Employment*, March.

Bureau of Labor Statistics (BLS) (1999a) *Report on the American Workforce*, Washington, DC: Department of Labor.

Bureau of Labor Statistics (BLS) (1999b) *Monthly Labor Review*, February, Washington, DC: Department of Labor.

Bureau of Labor Statistics (BLS) (1999c) *Monthly Labor Review*, March, Washington, DC: Department of Labor.

Bureau of Labor Statistics (BLS) (2000a) *Statistical Yearbook*, Washington, DC: Department of Labor.

Bureau of Labor Statistics (BLS) (2000b) *Earnings and Employment*, Washington, DC: Department of Labor.

Bureau of Labor Statistics (BLS) (2002) *Current Population Survey 1999* <http://stats.bls.gov/cps/home.htm>, (2002–06–04).

Calmfors, L. (1994) 'Active labour market policy and unemployment – a framework for the analysis of crucial design features', *OECD Economic Studies* 22: 7–47.

Calmfors, L. and J. Driffill (1988) 'Bargaining structure, corporatism and macro-economic performance', *Economic Policy* 6: 13–61.

Calmfors, L. and P. Skedinger (1995) 'Does active labour-market policy increase employment? Theoretical considerations and some empirical evidence from Sweden', *Oxford Review of Economic Policy* 11, 1: 91–109.

Campbell, R. M. (1991) *The Full Employment Objective in Canada 1945–85*, Economic Council of Canada.

Cantillon, B. (1997) 'The challenge of poverty and exclusion', in *Family, Market and Community: Equity and Efficiency in Social Policy*. OECD Socal Policy Studies, 21, Paris: OECD.

Carnoy, M., M. Castells, S. S. Cohen and F. H. Cordoso (1993) *The New Global Economy in the Information Age*, Philadelphia, PA: Pensylvania State University Press.

Carnoy, M. (1994) *Undoing Inequality: The Political Economy of Race in America*, New York and London: Cambridge University Press.

Carnoy, M and M. Castells (1997) 'Sustainable Flexibility. A Prospective Study on Work, Family and Society in the Information Age'. *OECD Working Papers* V, 29, Paris: OECD.

Carnoy, M., M. Castells and C. Brenner (1997) 'Labour markets and employment practices in the age of flexibility: A case study of Silicon Valley', *International Labour Review* 136: 27–48.

Carr Jr, W. Z., D. A. Cathcart and S. A. Kruse (1991) 'United States of America', in S. Bradley and B. Youngman (eds) *International Handbook on Contracts of Employment*, Deventer and Boston, MA: Kluwer.

Casey, B. and G. Bruche (1985) 'Active labor market policy: an international overview', *Industrial Relations* 24, 1: 37–61.

Castells, M. (1996) *The Information Age: Economy, Society and Culture. Volume I: The Rise of the Network Society.* London and Oxford: Blackwell Publishers.

Castells, M. and Y. Aoyama (1994) 'Paths towards the informational society: Employment structure in G-7 countries 1920–90', *International Labour Review* 135, 3–4: 5–33.

Castles, F. and J. Mitchell (1990) *Three Worlds of Welfare Capitalism or Four?*, Australian National University, Discussion Paper 21.

Charles, M. (1992) 'Cross-national variation in occupational sex segregation', *American Sociological Review* 57, August: 483–502.

Christie, I., G. England and B. W. Cotter, (1993) *Employment Law in Canada*, Toronto: Butterworths.

Christopherson, S. (1991) 'Trading time for consumption. The failure of working-hours reduction in the United States', in H. Karl, W. Roche and C. Sirianni (eds) *Working Time in Transition. The Political Economy of Working Hours on Industrial Nations*, Philadelphia; Temple University Press.

Christopherson, S. and M. Stroper (1989) 'The effects of flexible specialization on industrial politics and the labor market: The motion picture industry', *Industrial and Labor Relations Review* 42, 3: 331–47.

Clawson, D. and M. A. Clawson (1999) 'What has happened to the US Labor Movement?, *Annual Review of Sociology* 25: 95–119.

Clinton, A. (1997) 'Flexible labor: Restructuring the American work force', *Monthly Labor Review* 121, 8: 3–23.

Coenen, H. and P. Leisink (eds) (1993) *Work and Citizenship in the New Europe*, Brookfield: Edward Elgar.

Cohen, S. and J. Zysman (1987) *Manufacturing Matters: The Myth of the Postindustrial Economy*, New York: Basic Books.

Collins, R. (1979) *The Credential Society. An historical Sociology of Education and Stratification*, Orlando, FL: Academic Press, Inc.

Cornitz, M. (1988) 'The dark side of the "Employment Miracle" in the US', *Intereconomics* Jan.–Feb: 39–48.

Craven Hoglund, C. (1996) 'Canada', in R. Jeffers and T. Cox (eds) *International Handbook of Contracts and Employment*, Boston, MA: Kluwer.

Crouch, C. (1993) *Industrial Relations and European State Traditions*, Oxford: Clarendon.

Crouch, C. (1999) *Social Change in Western Europe*, Oxford: Oxford University Press.

Crouch, C. and W. Streeck (eds) (1997) *Political Economy of Modern Capitalism*, London: Sage Publications.

Cusack, T. R., T. Noterman and M. Rein (1989) 'Political-economic aspects of public employment', *European Journal of Political Research* 17: 471–500.

Davis, M. (1987) *Prisoners of the American Dream: Politics and Economy in the History of the US Working Class*, London: Verso.

Derber, M. (1984) 'Employers associations in the United States', in J. P. Windmuller and A. Gladstone (eds) *Employers Associations and Industrial Relations. A Comparative Study*, Oxford: Clarendon Press.

Dercksen, W. (1992) 'Job protection and flexibility in Western Europe', in A. Gladstone, H. Wheeler, J. Rojot, F. Eyraud and R. Ben-Israel (eds) *Labor Relations in a Changing Environment*, New York: Walter de Gruyter.

Dex, S. and A. McCulloch (1997) *Flexible Employment. The Future of Britain's Jobs*. Basingstoke and London: Macmillan.

Dex, S. and L. Shaw (1986) *British and American Women at Work: Do Equal Opportunity Policies Matter?* London: Macmillan.

Doeringer, P. and M. Piore (1971) *Internal Labor Markets and Manpower Analysis*, Lexington, MA: Lexington Books.

Drache, D. and M. S. Gertler (eds) (1991) *The New Era of Global Competition. State Policy and Market Power*, Montreal: McGill-Queen's University Press.

Due, J., J. S. Madsen and C. S. Jensen (1997) 'Major developments in danish industrial relations since 1980', in M. Mesch (ed.) *Social Partnership and Labour Relations in Western*

Europe, Aldershot: Edward Elgar.

Ebbinghaus, B. and J. Visser (1997) 'Der Wandel der Arbeitsbeziehungen in westeuropäischen Vergleich', in S. Hradil and S. Immerfall (eds) *Die westeuropäischen Gesellschaften in Vergleich*, Oplanden: Leske and Budrich.

Ebbinghaus, B. and J. Visser (2000) *The Societies of Europe: Trade Unions in Western Europe since 1945*. Series of historical data Handbooks. London: MacMillan.

Edin, P. and A. Holmlund (1993) *Effekter av anställningsskydd*. Rapport till 1992 års arbetsrättskommitté. In SOU 1993: 32, Stockholm.

Edlund, S. and B. Nyström (1988) *Developments in Swedish Labour Law*, Stockholm: The Swedish Institute.

Ehrenreich, B. and J. Ehrenreich (1979) 'The professional-managerial class', in P. Walker (ed.) *Between Labour and Capital*, Brighton: Harvester Press.

Elfring, T. (1988). *Service Sector Employment in Advanced Economies*, Aldershot: Gower Publishing.

Ellman, M. (1980) 'Against convergence', *Cambridge Journal of Economics* 4: 199–210.

Elmeskov, J. (1993) *High and Persistent Unemployment: Asssessment of the Problem and Its Causes*, OECD Economic Department, Working Paper, 130, Paris: OECD.

Elvander, N. (1980) *Skandinavisk arbetarrörelse*, Stockholm: Publica.

Emerson, M. (1988) 'Regulation or deregulation of the labour market. Policy regimes for the recruitment and dismissal of employees in the industrial countries', *European Economic Review* 32: 775–817.

Engelund, H. (1992) *Fleksibilitet på arbejdsmarkedet i Norden*, Kobenhavn: Socialforskningsinstituttet.

Esping-Andersen, G. (1985) *Politics Against Markets*, Princeton: Princeton University Press.

Esping-Andersen, G. (1990) *The Three Worlds of Welfare Capitalism*, Cambridge: Polity Press.

Esping-Andersen, G. (ed.) (1993) *Changing Classes: Stratification and Mobility in Post-industrial Societies*, New Delhi and London: Sage.

Esping-Andersen, G. (1999) *The Social Foundation of Post-Industrial Societies*, London and Oxford: Oxford University Press.

Esping-Andersen, G. and M. Regini (eds) (2000) *Why Deregulate Labour Markets?*, Oxford: Oxford University Press.

European Commission (1994) *Growth Competitiveness and Employment. White paper*, Luxembourg: Office for Official Publications of the European Communities.

European Commission (1998) *The Future of European Labour Supply*, Luxembourg: Office for Official Publications of the European Communities.

European Commission (1999) *Employment Performance in the Member States. Employment Rates Report 1998*, Luxembourg: Office for Official Publications of the European Communities.

Eurostat (1985) *Labour Force Survey, Results 1985*, Luxembourg: Eurostat.

Eurostat (1990) *Labour Force Survey, Results 1990*, Luxembourg: Eurostat.

Eurostat (1996) *Labour Force Survey, Results 1996*, Luxembourg: Eurostat.

Fagan, C. and J. Rubery (1999) *Gender and Labour Markets in the EU*, Manchester: UMIST, Working Paper.

Feldman, A. and W. Moore (1962) 'Industrialization and industrialism: convergence and differentiation', in *Transactions* from the Fifth World Congress of Sociology, Washington DC.

Ferner, A. and R. Hyman (eds) (1998) *Changing Industrial Relations in Europe*, Oxford: Blackwell Publishers.

Fine, B. (1995) 'Flexible production and flexible theory: The case of South Africa', *Geoforum* 26, 2: 107–19.

Finkin, M. W. (1994) 'Introduction', in M. W. Finkin (ed.) *The Legal Future of Employee Representation*, Ithaca, NY: ILR Press.

Flodgren, B. (1992) 'Co-determination at the workplace', in N. Bruun., B. Flodgren and M. Halvorsen (eds) *The Nordic Labour Relations Model: Labour Law and the Trade Unions in the Nordic Countries Today and Tomorrow*, Dartmouth: Aldershot.

Forbath, W. E. (1991) *Law and the Shaping of the American Labor Movement*, Cambridge, MA: Harvard University Press.

Forsman, A. (1984) *Det nya tjänstesamhället. De offentliga tjänsternas framväxt och framtid*, Gidlunds.

Freeman, R. B. (ed.) (1992) *Working under Different Rules*, New York: Russell Sage Foundation.

Freeman, R. B. (1999) 'Wages, employment and unemployment: An overview', in EC/DGV–OECD/DEELSA *Wages and Employment*, Luxenbourg: Office for Official Publications of the European Communities.

Freeman, R. B. and L. F. Katz (1994) 'Rising wage inequality: the United States vs. other advanced countries', in R. B. Freeman (ed.) *Working under Different Rules*, New York: Russell Sage Foundation.

Freeman, R. B and J. L. Medoff (1984) *What Do Unions Do?*, New York: Basic Books.

Furåker, B. (1987) *Stat och offentlig sektor*, Stockholm: Rabén and Sjögren.

Furåker, B. (1989) 'Inledning', in B. Furåker (ed.) *Välfärdsstat och lönearbete*, Lund: Studentlitteratur.

Furåker, B., L. Johansson and J. Lind (1990) 'Unemployment and labour market policies in the Scandinavian countries', *Acta Sociologica* 33, 2: 141–64.

Furåker, B. and R. Lindqvist (1992) *Arbetsrätt och offentlig sektor*, Lund: Arkiv.

Galenson, W. (1986) 'The historical role of American trade unionism', in S. M. Lipset (ed.) *Unions in Transition. Entering the Second Century*, San Fransisco, CA: ICS Press.

Gallie, D., C. Marsh and C. Vogler (eds) (1994) *Social Change and the Experience of Unemployment*, Oxford: Oxford University Press.

Gallie, D., M. White, Y. Cheng and M. Tomlinson (1998) *Restructuring the Employment Relationship*. Oxford: Clarendon Press.

Gallie, D. and S. Paugam (eds) (2000) *Welfare Regimes and the Experience of Unemployment in Europe*, Oxford: Oxford University Press.

Gera, S. (ed.) (1991) *Canadian Unemployment. Lessons from the 80s and Challenges for the 90s*, Ottawa: Ministry of Supply and Services Canada.

Gershuny, J. (1978) *After Post-Industrial Society? The Emerging Self-service Economy*, London and Basingstoke: Macmillan.

Getman, J. G. and B. B. Pogrebin (1988) *Labor Relations. The Basic Processes, The Law and Practice*, Westbury, NY: The Foundation Press.

Giddens, A. (1989) *Sociology*, Cambridge: Polity Press.

Giersch, H. (1985) *Eurosclerosis*, Kiel discussion papers 112, University of Kiel: Institut für Weltwirtschaftsforschung.

Ginsburg, N. (1992) *Divisions of Welfare. A Critical Introduction to Comparative Social Policy*, London: Sage.

Golden, M. (1993) 'The dynamics of trade unionism and national economic performance', *American Political Science Review* 87, 2: 439–54.

Golden, M. A., M. Wallerstein and P. Lange (1999) 'Postwar trade-union organization and industrial relations in twelve countries', in H. Kitschelt, P. Lange, G. Marks and J. D. Stevens (eds) *Continuity and Change in Contemporary Capitalism*, Cambridge: Cambridge University Press: 194–229.

Goldfield, M. (1987) *The Decline of Organized Labor in the United States*, Chicago: The University of Chicago Press.

Goldthorpe, J. H. (1971) 'Theories of industrial society: Reflections on the recrudescence of historicism and the future of futurology', *Archives Européennes de Sociologie* 12: 263–88.

Gonäs, L. (1995) *Vad händer med kvinnors arbete när den offentliga sektorn skärs ned?* Stockholm: Arbetslivsinstitutet.

Göransson, H. (1988) *Kollektivavtalet som fredspliktsinstrument,* Juristforlaget, Stockholm.

Gordon, D. M., R. Edwards and M. Reich (1982) *Segmented Work and Divided Workers. The Historical Transformation of Labour in the United States,* London and Cambridge: Cambridge University Press.

Gornick, J. C., M. K. Meyers and K. E. Ross (1997) 'Supporting the employment of mothers: Policy variation across fourteen welfare states', *Journal of European Social Policy* 7: 45–70.

Gould IV, W. B. (1994) *Agenda for Reform. The Future of Employment Relationships and the Law,* Cambridge, MA: The MIT Press.

Graafland, J. J. (1989) 'Can hysteresis explain different labour market operations between Europe and the United States?', *Applied Economics* 21, 1: 95–111.

Grenig, J. E. (1991) 'The dismissal of employees in the United States', *International Labour Review* 130, 5–6: 569–81.

Gullason, E. T. (2000) 'The dynamics of the U.S. occupational structure during the 1990s', *Journal of Labor Research* 21: 363–75.

Hakim, C. (1990) 'Core and periphery in employers' workforce strategies: Evidences from the 1987 ELUS survey', *Work, Employment and Society* 4: 157–88.

Hakim, C. (1996) *Key Issues in Women's Work: Female Heterogeneity and the Polarisation of Women's Employment,* London: Athlone.

Hall, S. and M. Jacques (eds) (1991) *New Times: The Changing Face of Politics in the 1990s,* London: Lawrence and Wishart.

Hamermesh, D. S. (1979) 'Entitlement effects, unemployment insurance and unemployment spells', *Economic Inquiry* 17, 3: 317–32.

Hamermesh, D. S. (1980) 'Unemployment insurance and labor supply', *International Economic Review* 21: 517–27.

Hammarström, O. and T. Nilsson (1998) 'Employment relations in Sweden', in G. J. Bamber and R. D. Lansbury (eds) *International and Comparative Employment Relations. A Study of Developed Market Economies,* revised edition, Newbury Park: Sage: 224–48.

Hansen, H. (2000) *Elements of Social Security,* Working Paper 2000:7, Copenhagen: The Danish National Institute of Social Research.

Harrison, B. (1994) *Lean and Mean: The Changing Landscape of Corporate Power in the Age of Flexibility,* New York: Basic Books.

Harrison, B. and B. Bluestone (1988) *The Great U-Turn: Corporate Restructuring and the Polarizing of America,* New York: Basic Books.

Heckscher, C. (1988) *The New Unionism. Employee Involvement in the Changing Corporation,* New York: Basic Books.

Henley, A. and E. Tsakalotos (1991) 'Corporatism, profit squeeze and investment', *Cambridge Journal of Economics* 15: 425–50.

Henrekson, M. (1998) 'En ond cirkel för tjänstesektorn', *Arbetsmarknad & Arbetsliv* 4, 2: 137–51.

Hernes, H. (1987a) *Welfare State and Women Power,* Oslo: Norwegian University Press.

Hernes, H. (1987b) 'Women and the welfare state: The transition from public to private dependence', in A. Showstack Sassoon (ed.) *Women and the State,* London: Hutchinson.

Heron, C. (1989) *The Canadian Labour Movement. A Short History,* Toronto: Lorimer and Co.

Heylen, F. (1993) 'Labour market structures, labour market policy and wage formation in the OECD', *Labour* 7, 2: 25–51.

Hibbs, D. (1977) 'Political parties and macroeconomic policy', *American Political Science Review* 71: 1467–87.

Hinrichs, K., W. Roche and C. Sirianni (1991) 'From standardization to flexibility: Changes in the political economy of working time', in K. Hinrichs, W. Roche and C. Sirianni (eds) *Working Time in Transition. The Political Economy of Working Hours on Industrial Nations*, Philadelphia, PA; Temple University Press.

Hirschhorn, L. (1997) *Reworking Authority: Leading and Following in the Post-Modern Organization*, Cambridge, MA: MIT University Press.

Holmlund, B. (1991) *Unemployment Persistence and Insider-Outsider Forces in Wage Determination*, Working Paper 92, Paris: OECD, Department of Economics and Statistics.

Holmlund, B. (1995) Livstidsjobb och korta jobb, *Arbetsmarknad and Arbetsliv* 1, 2, 149–55.

Holmlund, B. and A. Vejsiu (1998) *Labour Turnover in Boom and Slump: The Swedish Experience*, Paper prepared for the International Conference on Job Tenure and Labour Reallocation, April 24–25, London.

Holt, H. and I. Taulow (eds) (1996) *Reconciling Work and Family Life: An International Perspective on the Role of Companies*, Copenhagen: Danish National Institute of Social Research.

Hvinden, B. (1999) 'Activation: a Nordic perspective', in *Linking Welfare and Work*, Dublin: European Foundation, 27–42.

Huxley, C., D. Kettler and J. Struthers (1986) 'Is Canada's experience especially instructive?', in S.M. Lipset (ed.) *Unions in Transition. Entering the Second Century*, San Francisco, CA: ICS Press, 113–32.

Ilg, R. E. and S. E. Haugen (2000) 'Earnings and employment trends in the 1990s', *Monthly Labor Review*, March: 21–33.

ILO *Yearbook of Labour Statistics* (various years), Paris: OECD.

ILO (1990) *ISCO-88. International Standard Classification of Occupations*, Geneva: International Labour Office.

ILO (2001) *LABORSTA*, http://laborsta.ilo.org/cgi-bin/broker8.exe (15 July 2001). *Information* 1998–12–28.

Iversen, T. (1996) 'Power, flexibility and the breakdown of centralized wage bargaining: Denmark and Sweden in comparative perspective', *Comparative Politics* July: 399–436.

Jacobs. J. and S. T. Lim (1992) 'Trends in occupational and industrial sex segregation in 56 countries, 1960–1980', *Work and Occupations* 19, 4: 450–86.

Jacobsen, P. (1993) 'Denmark', in R. Blanpain (ed.) *Temporary Work and Labour Law*, Boston, MA: Kluwer.

Jacoby, S. M. (1982) 'The duration of indefinite employment contracts in the United States and England: An historical analysis', *Comparative Labor Law* 5, 1: 85–128.

Jägerskiöld, S. (1971) *Collective Bargaining Rights of State Officials in Sweden*, Ann Arbor, MI: Institute of Labor and Industrial Relations.

Jain, H. C. (1985) 'Canada', in R. Blanpain (ed.) *Bulletin of Comparative Labour Relations* Bulletin 14: 69–81.

Jain, H. C. (1992) 'Affirmative action, employment equity and visible minorities in Canada', in A. Gladstone, H. Wheeler, J. Rojot, F. Eyraud and R. Ben-Israel (eds) *Labor Relations in a Changing Environment*, New York: Walter de Gruyter.

Janoski, T. (1990) *The Political Economy of Unemployment*, Los Angeles: University of California Press.

Jessop, B., K. Nielsen and O. K. Pedersen (1993) 'Structural competitiveness and strategic capacities: Rethinking the state and international capital', in S. E. Sjöstrand (ed.) *Institutional Change: Theory and Empirical Findings*, New York: M. E. Sharpe.

Johannesson, J. and E. Wadensjö (eds) (1995) *Labour Market Policy at the Crossroads*, Stockholm: EFA, Minstry of Labour.

Johnsson, D. and J. Malmberg (1998) *Avtalsutveckling på arbetstidsområdet*, Arbetslivsrapport 1998: 2, Solna: Arbetslivsinstitutet.

Jones, J. (1985) 'USA', in R. Blanpain (ed.) *Bulletin of Comparative Labour Relations*, Bulletin 14: 69–81.

Jonung, C. (1993) 'Yrkessegregeringen på arbetsmarknaden', in *Kvinnors arbetsmarknad. 1990–talet – återtågets årtionde*. Ds 1993:8. Stockholm: Arbetsmarknadsdepartementet.

Jonung, C. (1996) 'Economic theories of occupational segregation by sex – implications for change over time', in P. Beckmann (ed.) *Gender-Specific Occupational Segregation*, BeitrAB 188, Nürenberg: Institut für Arbeitsmarkt und Berufsforschung der Bundesanstalt für Arbeit.

Kahn-Freund, O. (1972) *Labour and the Law*, London: Stevens & Sons.

Kamerman, B. and A. Kahn (eds) (1989) *Privatisation and the Welfare State*, Princeton, NJ: Princeton University Press.

Kassalow, E. M. (1992) 'Labour market flexibility: The US case in a comparative framwork', in A. Gladstone, H. Wheeler, J. Rojot, F. Eyrand and R. Ben-Israel (eds) *Labour Relations in a Changing Environment*, New York: Walter de Gruyter.

Kerr, C., J. T. Dunlop, F. H. Harbison and C. A. Myers (1960) *Industrialism and Industrial Man. The Problems of Labor and Management in Economic Growth*, Cambridge, MA: Harvard University Press.

King, D. (1999) *In the Name of Liberalism*, Oxford: Oxford University Press.

Kjellberg, A. (1983) *Facklig organisering i tolv länder*, Lund: Arkiv.

Kjellberg, A. (1997) *Fackliga organisationer och medlemmar i dagens Sverige*, Lund: Arkiv.

Kjellberg, A. (1998) 'Sweden: Restoring the model?, in A. Ferner and R. Hyman (eds) *Changing Industrial Relations in Europe*, Oxford: Blackwell Publishers.

Kjellberg, A. (1999) 'The multitude of challenges facing swedish trade unions', in R. Hoffman and J. Waddington (eds) *Trade Unions in Europe–Facing the Challenges*, Brussels: ETUI.

Kjellberg, A. (2000) 'Sweden', in B. Ebbinghaus and J. Visser (eds) *The Societies of Europe: Trade Unions in Western Europe since 1945*, Series of historical data handbooks, London: Macmillan.

Kjellberg, A. (2001) *Fackliga organisationer och medlemmar i dagens Sverige*, 2nd edition, Lund: Arkiv.

Knijn, T. and M. Kremer (1997) 'Gender and the caring dimension of welfare states: Towards inclusive citizenship', *Social Politics* 4, 3: 328–62.

Kochan, T. A. (1985) *Challenges and Choices Facing American Labor*, Cambridge, MA and London: The MIT Press.

Korpi, W. (1983) *The Democratic Class Struggle*, London: Routledge and Kegan Paul.

Korpi, W. (1991) 'Political and economic explanations for unemployment: A cross-national and long-term analysis', *British Journal of Political Science* 21: 315–48.

Korpi, W. (1996) 'Eurosclerosis and the sclerosis of objectivity. On the role of values among economic policy experts', *Economic Journal* 106: 1727–46.

Korpi, W. (2000) 'Faces of inequality. Gender, class and patterns of inequality in different types of welfare states', *Social Politics* Summer: 127–91.

Korpi, W. and J. Palme (1998) 'The paradox of redistribution and strategies of equality: Welfare state institutions, inequality and poverty in the Western countries', *American Sociological Review* 63, 5: 661–87.

Kuhn, P. (1993) 'Employment protection laws: Policy issues and recent research', *Canadian Public Policies – Analyse de Politique* XIX, 3: 279–97.

Kumar, K. (1988) *The Rise of Modern Society. Aspects of the Social and Political Development of the West*, Oxford: Basil Blackwell.

Kumar, K. (1995) *From Post-Industrial to Post-Modern Society. New Theories of the Contemporary World*, Oxford and Cambridge, MA: Blackwell.

Kumar, P. (1993) '*Canadian Labour's Response to Work Reorganization*', Queen's University of Kingston: Working Papers Series QPIR 1993–6.

Lash, S. and J. Urry (1987) *The End of Organized Capitalism*, Cambridge: Polity Press.

Layard, R., S. Nickell and R. Jackman (1991) *Unemployment*, Oxford: Oxford University Press.

Lehmbruch, G. (1984) 'Concertation and the structure of corporatist networks', in J. H. Goldthorpe (ed.) *Order and Conflict in Contemporary Capitalism*, London: Clarendon Press.

Leisink, P., J. van Leemput and J. Vilrokx (1996) *The Challenges to Trade Unions in Europe*, Cheltenham and Brookfield: Edward Elgar.

Levy Jr., M. (1966) *Modernization and the Structure of Societies*, Princeton, NJ: Transaction.

Lewin, D. (1986) 'Public employee unionism and labor relations in the 1980s: An analysis of transformation', in S. M. Lipset (ed.) *Unions in Transition. Entering the Second Century*, San Fransisco, CA: ICS Press, 241–64.

Lewis, J. (1992) 'Gender and the development of welfare regimes', *Journal of European Social Policy* 2, 3: 159–73.

Lindbeck, A. (1992) *The Welfare State*, London: Edward Elgar.

Lindbeck, A. and D. J. Snower (1988) *The Insider–Outsider Theory of Employment and Unemployment*, Cambridge, MA: MIT Press.

Lindqvist, R. (1992) 'Arbetsrättens utveckling i den offentliga sektorn', in B. Furåker and R. Lindqvist, *Arbetsrätt och offentlig sektor*, Lund: Arkiv.

Lindqvist, R. and S. Marklund (1995) 'Forced to work and liberated from work. A historical perspective on work and welfare in Sweden', *Scandinavian Journal of Social Welfare* 4: 224–37.

Lipset, S. M. (ed.) (1986) *Unions in Transition. Entering the Second Century*, San Fransisco, CA: ICS Press.

Lipset, S. M. (1990) *Continental Divide: The Values and Institutions of the United States and Canada*, New York and London: Routledge.

Lipset, S. M. (1996) *American Exceptionalism. A Double-Edged Sword*, New York: W.W. Norton & Company.

Lipsett, B. and M. Reesor (1997) *Flexible Work Arrangements: Evidence from the 1991 and 1995 Survey of Work Arrangements*, 1st Internet edition, Quebec: Human Resources Development Canada.

Lister, R. (1994) 'She has other duties – women, citizenship and social security', in S. Baldwin and J. Falkingham (eds) *Social Security and Social Change: New Challenges to the Beveridge Model*, New York: Harvester Wheatsheaf.

Lister, R. (1997) *Citizenship: Feminist Perspectives*, London, Macmillan.

Little, D. (1998) *Employment and Remuneration in the Service Industries since 1984*, Ottawa: Statitics Canada.

Locking, H. (1995) *Essays on Swedish Wage Formation*, Gothenburg, Handelshögskolan vid Göteborgs Universitet.

MacDonald, K. M. (1995) *The Sociology of the Professions*, London: Sage Publications.

Madsen, P. Kongshøj (1995) *Phillips Revisited. A Comparative Study of Wage Flexibility, Labour Market Institutions and International Inflationary Linkages*, Forskningsrapport 1995/7, Copenhagen: Department of Political Science.

Madsen, P. Kongshøj (1999): *Denmark: Flexibility, Security and Labour Market Success*, Employment and Training Papers 53, Geneva: ILO:
<http://www.ilo.org/public/english/employment/strat/publ/etp53.htm>.

Marable, M. (1996) 'Staying on the path to racial equality', in G. E. Curry (ed.) *The*

Affirmative Action Debate, Reading, MA: Addison-Wesley.

Martin, A. (1979) 'The dynamics of change in a Keynesian political economy: The Swedish case and its implications', in C. Crouch (ed.) *State and Economy in Contemporary Capitalism*, London: Croom Helm.

Martin, A. (1984) 'Trade unions in Sweden: Strategic responses to change and crisis', in P. Gourevitch (ed.) *Unions and Economic Crisis: Britain, West Germany and Sweden*, London: Allen and Unwin.

Martin, B. (1993) *In the Public Interest? Privatisation and Public Sector Reform*, London: Zed Books.

Martin, J. P. (2000) 'What works among active labour market policies: Evidence from OECD countries' experiences', *OECD Economic Studies* 30: 79–113.

Martin, J. P. and D. Grubb (2001) *What Works and for Whom: A Review of OECD Countries' Experiences with Active Labour Market Policies*, Working Paper 2001: 14, Uppsala: Office of Labour Market Policy Evaluation.

Marx, I. and G. Verbist (1997) *Low-Paid Employment and Poverty: Curse and Cure?* paper presented at the European Low-Wage Employment Research Network Conference, 31 January–1 February, Bordeaux.

McLaughlin, E. and C. Glendinning (1994) 'Paying for care in Europe: Is there a feminist approach?', in L. Hantrais and S. Mangen (eds) *Family Policy and the Welfare of Women*, Loughborough: Cross-National Research Group.

Mead, L. (1992) *The New Politics of Poverty*, New York: Basic Books.

Meisenheimer II, J. R. (1998) 'The services industry in the "good" versus "bad" jobs debate', *Monthly Labor Review* 121: 22–47.

Menger, P.-M. (1999) 'Artistic labor markets and careers', *Annual Review of Sociology* 25: 541–74.

Meulders, D., O. Plasman and R. Plasman (1997) *Atypical Employment in the EC*, Aldershot: Dartmouth.

Meulders, D. and L. Wilkin (1987) 'Labour market flexibility: Critical introduction to the analysis of a concept', *Labour and Society* 12, 1: 3–17.

Meyer, A. G. (1970) 'Theories of convergence', in C. Johnson (ed.) *Change in Communist Systems*, Stanford, CA: Stanford University Press.

Michel, L. and J. Bernstein (1994) *The State of Working America 1994–95*, New York and London: M. E. Sharpe.

Milkman, R., E. Reese and B. Roth (1998) 'The macro-sociology of paid domestic labor', *Work and Occupations* 25: 483–510.

Mills, C. W. (1958) *The Causes of World War Three*, New York: Simon and Schuster.

Ministry of Finance, Denmark (1998) 'Availability criteria in selected OECD-countries', *Working Paper* 6.

Ministry of Finance, Denmark (1999) Adam-database, Copenhagen.

Mishel, L. and J. Schmitt (eds) (1995) *Beware the U.S. Model. Jobs and Wages in a Deregulated Economy*, Washington DC: Economic Policy Institute.

Mishra, R. (1999) *The Globalisation and the Welfare State*, Northampton, MA: Edward Elgar.

Mitchell, D. B. (1993): 'Keynesianism, old Keynesianism and new Keynesian wage nominalism', *Industrial Relations* 32, 1: 1–29.

Moody, K. (1997/2001) *Workers in a Lean World: Unions in the International Economy*, London: Verso.

Mosley, H. G. (1994) 'Employment protection and labour force adjustment', in G. Schmid (ed.) *Labor Market Institutions in Europe. A Socio-economic Evaluation of Performance*, New York: M.E. Sharpe.

Myles, J. (1996) 'When markets fail: Social welfare in Canada and the United States', in

G. Esping-Andersen (ed.) *Welfare States in Transition*, London: Sage.

Nätti, J. (1994) *Part-Time Employment in the Nordic Countries: A Trap for Women?*, Paper presented at the 13th World Congress of Sociology, Bielefeld, Germany.

Nermo, M. (1999) *Structured by Gender. Patterns of Sex Segregation in the Swedish Labour Market. Historical and Cross-National Comparisons*, Stockholm: Swedish Institute for Social Research.

Nickell, S. (1997) 'Unemployment and labor market rigidities: Europe versus North America', *Journal of Economic Perspectives* 11, 3, Summer: 55–74.

Nickell, S. and R. Layard (1999) 'Labor market institutions and economic performance', in O. Ashenfelter and D. Card (eds) *Handbook of Labor Economics*, Amsterdam: Elsevier, 3: 3029–84.

Nielsen, R. (1992) 'Protection of employment rights', in N. Bruun, B. Flodgren, M. Halvorsen, H. Hydén and R. Nielsen (1992) *The Nordic Labour Relations Model: Labour Law and the Trade Unions in the Nordic Countries Today and Tomorrow*, Dartmouth: Aldershot.

Nielsen, R. (1995) *Equality in Law between Men and Women in the European Community. Denmark*, The Hague: Martinus Nijhoff.

Nilsen, S. R. (2001) *Unemployment Insurance-Role as Safety Net for Low-Wage Workers Is Limited*, FDCH Government Account Reports, Washington, DC: Media Millworks inc.

Norwood, J. (1983) 'Labor market contrasts: United States and Europe', *Monthly Labor Review* 106, 8: 3–70.

Noyelle, T. (1987) *Beyond Industrial Dualism*, London and New York: Westview Press.

Numhauser-Henning, A. (1988) *Arbetshandikappad med rätt till arbete?*, Stockholm: Norstedts.

O'Connor, J. S. and G. M. Olsen (eds) (1998) *Power Resources Theory and the Welfare State. A Critical Approach*, Toronto: University of Toronto Press.

OECD database (various years).

OECD (1985) *Economic Outlook*, Paris: OECD.

OECD (1989a) *Labour Market Flexibility. Trends in Enterprises*, Paris: OECD.

OECD (1989b) *Employment Outlook*, Paris: OECD.

OECD (1990) *Employment Outlook*, Paris: OECD.

OECD (1991a) *National Accounts 1977–89*, Paris: OECD.

OECD (1991b) *Employment Outlook*, Paris: OECD.

OECD (1992) *Employment Outlook*, Paris: OECD.

OECD (1993) *Employment Outlook*, Paris: OECD.

OECD (1994a) *Employment Outlook*, Paris: OECD.

OECD (1994b) *The OECD Job Study, Part I: Labour Market Trends and Underlying Forces of Change*, Paris: OECD.

OECD (1994c) *The OECD Job Study, Part II: The Adjustment Potential of the Labour Market*, Paris: OECD.

OECD (1994d) *Measuring Public Employment in OECD Countries: Sources, Methods and Results*, Paris: OECD.

OECD (1995) *Employment Outlook*, Paris: OECD.

OECD (1996a) *SMEs: Employment, Innovation and Growth – the Washington Workshop*, Paris: OECD.

OECD (1996b) *Education at a Glance. OECD Indicators*, Paris: OECD.

OECD (1996c) *Employment Outlook* Paris: OECD.

OECD (1997a) *Family, Market and Community. Equity and Efficiency in Social Policy*, OECD Social Policy Studies, No. 21, Paris: OECD.

OECD (1997b) *Labour Force Statistics*, Paris: OECD.

OECD (1997c) *The Definition of Part-Time Work for the Purpose of International Comparisons*, Labour Markets and Social Policy, Occasional Paper No. 22, Paris: OECD.

OECD (1997d) *Employment Outlook*, Paris: OECD.

OECD (1997e) *Labour Market Policies: New Challenges*. Policies for Low-Paid Workers and Unskilled Job-Seekers, Paris: OECD.

OECD (1998a) *Employment Outlook*, Paris: OECD.

OECD (1998b) *Education at a Glance. OECD Indicators*, Paris: OECD.

OECD (1999a) *Economic Outlook*, No. 66, Paris: OECD.

OECD (1999b) *Employment Outlook*, Paris: OECD.

OECD (1999c) *Historical Statistics 1960–1998*, Paris: OECD.

OECD (1999d) *Economic Survey, Sweden*, Paris: OECD.

OECD (1999e) *Economic Survey, Denmark*, Paris: OECD.

OECD (2000a) *Employment Outlook*, Paris: OECD.

OECD (2000b) *Historical Statistics, 1970–2000*, Paris: OECD.

OECD (2000c) *Labour Force Statistics*, Paris: OECD.

OECD (2001a) *Economic Outlook*, No. 69, Paris: OECD.

OECD (2001b) *Employment Outlook*, Paris: OECD.

Offe, C. (1984) *Contradictions of the Welfare State*, London: Hutchinson.

Offe, C. (1985) *Disorganised Capitalism: Contemporary Transformations of Work and Politics*, Cambridge: Polity Press.

Olafsson, S. (1992) 'The rise or decline of work in the welfare state? Equality and efficiency revisited', in J. E. Kolberg (ed.) *Between Work and Social Citizenship*, Armonk, NY: M. E. Sharpe.

Olsen, G. M. (1994) 'Locating the Canadian welfare state: Family policy and health care in Canada, Sweden and the United States', *Canadian Journal of Sociology* 19, 1: 1–20.

O'Reilly, J. and C. Fagan (eds) (1998) *Part-Time Propects: An International Comparison of Part-Time Work in Europe, North America and the Pacific Rim*, London: Routledge.

Orloff, A. S. (1993) 'Gender and the social rights of citizenship: the comparative analysis of gender relations and welfare states', *American Sociological Review* 58: 303–28.

Osterman, P. (1988) *Employment Futures: Reorganization, Dislocation and Public Policy*, New York: Oxford University Press.

Panitch, L. and D. Swartz (1988) *The Assault on Trade Union Freedoms. From Consent to Coercion Revisited*, Toronto: Garamond Press.

Pateman, C. (1988) 'The patriarchal welfare state', in A. Gutmann (ed.) *Democracy and the Welfare State*, Princeton, NJ: Princeton University Press.

Peck, J. (1994) 'Regulating labour: The social regulation and reproduction of local labour markets', in A. Amin and N. Thrift (eds) *Globalization, Institutions and Regional Development in Europe*, Oxford: Oxford University Press.

Perkin, H. (1996) *The Third Revolution. Professional Elites in the Modern World*, London and New York: Routledge.

Petersen, H. (1987) *Ledelse og loyalitet. Kollektiv arbejdsret i den offentlige sektor*, Copenhagen: Akademisk forlag.

Peterson, J. (1993) 'Part-time employment and women: A comment on Sundström', *Journal of Economic Issues* XXVII, 3: 909–15.

Pfeffer, J. (1994) *Competitive Advantage through People: Unleashing the Power of Work Force*, Boston, MA: Harvard Business School Press.

Pfeffer, J. and J. N. Baron (1988) 'Taking the workers back out: Recent trends in the structuring of employment', *Research in Organizational Behavior* 10: 257–303.

Piore, M. (1975) 'Notes for a theory of labor market stratification', in R. C. Edwards, M. Reich and D. M. Gordon (eds) *Labor Market Segmentation*, Lexington, MA: D. D. Heath.

Piore, M. and C. Sabel (1984) *The Second Industrial Divide*, Cambridge, MA: MIT Press.

Polanyi, K. (1957) *The Great Transformation*, Boston, MA: Beacon Press.

Polivka, A. E. (1996a) 'A profile of contingent workers', *Monthly Labor Review* 119, 10: 10–21.

Polivka, A. E (1996b) 'Into contingent and alternative employment: By choice?', *Monthly Labor Review* 119, 10: 55–74.

Polivka, A. E. and T. Nardone (1989) 'On the definition of "Contingent Work"', *Monthly Labor Review* 112, 12: 9–14.

Pollard, J. S. (1995) 'The contraditions of flexibility: Labour control and resistance in the Los Angelos banking industry', *Geoforum* 26, 2: 121–38.

Pollert, A. (1988) 'The flexible firm: Fixation or fact?', *Work, Employment and Society* 2: 281–316.

Pollert, A. (ed.) (1991) *Farewell to Flexibility?* Oxford: Blackwell.

Ponak, A. (1982) 'Public-sector collective bargaining', in J. C. Anderson and M. Gunderson (eds) *Union–Management Relations in Canada*, Toronto: Addison-Wesley, 343–77.

Pontusson, J. (1987) 'Radicalization and retreat in Swedish Social Democracy', *New Left Review* 165: 5–33.

Poole, M. (1981) *Theories of Trade Unionism. A Sociology of Industrial Relations*, London: Routledge and Kegan Paul.

Porter, M. E. (1990) *The Competitive Advantages of Nations*, New York: The Free Press.

Presser, H.(1995) 'Job, family and gender: Determinants of nonstandard work schedules among employed Americans in 1991', *Demography* 32, 4, Nov.: 577–99.

Raskin, C. (1994) 'Employment equity for the disabled in Canada', *International Labour Review* 133, 1: 76–88.

Regini, M. (ed.) (1994) *The Future of Labour Movements*, London: Sage.

Reich, R. (1992) *Work of Nations: Preparing Ourselves for 21st Century Capitalism*, New York: Vintage Books.

Reissert, B. and G. Schmid (1994) 'Unemployment compensation and active labour market policy', in G. Schmid (ed.) *Labor Market Institutions in Europe. A Socioeconomic Evaluation of Performance*, New York: M. E. Sharpe.

Reskin, B. (1993) 'Sex segregation in the workplace', *Annual Review of Sociology* 19: 241–70.

Robinson, P. (2000) 'Active labour-market policies: A case of evidence-based policy-making?', *Oxford Review of Economic Policy* 16,1: 13–26. .

Rodgers, G. and J. Rodgers (eds) (1989) *Precarious Jobs in Labour Market Regulation: The Growth of Atypical Employment in Western Europe*. Geneva: ILO.

Roos, P. A. (1985) *Gender and Work: A Comparative Analysis of Industrial Societies*, New York: State University of New York Press.

Rose, R. (1985) *Public Employment in Western Nations*, Cambridge: Cambridge University Press.

Rosen, S. (1996) 'Public employment and the welfare state in Sweden', *Journal of Economic Literature* 34: 729–40.

Rosenberg, S. (1989) 'From segmentation to flexibility', *Labour and Society* 14, 4: 363–407.

Rosenberg, S. (1994) 'United States of America', in G. Bosch, P. Dawkins and F. Michon (eds) *Times Are Changing – Working Time in 14 Industrialised Countries*, Geneva: International Institute for Labour Studies.

Rosenfeld, R. and G. E. Birkelund (1995) 'Women's part-time work: A cross-national comparison', *European Sociological Review* 11: 111–34.

Rosenfeld, R. and A. Kalleberg (1991) 'Gender inequality in the labor market: A cross-national perspective', *Acta Sociologica* 34, 3: 207–25.

Rothstein, D. S. (1996) 'Entry into and consequences of nonstandard work arrangements', *Monthly Labor Review* 119, 10: 75–82.

Rubery, J. (1989) 'Labour market flexibility in Britain', in F. Green (ed.) *Restructuring and the*

UK Economy, Brighton: Harvester-Wheatsheaf.

Rubery, J., M. Smith, C. Fagan and D. Grimshaw (1998) *Women and European Employment*, London and New York: Routledge.

Rubery, J., M. Smith and C. Fagan (1999) *Women's Employment in Europe: Trends and Prospects*. London and New York: Routledge.

Sabel, C. and M. Zeitlin (eds) (1997) *World of Possibilities. Flexibility and Mass Production in Western Industrialization*, New York and Cambridge: Cambridge University Press.

Sainsbury, D. (ed.) (1994) *Gendering Welfare States*, London: Sage.

Sainsbury, D. (1996) *Gender, Equality and Welfare States,* Cambridge: Cambridge University Press.

Saraceno, C. (1997) 'Family change, family policies and the restructuring of welfare', *Family, Market and Community. Equity and Efficiency in Social Policy,* OECD Social Policy Studies, No. 21, Paris: OECD.

Saunders, P. and C. Harris (1994) *Privatisation and Popular Capitalism*, Buckingham: Open University Press.

Saunders, P. and F. Klau (1985) 'The role of the public sector', *OECD Economic Studies* 4.

Sayer, A. and R. Walker (1992) *The New Social Economy: Reworking the Division of Labor*, Cambridge, MA and Oxford: Backwell.

Scarpetta, S. (1996) 'Assessing the role of labour market policies and institutional settings on unemployment: A cross-country study', *OECD Economic Studies* 26: 43–98.

SCB (various years) *Arbetskraftsundersökningen. Årsmedeltal*, Stockholm.

SCB (1989) *Arbetstider. Omfattning och förläggning*, Information om arbetsmarknaden 1989: 2, Stockholm: Statistics Sweden.

SCB (1992) *Statistiska Meddelanden*. AM 10, Stockholm.

SCB (1994) *Hur arbetstiden är förlagd*. Information om arbetsmarknaden 1994: 1, Stockholm: Statistics Sweden.

SCB (1996a) *Nu och då. Dagens arbetsmarknadsläge jämfört med situationen före krisen*, Stockholm: Statistics Sweden.

SCB (1996b) 'The Swedish labour force survey', *Bakgrundsfakta till arbetsmarknads- och utbildningsstatistiken* 1996: 3, Stockholm: Statistics Sweden.

Scheuer, S. (1991) *Leaders and Laggers: Who Goes First in Bargaining Rounds*, University of Warwick, UK: Industrial Relations Research Unit.

Scheuer, S. (1997) 'Collective bargaining coverage under trade unionism: A sociological investigation', *British Journal of Industrial Relations* 35, 1: 65–86.

Scheuer, S. (1998) 'Denmark: A less regulated model', in A. Ferner and R. Hyman (eds) *Changing Industrial Relations in Europe*, Oxford: Blackwell Publishers.

Schmid, G. (1994a) 'Introduction', in G. Schmid (ed.) *Labor Market Institutions in Europe. A Socioeconomic Evaluation of Performance*, New York: M. E. Sharpe.

Schmid, G. (ed.) (1994b) *Labor Market Institutions in Europe. A Socioeconomic Evaluation of Performance*, New York: M. E. Sharpe.

Schmid, G., B. Reissert and G. Bruche (1992) *Unemployment Insurance and Active Labour Market Policy. An International Comparison of Financing Systems*, Detroit, MI: Wayne State University Press.

Schmid, G. and K. Schömann (1994) 'Institutional choice and flexible coordination', in G. Schmid (ed.) *Labor Market Institutions in Europe. A Socioeconomic Evaluation of Performance*, New York: M. E. Sharpe.

Schragge, E. (ed.) (1996) *Workfare: Ideology for a New Underclass*, Toronto: Garamond Press.

Schömann, K., R. Rogowski and T. Kruppe (1998) *Labour Market Efficiency in the European Union*, London: Routledge.

Schönemann-Paul, H., E. Körmendi and T. Gelting (1992) *Den faste arbeidstid er fortid. Om danskernes arbejdstidsmonstre og om den faglige og geografiske kleksibilitet på arbejdsmarkede,* Copenhagen: Spektrum.

SFS 1991:433 *Act Concerning Equality Between Men and Women,* Stockholm.

Singelmann, J. (1978a) 'The sectoral transformation of the labor force in seven industrialized countries, 1920–1970', *American Journal of Sociology* 83, 5: 1224–34.

Singelmann, J. (1978b) *The Transformation of Industry: From Agriculture to Service Employment,* Beverly Hills, CA: Sage.

Smucker, J. (1980) *Industrialization in Canada,* Scarborough, Ontario: Prentice-Hall.

Sohlman, Å. (1996) *Framtidens utbildning. Sverige i internationell konkurrens,* Stockholm: SNS Förlag.

Sorokin, P. (1964) *The Basic Trends of Our Times,* New Haven, CT: College and University Press.

Sorrentino, C. (2000) 'International unemployment rates: how comparable are they?', *Monthly Labor Review* June: 3–20.

Soskice, D. (1990) 'Wage determination. The changing role of institutions in advanced industrial countries', *Oxford Review of Economic Policy* 6, 4: 36–61.

SOU 1975:1, *Demokrati på arbetsplatsen* (Report from the Government Committee on Labour Law), Stockholm.

SOU 1989: 53, *Arbetstid och välfärd* SOU (Report on Working Time and Welfare), Stockholm.

SOU 1996: 56, *Hälften vore nog–om kvinnor och män på 90-talets arbetsmarknad* (Half could be Enough), Stockholm.

SOU 2000: 3, *Välfärd vid vägskäl. Delbetänkande från välfärdskommittén* (Welfare at the Crossroads), Stockholm.

Statistics Canada (various years) *The Labour Force Survey,* Ottawa.

Statistics Canada (1998) *Work Arrangements in the 1990s,* Analytic Report No. 8, Labour and Household Surveys Analysis Division, Ottawa.

Statistics Denmark (1984–2000) *Arbejdsstyrkeundersøgelserne* (Labour Force Survey) Statistiske Efterretninger: Arbejdsmarked. Serial Publication. Copenhagen.

Statistics Denmark (1999) *Statistisk Tiårsoversigt* (Ten YearsOverview), Copenhagen.

Statistics Sweden (1998) *Arbetskraftundersökningen* (Labour Force Survey), Stockholm.

Stephens, J. D. (1979) *The Transition from Capitalism to Socialism,* Urbana and Chicago: University of Illinois Press.

Stephens, J. D. (1994) 'Welfare states and employment regimes', *Acta Sociologica* 37: 207–11.

Stephens, J. D. (1996) 'The Scandinavian welfare states: Achievements, crises and prospects', in G. Esping-Andersen (ed.) *Welfare States in Transition. National Adaptations in Global Economies,* London: Sage, 32–65.

Storey, J. R. and J. A. Neisner (1997) 'Unemployment compensation in the group of seven nations', in C. J. O'Leary and S. A. Wandner (eds) *Unemployment Insurance in the United States, Analysis of Policy Issues,* Kalamazoo, MI: W. E. Upjohn Institute for Employment Research.

Storrie, D. (1997) *Flexible Employment Contracts in Sweden 1987–1996,* paper presented at the conference Flexibility in the Nordic Labour Markets, The Research Institute of the Finish Economy (ETIA) and The Nordic Council of Ministers.

Storrie, D. (2002) *Temporary Agency Work in the European Union.* Dublin: European Foundation for the Improvement of Living and Working Conditions.

Streeck, W. (1988) 'Comments on Ronald Dore: Rigidities in the labour market', *Government and Opposition* 23, 4: 413–23.

Sundström, M. (1991) 'Part-time work in Sweden: Trends and equality effects', *Journal of Economic Issues* XXV, 1, March: 167–76.

Therborn, G. (1986) *Why Some People Are More Unemployed than Others*, London: New Left Books.

Thompson, M. (1998) 'Employment relations in Canada', in G. J. Bamber and R. D. Lansbury (eds) *International and Comparative Employment Relations. A Study of Developed Market Economies*, revised edition, Newsbury Park: Sage, 89–109.

Thurow, L. C. (1996) *The Future of Capitalism. How Today's Economic Forces Shape Tomorrow's World*, New York: William Morrow and Company.

Tilly, C. (1996) *Half a Job: Bad and Good Part-Time Jobs in a Changing Labor Market*, Philadelphia, PA: Temple University Press.

Tilly, C. and C. Tilly (1998) *Work Under Capitalism*, Boulder, CO: Westview Press.

Tobisson, L. (1973) *Framväxten av statstjänstemännens förhandlingsrätt*, Stockholm: Jurist- och samhällsvetareförbundets förlag.

Toffler, A. (1980) *The Third Wave*, New York: William Morrow and Company.

Touraine, A. (1969) *La société post-industrielle*, Paris: Denoël.

Touraine, A. (1971) *The Post-Industrial Society. Tomorrow's Social History: Classes, Conflicts and Culture in the Programmed Society*, New York: Random House.

Traxler, F. (1994) 'Collective bargaining: levels and coverage in OECD', *Employment Outlook*, Paris: OECD, 167–94.

Traxler, F., S. Blaschke and B. Kittel (2001) *National Labour Relations in Internationalized Markets: A Comparative Study of Institutions, Change and Performance*, Oxford: Oxford University Press.

Troy, L. (1986) 'The rise and fall of American trade unions: The labor movement from FDR to RR', in S. M. Lipset (ed.) *Unions in Transition. Entering the Second Century*, San Fransisco, CA: ICS Press, 75–112.

Turner, D. and E. Seghezza (1999) *Testing for a Common OECD Phillips Curve*, Economic Department Working papers No. 219. Paris: OECD.

US Department of Labor (1999) *Report on the American Workforce*, Washington, DC.

Usui, C. (1996) 'Welfare state development in a world system context: Event history analysis of first social insurance legislation among 60 countries 1880–1960', in T. Janoski and A. M. Hicks (eds) *The Comparative Political Economy of the Welfare State*, New York: Cambridge University Press.

Vallas, S. (1999) 'Rethinking post-Fordism: The meaning of workplace flexibility', *Sociological Theory* 17, 1: 68–101.

Valenzuela, S. J. (1994) 'Labour movements and political systems: Some variations', in M. Regini (ed.) *The Future of Labour Movements*, London: Sage, 53–101.

Vejsiu, A. (1997) *Job Stability in Sweden 1968–1991*, Manuscript, Uppsala University, Department of Economics.

Visser, J. (1991) 'Trends in trade union membership', in OECD *Employment Outlook*: Paris: OECD, 97–134.

Visser, J. (1994) 'The strength of union movements in advanced capitalist democracies: Social and organizational variations', in M. Regini (ed.) *The Future of Labor Movements*, London: Sage.

Visser, J. (1998) 'The Netherlands: The return of responsive corporatism', in A. Ferner and R. Hyman (eds) *Changing Industrial Relations in Europe*, Oxford: Blackwell Publishers.

Visser, J. (2001) 'Industrial relations and social dialogue', in P. Auer (ed.) *Changing Labour Markets in Europe: The Role of Institutions and Policies*, Geneva: ILO.

Weber, M. (1978) in G. Roth and C. Wittich (eds) *Economy and Society*, Berkeley, CA, Los Angeles, CA, and London: University of California Press.

Weiler, P. C. (1990) *Governing the Workplace. The Future of Labor and Employment Law*, Cambridge, MA: Harvard University Press.

Weir, M. (1992) *Politics and Jobs. The Boundaries of Employment Policy in the United States*,

Princeton, NJ: Princeton University Press.

Westergaard-Nielsen, N. (1999) 'Wage dispersion, employment and unemployment: Possible trade-offs, in *EC/DGV–OECD/DEELSA seminar: Wage and Employment*, Luxembourg: Employment and Social Affairs, European Commission.

Western, B. (1995) 'A comparative study of working-class disorganization: Union decline in eighteen advanced capitalist societies', *American Sociological Review* 60: 179–201.

Western, B. (2000) *Between Class and Market: Postwar Unionization in the Capitalist Democraties*, Princeton, NJ: Princeton University Press.

Western, B. and K. Beckett (1999) 'How unregulated is the U.S. labor market? The penal system as a labor market institution', *American Journal of Sociology* 104, 4: 1030–60.

Wheeler, H. N. (1992) 'Introduction', in A. Gladstone, H. Wheeler, J. Rojot, F. Eyrand and R. Ben-Israel (eds) *Labour Relations in a Changing Environment*, New York: Walter de Gruyter.

Wheeler, H. N. and J. A. McClendon (1998) 'Employment relations in the United States', in G. J. Bamber and R. D. Lansbury (eds) *International and Comparative Employment Relations. A Study of Developed Market Economies*, revised edition, Newbury Park: Sage, 63–80.

Whitfield, D. (1992) *The Welfare State. Privatisation, Deregulation, Commercialisation of Public Services: Alternative Strategies for the 1990s*, London: Pluto Press.

Williams, K., T Cutler, J. Williams and C. Haslam (1987) 'The end of mass production', *Economy and Society* 16, 3: 405–39.

Wise, L. (1988) *Labor Market Policies and Employment Patterns in the United States*, Stockholm: Department of Labour, EFA 18.

Wood, S. (ed.) (1989) *The Transformation of Work?*, New York and London: Routledge.

Xu, J. (1997) *Sex Discrimination in The Swedish Labor Market*, Stockholm: Swedish Institute for Social Research, Working Paper 5/1997.

Index